INTERNATIONAL LAW FROM BELOW

Development, Social Movements, and Third World Resistance

The emergence of transnational social movements as major actors in international politics – as witnessed in Seattle in 1999 and elsewhere – has sent shockwaves through the international system. Many questions have arisen about the legitimacy, coherence and efficiency of the international order in the light of the challenges posed by social movements. This groundbreaking book offers a fundamental critique of twentieth-century international law from the perspective of Third World social movements – the first ever to do so. It examines in detail the growth of two key components of modern international law – international institutions and human rights – in the context of changing historical patterns of Third World resistance. Using a historical and interdisciplinary approach, Rajagopal presents compelling evidence challenging current debates on the evolution of norms and institutions, the meaning and nature of the Third World as well as the political economy of its involvement in the international system.

B. RAJAGOPAL is the Ford International Assistant Professor of Law and Development and the Director of the Program on Human Rights and Justice at the Massachusetts Institute of Technology, Cambridge, MA. He served with the United Nations in Cambodia for many years as a human rights lawyer and has been a legal and human rights advisor to international organizations and non-governmental organizations. He has published many scholarly articles in leading law journals.

INTERNATIONAL LAW FROM BELOW

Development, Social Movements, and Third World Resistance

B. RAJAGOPAL

Ford International Assistant Professor of Law and Development and Director, Program on Human Rights and Justice Massachusetts Institute of Technology Cambridge, MA

CAMBRIDGE
UNIVERSITY PRESS

PUBLISHED BY THE PRESS SYNDICATE OF THE UNIVERSITY OF CAMBRIDGE
The Pitt Building, Trumpington Street, Cambridge CB2 1RP, United Kingdom

CAMBRIDGE UNIVERSITY PRESS
The Edinburgh Building, Cambridge, CB2 2RU, UK
40 West 20th Street, New York, NY 10011–4211, USA
477 Williamstown Road, Port Melbourne, VIC 3207, Australia
Ruiz de Alarcón 13, 28014 Madrid, Spain
Dock House, The Waterfront, Cape Town 8001, South Africa

http://www.cambridge.org

First published 2003
Reprinted 2004

Printed in the United Kingdom at the University Press, Cambridge

Typeface Adobe Minion 10.75/12.75 pt. *System* LaTeX 2_ε [TB]

A catalogue record for this book is available from the British Library

Library of Congress Cataloguing in Publication data
Rajagopal, B. (Balakrishnan)
International law from below : development, social movements, and Third World resistance / B. Rajagopal.
p. cm.
Includes bibliographical references and index.
ISBN 0-521-81646-7 – ISBN 0-521-01671-1 (pb.)
1. International law – History. 2. International agencies – History. 3. Human rights – History. 4. Economic development – History. 5. Social movements – History. I. Title.
KZ1242.R35 2003
341′09 – dc21 2003043923

ISBN 0 521 81646 7 hardback
ISBN 0 521 01671 1 paperback

CONTENTS

ABBREVIATIONS

AAA	American Anthropological Association
ADB	Asian Development Bank
ASEAN	Association of Southeast Asian Nations
BWIs	Bretton Woods Insitutions
CIDA	Canadian International Development Agency
DANIDA	Danish Agency for Development Assistance
DRD	Declaration on the Right to Development
EAD	Electoral Assistance Division of the United Nations
EBRD	European Bank for Reconstruction and Development
ECLA	Economic Commission for Latin America
ECOSOC Res.	Resolution of the Economic and Social Council of the United Nations
ESCAP	United Nations Economic and Social Commission for Asia and the Pacific
FAO	Food and Agriculture Organization
FTAA	Free Trade Area of the Americas
GAOR	United Nations General Assembly Official Records
GATT	General Agreement on Tariffs and Trade
GSP	Generalized System of Preferences
ICCPR	International Covenant on Civil and Political Rights
ICESCR	International Covenant on Economic, Social and Cultural Rights
ICJ	International Court of Justice
ICNW	Indian Cooperative Network for Women
IDA	International Development Agency
IFC	International Finance Corporation
IFES	International Foundation for Election Systems
ILO	International Labor Organisation
IMF	International Monetary Fund
JVP	Janata Vimukti Peramuna

LTTE	Liberation Tigers of Tamil Eelam
MIGA	Multilateral Investment Guarantee Agency
NABARD	National Bank for Agriculture and Rural Development
NADB	National Development Bank
NAFTA	North American Free Trade Agreement
NAM	Non Aligned Movement
NAPHR	National Action Plan on Human Rights
NATSR	National Alliance for Tribal Self Rule
NBA	Narmada Bacho Andolan
NED	National Endowment for Democracy
NFF	National Fishworkers Federation
NIEO	New International Economic Order
NOVIB	Netherlands Organization for International Development Cooperation
NUWW	National Union of Working Women
OAU	Organization of African Unity
OECD	Organization for Economic Cooperation and Development
OPEC	Organization of the Petroleum Exporting Countries
PCIJ	Permanent Court of International Justice
PCN	Process of Black Communities
PMC	Permanent Mandates Commission
PSNR	Permanent Sovereignty over Natural Resources
SERNAM	Servicio Nacional de la Mujer
SIDA	Swedish International Development Agency
SIDBI	Small Industries Development Bank of India
SUNFED	Special United Nations Fund for Economic Development
UNCTAD	United Nations Conference on Trade and Development
UNDP	United Nations Development Program
UNFPA	United Nations Population Fund
UNHCHR	United Nations High Commissioner for Human Rights
UDHR	Universal Declaration of Human Rights
UNGA	United Nations General Assembly
UNGA Res.	Resolution of the United Nations General Assembly
UNICEF	United Nations Children's Fund
UNSG	United Nations Secretary General

UNTS	United Nations Treaty Series
USAID	United States Agency for International Development
WHO	World Health Organization
WTO	World Trade Organization
WWF	Working Women's Forum

PREFACE AND ACKNOWLEDGMENTS

The role of non-state actors, particularly NGOs and social movements, has become more important in international relations and in domestic policy. The well-known protests against the World Trade Organization in Seattle in 1999 and against other global economic institutions since then have firmly introduced social movements into the debate on global governance. The violent attacks against targets in the US on September 11, 2001, have even introduced the idea of networks of non-state actors into analyses of peace and security. Indeed, recent work in several disciplines including international relations, comparative politics, sociology and anthropology has attempted to come to grips with these new phenomena.[1] Despite this, legal scholarship in general, and international legal scholarship in particular, have been slow to respond to these changes. Despite recent work in law and society that examines the importance of social mobilization for legal transformation,[2] international legal scholarship has remained largely isolated from this body of work. A principal purpose of this book is to fill this gap by systematically addressing the role of social movements in international legal transformation.

However, this is a hard task. There are two ways of seeing and interpreting international legal transformation – from above as most lawyers do when they focus on formal sources, judicial opinions, and treaties exclusively – or from below when we focus on the lived experience of ordinary people with international law when they encounter international institutions, frame their demands in international legal terms, and network for influencing international or domestic policy. The latter genre of work is not usual in international law, partly because there is no tradition of socio-legal research in international law as there is in domestic law. Therefore, "thicker" descriptions of how norms and institutions evolve – for instance, through ethonography – are not common. But it is clear that there is a greater need for such scholarship in international law now more

[1] See e.g., Keck and Sikkink (1998).

[2] See e.g., Epp (1998); Rosenberg (1991).

than at any other time. This book is a modest contribution to such an effort. It describes how the growth of modern international law (especially international institutions and human rights, its two most cosmopolitan achievements of the twentieth century) is a product of an ambivalent and complex interaction between international law and social movements of people in the Third World faced with a process of enormous transformation unleashed in their territories called "development."

The telling of this story is also targeted at the ideological and political structure of standard narratives about how international legal transformation happens. In this traditional analysis, legal change is either "internal," driven by the structure of norms, the function of institutions, and the interests of states. Or legal change is "external," driven by changes in community values, interests, or power. In either case, this story-telling has been characterized by two major sets of bias: a bias towards the West, rarely treating the Third World as a maker of legal transformation; and a bias towards the elites in legal transformation, ignoring the importance of the role played by ordinary people. This book challenges these sets of bias and argues that it is impossible to understand how international law and institutions have evolved in the modern period (since the League of Nations) without taking Third World social movements, into account. To that extent, this study is also a contribution to a tradition of Third World scholarship in international law. But it is also a challenge to traditional Third World scholarship in international law that remained focused on the state, by examining the relation between states, social movements, and international norms and institutions.

This book is the outgrowth of my doctoral dissertation at Harvard Law School submitted in June 2000, but reflects several years of engagement with the themes presented here during my human rights and legal work with the United Nations. Writing this book would not have been possible without the help of a very large number of individuals. First among them is David Kennedy, my doctoral supervisor, whose personal encouragement to "return" from the field of activism and undertake the arduous task of writing a doctoral thesis, is gratefully acknowledged. More than that, his scholarship has provided a singular inspiration for my work and challenged me to engage in critical reflection in a way that I myself would never have imagined possible.

This work also importantly benefited from the guidance of my doctoral committee consisting of Amartya Sen, William Fisher, and Joseph Singer as well as detailed criticism from the external reader, Richard Falk. I thank them all for their critical, yet constructive, comments and support.

I wish to thank the network of scholars assembled under the acronym "New Approaches to International Law," whose important work has provided the ideal setting for developing my arguments. Thanks to David Kennedy and Duncan Kennedy for introducing me to this remarkable group. I also wish to thank the network of international legal scholars who have collectively pursued "Third World Approaches to International Law," whose work has been important and inspiring, and into which genre this book falls.

I have also benefited greatly from the comments and criticism of some fellow Third World travelers including Anthony Anghie, Bhupinder Singh Chimni, James Gathii, Amr Shalakany, Hani Sayed, and Celestine Nyamu. In no particular order, the following individuals have had a major influence on this work and with whom I have had the pleasure of discussing many of the themes presented here: Nathaniel Berman, Duncan Kennedy, Gerald Frug, (the late) Abe Chayes, Henry Steiner, Lucy White, Frank Michelman, Martha Minow, Anne-Marie Slaughter and William Alford. I thank them all for their generosity. Martti Koskenniemi and Jan Klabbers provided detailed criticism and comments on the whole manuscript and I am particularly grateful to them. Martti's work has been singularly inspiring for mine. I am also deeply grateful to the detailed comments of the two anonymous reviewers of Cambridge University Press on the whole manuscript.

At various stages, the following people sharpened my understanding of the themes presented here through discussions and I thank them deeply: Kerry Rittich, Robert Wai, Obiora Okafor, Annelise Riles, Karen Knop, Chantol Thomas, Karen Engle, Diane Otto, Hilary Charlesworth, Susan Marks, Philip Allot, Makau Mutua, Benedict Kingsbury, Tom Farer, Tayyab Mahmud, Arturo Escobar, Smitu Kothari, Gustavo Esteva, Ashis Nandy, Stephen Marglin, Justice C. G. Weeramantry, Greg Fox, Frank Garcia, Eva Thorne, Sanjeev Khagram, Ed Morgan, Joel Ngugi, Keith Aoki, Liliana Obregon, Lan Cao, Upendra Baxi, and Vasuki Nesiah.

At MIT, the following colleagues have been kind enough to discuss and sometimes offer comments on either ideas presented here or on various parts of this book: Judith Tendler, Bish Sanyal, Diane Davis, Alice Amsden, Karen Polenske, John DeMonchaux, Larry Susskind, Dara O'Rourke, Martin Rein, Larry Vale, Noam Chomsky, Susan Silbey, Jean Jackson, Suzanne Berger, Michael Piore, and Evelyn Fox-Keller. I thank them all for their generosity

I am grateful to the students and faculty who participated in the "New social movements and international law" workshop that I taught at

Harvard Law School as a Senior Fellow in 1997–98, the students in the "Economic development and international institutions" seminar at University of Oklahoma Law School in fall 1998 that I taught as Crowe and Dunlevy Visiting International Professor, the students in the summer seminar on international law at the University of Helsinki Faculty of Law in 2000 and the students in my "Law, social movements and public policy" course at MIT. The work on this book was supported by several fellowships: the Samuel Morse Lane Fellowship, the Senior Fellowship and the Reginald Lewis Fellowship, all at Harvard Law School and the Soros Justice Senior Fellowship. I thank them all.

My editors at Cambridge University Press, Finola O'Sullivan and Jennie Rubio, were pillars of support and showed enormous enthusiasm and patience while prodding me along. My production editor, Jackie Warren, was superbly efficient. I thank them. I am grateful to Marisa Cravens for her help with the list of references.

Some chapters from this book have been previously published in whole or in part in journals or books, often in substantially different form. The publications are:

"International Law and Social Movements: Challenges of Theorizing Resistance," *Columbia Journal of Transnational Law* 42 (2003), 397

"From Modernization to Democratization: the Political Economy of the "New" International Law," in eds., Richard Falk, Lerter Ruiz, and R. B. J. Walker *Reframing International Law for the Twenty-first Century* (Routledge, 2002)

"From Resistance to Renewal: the Third World, Social Movements and the Expansion of International Institutions," *Harvard International Law Journal* 41(2) (Symposium Issue on International Law and the Developing World: a Millenial Analysis, Spring 2000), 529.

"International Law and the Development Encounter: Violence and Resistance at the Margins," 93rd American Society of International Law Proceedings (1999), 16.

This book is dedicated to my wife, Anu and our children, Mekala and Muhil, whose love and affection in the face of my obvious failings makes all the work so important. Finally, this book and all my work would not have been possible without the love and support of my mother, Kalyani, and the faith of my father, S. R. Balakrishnan, who inspired the love of law and scholarship in me.

Introduction

This book chronicles the complex relationship between international law and the Third World, during the twentieth century. It does so by suggesting that it is impossible to obtain a full understanding of this complex relationship unless one factors in two phenomena: first, a focus on development discourse as the governing logic of the political, economic, and social life in the Third World; and second, an appreciation of the role of social movements in shaping the relationship between Third World resistance and international law. The suggestion in this book is that dominant approaches to international law are deficient because they neither take development discourse to be important for the very formation of international law and institutions, nor do they adopt a subaltern perspective that enables a real appreciation of the role of social movements in the evolution of international law. The central concern then is: how does one write resistance into international law and make it recognize subaltern voices? In particular, international law has been crucially shaped during the twentieth century by the nature and the forms of Third World resistance to development. This has happened at at least two levels: first, substantial parts of the architecture of international law – international institutions – have evolved, in ambivalent relationship with this resistance; second, human-rights discourse has been fundamentally shaped – and limited – by the forms of Third World resistance to development. The focus on these two areas of international law – international institutions and human rights – is simply due to the centrality of these areas of law in modern international law, that is, from the League of Nations. By showing that the central aspects of modern international law cannot be understood without taking due account of the impact of development and Third World social movements, this work challenges traditional narratives of how international legal change has come about and how one might understand the place of law in progressive social praxis. I argue that international law needs to be fundamentally rethought if it is to take the disparate forms of Third World resistance seriously.

At a fundamental level, this work is an attempt to explore how international law relates to the 'base,' how the functional and pragmatic cosmopolitan relates to 'culture,' to the Other across the barrier of civilization and rationality. International law has traditionally not concerned itself with this relationship except to repress/suppress the existence of such relationships. But, it now seems urgent to abandon such narrow views as partial, partisan, and ideological. International law is no longer a marginal discipline that figures occasionally in diplomatic disagreements about war and peace. Rather, it is now an ensemble of rules, policies, institutions, and practices that directly and indirectly affects the daily lives of millions of people all over the world, in the areas of economy, environment, family relationships, and governmental performance. Yet, extant approaches to international law do not seem to ask the elemental question of for whom international law exists. Rather, the mainstream – both the apologist and the utopian[1] – seem to function within specific paradigms of western modernity and rationality, that predetermine the actors for whom international law exists. These include political actors such as state officials, economic actors such as corporations and cultural actors such as the atomized individual who is the subject of rights. This actor-based approach of international law simply privileges what happens in certain institutional arenas. While that may be important for some purposes, most of the people in the Third World live and interact in non-institutional spaces: in the family, the informal economy, and non-party political spaces. This dynamic is of great relevance at the beginning of the twenty-first century due to the rapid mobility of people and capital across borders and the resultant overlapping and interchangeability of identities and values, a dynamic that is sometimes partially captured by the word "globalization." International law, either in its statist realist version, or in its cosmopolitan liberal version, falls short of providing a viable framework for thinking about these issues. It is suggested that a social movement perspective may assist in developing that framework, but only at the cost of a fundamental rethinking of international law.

At a second level, this work investigates how Third World resistance is analyzed within international law. Extant approaches look at Third World resistance in purely statist terms, for example as it manifested through the Third World coalition at the UN in the 1960s and 1970s. In my view, this is no longer an adequate or accurate way to analyze patterns of Third World resistance to international law. Patterns of the Third World's interaction

[1] These refer to the framework adopted in Koskenniemi (1989).

with international law have changed significantly and can no longer be analyzed within the statist paradigm alone. Nor can such patterns be analyzed through the liberal rights paradigm alone, as the rights paradigm is also a statist one, and, besides, it overlooks the continuing relevance of public action to international law's relationship with the Third World. The attempt here to use a social movement perspective to analyze Third World resistance to international law is the first known attempt to systematically engage with changing patterns of the Third World's interaction with international law.

Thirdly, this work seeks to displace development as a progressive Third World narrative. Traditionally, international law scholarship – both utopian mainstream and previous Third World approaches – saw development in positive, glowing terms due to its supposed potential to assist in the nation-building project or to promote liberal objectives. Instead, I approach development discourse as a particular ensemble of norms, practices, and institutions in which there is a general loss of faith in the Third World exhibited most clearly through the agitations of social movements. This is in large part due to the realization among social movements and progressive intellectuals that it is not the lack of development that caused poverty, inflicted violence, and engaged in destruction of nature and livelihoods; rather it is the very process of bringing development that has caused them in the first place. As such, social movements seek to construct alternative visions of modernity and development that constitute valid Third World approaches to international law. The mainstream and past Third World approaches must be questioned for rendering such alternative practices invisible. In this sense, this book is not concerned with traditional topics such as 'international development law.' Rather, it is more concerned with the role of international law in shaping the ideas and practices in the field of development and with the role of ideas and practices in the field of development in shaping international law.

At a theoretical level, this book builds on the insights of postcolonial theory, poststructuralism, postmodernism, critical race theory, critical development theory, and critical Third World scholarship loosely identified by the acronym TWAIL (Third World Approaches to International Law). Methodologically, it adopts an eclectic mixture of an internal critique (based on discourse analysis) and an external critique (bringing insights and evidence from outside international law, buttressed by a case study and several examples of social movements). The work itself falls into a genre of scholarship that straddles established fields including international law and law and society, a new kind of socio-legal international legal scholarship that attempts to offer thicker descriptions of legal transformations. Two limitations must be noted. First, it does not claim to do a complete mapping of all the critical moments of Third World resistance to international law, but only those moments that are considered crucial. Second, it does not chart out all the relevant social movements that have ever had an impact on international law,[2] but only those that are relevant to my inquiries, for example in the area of environment. It must also be noted that this is not a book on the role of NGOs and non-governmental networks in international law; rather, its major purpose is to contest particular ways of explaining international legal change. In the final analysis, the work on social movements in the Third World and their complex relationship with global political and legal change is born out of a search for culturally legitimate forms of resistance that nevertheless do not fall into the trap of nativism.

The following chapters expand and build upon these and related themes. Part I offers an introduction to the question of theorizing resistance as an analytical category in international law and an analysis of the ways in which 'development' was received by international lawyers after World War II. Part II explores four critical moments of international institutional expansion: the Mandate system of the League of Nations, the establishment of UN development agencies and their expansion by the Third World coalition in the 1960s and 1970s, the expansion of Bretton Woods institutions, and the evolution of post-Cold-War institutions to promote democracy and peace. All of these cannot be understood, I suggest, without an appreciation of how the ideology of development was deployed and how the Third World resisted it. In the course of these evolutions, the nature of Third World resistance underwent many changes as well, from anticolonial nationalist to statist, to that of social movements. Part III offers a critique of human rights discourse as the sole approved discourse of resistance and an analysis of the fundamental theoretical challenges that social movements pose for international law. I illustrate the arguments made in this Part with a case study of the Working Women's Forum, India's largest women's movement. Part IV concludes with some reflections on the challenges that confront international lawyers if they wish to build an international law that takes the resistance of social movements seriously. A central conclusion is that while the most important aspects of cosmopolitan international law of the twentieth century have

[2] A prominent example is the peace movement of the nineteenth and twentieth centuries, which has had a profound effect on humanitarian law.

been ineluctably shaped by Third World resistance including through social movements, it has repressed and excluded this resistance from the story of its formation. A call to write that resistance into international law – a task undertaken here – should ideally lead to a fundamental rethinking of how global change at the present time can be achieved and what role, if any, international law should play in that process.

PART I

International law, development, and Third World resistance

1

Writing Third World resistance into international law

> Provided the imperial power is itself prepared to set the pace for self-government and does not have to be forced out by pressure from below, the legacies of the past can quickly be transformed from a serious handicap in world affairs into a priceless diplomatic and political advantage.[1]

> That is the partial tragedy of resistance, that it must to a certain extent work to recover forms already established or at least influenced or infiltrated by the culture of empire.[2]

There are several themes that run through this book which attempt to rethink Third World resistance to international law. Let me outline some of them here. First, a straightforward Saidian theme:[3] when international law, as a cultural category, encounters resistance, it can engage with it only by adopting certain unchanging essences of western or Third World-ness, as well as images of legitimacy and redemption. The result of this can be seen in the ways in which certain types of resistance are chosen as legitimate and certain other types are not in international law, and the power that makes this choice possible. This can be seen, for example, in the invisibility of Third World environmental movements to progressive Third World legal scholarship or in the attribution of the success of public enterprises (town and village enterprises or TVEs) in China to kinship ties (rather than economic rationality) by the World Bank.

Second, just as colonialism as a system sanctioned legitimacy to only certain forms of anticolonial resistance (mild nationalism), only certain forms of resistance in the Third World have been granted legitimacy. The main filter through which Third World resistance is admitted to be legitimate is the discourse of human rights. Indeed, human rights has emerged as the sole approved discourse of resistance. I do not claim that resistance through rights is not legitimate or that other forms of resistance

[1] Kenneth Younger, former minister of state in the Foreign Office of Great Britain, "The colonial issues in world politics" in Creech Jones (1959) 53.

[2] Said (1993) 210. [3] Said (1978).

are more 'authentic' and therefore more legitimate. I merely point out the ideological/imperial character of this exercise of power by the discourse of rights, and explore if alternative forms of resistance through the praxis of social movements may recode resistance in international law.

Third, I am interested in the relationship between resistance and institutions. This is very important for law, as it is the language of institutions. I explore this theme at two levels. First, I examine whether it is more useful to study in greater detail the systemic nature of resistance. Many, if not most, social movements shape and are shaped by the environment in which institutions and their politics develop. This is true even if these movements 'fail,' due to unintended consequences as well as intended but unrealized consequences. For example, environmental, human rights, and other movements have driven the evolution of the agendas of the World Bank, and trade unions and women's movements have fed off each other in India. Another way of stating this is that resistance continues even after successful institutionalization of its goals – nationalism does not represent the final fruit of anticolonial struggle. But law pays no attention to this dynamic, preferring to view institutions as functional embodiments of legal rationality and resistance as an aberration and in need of repression. It seems to me that law and institutions very much depend on resistance.

At the second level, I note the somewhat tragic reality that resistance must work, to some extent, within the parameters established by that which is being resisted. This has the constant danger of making resistance a cooptive/coopted enterprise. Progressive Third World scholarship is aware of this danger and attempts two ways to deal with it: first, scholars reject the parameters set by that which is being resisted, in favor of a culturally 'authentic' way of resistance. Certain proponents of strong cultural relativism in human rights, as well as many social movement theorists, take this approach as they seek to counterpose alternative visions of modernity to that of the hegemonic discourse which is being resisted. A second approach would be to treat resistance and its antithesis as mutually overlapping, constitutive, and a dialectic, and therefore to show that the object of resistance is not as imperial and internally strong as it appears. These are the Saidians. I trace both tendencies of Third World resistance to international law.

The fourth theme is the idea that resistance is not merely always a reaction to hegemony, but is in fact a complex multitude of alternative visions of social relationships and therefore, of human history. This theme is based on two propositions about the nature of resistance: first, I reject the absolute wall of separation between resistance and forms of hegemony. Another way of stating this is that there is no such thing as an absolute modern v. tradition, primitive v. advanced, or developed v. underdeveloped dichotomy. Second, viewing forms of resistance as various valid ways of conceiving the world rejects the dogma that to be legitimate resistance must either work within existing theories of human liberation or formulate an entirely new 'universal' paradigm that is applicable across time and space. Yet, this is precisely how legal scholarship works. An example would be Abdullahi An-Na'im's contrived attempt to fit Islam into a human rights framework.[4]

Resistance as an analytical category in international law

Traditional international law did not concern itself with the resistance of mass action unless it was directed at the creation of states in the form of movements that asserted the right to self-determination. Even in such cases, international law usually left the murky terrain and 'returned' only to welcome the victor as the legitimate representative of state sovereignty.[5] This doctrinal position enabled European and American colonial empires to defeat the legal claims of Third World anticolonial nationalist movements for independence under international law. No matter how much 'resistance' the natives posed – for example the Mau Mau rebellion in British Kenya – international law had no vocabulary for understanding and accommodating it. This enabled the colonial authorities to treat anticolonial resistance as criminal acts and deal with them through law-enforcement measures, especially through the doctrine of emergency. Indeed, traditional international law was notorious for the ease with which it sanctioned violence against non-western peoples. As Professor Anthony Anghie has emphasized about nineteenth-century positivism,

[4] An-Na'im (1990) 17. For an entirely different take on the issue of universality of human rights and its relationship to culture, see Panikkar (1982). An-Na'im is not without ambivalence: in later publications, he has taken a strong relativist perspective. See An-Na'im (1992) 37.

[5] See Aalands Islands Case, *Official Journal of the League of Nations*, Supp. No.3 (1920), 6 (stating that, when a state undergoes transformation or dissolution, its legal status is uncertain). For a trenchant critique of this case and self-determination doctrine, see Berman (1988). See also Rajagopal (1992) 666–74.

> The violence of positivist language in relation to non-European peoples is hard to overlook. Positivists developed an elaborate vocabulary for denigrating these peoples, presenting them as suitable objects for conquest, and legitimizing the most extreme violence against them, all in the furtherance of the civilizing mission – the discharge of the white man's burden.[6]

The hope that formal political independence for the colonized territories will quickly lead to the creation of a new international law was dashed as the efforts by the newly independent countries to create a New International Economic Order (NIEO) in the 1970s ground to a halt.[7] During the last couple of decades, it has become increasingly hard to place much hope in the capacity of Third World states to act as real guarantors of the democratic aspirations of the masses in the Third World, as state sovereignty has been parceled out up (to international institutions such as the World Trade Organization – WTO – and Bretton Woods institutions) and down (to market actors and NGOs). The idea of development, with its catching-up rationale, that provided the motivation for nation-building in the post-War period, has come to be seen as an ideological enterprise with profoundly dangerous implications for the most vulnerable and voiceless in society. In addition, the Third World state has come to colonize all life spaces in civil society and has effectively championed the interests of the global elite that runs the world economy. The democratic deficit experienced by global governance processes has been exacerbated due to the democratic deficit of Third World states that act as the agents of the globalitarian class. The reformist sensibility in international law during the post-War period, which revolved around a commitment to individual human rights, and an expanded concept of international development including the law of welfare, also failed to reverse the rot in the system. As I argue in later chapters, the idea of human rights has proved to be blind to the tremendous variety that human-rights struggles take in the form of social movement resistance in the Third World, while the idea of development has proved to be associated with the containment of mass resistance (especially anticommunist peasant) and a destructive modernity. The post-War 'settlement' of the colonial question through the grant of political sovereignty did not end mass movements in the Third World. Instead, this resistance took myriad other forms through social

[6] Anghie (1999) 7.

[7] This took the form of a number of UN General Assembly resolutions and declarations whose legal status was contested by western international lawyers. See United Nations (1974a), United Nations (1974b). On the NIEO, see Bedjaoui (1979).

movement action that have not been sufficiently understood by international lawyers, partly due to their own disciplinary limitations that are discussed in this book. It is now becoming obvious that Third World social movements represent the cutting edge of resistance in the Third World to antidemocratic and destructive development. It is important for international lawyers to try to develop a theory of resistance that would enable them to at least partially respond to it.

A theory of resistance in international law must pay particular attention to the rearticulation of four issues: against what? (the nature of the exercise of power in current international society including by the modern state); towards what end? (the nature of human liberation that is aimed, including the relationship between resistance and the psychology of deprivation); using what strategies? (the relationship between reformist and radical resistance); and what should be the role of the postcolonial state in resistance? (state as a plural, fragmented, and contested terrain). While this project has not yet truly begun, some possible inspirations for building such a theory of resistance can be identified.

Michel Foucault

A first such source of inspiration is the notion of governmentality or governmental rationality, expounded by Michel Foucault in a set of lectures in late 1970s.[8] This notion helps us in better understanding the nature of particular exercises of power that a theory of resistance must focus on. As he defines it, governmentality means:

1 The ensemble formed by the institutions, procedures, analyses and reflections, the calculations and tactics that allow the exercise of this very specific albeit complex form of power, which has as its target population, as its principal form of knowledge political economy, and as its essential technical means apparatuses of security.
2 The tendency which, over a long period and throughout the West, has steadily led towards the pre-eminence over all other forms (sovereignty, discipline, etc.) of this type of power which may be termed government, resulting, on the one hand, in the formation of a whole series of specific governmental apparatuses, and on the other, in the development of a whole complex of *savoirs*.
3 The process, or rather the result of the process, through which the state of justice of the Middle Ages transformed into the administrative

[8] See Gordon, Burchell, and Miller (1991).

state during the fifteenth and sixteenth centuries, gradually becomes 'governmentalized.'[9]

The nature of the exercise of power in the Third World makes it clear that it is a mistake to regard power emerging from the state as the principal one. Rather, most effective power has shifted to apparatuses of government that are both above and below the state as well as to private actors, both domestic and transnational. As such we need a theory of power in the Third World that is broader than that which emerges from state institutions. Also, the form of exercise of power in the Third World has a particular bureaucratic aspect to it, consisting of techniques designed to observe, monitor, shape, and control the behavior of individuals, especially of the poor, situated within the state.[10] This focus on the population is particularly intense with regard to the poor who constitute a main domain of the exercise of governmental rationality. This is nothing new, of course. As a mid-nineteenth-century French author puts it, "assisting the poor is a means of government, a potent way of containing the most difficult section of the population and improving all other sections."[11] In addition, Foucault's definition is useful for developing a theory of resistance that moves away from a fetishism of the state. Traditional state theory in the Third World, influenced by Marxism, holds that the modern activities of government must be deduced from the properties and propensities of the state.[12] Foucault reverses that presumption and suggests that the nature of state institutions is a function of changes in the practice of government. This has the salutary effect of moving the focus of political theory from an excessive attention on institutions to practices.[13] Finally, Foucault's definition allows for a focus on the micropolitics of power relations and their strategic reversibility. The former permits a theory of resistance to take into account how individuals and groups experience power relations, thus enabling international law to accommodate the feminist slogan 'Personal is Political' without theoretical discomfort.[14] The strategic reversibility of power relations essentially shows the contestability

[9] Foucalt (1991) 102–03.

[10] The practice of Bretton Woods institutions in recent years is a good example of this new popularity of poverty alleviation. Even the IMF has embraced this as its governing mantra, launching the Poverty Reduction and Growth Facility (PRGF) in 1999. See http://www.imf.org/external/np/exr/facts/prgf.htm.

[11] Firmin Marbeau, cited in Procacci (1991) 151.

[12] Gordon, Burchell, and Miller (1991) 4.

[13] Ibid.

[14] For an example of discomfort with feminist approaches to international law, see Teson (1993).

of seemingly entrenched power structures by showing how governmental practices themselves can be turned around into focus of resistance, in what Foucault calls the "history of dissenting 'counter-conducts.'"[15] This focus on micropolitics and strategic reversibility offers a richer basis for articulating a theory of resistance that focuses on social movements.

Frantz Fanon

A second question in the articulation of a theory of resistance is towards what end the resistance must aim. In two of his well-known essays, "Concerning Violence" and the "Pitfalls of National Consciousness,"[16] Fanon lays out the psychological aspects of colonialism as well as that of anticolonial resistance. There are three themes that arise from his work that are relevant to the articulation of a theory of resistance that engages with Third World social movement action. The first theme is that human liberation cannot be confined within the nationalist paradigm. As Amilcar Cabral stated, "national liberation is an act of culture."[17] This basic lesson is amply illustrated by the emergence of thousands of social movements of farmers, peasants, urban poor, indigenous peoples, women, and workers, who have felt let down during the nation-building project during the postcolonial period. The idea that nationalism is a total response to colonialism has proved inadequate. As Fanon says, "history teaches us that the battle against colonialism does not run straight away along the lines of nationalism."[18] Instead, he advocates a range of measures that can be adopted to avoid the dangers of nationalist consciousness, including that of that singular postcolonial institution, the political party, which rests on the western assumption that the masses are incapable of governing themselves.[19] These views have profound importance for articulating the ends of mass resistance in already-independent nation states as they move us away from the ends that are traditionally postulated for mass movements in international law such as secession. Indeed, the practice of several social movements such as the Zapatistas in Mexico and the National Alliance for Tribal Self Rule (NATSR) in India, have moved away from nationalist framings of their demands. Nevertheless, these movements often see their strategies as contributing to a vision of human liberation that is as profound as anticolonial nationalism. As Pradip Prabhu, one of the conveners of the NATSR remarked about the passage of a law in India

[15] Gordon, Burchell, and Miller (1991) 5. [16] Fanon (1963) 35–106 and 148–205.
[17] Cabral (1970) 6. [18] Fanon (1963) 148. [19] Ibid. 188.

in 1996 that extended village self-rule to tribal areas, "it is the first serious nail on [sic] the coffin of colonialism."[20]

A second theme that emerges from the work of Fanon relates to resistance and economic power. A traditional understanding of mass action holds that, to be viable, mass action must rest on economic strength. This economic theory of violence is derived from Marxist theory, which holds that economic substructure determines all social outcomes. As Engels states, "to put it briefly, the triumph of violence depends upon the production of armaments, and this in turn depends on production in general, and thus . . . on economic strength, on the economy of the State and in the last resort on the material means which that violence commands."[21] It is this logic that drives accumulation of economic power by nation states and that forms the core of the catching-up rationale in the development paradigm. It is also this logic behind the traditional Third World lawyers' response to colonialism as a peculiar economic exploitation (as opposed to racial or religious domination) which could, they believed, be reversed through doctrines such as Permanent Sovereignty over Natural Resources.[22] But, as I argue below, mass action in the Third World is often a combination of struggles over material resources and symbolic meanings. It is simultaneously cultural and economic. Fanon recognizes the importance of this aspect. On the one hand, he bluntly states that in the colonies, "the economic substructure is also the superstructure. The cause is the consequence; you are rich because you are white, you are white because you are rich."[23] In the postcolonial context, the intersecting relation between caste, racial, ethnic, or religious dominance with economic dominance is a fact of life. It is also a fact of life in international relations. On the other hand, Fanon also notes that even economic and military dominance has not historically assured colonial countries of victories over the colonized peoples partly due to tactics such as guerilla warfare.[24] Fanon's theory helps us avoid the underestimation of mass resistance in a non-hegemonic context, which includes most social movements action. It is especially germane in international relations in the post 9/11 era of asymmetric threats from well-organized movements such as al Queda.

A third theme that is relevant to a theory of resistance is Fanon's understanding that the new forms of capitalism in the Third World have

[20] Personal communication, Fall 1997. [21] Cited in Fanon (1963) 64.

[22] G.A.Res. 1803, U.N. GAOR, 17th Sess., Supp. No.17 at 15, U.N.Doc. A/5217 (1962). See also Hossain and Chowdhury (1984).

[23] Fanon (1963) 40. [24] Ibid. 64–65

transformed the political space for governance and resistance. Though he was writing well before the advent of the new global economy, Fanon notes that as the colony is transformed from a sphere of exploitation to a market for goods, blind domination of the natives based on slavery is replaced by a desire to protect the market including the 'legitimate interests' of the colonial business elite.[25] This creates, in his view, a sort of "detached complicity" between capitalism and anticolonial resistance.[26] In addition, the creation of a worker force in the colony leads to a politics of reformism wherein strikes and boycotts take the place of anticolonial rebellion.[27] This analysis has much to offer to understand how contemporary global capitalism works and how resistance to it is structured. On the one hand, global capitalism works to create and protect markets and increasingly, the 'rights' of the consumers. Its presence in Third World societies creates workers and others who directly benefit from it and whose politics is aimed at reformism. This analysis reveals how the spread of free markets is so often equated with the spread of freedom in general. For articulating a theory of resistance under conditions of globalization, there must be an acute understanding of how globalization structures opportunities for resistance. Fanon's work offers some clues as to how to proceed.

Antonio Gramsci

A third inspiration for a theory of resistance in international law that sheds light on the various strategies of resistance, is the well-known work of Antonio Gramsci in the "Prison Notebooks."[28] Though eurocentric[29] like his contemporaries, Gramsci postulates three ideas that are of enormous value for articulating a theory of resistance that focuses on the practice of social movements. The first is his notion of 'hegemony,' which he defines as

1 The spontaneous consent given by the great masses of the population to the general direction imposed on social life by the dominant fundamental group; this consent is "historically" caused by the prestige (and consequent confidence) which the dominant group enjoys because of its position and function in the world of production;
2 The apparatus of state coercive power which "legally" enforces discipline on those groups who do not "consent" either actively or passively.

[25] Ibid. 65. [26] Ibid. [27] Ibid. 66. [28] Gramsci (1971).
[29] Ibid. 416 (noting the 'hegemony of western culture over the whole world culture' and certifying that European culture is the only 'historically and concretely universal culture').

> This apparatus is, however, constituted for the whole of society in anticipation of moments of crisis of command and direction when spontaneous consent has failed.[30]

Hegemony to him, then, is an active process involving the production, reproduction, and mobilization of popular consent, which can be constructed by any "dominant group" that takes hold of it and uses it. This meaning is different from the more common understanding of 'hegemony' as domination through force, and corresponds realistically to the global process of governance, which does not rest only on brute military force but on the confluence between force and moral ideas. Thus, currently it is the case that great power interests are sought to be justified by the language 'humanitarian intervention' and containment of mass resistance is justified through 'poverty alleviation.' As such, the 'consent' given by the international society of states to the general direction imposed on world affairs is a function of the domination of the force and ideas of the west. Until recently, this hegemony was unshakeable. However, after decolonization and the rise in the economic power of Asia, as well as the emergence of multiple voices of dissent from within western societies, political opportunities have existed for some decades for creative political and legal strategies for the Third World. Social movements, including those directed at corporate accountability for environmental and human-rights abuses and single-issue movements such as those for banning anti-personnel landmines, have attempted to manufacture the consent of the population for alternative paths of sustainable development, peace, or democracy. While these movements continue to lack the state's coercive apparatus for enforcing discipline on those who do not consent, it is arguable that this part of Gramsci's definition does not apply to international affairs, and never has, as it has always lacked an enforcement mechanism. It is plausible to argue that in international law and relations, the conditions under which 'spontaneous consent' can be manufactured are as imporant if not more important than the existence of forceful enforcement mechanisms. One could see this idea in the disciplinary sensibility that states obey most rules of international law most of the time even in the absence of enforcement,[31] or in the recognition

[30] Ibid. 12.

[31] See Henkin (1979). Admittedly, the reason given for this does not rest on a Gramscian framework, but on an understanding of legal process. Nevertheless, this perspective sees the value of maintaining western 'hegemony' through the application of a legal process that produces consent. See also Koh (1997).

of the increasingly important role that transnational advocacy networks play in international politics.[32]

A second theme articulated by Gramsci relates to the definition of 'passive revolution' and the distinction between 'war of position' and 'war of movement/maneuver.' This theme is critical for understanding the relationship between civil society and the state broadly, and for theorizing about the tactical efforts of social movements to influence global law and policy. He defines passive revolution in two ways: as a revolution without mass participation and as a "molecular" social transformation that takes place beneath the surface of society where the progressive class cannot advance openly.[33] The latter meaning, for which he cites Gandhi's non-violent movement against the British rule as an example,[34] helps to introduce the everyday forms of resistance to economic and political hegemony into political theory. Although he is critical of passive revolution as a political program, he uses the term ambiguously enough to indicate that when frontal attack may be impossible, a passive revolution may be taking place: that despite the surface stability of particular regimes or, indeed, the global order, class and other forms of struggle continue even if at an interpersonal level.[35] This perspective is important for expanding the analysis of international law and politics to include thick descriptions of the micropolitics of change. Without engaging with social movement literature and the tools of anthropological analysis that it provides, international law and relations cannot hope to accomplish this.

It is important to note the distinction between 'war of position' and 'war of movement/maneuver' in Gramscian thought. Gramsci uses 'war of position' to mean a muted form of political struggle that alone is possible during periods of relatively stable equilibrium between fundamental classes.[36] In particular, he emphasizes that this struggle takes the form of winning over civil society before taking on the state. As he puts it, "a social group can, and indeed must, already exercise 'leadership' before winning governmental power (this indeed is one of the principal conditions for winning of such power)."[37] A 'war of movement/maneuver' on the other hand, is a frontal attack that aims to take over the institutions of hegemony. Boycotts are a form of war of position, strikes of war of movement.[38] The same struggle can constitute both a war of position and war of movement

[32] See Keck and Sikkink (1998). [33] Gramsci (1971) 46. [34] Ibid. 107.

[35] Ibid. 47. Partha Chatterjee suggests that passive revolution is in fact the general framework of capitalist transformation in societies where bourgeois hegemony has not been accomplished in the classical way. See Chatterjee (1993) 212.

[36] Ibid. 206. [37] Ibid. 57. [38] Ibid. 229.

at the same time. Thus he notes that Gandhi's passive resistance in India was a war of position, which at certain times became a war of movement and, at others, underground warfare.[39] Social movement action is mostly a passive revolution, which can, at times be a war of position (as when transnational movements press demands for boycotts of brands or insist on eco-labeling) or a war of movement (as when ethical investors divest stocks of companies that are deemed by social movement actors to be unfriendly to environmental or human-rights concerns). A political theory of international law that ignores the role of passive revolution or war of position is in danger of becoming irrelevant or worse, being blind to the role of non-state groups that do not qualify as NGOs.

A third issue that is important to a theory of resistance is the relationship between the masses and intellectuals. Several social movements that arose during the 1990s have revealed the existence of a symbiotic relationship between mass action and movement intellectuals who act as mediators between the movements and the global cosmopolitan class. Some intellectuals have assumed leadership positions themselves in social movements. Examples include Gustavo Esteva (Zapatistas), Vandana Shiva (ecological feminism), and Arundhati Roy (Narmada Bachao Andolan in India). However, there are few, if any, international lawyers who are associated with social movements. This notable fact makes even progressive international lawyers rather clubby and elitist with no real connection with the most important mass struggles of our time. This is especially the case in the Third World where international lawyers have an ethical responsibility to the masses but remain committed to highly formalistic and statist analyses of the international order. This leads them to take positions on international legal issues that reflect state positions while entirely ignoring social reality. An example would be the ready acceptance by Third World international lawyers in the 1970s of the developing countries' position that environmental concerns were those of the rich and poverty was the greatest polluter, while entirely overlooking the ongoing peoples' movements around the environment in their own societies.[40]

Gramsci's analysis helps us formulate a theory about the proper relationship between international lawyers (as intellectuals) and social movements. He explains that the supremacy of the social group manifests itself

[39] Ibid.

[40] See e.g., Anand (1980). Several environmental movements such as Chipko had been already ongoing in India since the early 1970s. See Guha (1989).

in two ways, as "domination" and as "intellectual and moral leadership."[41] As such, it is imperative for a struggle to encompass the capture of intellectual and moral leadership and this opens a role for intellectuals. Agreeing with Lenin that the division of labor between intellectuals and the working class is false,[42] he suggests that the working class is capable of developing from within itself "organic intellectuals" who have a dual role: that of production and organization of work and of a "directive political" role.[43] This approach has the salutary effect of drawing attention to the class character and other ruling characteristics of international lawyers while recognizing the connection between their role in 'producing' legal knowledge and the dominant group of which they are a part. It is imperative that a theory of resistance in international law pay close attention to these aspects of elite–non-elite and law–social interaction to remain effective and credible.

Partha Chatterjee

One of the most important issues for articulating a theory of resistance in international law concerns the role of the state. The sanctioned language of resistance in international law, human rights, is generally thought to be an anti-state discourse, though this is now increasingly recognized as an inaccurate description.[44] Given that many Third World social movements arose as a result of the pathologies of the developmental state, as I argue below, what is and should be the relationship between resistance and the state? Should the state be a target or an ally? It is impossible to answer this question in the abstract as it depends on the particular relationship between states and social movements on particular issues. Nevertheless, some clues can be drawn from the work of Partha Chatterjee[45] about the nature of the postcolonial state in order to develop some understanding of how social movements relate to Third World states.

A first theme that Partha Chatterjee develops is the centrality of the ideology of development for the very self-definition of the postcolonial state.[46] This directly resulted from an economic critique of colonial rule, that it was illegitimate because it resulted in the exploitation of the

[41] Gramsci (1971) 57. [42] Ibid. 3–4. [43] Ibid. 4.

[44] This is due to the increasing salience of economic, social and cultural rights which require an active role for the state, as well as the recognition that effective protection of human rights and rule of law sometimes requires state-building. On the first, see UNDP (2000). On the second, see Fox (1999).

[45] See Chatterjee (1993). [46] Ibid. 202–05.

nation.[47] The state represents the only legitimate form of exercise of power because it is a necessary condition for the development of the nation. In this view, the legitimacy of the state does not come merely from elections or its democratic character; rather it comes from its rational character to direct a program of economic development for the nation.[48] As such, the challenge posed by social movements to the developmental ideology of the state, whether it be through environmental or human-rights critiques of its developmental activities, is seen as anti-national.[49] What is required instead, is a theory of resistance that questions the development ideology of the state and seeks to build alternative sources of legitimacy for the state.

A second theme relates to the supposed neutrality of the state in the development process. The postcolonial goal was to establish a Hegelian rational state that would engage in planning for and implementation of development. This soon proved to be difficult as the state itself proved to be a contested terrain where the power relations that it seeks to reorder through development planning are already shaping the very identity of the state[50] and of civil society. This means that the objects and subjects of planning merge into each other and politics is never just an external constraint on the state in the development process.[51] Rather, politics deeply interpenetrates the state even as the state constitutes itself as the chief agent of development. This insight has deep implications for international law, as it too assumes a neutral state that undertakes to execute legal obligations in a technical-rational manner, regarding objects of intervention that are located in politics. A theory of resistance in international law must allow for the inter-penetrability of state and society, of domestic and international, and of law and politics. In fact, social movement practice shows that this has already been happening. For example, the leaders of social movements and the state agencies in Latin America in areas such as environment and women's rights constantly switch jobs and blur the lines between the state and the objects of its intervention. Often, social movements and the states have complex, inter-penetrating relationships, such as SERNAM (Servicio Nacional de la Mujer) in Chile,[52] which is a National Women's Bureau, or the Venezuelan ecology movement that began with a state Organic Law on the Environment in 1976.[53] This complexity shows

[47] Ibid. 202. [48] Ibid.

[49] For example, the critics of the Narmada dam project in India have been dubbed by its Home Minister as foreign elements. For a critique, see Rajagopal (2000b).

[50] Chatterjee (1993) 207–08. [51] Ibid. 208. [52] See Schild (1998) 101.

[53] See Garcia (1992) 151.

that a theory of resistance in international law must treat the state as a plural and fragmented terrain of contestation rather than as a monolith.

The call for a theory of resistance that addresses a need to understand social movement action should not be misunderstood as a call for a rejection of international legal order. Rather, international law and institutions provide important arenas for social movement action, as they expand the political space available for transformative politics. For international lawyers, the ability to engage with social movement literature and to develop the sensibility as concerned activists who are motivated by the best cosmopolitan ideals of the discipline awaits. Mass action is a social reality in contemporary society and international lawyers cannot remain disengaged from it. A new Third World approach to international law, will have to engage with social movements to transcend the impasse in which it finds itself. This new international law has the potential to contribute to a new understanding of not only the doctrines and ideas of international law, but also the very ethical purpose of the discipline. In this chapter, I have traced some theoretical challenges faced by international lawyers as they encounter social movements. I have also suggested some preliminary considerations for articulating a theory of resistance in international law. For too long, during almost its entire life, international law has remained too western, elitist, male-centered, and imperial, and the encounter with social movements offers an opportunity to fundamentally transform itself.

2

International law and the development encounter[1]

This chapter describes some of the historical aspects of how development was received by international lawyers in the inter-war and post-WWII period and the impact this had on the generation of particular forms of Third World resistance. This sets the stage for the chapters that follow. Let me begin by noting that there are at least three key moments in the evolution of development ideology in international law, overlapping between the desire to advance the 'primitive' to civilization in a purely cultural sense, and the attempt to develop the 'backward' to well-being in a material, developmental sense. The first moment was the positing of a cultural divide, articulated in a pre-modern, theological sense, between the Christians and the infidels. This was first seen in the work of Pope Innocent IV (1243–54 AD) in the argument over whether the lands of the infidels could justly be taken by Christians,[2] an argument that became central in the founding texts of international law, such as those by Francisco de Vitoria, that have deeply influenced the evolution of the doctrine of sovereignty.[3] This moment was repeated over time in the work of the naturalists and could be seen at work in contemporary international law in the doctrines of humanitarian and pro-democratic interventions[4] as well as in the advocacy of trusteeships for so-called failed states.[5]

The second moment was the construction of a civilizational divide, articulated in pre-modern, but economic, sense between the people of commerce and others, or in the words of A. O. Hirschman, the "*doux commerce* thesis".[6] This constructed a nexus between civilization and capitalism and gave a moral motivation for commercial expansion into the colonies as James Mill noted in his *History of British India*.[7] This moment,

[1] This section draws on Rajagopal (1999a).

[2] For a description, see Muldoon (1979). [3] See Anghie (1996).

[4] For advocacy, see Teson (1997). See also International Commission on Intervention and State Sovereignty (2001).

[5] See Gordon (1997). [6] Hirschman (1977), especially 56–63. [7] Mill (1820).

which could be seen at work in the writings of Samuel Pufendorf[8] as well as nineteenth-century positivists, is at work in contemporary international order in the form of the "convergence thesis"[9] or the internally coherent nature of liberal democratic capitalism.[10]

The third moment was the development of an apparatus of management of anticolonial resistance struggles by colonial powers from the 1940s to the 1950s[11] that would be able to manage the dynamics unleashed by the operation of the first two moments. This apparatus of management consisted not only of domestic techniques relating to constitutional devolution of powers and techniques of law and order such as emergencies, but also of a complex configuration of powers between various levels of international, national, metropolitan, and local authorities. Between them, these three dynamics have set the dominating course of twentieth century international law's encounter with the Third World.

At the end of WWII, the colonial world had begun crumbling. Independence movements had secured or were about to secure political independence for former colonies. But more importantly, colonialism as an idea, even in its more 'humane' form found in the Mandate system, had been thoroughly discredited. Popular politics – the emergence of ordinary people of the Third World as political actors who could no longer be ignored – was transforming the relations between the West and the Third World. Henceforth, the relationship between the West and the Third World would be governed not by colonialism, but by a new discipline called development which replaced the colonizer–colonized relationship with the developed–underdeveloped one. Indeed, the term "Third World" was coined by the French demographer Alfred Sauvy in 1952 to reflect this new hierarchical relationship.[12] This new relationship was characterized by a humanitarian urge to uplift the backward peoples of these new nations and a belief in the capacity of western science and technology to accomplish that task – in other words, the techniques invented by the Mandate system of the League were to be fully deployed, albeit in a changed political setting. All this was accomplished, not by a clean and single break with colonialism, but by a complex process of dealing with, suppressing, and coopting Third World resistance that stretched out over decades. For instance, Britain was fighting colonial

[8] Pufendorf (1703). See also Williams (1990) 3–5. [9] Unger (1996).

[10] Bowles and Gintis (1986); for such an argument, see Sen and Wolfensohn (1999) 3.

[11] Furedi (1994).

[12] Attributed by the *Penguin Dictionary of Third World Terms*, cited in Kapur, Lewis, and Webb (1997) 97.

wars – indeed was just beginning to enter the most confrontationist phase – in Kenya, Malaya, and a host of other countries even as it signed the UN Charter proclaiming self-determination, and continued to do so for decades.

This new mantra of development suited the new nations, which ardently believed and invested in the project of nation building in the image of the West. The most important decision for these new nations, as they entered the UN, was to decide upon their political and economic organization. It is well known that the Europeanized elites who led these countries chose to follow western models of polity and economy (including the Soviet command model), despite serious internal debates within countries such as India about whether western models must be renounced in favor of an indigenous one.[13]

This triumph of development as the new ideology of governance in the colonized world did not leave international law untouched. For First World lawyers, the entry of new states into international relations and their desire to develop, provided an opportunity to renew the discipline which was suffering from a loss of credibility after the collapse of the League.[14] For the Third World lawyers, international law provided an opportunity to use its institutions and techniques to advance the nation-building project. It is my suggestion that most, if not all, of these international lawyers of the post-WWII period shared an essential belief in the emancipatory ideas of western modernity and progress embedded in the new discipline of development, and looked upon international institutions as embodiments of the peculiar western modernity that would advance their respective projects. This convergence – in pragmatism and institutionalism – played a major role in consolidating international institutions as apparatuses of management of social reality in the Third World. Such convergence ensured that even the most radical critiques of international law by Third World lawyers were not directed at development or international institutions,[15] while the renewalist attempts by First World lawyers were also firmly located within this dialectic of institutions and development. In the following chapters, I analyze how this was accomplished. I also analyze the responses of these lawyers to the violence of development as it claimed millions of lives in the nation-building and

[13] For Gandhi's views, see M. K. Gandhi (1997); for the Gandhi-Nehru debate, see Chatterjee (1993) 201–02.

[14] Kennedy (1987).

[15] See, e.g., Bedjaoui (1979). These critiques were, in fact, formulated in a way that would expand the province of development and institutions. For a discussion and critique, see chapter 4.

renewalist projects. In particular, I am interested in the intellectual and social conditions that led to the emergence of the discourse of human rights as the sole legitimate discourse of resistance in the Third World, and the impact of this 'approved' resistance discourse on other possible discourses of resistance.

In this chapter, I make two interrelated claims. First, international law, understood as that body of rules, doctrines, institutions, and practices, has played a crucial, perhaps even a central, part in the evolution of the ideology and practice of development in the post-WWII period, and, conversely, that development ideology has been a driving force behind the expansion of international law. Development writers as well as international lawyers have, I suggest, overlooked this fact in general. Development writers have generally treated international law, if at all, as epiphenomenal – as mainstream development thinking treats law in general. International lawyers have, on the other hand, seen development as a specific set of socio-economic transformations occurring in the so-called newly independent states, for which international law must somehow adjust – for example, by acquiring a social character, in the words of Wolfgang Friedman[16] – rather than understanding international law as deeply implicated in and intertwined with the very project of development. The new international law, with its focus on the status of individuals and a truly global community, was seen as constituting a clean epistemological break with the pre-war international law's subservience to power and ethnocentrism. With very few exceptions, the image of international law, according to its leading practitioners, is that of a pre-development, pre-Third World, body of rules, doctrines, and institutions, that must somehow adapt to the new realities of development in the Third World. This image appears to be wrong because it is simplistic and ahistorical. Instead, the new international law was as much caught up in the discursive and ideological embrace of modernity, as the pre-war colonial international law, mainly through the institutions and practices of development which were invented after the war to control, manage, order, and reproduce social reality in the so-called Third World. The specific ways in which this complex dialectic emerged between international law and development discourses, and the particular problems that it gave rise to, form a focus of my inquiry.

The second claim consists of two parts: in the first part, I suggest that contrary to the received ways in which mainstream international lawyers have generally treated development and human rights – as antithetical

[16] Friedman (1964). See also Röling (1960).

to each other – they should be seen as deeply implicated in each other and functioning within common parameters. This claim, rather than appearing to smooth out the relationship between human rights and development – as might appear at a first glance – makes that relationship highly problematic and contradictory. In particular, it is suggested that the mainstream human-rights discourse remains too deeply mired within the progressivist and teleological imperatives set by the development discourse, and therefore can not be counted upon in an unproblematic way as an emancipatory narrative of resistance to violence and oppression unleashed by the development encounter. In chapter 7, I shall substantiate this through a discussion of particular legal doctrines that enable the violence of development to continue legitimately even as they control and order the resistance to that violence. Such doctrines include the concept of emergency in the International Covenant on Civil and Political Rights (ICCPR), as well as various economic and social rights that are premised on the ideal of a developmentalist welfare state.

Secondly, social movements of various kinds in the Third World have posed effective challenges to development. They have used aspects of international law to achieve this, including through international human-rights law and the rhetoric of autonomy and democratization to resist the violence of the developmental state. Despite this, the praxis of various popular movements and community initiatives that have quite successfully struggled against the violence of development remain invisible in human rights and international legal scholarship. The politics of knowledge production in international law that has so far ensured such invisibility of the struggles waged by subaltern groups such as women, peasants, and indigenous people must be questioned in the light of this.

Receiving development

In his inaugural address as President of the United States on January 20, 1949, President Truman announced the arrival of the age of development with the following ringing declaration aimed at solving the problem of the "underdeveloped" areas:

> More than half the people of the world are living in conditions approaching misery. Their food is inadequate, they are victims of disease. Their economic life is primitive and stagnant. Their poverty is a handicap and a threat both to them and to more prosperous areas. For the first time in history humanity possesses the knowledge and the skill to relieve the

> suffering of these people... I believe that we should make available to peace-loving peoples the benefits of our store of technical knowledge in order to help them realize their aspirations for a better life... What we envisage is a program of development based on the concepts of democratic fair dealing... Greater production is the key to prosperity and peace. And the key to greater production is a wider and more vigorous application of modern scientific and technical knowledge.[17]

Thus, the objective of developing the underdeveloped was firmly placed within the progressivist parameters of the project of modernity, deploying its main tools of science and technology. Before this, it had not been the international policy objective of the imperial and colonial powers to bring economic development to the natives. Indeed, the native was seen as incapable of development since he/she was seen as lazy, lacking in dynamism or impeded by the wrong cultural values. But the modernist desire to embrace the Other initiated during the early part of the century, coupled with the cosmopolitan desire to advance the uncivilized, particularized in the institution of the Mandates, started having a profound transformation on the relationship between the colonial powers and the colonized. Important signals of the change could be detected by the work of the International Labour Organization (ILO) banning slavery and forced labor in the inter-war period. With the 1939 British Law of Development and Welfare of the Colonies, which changed its name from the Law of Development of the Colonies, the focus of colonial administration had significantly changed. In it, the British argued for the need to ensure minimum levels of nutrition, health, and education to the natives. Now, the welfare dimension was introduced as an essential part of the Mandate, thereby providing a moral basis for the economic side of colonialism while simultaneously providing an economic rationale for the cultural project of civilizing the natives. With the declaration of the age of development by Truman in 1949, this dual mandate had collapsed into one secular theory of salvation:[18] namely, development.

When the age of development dawned in 1949, international law had been in crisis. It had been assailed as either too utopian because it harbored ambitions of building a world government or as too subservient to power because of excessive realism – in other words, both naturalism and positivism stood discredited as theoretical approaches to the age-old

[17] Harry Truman, *Public Papers of the Presidents of the United States: Harry S. Truman*, Washington DC, US Government Printing Office (1964) cited in Escobar (1995).

[18] I borrow this term from Nandy (1983).

problems of order v. liberty and autonomy v. community in international social life. In addition, the emergence of the Soviet approach to international law, combined with the entry of non-western states into the UN, led to calls for reinforcing the universality of international law in a world of legal, cultural, and ideological pluralism.[19] A new approach, and a new way of thinking about international law was badly in need and that was supplied by the discourse of development in the form of a new emphasis on pragmatism, functionalism, and institutionalism. International lawyers from the First World as well as those from the newly independent Third World approached the challenges offered by international law's encounter with development in ways that differed due to their motivations but still shared many similarities.

Response of First and Third World lawyers

At the political level, the most visible aspect of the changed attitude towards underdeveloped areas from the Mandates, was the formal achievement of political independence of colonized territories. First World international lawyers such as Hersch Lauterpacht, Wilfred Jenks, and Wolfgang Friedman received this political phenomenon – of the entry of states with divergent cultures into international law – as an opportunity to renew the discipline. In classic modernist fashion,[20] they attempted to channel the energy provided by the entry of new states into a constructivist project that attempted to build a more universal basis for international law at a theoretical level, while adopting a functional and pragmatist approach by focussing on international institutions. As described by one of the prominent post World War II international lawyers, Wilfred Jenks:

> The strains which now confront us represent a challenge of the first order to the science of international law; but it is a challenge which arises from a crisis of growth and which affords an opportunity for imaginative reappraisal unparalleled since the time of Grotius. Politically we have for the first time the formal framework of a universal world order; our problem is to create a political reality within this framework. Legally we have for the first time the formal elements of a universal legal order; our problem is to fuse these elements into a body of law which expresses and protects the common interests of a universal community.[21]

[19] See Kunz (1955); Jenks (1958), chapter 2; McDougal and Lasswell (1959).
[20] Berman (1992). [21] Jenks (1958) 80.

Thus, for the First World international lawyers, the independence of Third World states as well as their problems of poverty, illiteracy and social backwardness provided the raw material for the renewal of the discipline. In other words, they tended to view the phenomenon of development and the emergence of the Third World from within the discipline, imagining international law and its context as different worlds. This worldview implied that nineteenth century positivism as well as Wilsonian utopianism could be transcended somehow due to the new social character of international law, with its focus on the individual and international organizations. However, a different view could be that it is dubious if the new context could liberate international law from the grip of failed paradigms since the new context itself is the result of old international law; in other words, the language of infidels of medieval law, the language of natural rights of Vitoria, the language of civilization of Westlake, and the language of sacred trust of the Mandate system, had simply been replaced by the language of developed and underdeveloped.

These were not the concerns of Third World international lawyers in the post-War period, who, having been educated in the West, shared the belief in the idea of progress and modernization. For these Europeanized elites, the central concerns were two: a meta-disciplinary concern about expanding the cultural bases of international law so that it is legitimate for them to be part of its aspirations;[22] and second, an instrumental concern about defending Third World sovereignty by deploying the newly found weapon of international law.[23] Thus, for them, development was not a world-view imposed on them, but the essential element in the establishment of better living standards and elimination of poverty. If decolonization was the political aspect of their emancipation from foreign rule, development was the socio-economic aspect that would make the struggle for emancipation real. In attempting to realize these aspirations, Third World international lawyers viewed international law from within the social reality called the Third World, created by the development discourse. Their intention was to recast the discipline in the light of their own needs to develop.

The best example of this is the Declaration on the Establishment of the New International Economic Order (NIEO). Firmly anchored within the teleological imperative of "catching-up" set by the development discourse, it declares that the NIEO "shall correct inequalities and redress existing

[22] This usually took the form of the argument that non-western cultures had also "contributed" to international law, historically. See e.g., Chacko (1958).

[23] Much of the rest of the Third World scholarship falls into this category. For a sampling, see Sathirathai and Snyder (1987).

injustices, making it possible to eliminate the widening gap between the developed and the developing countries and ensure steadily accelerating economic development."[24] First, the very idea that a difference in wealth between countries could be described as inequality presupposed the existence of a global economic system in which the Third World was ready to participate. As put by Douglas Lummis, "the accusation of injustice can not traditionally be made against inequalities between systems, but only within a system."[25] Second, the NIEO declaration said nothing about either the violence of development (which was fairly well known by the 1970s) on marginalized communities or the need to preserve cultural spaces that would protect diversities of culture and life from the onslaught of development. Nor did it talk about leveling the living standards down, but only about leveling them up. In other words, instead of targeting the over consumption of the rich, the NIEO declaration may have focused on the under consumption of the poor.

There were several commonalties between the First and Third World lawyers' attitudes to development, but two of them stand out. First, they both believed in the centrality of international institutions in a progressive world order committed to development and prosperity. Thus, lawyers such as Wilfred Jenks, Louis Sohn, and Wolfgang Friedman firmly believed that focusing on international institutions would move the discipline away from sovereignty, towards pragmatic problem-solving and ever-greater prosperity. Indeed, this belief in the capacity of international institutions was not new in the West: as early as 1920, John Maynard Keynes had argued that the epoch of continent-wide prosperity before the first World War was maintained by the "delicate organization" of international institutions including Public International Unions, intergovernmental conferences and public and private international agreements.[26] For the Third World international lawyers, international institutions became central to their objective of attempting to recast the discipline by making law through the UNGA, asserting their new sovereignties, as well as to focus the institutions towards resolving the concrete problems of the Third World.

A second commonality was their focus on human rights. For the First World liberal international lawyers, a focus on the individual in international law heralded the much-awaited move away from state-centered

[24] United Nations (1974b), Preamble. [25] Lummis (1992) 44.

[26] J. M. Keynes, The Economic Consequences of the Peace (1920) 10, cited in Murphy and Augelli (1993) 71.

positivism to human-centered naturalism. For the Third World lawyers, human rights represented the perfect weapon in their struggle to decolonize and modernize their own countries. Thus from the Bandung Conference to the negotiation of both the human rights Covenants in 1966 to the introduction of economic and social issues on the human-rights agenda, the Third World lawyers argued within the paradigm of human rights for a different emphasis on the role of the state in the economy. Their quarrel was not over the universality of human rights or about Asian values in the beginning, but about which sets of rights had to be prioritized in their march towards development. As a result, the First and Third World lawyers argued over whether economic and social rights (understood as the result of development) had priority over civil and political rights.[27] These arguments were essentially disagreements about the proper role of the state in the economy – Plan v. Market – rather than radical disagreements about the goal and direction of development, which was always to modernize the primitives.

On why these attitudes were misguided

The attitudes of First and Third World lawyers examined above were misguided because they were simplistic and ahistorical. First, both of them did not take into account the economic/systemic nature of inter-state violence, exemplified in the conflicts that resulted from the gradual integration of colonized territories into a world economy over the last four hundred years. This meant that contrary to the hopes of Keynes and the legion of post-War international lawyers, the attempt to bring prosperity through development will increase and not decrease the root causes of violence. As Richard Ashley puts it, "technical-rational action has brought progress – progress toward destruction of all it has built."[28] This was inevitable in the logic of enlightenment: as Foucault said, "the Enlightenment which discovered the liberties also invented the disciplines."[29]

The best example of this counter-tendency in international law can be found in the material conditions that gave rise to the Drago and Calvo doctrines in Latin America in the early part of the twentieth century. In December 1902, the military forces of England, Germany, and Italy seized the Venezuelan fleet, bombarded several cities, and established a rigorous

[27] The literature on this is voluminous, but for an analysis that is relevant to the arguments developed here, see Jhabvala (1987).
[28] Ashley (1980) 14. [29] Foucault (1979) 222.

blockade off the coast, for the settlement of several claims, including, chiefly, the collection of deferred interest on foreign public debt, outstanding in the form of bonds issued by the Venezuelan government for the construction of railways and other public works. This use of military force to resolve the debt crisis was strongly opposed by Argentina which sent a diplomatic note to the US on the subject. The whole episode is analyzed well by Luis Drago who, after arguing against the use of force to collect debts on private and public law grounds, including the rules of caveat emptor and sovereign immunity, puts the whole discussion in the context of colonialism and racism, by citing Juan Garcia:

> the events in Venezuela are not isolated facts, measures of policy or reparation of wrongs, but the opportunity which materialized a tendency latent in Europe since the middle of the past century which in the last years has been emphasized and fortified by the new economic necessities, the idea of races supposedly predestined successors of the Roman Empire that has been made familiar through Germanic philosophy. Long before this tendency appeared there was begun in the German Universities the work of transmutation of moral values, needed to root out the scruples and doubts which made the work difficult and which shattered the efficacy of the iron glove. The morality, right and justice of the conquerors (sic) are harmonized with the philosophy of Darwin, Hegel, Savigny, von Hering, DeSybil and Mommsen.[30]

In the latter half of the twentieth century the physical violence of the western intervention was replaced by the economic violence of structural adjustment and the debt crisis, mediated by the International Monetary Fund (IMF) and the World Bank. It is not the nature of violence then, but the locus of violence that has changed, from inter-state to intra-state. But more importantly, the idea of superiority of races lives on, most concretely through the idea of development. This was/is completely overlooked by First and Third World lawyers' generally enthusiastic responses to development.

Second, it was a mistake on the part of First and Third World lawyers to rely on human rights as the terrain on which they could disagree about the role of the state in the economy. This entirely overlooked the colonial origins of mainstream human-rights discourse, particularly with respect to the doctrine of responsibility of states for injuries to aliens, which is commonly cited as one of the intellectual strands in the historiography

[30] Cited in Drago (1907). On Calvo and Drago doctrines generally, see Hershey (1907).

of mainstream human-rights discourse.[31] According to this mainstream telling, this doctrine was one of the ways in which the individual came partially within the scope of old international law, even though the individual was traditionally seen only as an object and not a subject of law in this sense.[32] However, as pointed out by Guha-Roy, this Vattelian fiction was the result of imperialism and could not be reconciled with the idea of universal human rights, as it was based on "special additional rights accorded to aliens."[33] This meant that instead of expecting that this doctrine would universally apply everywhere, it was more appropriate to investigate the conditions that made it such a sensitive issue in the developing countries: the consolidation of vast economic interests in the hands of the nationals of imperial powers during the colonial period. It was/is almost perverse to argue that an emancipatory discourse such as human rights is based, inter alia, on this doctrine. More importantly, the connection between this doctrine and the human-rights discourse also reveals some of its liberal bias towards the role of the state in the economy: the Third World states were not expected to intervene in the economy to the prejudice of First World economic interests. But, in addition, it must be pointed out that the Third World response – in the form of the doctrine of Permanent Sovereignty over Natural Resources (PSNR) – only resulted in replacing one form of economic interests with another, rather than enabling communities whose resources were being destroyed to exercise meaningful control. Given this historiography, the human-rights discourse is hardly the terrain on which lawyers should disagree about the role of the state in the economy, for such disagreement only conceals a broad agreement about the goals and the direction of development as centrally directed, either by the state or the market.

Third, the responses by First and Third World lawyers that focused on the role of individuals and international institutions maintain a totality of silence towards the role played by social movements in the Third World and even in Europe and the US during the colonial period. In other words, First and Third World lawyers could have been much more critical of development as a master narrative of ensuring human dignity through market-led global prosperity, if they had paid more attention to the radical democratic tradition in the Third World and the West. These traditions include the seventeenth-century levelers, the eighteenth-century *sans culottes*, the nineteenth-century chartists and agrarian populists, the

[31] See e.g., Steiner and Alston (1996) 59. [32] Oppenheim (1960).
[33] Guha-Roy (1961), citing Philip Jessup (1948) 101.

nineteenth-century peasant rebellions in the colonies, and twentieth-century women's movements and advocates of worker councils and environmental justice.[34] These movements were/are based on two critical themes that do not find their place in the nationalist/developmentalist literature: first, that the economy and the family are no less arenas of domination than is the state; and second, that politics is not just a fight over resources but also over cultural identities, about who we are to become.[35] Taking these progressive movements seriously as historical actors would, I suggest, destabilize the liberal understanding of the harmony between development and the 'new' international law. Several historical studies of such social movements by Eric Hobsbawm, Charles Tilly, George Rudé, and others have shown the role played by ordinary men and women in them, contrary to elite historiographies that stress the role of vanguards, historical agents and structural transformations. In addition, rethinking the historiography of many anticolonial/nationalist movements in the light of ordinary peoples' resistance to the modernizing imperatives of colonialism, would also problematize the smooth incorporation of decolonization into a forward-looking progressivist narrative of international law. Such work has hardly begun.

[34] Bowles and Gintis (1986) 8.

[35] Ibid. One exception to the traditional nationalist orientation towards western-style development was M. K. Gandhi, who clearly understood that true liberation from colonial rule meant recovering the selves which had been lost, through a cultural and political struggle. This meant that western-style industrial development was inappropriate as a nation-building strategy. For this argument, see M. K. Gandhi (1997).

PART II

International law, Third World resistance, and the institutionalization of development: the invention of the apparatus

The Commission must be so constituted that it can constantly bear in mind three points of view: international interests, since in modern civilization what affects one region of the world has repercussions in every other portion; national interests, since the rights and dignity of the Mandatory Power or the Mandatory Dominion are intimately concerned; native interest, since the promotion of the welfare of the Mandated Territories is the primary object.

Hon. Ormsby-Gore, *The League of Nations Starts, an Outline by its Organizers* (London, 1920), 116.[1]

The 'native interest' was truly born with the invention of the Mandate system in the League of Nations. Even though the 'humanitarian' idea that the welfare of the natives in various colonies must be promoted had been animating the imperial European conquest of Asia and Africa throughout the nineteenth century, international law had not truly been prepared for that task until the League. Indeed, the natives were seen as lazy, lacking in dynamism and entrepreneurship and were considered to lack the character necessary for capitalism, including by many social scientists in the nineteenth century.[2] This was important, since (as mentioned in the introductory chapter) the route to civilization now lay in the transition of traditional economies into modern ones. An effort to bring welfare and development to the natives could then be justified more easily on the more culturally neutral terms of the '*doux commerce*' thesis, rather than the more imperial, theological imperative to bring the true faith to the infidels. This also coincided with the move away from the missionary

[1] Hon. Ormsby-Gore, *The League of Nations Starts, an Outline by its Organizers* (London, 1920), 116, cited in Wright (1930) 137. Ormsby-Gore, a member of the British Parliament, was later to become a member of the Permanent Mandates Commission and then Under-secretary of the Colonies. Ibid.

[2] This was most clearly visible in the evolutionary perspective that economic and social forms of organization in primitive societies were destined to disappear with the advance of modern capitalism. Marx (1959) 480; Weber (1958).

humanism and rigid formalism of many early internationalists to a pragmatist orientation, formulated during the inter-war years, but fully flowering after the second World War.[3]

The challenge was how to effect this massive social, political, and cultural transformation of the colonies. What were lacking were not merely the apparatuses – the institutions and processes – but also the techniques that are taken for granted in development discourse today such as labor and land-use data, health policy and other social aspects of the natives' lives, as well as good governance strategies that seek to re/construct judiciaries, civil societies, and Parliaments. It is recognized that many of these planning policies and practices were developed from the beginning of the nineteenth century in western countries, through town planning, social planning, and the institutionalization of the market.[4] But the progressive internationalization of these techniques, apparatuses, and processes remains a murky area of inquiry, especially in terms of the role that international law and institutions played in it. In other words, did international law play any role in the progressive bureaucratization of social life in the colonies and (now) in the Third World? Existing analyses of international law treat development, if at all, as epiphenomenal, while development writers pay no attention to international law. Yet, international law and institutions have evolved rapidly during the same period of the emergence of development discourse to govern the relationship between the West and the Rest. What then was the relationship between these two phenomena? In addition, I am also interested in exploring the relationship between the move to pragmatism as a methodological approach in post World War II international law, and the constitution of a new discourse of development to manage the social and political evolution of the erstwhile colonies.

Pragmatism is the credo of international institutions. It explains why they come into being and how they evolve over time. Institutions represent the concrete manifestations of the normative aspirations of law in the international system. As such, their expansion is the expansion of the domain of the "international" itself. The most significant aspects of twentieth-century international law are its institutionalization, through international courts and bureaucracies, and its development, from international economic law to human-rights law. How has this expansion occurred? What factors have propelled the institutionalization of global

[3] For a discussion, see Kennedy (1994). [4] Escobar (1992) 132.

cosmopolitanism? What role, if any, has the Third World[5] played in this expansion at all? And what can we foretell about the future?

These are large, ambitious questions, and they cannot be answered here in detail. Rather, this part will examine four key moments of international institutional expansion to see what factors propelled it: the Mandate system of the League of Nations; the creation of a dense network of UN agencies, in particular, the UN Conference on Trade and Development (UNCTAD), during the 1960s and 1970s by the Third World coalition; the expansion and proliferation of the Bretton Woods institutions, particularly since 1961; and the expansion of international institutions during the post-Cold-War period to promote democracy, human rights and peace. By examining these institutional expansions, I hope to raise some fundamental questions about how international institutional change is explained within the discipline of international law, and whether such explanations take the "local" or the "subaltern" seriously as agents of change.[6] Ignoring the role of the "local" as an agent of institutional transformation is, I suggest, inseparable from the hegemonic nature of international law as an elitist discipline.

The first set of questions that is raised concerns the functionalist explanation of international institutions. Stemming from David Mitrany's work in the 1940s,[7] this theory explains the emergence of international institutions as a result of a pragmatic necessity to serve concrete functions relating, for example, to trade, postal services, or regulation of rivers. This explanation has remained theoretically dominant in international affairs for over fifty years.[8] The central proposition of this theory is that

[5] I deliberately use the term "Third World" rather than "developing countries" for reasons already indicated, but it can be noted here that I do not use it to mean the exclusivist, politico-territorial space of states, but, rather, a contingent and shifting cultural-territoriality which may encompass states and social movements. The boundaries that matter here are not those of states, but of forms of life. In addition, I wish to avoid the teleology that is implied in the term "developing." See Rajagopal (1998–99) (developing this understanding of the "Third World" as it applies to international law and international relations).

[6] In pursuing this line of inquiry, I am influenced by the work of the Subaltern Studies Collective. See Guha and Spivak (1988). The central element of this critique is that the elitist historiography is constituted by hidden "cognitive failures," which is inseparable from domination, and that the agency of change is located in the 'subaltern'. Ibid. at 3, 6. I use the term "local" to mean social movements in the way I have described below. See note 13 below and the accompanying text.

[7] Mitrany (1933); Mitrany (1946).

[8] One can distinguish at least two other theoretical approaches to international institutions. The first is the "realist" school beginning with Hans Morgenthau, treating international institutions as instruments of state power. The second is the global cosmopolitan school,

institutions are born and expand due to top–down policy decisions that correlate with the functional needs of international society. This theory does not recognize grassroots groups, individuals, or social movements as agents of institutional transformation or international legal history. This theory must be questioned on empirical and theoretical grounds, both for its accuracy and for its political effects. The claim is not so much that functionalism fails as a theory of international institutions in all circumstances – it may well remain relevant in certain areas of international life such as the regulation of postal services, for example. Rather, it is suggested that functionalism is seriously deficient in explaining the evolution of many important politically charged international institutions such as the Bretton Woods institutions (BWIs). To the extent that international legal scholarship continues to reiterate this apolitical and technical image of BWIs, it remains trapped in functionalism.[9]

The second set of questions relates to the particular place of international institutions vis-à-vis the Third World. In some ways, international institutions and the Third World are like Siamese twins: one can not even imagine them as separate from one another because development, human rights, environmental, and other institutions operate mostly in the Third World. As the Third World decolonized and "entered" international society in the middle of the twentieth century, international institutions were truly becoming consolidated in a wave of pragmatism. Despite this temporal coincidence, leading accounts of international institutions say nothing about the influence that the Third World may have had on their evolution or vice versa.[10] In this view, institutions evolve due to their own functionalist logic, while grand politics of decolonization and development takes place elsewhere. Indeed, to the extent that the Third World is discussed as an entity in relation to institutions, it is criticized for "politicizing" them and preventing their effective operation.[11] The "failure" of Third World resistance to achieve its objectives – such as the New International

rooted in Wilsonite sensibilities, that sees international institutions as the antithesis of state power. Many of the latter also share the functionalist perspective in that they look at international institutions as technical, problem-solving, apolitical inventions that provide a real alternative to arbitrary state power. The latter predominate in the international law field. For an example of the former, see Morgenthau (1940). For examples of the latter, see Haas (1964); Jessup (1956); Kunz (1957); Friedman (1964); Falk (1983); Chayes and Chayes (1995).

[9] See, e.g., Carter and Trimble (1995) 528 ("both the IMF and the World Bank are supposed to be apolitical").

[10] See generally Kirgis, Jr. (1993); Schermers (1980).

[11] This charge was most common in the field of human rights. See, e.g., Donnelly (1988).

Economic Order proposals of the 1970s at the United Nations – is explained away by the unrealistic "radicalism" of its proposals.[12] This Part proposes to question these suppositions regarding the role that the Third World has or has not played in the expansion and consolidation of international institutions. I do this by examining key elements in the discourses of colonialism and development, which have been the central governing discourses of the Third World since the inter-war period, and highlighting moments of local resistance from the Third World that are not captured in traditional international law narratives about the Third World.

The expansion and renewal of international institutions cannot be understood in isolation from Third World resistance, whether in the form of 'new social movements,' such as environmental movements, or in the form of 'old social movements,' such as nationalist movements. This may be more obvious in the contemporary proximity of international institutions to grassroots activism, but "the Third World" masses were constantly evoked by legal cosmopolitans in the part to expand the sphere of activity of international organizations. Not only have social movements from the Third World such as peasant rebellions, environmental movements, and human-rights movements, propelled the expansion of international institutions since the 1960s, the "Third World" as a category has been central to the expansion of the domain of the "international" itself. In other words, the very architecture of contemporary international law has been constituted by its continuous evocation of and interaction with the category "Third World," which has included not only states, but also these social movements. The invocation of the "Third World masses," whether real or imaginary, was essential to the expansion of international institutions.

In putting forth this view, this Part departs in a number of significant ways from extant analyses of international institutions. First, it introduces "social movements"[13] as a theoretical category in international law

[12] See Franck (1986) 82.

[13] The term "social movements" is not new in sociology and social theory. However, in recent times, "social movements research," particularly under the rubric of "new social movements," has moved to the center of social theory. Roughly speaking, this literature can be divided into two theoretical approaches. The first, known as Resource Mobilization theories, predominates in the Anglo-Saxon world and is primarily concerned with strategy, participation, organization, rationality, etc. The second, known as the New Social Movements Approach, predominates in Europe, Latin America, and South Asia, and emphasizes the cultural and symbolic aspects of identity formations as central to collective mobilizations. The latter is also heavily influenced by poststructuralism, post-Marxism, and to some extent, postmodernism.

in order to enable an understanding of the complex relationship between the Third World and international institutions. This is important because the "Third World" that international institutions deal with now is no longer the "Third World" of the post-independence period.[14] Indeed, the very meaning of the "Third World" has undergone a radical change since the 1950s and 1960s, when it meant only an agglomeration of newly independent states. Now, "Third World" means a collection of peasant movements, environmental movements, feminist movements, and a host of others who are in global and regional alliances with states, individuals, international institutions, and private groups. It is this "Third World" from which international institutions such as BWIs are now facing opposition and resistance. As the collapse of the WTO talks in Seattle in 1999 showed, international institutions are now openly confronted with mass resistance.[15] But of equal importance was the invocation of the "natives" as the driving force behind the Mandate system, or the "Third World masses" as the key driving force behind the expansion of the BWIs, even during the apogee of Third World "radicalism" at the United Nations in the 1960s and 1970s. In other words, while the BWIs formally engaged with the representatives of the Third World States, they were also simultaneously engaging with the "Third World masses," invoking the concept

For recent works on social movements, see Alvarez, Dagnino, and Escobar (1998); Eder (1993); Escobar and Alvarez (1992); Wignaraja (1993); Slater (1985); Oberschall (1993); Omvedt (1993); Tarrow (1994); Touraine (1988).

International law has remained virtually isolated from this literature. One notable exception is Falk (1987). Very recent critical international law scholarship, has begun engaging with the social movements literature. See Stammers (1999). For a partial attempt to engage with this literature, see Otto (1996b). International relations theory has attempted to engage with the rich theoretical issues emerging from "social movements research" literature under the rubric of "global civil society," "networks," and "globalization," though it has not fully engaged with the cultural critique of the theories. See Burbach et al. (1997); Ghils (1992); Lipschutz (1992); Shaw (1992); Sikkink (1993); Spiro (1995); Wapner (1994).

In democratic and political theory, new research has made important and striking contributions, borrowing from radical social movement approaches. See, Benhabib (1996); Kothari (1996); Laclau and Mouffe (1985); Sheth and Nandy (1996). Of all the specific disciplines, feminist studies and environmental studies have gone the farthest in developing critiques in the social movements tradition, most of them in the context of pursuing a critique of "development." See Basu (1995); Guha (1989); Omvedt (1993) 127–149; Fisher (1995); Linkenbach (1994); Sethi (1993); Sternbach (1992). Of most interest is a recent stream of literature on what I would call "critical development theory," which builds on radical social movement critiques in the area of development studies. See Sachs (1992); Escobar (1995); Rahnema and Bawtree (1997); Banuri (1990).

[14] For a discussion and critique of existing notions of the "Third World" in international law, see Rajagopal (1998–99).

[15] Rajagopal (1999b).

as if it were a totem, exoticizing it, responding to it, and being shaped by it. It is this elusive "Third World" that I seek to capture in this Part.

Second, it is suggested that the architecture of modern international law has been ineluctably shaped by popular, grassroots resistance from the Third World. This contrasts with traditional accounts of the birth of international institutions that emphasize the role of leading individuals,[16] or states, or simply functional needs that propelled institutional behavior. If the account offered here is correct, a number of important implications follow. The "eurocentric" history[17] of international institutions – and therefore of international law – must be rewritten to reflect accurately the role played by various subaltern[18] groups. Indeed, recent historical work by various scholars has already begun this process. For example, David Kennedy has demonstrated the role that women's peace movements played in the creation of the League of Nations as well as their subsequent exclusion from the League.[19] On the other hand, an extreme anti-imperialistic critique of international institutions – such as BWIs – should also reconsider the role they play in receiving, encouraging, countering, and coopting popular resistance of various kinds.

Third, reassessing the relationship between resistance and institutional change can also serve to lessen some of the bias in international law against popular resistance as such. In particular, I am interested in how one might de-elitize international law by writing resistance into it, to make it recognize subaltern voices. As is well known, international law has never been concerned primarily with mass protest or social movements, except in the context of self-determination and the formation of states.[20] It has treated all other popular protests and movements as outside the state and, therefore, as illegitimate and unruly. This division has been based on a liberal conception of politics, which sharply distinguishes between routine institutional politics and other extra-institutional forms of protest.[21] While there may have been some previous justification for this attitude, this model of politics bears no resemblance to reality in an increasingly cosmopolitan world of information flows, economic grids,

[16] The most famous example of this is perhaps the role played by J. M. Keynes and H. D. White in the formation of the BWIs. See Dam (1982).

[17] This is, of course, hardly a new claim in Third World international law scholarship. For an incisive, early discussion of eurocentricity in international law, see Baxi (1972). For a more recent account, see Gathii (1998).

[18] The term "subaltern" is, of course, borrowed from the scholarship of postcolonial theory. See Spivak (1988).

[19] See Kennedy (1987) 878.

[20] See, e.g., Cassesse (1995); Crawford (1979); Quaye (1991).

[21] See Bright and Harding (1984).

and NGO networks, and stands heavily criticized in the social sciences[22] and the law.[23] Due to its liberal conception of politics and its inability or unwillingness to factor in the impact of collective movements and forms of identity struggles other than nationalism, international law has remained strangely artificial and narrow. The approach proposed here offers one way of overcoming this difficulty.

This attempt to compel international law to take Third World resistance seriously could be misinterpreted easily as a standard liberal argument that calls for the replacement of the statist paradigm with 'new' paradigms such as civil society, that the state is being marginalized or even supplanted by these new actors.[24] It is not the intention here to make such an argument. Rather, it is argued that many forms of extra-institutional forms of resistance generated in the Third World remain invisible to international law, even though its own architecture is a product of an intense and ambivalent interaction with that resistance.

Methodologically, this Part advances a critique that aims to rethink the place of the "Third World" in international law, as part of an emerging TWAIL scholarship.[25] While the theoretical similarities and contradictions between this new international law literature and the literature on social movements are not elaborated on here, some caveats should be noted to more precisely delineate the scope of the inquiry in this Part. First, this Part does not attempt to present a systematic ethnography of all social movements that have ever propelled international institutional evolution. The focus in this Part is only on the most significant movements in some notable areas of institutional expansion, such as in poverty

[22] Ibid. [23] See Koskenniemi (1989) 52–131; Unger (1975).

[24] Much of recent international relations theory is in this vein, focusing on civil society. See sources cited in note 13. In international law, see, Weiss and Gordenker (1996); Khan (1996); Falk (1998); Charnowitz (1997); Schreuer (1993); McCormick (1993); Symposium Issue (1996); Symposium Issue (1993). But see Schachter (1997) (concluding that the state is unlikely to disappear soon).

[25] I loosely identify this new scholarship with the emerging intellectual identity of TWAIL that is challenging the statist, elitist, colonialist, eurocentric, and masculine foundations of international law. See TWAIL Mission Statement, Conference on New Approaches to Third World Legal Studies (March 7–8, 1997, Harvard Law School). Of course, this joins an ongoing genre of scholarship in the Third World tradition. Scholars in this genre, both young and well-established include (in alphabetical order): Helena Alviar, Anthony Anghie, Keith Aoki, Upendra Baxi, Lan Cao, B. S. Chimni, James Gathii, Yash Ghai, Ruth Gordon, Shadrack Gutto, Hope Lewis, Tayyab Mahmoud, Makau Wa Mutua, Vasuki Nesiah, Joel Ngugi, Celestine Nyamu, Liliana Obregon, Obiora Okafor, Joe Oloka-Onyango, Diane Otto, Neil Stammers, Kerry Rittich, Hani Sayed, B. de Sousa Santos, Amr Shalakany, Issa Shivji, Chantol Thomas and C. G. Weeramantry. For a recent attempt in this genre, see Mickelson (1998); see also, Rajagopal (1998–99).

alleviation and environmental protection. Second, without presuming to speak on behalf of the peasants, environmentalists, women, and other individuals who were active participants in these social movements, I have attempted to construct a more textured and complex narrative about patterns of institutional change in international law. It may be political to thus represent the "Other," but it is no less political to maintain silence about the "Other." Third, there is also a danger of romanticizing the "local," and constructing enlightenment-style progress narratives about movements as the grand successors of states. It is not intended to present social movements in these terms; indeed, what makes them interesting is precisely the context-specific, shifting, and contingent aspects of each movement as it has engaged with the global space occupied by the BWIs. This sets such movements apart from the reductionist and totalizing narratives of international law. Fourth, focusing attention on "new" identities in the chapter on BWIs, such as the environment, is not meant to suggest that the "old" identities based on class or nation are now irrelevant. Particularly during this era of globalization, preserving local spaces is increasingly dependent on notions of sovereignty, which remains a cardinal doctrine in international law.[26] However, this Part rests on the conviction that traditional understandings of sovereignty are no longer adequate for the defense of local spaces, and that an understanding of the role of social movements in international law is imperative to reverse the extant bias in favor of the "global" over the "local." Finally, the fact remains that various social movements organized around multiple identities such as gender, environment, ethnicity, and class are the most potent popular mobilizations in the world today, and the question is in what ways international law has shaped and been shaped by these movements. Telling their story is a simple process of narrating a "history from below."[27]

International institutions must then be viewed as independent variables, as discursive terrains, which provided the apparatus and techniques for the formulation, and transmission of such policies and practices of colonialism and development. Existing analyses of the origins of development do not take international institutions into account.[28] In this analysis, international institutions must be treated as irreducible and self-contained wholes, which cannot be reduced to a causal relationship to either economic or ideological factors.[29] This means that international

[26] For important recent discussions of sovereignty in international law, see Kennedy (1999); Kingsbury (1998); Schachter (1997).

[27] I borrow this phrase from Krantz (1985).

[28] An exception is Murphy and Augelli (1993).

[29] Here I rely on North (1990).

institutions cannot be seen as mere vehicles for the implementation of whatever development 'paradigm' happens to be dominant at any given time. Rather, they must be seen as independent actors, with their own internal dynamics and politics. These institutions must then be viewed as terrains on which both First World domination and Third World resistance played out in the twentieth century.[30]

Following this view, international institutions have played a crucial role in mediating and often deradicalizing the contentious relationship between development interventions and many non-European societies.[31] In particular, international institutions have often served to absorb and channel the resistance unleashed by mass movements – whether they be movements for national independence in the inter-war period, the Marxist revolutions of the post World War II period, the new social movements of the 1970s and 1980s or the democratic, nationalist, and other identity-based movements of the 1980s and 1990s. In each of these periods, international institutions have functioned as crucial shock absorbers against mass resistance.

Chapter 3 describes the Mandate system of the League and the particular techniques and processes that it invented to tackle the populations in the colonial areas, which laid crucial groundwork for subsequent development interventions. Chapter 4 examines the invention of new institutions by the Third World countries at the UN from the mid-1960s to the mid-1970s, as a moment of radical challenge/resistance to international law, which revealed the extent to which international institutions had become a terrain of resistance, but, in addition, the limitations of that resistance. As examples, I analyze the Bandung Conference, the formation of UNCTAD and the writings of Mohammed Bedjaoui. Chapter 5 provides a synopsis of the fundamental changes in the nature Third World resistance, and thereby the very meaning of the "Third World" in international law. It is then analyzed how this new Third World resistance was sought to be neutralized by the West, primarily through the BWIs since the 1970s. In that process, it is suggested, the BWIs have acquired a 'new' character and a lease of life, that have transformed them

[30] This view of international institutions is hardly new. See, e.g., Claude, Jr. (1971), especially chapter 16. What is different here is the explanation I provide for why this is so and what the implications might be for international law.

[31] On this theme, I draw inspiration from the pioneering work of Kennedy (1987), which drew attention to the complex relationship between the facts (constituted by the local incidents) and the law (constituted by internal workings of the bureaucracy), though not in the specific context of the Third World.

into Foucaultian "complete and austere institutions" that have a complex relationship with mass resistance. In particular the BWIs have acquired their present agenda of sustainable human development, with its focus on poverty alleviation[32] and environmental protection, as a result of their attempt to come to grips with grassroots resistance from the Third World in the 1960s and 1970s. Chapter 6 examines the new role that international institutions have assumed in promoting democracy and political order in developing countries as the *sine qua non* for development in the 1990s and how this politicization of these institutions is interacting with, and sometimes transforming and sometimes containing mass resistance of social movements. In effect, the turn to democracy in the 1990s by international institutions has been necessitated by the political challenges posed by the rise of mass movements. With this, the institutionalization of development is complete. As examples, I look at peace operations as 'development' interventions, and examine the World Bank's new doctrine of Comprehensive Development Framework.

[32] The World Bank (1992) Operational Directive 4.15.

3

Laying the groundwork: the Mandate system

The developing countries have undergone extraordinary social, political, legal, cultural, and economic transformations under the banner of 'development,' during the last fifty years, following decolonization. 'Modern' institutions, norms, and practices have sought to displace 'traditional' ones for the sake of achieving efficiency, justice, or prosperity. So powerful is 'development' as a regime of representation, that everything that relates to the non-western world is governed by its logic, from popular media images (slums and hungry children) to virtually all governmental practices. Indeed, the very term 'developing world,' reflects the power of the idea. According to received understandings of how this extraordinary social transformation came about, development discourse is entirely the product of the political, institutional, and moral sensibilities of the post-WWII era. In this view, colonialism as a politico-economic system was succeeded by development, in a clean break somewhere around the 1950s, as the colonial territories were gaining independence and began to focus on nation-building.

This narrative of the historical evolution of development as a discourse has puzzled development scholars: how did/could such a sophisticated and complex regime of representation as development suddenly come about and take root as the governing logic of the international system? As one recent critical study of development puts it, "generally speaking, the period between 1920 and 1950 is still ill understood from the vantage point of the overlap of colonial and developmentalist regimes of representation."[1] It is the argument in this chapter that it is the Mandate system of the League of Nations that provides the institutional link in the transition between colonialism and development. In particular, it is suggested that the whole range of post-WWII international institutions – from developmental, trade to human-rights ones – owes its origins to the Mandate system. This argument is substantiated through an analysis

[1] Escobar (1995) 27.

of the specific techniques that the Mandate system invented to deal with 'natives' in the mandated territories of the League, ranging from traditional developmental planning tools to petition processes. Indeed, this expansion of the activities of the Mandate system was made possible by a continuous evocation of and interaction with the "natives," a precursor to the "Third World." Thus, the discipline of international institutions was fundamentally shaped by the experience of the Mandate system in dealing with the Third World.

The Mandate system was established by the League of Nations to manage the non-European territories and peoples that were under the control of Germany and Turkey before World War I. As described by M. Rappard, director of the mandates section of the Secretariat of the League, "the mandatory system formed a kind of compromise between the proposition advanced by the advocates of annexation, and the proposition put forward by those who wished to entrust the colonial territories to an international administration."[2] Even though international conference diplomacy had laid the basis in the nineteenth century for the evolution of international administration, at the time of the establishment of the League, it was a wholly novel experiment and this was pointed out by leading commentators.[3] Admittedly, their primary concern was over the issue of sovereignty, viz., where did the sovereignty of the mandated territories lay; how the sovereignty of the mandatories was shared with the League and so on. My own concern, on the other hand, is over some other aspects of the Mandate system which introduced a new actor in the political relationship between European and non-European peoples: the international institution.[4]

[2] Cited in Wright (1930) 24. Wright's work is generally considered to be the definitive study on the Mandate system. For other works, see White (1926); Margalith (1930); Bentwich (1930); Hall (1948). There were other works during the inter-war period that tackled the Mandate system from the perspective of the capacity for independence that the 'natives' possessed. See, e.g., Ritsher (1934). There have also been country-specific studies of the Mandate system. See, e.g., Dore (1985). For a more recent and lucid exploration of the mandate system, see Weeramantry (1992).

[3] Claude, Jr. (1971) 41 ("the League of Nations provided the parentage of international organization as we know it today"). For an extensive discussion, see Kennedy (1987).

[4] My ideas in this chapter are influenced by the work of Anthony Anghie on the relationship between the Mandate system, colonialism, and sovereignty. See Anghie (1995), chapter 5. My attempt in this chapter is to build on his work and argue that the Mandate system not only contributed to the building of a new type of sovereignty and nation state, as he argues, it also provided an important institutional bridge between colonialism and development discourse, and marked the origin of the quintessential twentieth-century international institution.

With the establishment of the League, international law acquired the apparatus of international administration that would enable the colonial powers to perform two tasks: first, it created a network of international agencies who could systematically collect information on the social, economic and political conditions in the colonies. Such agencies included not only the Permaneat Mandates Commission (PMC), and the ILO, but also various special commissions relating to slavery, health, and armaments, as well as various ad hoc commissions of inquiry.[5] Even though colonial powers had begun surveying all aspects of natives' lives in the colonies through census and similar devices in the nineteenth century,[6] the establishment of international institutions under the League with special responsibility for collecting and analyzing such information quickened and solidified the technocratization of power in the colonial relationship. In essence, the experience of the Mandate system laid the groundwork for the more intensive international bureacratization of social life in the Third World after the Second World War.[7] In addition, the information that was collected was measured against "standards" that were established by the PMC, modeled on European standards, in areas as diverse as immigration, labor, education, health, and land policy.[8]

Second, the Mandate system began the process that enabled the colonial powers to shift the moral burden for the administration of the colonies from themselves to a technocratic, faceless bureaucracy. This marked a very important innovation: as domestic public opposition to colonialism had eaten away the moral foundations of colonial empires, they were eager to find an alternative way of managing the administration of these territories in order to keep them open for trade and exploitation.[9] The colonial powers suffered from a moral or legitimacy crisis during the inter-war years, due to complicated domestic and international reasons, and they needed to "recover their moral initiative", as described by Wilfred Jenks.[10]

[5] Wright (1930) 178–84; Berman (1993) (on ad hoc commissions of inquiries during the inter-war period).

[6] For example, see the discussion in Chatterjee (1993), chapters 2 and 10.

[7] See Escobar (1995). [8] Wright (1930) 219–64.

[9] As Sir Frederic Lugard suggested, "the democracies of to-day claim the right to work, and the satisfaction of that claim is impossible without the raw materials of the tropics on the one hand and their markets on the other." See Lugard (1922) 61. Lugard was an experienced British colonial administrator in West Africa (Nigeria) who also became a member of the Permanent Mandates Commission of the League of Nations. Indeed, a major reason for the refusal of the US to join the League of Nations was because of the League's failure to ensure an 'open door' trade policy, especially with regard to Middle East oil. See Wright (1930) 48–56. For a discussion of the Mandate system and the refusal of the US to join the League, see Logan (1945), Batsell (1925).

[10] Jenks (1958) 246–48.

They found the solution in the form of a new actor in international relations, viz., international institutions. This is important to bear in mind, as it underlines the crucial role that international institutions played in the transition from colonialism to development. I shall illustrate this by an analysis of the bureaucratic maneuvers that constituted the establishment of standards in the PMC.

Four aspects of the Mandate system are relevant here from the perspective of analyzing how international institutions played the crucial mediating role in the transition between colonialism and development and, in that process, helped manage mass resistance. The first aspect is really a puzzle: what constellation of factors enabled the evolution of the welfare of the natives as a prime consideration of international policy, when nineteenth-century colonialism is best remembered for its cruelty towards the natives? The second aspect is concerning the crucial components of the Mandate system that formed the foundations of the apparatus of development, particularly how the science of 'finding the facts' about the natives, was converted into a technocratic program that generated a new type of law that was fused with administration. In other words, there was a professionalization and institutionalization of development, through the Mandate system, even before the emergence of development as an academic discipline and political practice after WWII. The third issue is the creation of a dynamic for institutional expansion, through the establishment of European 'standards' in areas ranging from labor policy to armaments, that the natives were destined to aspire to. The focus here is not on the creation of this gap between 'facts' and 'standards' per se, but how the creation of this very gap was converted into institutional practice in a self-regenerating way. I shall suggest that this self-regenerative aspect of the PMC's work is an essential feature of international institutions as they struggle to balance cooperation versus supervision of governments. This internal dynamic, I shall claim, provides the field of autonomy for international institutions and it also explains their deradicalizing nature as they convert encounters with the 'reality' into institutional practice. The final aspect is the establishment of mechanisms that were intended to make the system 'accountable' by building safeguards against abuse of the natives, particularly the petition process which enabled complaints to be filed by natives to the PMC. My focus is on how this early precursor to petition mechanisms in modern international law, such as the 1503 procedure,[11] functioned as the intermediary between the politics of the 'local' which generates the petitions and the politics of the 'global' which

[11] See United Nations (1970).

is represented by the League, and how in that process the contents of the petitions become bureaucratized and deradicalized.

The invention of 'well-being and development' as a first principle

Article 22 (1) of the League Covenant states the principle of development of the native peoples through the Mandate system in simple terms:

> 1. To those colonies and territories which as a consequence of the late war have ceased to be under the sovereignty of the States which formerly governed them and which are inhabited by peoples not yet able to stand by themselves under the strenuous conditions of the modern world, there should be applied the principle that the well-being and development of such peoples form a sacred trust of civilization and that securities for the performance of this trust should be embodied in this Covenant.
> 2. The best method of giving practical effect to this principle is that the tutelage of such peoples should be intrusted to advanced nations, who, by reason of their resources, their experience or their geographical position, can best undertake this responsibility, and who are willing to accept it, and that this tutelage should be exercised by them as Mandatories on behalf of the League.[12]

This text marks a momentous event in the relationship between the West and the Third World. First, at the level of international law, the principle of "sacred trust of civilization," formulated as a duty of colonial powers, marked a turn from the narrow confines of European international law of the nineteenth century to the broader reaches of twentieth-century cosmopolitanism.[13] Surely it was not the first time this principle was enunciated: as early as 1783, Edmund Burke, in his speech in the House of Commons on Fox's India Bill, had formulated the principle of trusteeship in terms of the duties of a colonial power: "all political power which is set over men . . . ought to be some way or other exercized ultimately for their benefit. If this is true with regard to every species of political dominion, and every description of commercial privilege, none of which can be original self-derived rights, or grants for the mere private benefit of the holders, then such rights or privileges, or whatever else you chuse to call them, are all, in the strictest sense, a trust; and it is of the essence of every trust to be rendered accountable."[14] Chief Justice

[12] Covenant of the League of Nations, article 22(1). See League of Nations Covenant, reprinted in Israel (1967).

[13] Anghie (1995) 227. Kennedy (1996).

[14] Lindley (1926) 330.

Marshall of the US Supreme Court had also characterized the Indian populations as wards of the US government: "They (the Indians) are in a state of pupilage. Their relation to that of the United States resembles that of a ward to his guardian."[15] Indeed, the infantilization of subject-races was a standard practice in international law since the seventeenth century.[16]

In addition, there were some other historical precedents of the Mandate system: Article 6 of the General Act of the Berlin Conference in 1885 provided that the European powers exercising sovereign rights in the Congo region, "bind themselves to watch over the preservation of the native tribes, and to care for the improvement of the conditions of their moral and material well-being, and to help in suppressing slavery, and especially the Slave Trade."[17] The hypocrisy of this is that, rather than protecting the welfare of the natives, the Berlin Conference paved the way for the African scramble, and the systematic exploitation and killing of Congolese by Belgian King Leopold's henchmen, led by the American mercenary, Henry Morton Stanley. Recent accounts of that period estimate that more than 10 million were massacred in what is perhaps the world's worst known genocide.[18] In addition, historical precedents of the Mandate system could be found in the Brussels Act 1892,[19] and in the colonial practices of Great Britain,[20] Italy, Japan, and the US.[21]

But there were two clear innovations: for the first time, this principle of "sacred trust of civilization" was formulated in terms of an international administration, viz., the League organs and other specialized agencies such as the ILO. This had the effect of transforming a principle into a program. As the International Court of Justice put it in the *International Status of South West Africa Case*, the mandate "was created, in the interests of the inhabitants of the territory, and of humanity in general, *as an international institution with an international object* – a sacred trust of civilization."[22] Second, the "well-being and development" of the natives

[15] *Cherokee Nation v. Georgia*, 5 Peters at 17, cited in Lindley (1926) 330.

[16] Anghie (1996) for a description of Francisco Vitoria's description of Indians as childlike during the colonial encounter with the Spanish. Indeed, Ashis Nandy has pointed out the important parallels between the development of colonialism and the development of the modern concept of childhood in the seventeenth century. See Nandy (1983) 14–15. See also Nandy (1987). For a discussion of these themes, see Rajagopal (1998–99).

[17] Cited in Lindley (1926) 333.

[18] See Hochschild (1998). See also Wright (1930), f.n. 42, p.19.

[19] Lindley (1926) 333.

[20] See the use of the language of mandates with regard to Kenya under British rule in Lindley (1926) 335.

[21] Wright (1930) 19–20. With regard to Japan, Wright refers to discussions in Japan of a possible Mandate system in Manchuria.

[22] ICJ Reports (1950) 132.

was explicitly spelled out as the goal of the Mandate system, thereby adopting a humanitarian hue that had existed until then only at the periphery.[23] This converted humanitarianism from a principle of domination and resistance to one of governance.

These were no mean achievements. After all, nineteenth-century positivism had used the language of civilization as an exclusionary device to keep non-western countries out of international law.[24] Now the League Covenant introduced the language of civilization as a language of responsibility of the civilized (western powers) to ensure the humane transition of non-western peoples from tradition to the "strenuous conditions of the modern world." This responsibility was the result of a conjunction between the economic desire to bring non-western territories within the world economic system, especially by avoiding disputes over access between the colonial powers, and humanitarianism towards the dark and uncivilized masses.[25] This conjunction was clearly noted in one of the earliest reports to the Paris Peace Conference in 1918 by G. L. Beer: "Under modern political conditions apparently the only way to determine the problem of politically backward peoples, who require not only outside political control but also foreign capital to reorganize their stagnant economic systems, is to entrust the task of government to that state whose interests are most directly involved. . . . If, however, such backward regions are entrusted by international mandate to one state, there should be embodied in the deed of trust most rigid safeguards both to protect the native population from exploitation and also to ensure that the interests of other foreign states are not injured either positively or negatively."[26] This conjunction is, of course, clearly reflected in the phrase, "well-being and development" in Article 22 of the Covenant.

This economic humanitarianism was not the result of a fortuitous coincidence. Rather, it was based on the lessons learned by experienced colonial administrators, particularly the British, such as Sir Frederic Lugard, that the natives had to be made into productive economic resources rather than be brutally exploited. As described by Quincy Wright, "with thickly settled acquisitions like India or tropical acquisitions like

[23] For discussion of humanitarian antecedents of the Mandate system including the principles of sacred trust and trusteeship, see Hall (1948) 97–100, Wright (1930) 9, Margalith (1930) chapter 4. See also *Legal Consequences for States of the Continued Presence of South Africa in Namibia (South West Africa) notwithstanding Security Council Resolution 276* (1970), ICJ Reports (1971), 12, 28–29, para. 46 ("this trust had to be exercised for the benefit of the peoples concerned, who were admitted to have interests of their own").

[24] Gong (1984); Anghie (1995), chapter 2; Bedjaoui (1979); Bull and Watson (1984) 217.

[25] Wright (1930) 9–10.

[26] Cited in Wright (1930) 22.

Central Africa it began to be seen that the native was an important economic asset. Without his labor, the territory could not produce. Thus the ablest administrators like Sir Frederic Lugard in Nigeria began to study the native and cater not only to his material but to his psychological welfare with highly gratifying economic results. Everywhere the devastating and uneconomic effects of trade in spirits and firearms among the natives came to be recognized and their importation controlled. In some parts of Africa, especially the west coast, the more fundamental problems of an equitable land system and a liberal and humane labor policy were studied and in a measure solved."[27] Indeed this was the very logic behind the 'indirect rule' of the British Empire, contrasted to the 'direct rule' of the French.

The 'liberal and humane' aspect of colonial policy, or the inspiration of colonial policy by humanitarian ideals was not an invention of the modern age, but was as old as colonial rule.[28] Nor is the case that the Mandate system was purely the result of "humanitarianism and liberal idealism", as is often believed.[29] Rather it was the result of a combination of humanitarian factors, a desire to maintain a minimum level of moral authority in colonialism and the political exigencies of the relations between large western powers.

But what made the Mandate system truly significant in the context of international law was that it coincided with the creation of an international administration that helped transform a principle into a program. This was noted by several commentators who drew distinctions on this ground between the Mandate system and other international arrangements such as the Berlin Conference of 1885 or the Algiciras Conference of 1906.[30]

Importantly, this economic-humanitarianism conjunction in international law also coincided with significant developments in western political and social thought, which made the idea of 'development and well-being' of the natives, a powerful force. First, it was increasingly recognized, in the writings of authors such as J. A. Hobson and in the practice of colonial powers such as Great Britain, that colonialism was inefficient

[27] Wright (1930) 10. On the elaboration of this "dual mandate," see Lugard (1922). As he puts it, "let it be admitted at the outset that European brains, capital, and energy have not been, and never will be, expended in developing the resources of Africa from motives of pure philanthropy; that Europe is in Africa for the mutual benefit of her own industrial classes, and of the native races in their progress to a higher plane; that the benefit can be made reciprocal, and that it is the aim and desire of civilized administration to fulfill this dual mandate" (Ibid. 617).

[28] Furnivall (1956) 289. For a general discussion of the crucial role played by liberalism in colonial rule, see 282–90.

[29] Hall (1948) 8. [30] Temperley (1969), cited in Wright (1930) 23.

economically and unstable politically and therefore must be modified to enable less friction and more free trade between the European powers.[31] According to Lugard, this was crucial since colonialism was far too important for the ordinary masses of European states, as a source of resources and jobs. This contradicted the then prevailing view among significant sections of left-wing liberals that colonialism was an elite enterprise engaged in only by rich capitalists.[32]

Second, the system of indirect rule popularized by British administrators such as Lugard, when combined with Wilsonian idealism, produced a powerful current of opinion in favor of allowing the natives to 'develop' both economically and politically, as long as the economic interest of the colonial powers were secure. The most powerful manifestation of this was the system of native chiefs, in creating what Mahmoud Mamdani has tellingly described as "decentralized despotism."[33] As Furnivall says, "indirect rule through a native chieftain is the simplest and cheapest way by which a western power can obtain economic control."[34] This was clearly understood by the administrators of the PMC. As M. Yanaghita, the Japanese representative put it: "We find that under this system many chiefs, both great and small, are given charge of matters of minor importance connected with village administration. They are permitted to carry out these duties in a most imposing manner, taking advantage of the great traditional respect which they still receive from those under them. Scarcely aware of the fact that their little sovereignty has been transferred to a higher group, they will assist in the work of the mandatory government and will be content with the empty title and the modest stipend."[35]

Third, the notion of 'development' had acquired a scientific aura after Marx. The biological meaning of this term – derived from Darwinism – which came to mean the process through which the full potentialities of an organism are released, until it reaches its natural, complete and predestined form, had been imported into the social sphere in late eighteenth century.[36] This concept interacted with the Hegelian concept of history as a linear process of unfolding events, and manifested itself in Marxian economic theory. As a result, 'development' had become respectable among the critics of nineteenth-century capitalism as well.

Fourth, by the beginning the twentieth century, the word "development" came to be used frequently, in relation to "urban development," or the problems associated with the mass migration of poor to cities, and

[31] Anghie (1995) 258. [32] Lugard (1922), chapter 31. [33] Mamdani (1996), passim.
[34] Furnivall (1948) 277. [35] PMC, Min., III, at 283, cited in Wright (1930) 245.
[36] Esteva (1992) 8.

the social and political problems associated therewith, in Europe and the US.[37] The practices associated with this new field – including the use of the bulldozer, and the massive, homogenized production of industrial spaces – came to define civilization in a powerful way.[38] This made it easier to understand the appeal of the deployment of 'development' as a metaphor to deal with the heathens who needed to be saved; but more importantly, this also enables one to understand the particular forms that the economic meaning of 'development' took in the subsequent decades in the colonies.

Thus, the invention of 'well-being and development' of the natives in the Mandate system of the League was made possible by a number of factors, some of which were internal to the discipline of international law itself, while the others were outside of the discipline. Whatever these factors may have been, humanitarianism had joined economic interest as a powerful tool of governance.

'Finding facts': the creation of the apparatus

When the League was established in 1919, international law, and to some extent law itself, had been in crisis: the Great War had shown international law to be powerless against sovereignty; a legal revolution was sweeping American and French legal academies which called into question the whole edifice of nineteenth-century formalism;[39] progressive international lawyers, particularly those from Latin America, called into question not only the universality of international law, but also the legal methods of nineteenth-century positivism which placed emphasis on legal rules and sovereign consent.[40] The establishment of the League was therefore seen by progressive international lawyers of the time such as Wright, Corbett, and Alvarez as an opportunity to renew the discipline by breaking with the old.[41]

This attempt to renew the discipline was not attempted in a political vacuum, but within the context of the practical issues that arose from the establishment of the League institutions to study the conditions of lives

[37] Ibid. 9.

[38] Ibid. For a brilliant analysis of the relationship between the production of geographical spaces in urban development and colonialism, see Sibley (1995); see also the analysis in Rajagopal (1998–99).

[39] See Kennedy (1996) 397; Horowitz (1992), chapter 6; Belleau (1990).

[40] Drago (1907); Alvarez (1929).

[41] Kennedy (1987) 845; Alvarez (1929); Corbett (1924).

of the natives. The need to study those conditions, or to 'find the facts,' was a corollary of the objective of article 22, which was to improve the conditions in the mandated areas. To improve the conditions, the League organs had to know all the facts about the territories and have some standards by which the performances of mandatories could be judged.[42] This was then a wholly different enterprise from colonial rule, under which the information collected about the territories was not compared to some standards and judged. In this sense, the task of 'finding the facts' was itself an assertion of the autonomy and the superiority of law, as well as the 'international,' represented by the League.

The League had many different ways to discover facts about the natives. They included: (a) written reports of mandatories; (b) information resulting from oral hearings of their representatives; (c) written petitions; (d) reports of special committees and commissions; and (e) miscellaneous materials gathered by the Secretariat of the League, including press reports and travel accounts.[43]

The whole gamut of facts thus gathered by the League was enormously wide. It included, for example, information emerging from the administration of colonial territories stretching from Nauru to Southwest Africa to Syria, among other areas[44] (I provide snapshots of information in several areas to show the range of information collected):

Population: French Togoland population increased 7% from 1921 to 1927, whereas in Palestine, there was an excess of births over deaths, despite heavy infant mortality, of 2.20%;

Health: In 1926, per capita health expenditures were $0.06% in French Cameroons, and the health budget was 9% in Tanganyika;

Land Tenure and Wages: Between 1924–26, in Palestine, Jewish unskilled labor was three times more expensive than Arab labor (Jewish: $100–$125; Arab: $30–$50 per month), compared to wages in East Africa of $2–$5 a month;

Education: The number of school children in Tanganyika in 1925 was about equal to that under Germany in 1914 – about 2.4% of the population, compared to 1.7% for Kenya and 5.5% in Uganda;

Security: Not susceptible to statistics, but the PMC's interest in colonial policy extended to maintenance of native customs and institutions, prevention of forced labor, and elimination of conscription except for police purposes, law and order, and justice;

[42] Wright (1930) 190. [43] Wright (1930) 159; Hall (1948), chapters 12 and 13.
[44] This information is from Wright (1930) 549–79.

External trade: Per capita foreign trade in 1926 of Syria was $28, Ruanda-Urundi was $0.18, and $7 for Belgian Congo;
Investments, loans, and subsidies: Belgian government made loans of $60,000 a year to Ruanda-Urundi, whereas French Togoland lent $250,000 to French Cameroons in 1927 out of its surplus;
Public revenues: Per capita revenue in Syria in 1926 was $5.65, whereas the revenue of British Togoland rose 2,000% from 1919 to 1925;
Public works and services: In 1925, Southwest Africa had 4 miles of railroad per thousand square miles of area, whereas French Cameroons had 2 miles per thousand.

The colonial powers had collected statistics on native populations at least since the nineteenth century, in order to know them better and therefore to govern them.[45] But the chief innovations of the Mandate system were two: first, these extensive data were *compared systematically* to draw lessons and formulate standards and principles in these areas. Comparative statistical and informational analysis, which is one of the essential prerequisites to global governance, was systematized in the Mandates. Second, as a corollary of this, a new "science of colonial administration" at the international level, based on a deductive and experimental method, was born.[46] This science of colonial administration was, I suggest, the essential precursor to the science of development, administered through a complex apparatus of international institutions after WWII. In other words, without the practical experience of the mandate system in the collection and analysis of comparative data, and the evolution of a new science of administration, international institutions could not have assumed the all-encompassing role that they did in Third World development after WWII. 'Native well-being' and 'development' had started to become professionalized and institutionalized during the inter-war years, much earlier than the emergence of development as an academic discipline and political practice.[47]

The other important aspect that emerges from the analysis of these new responsibilities of the League, is that international law itself acquired a different character in the interaction between, law, administration, public

[45] For a geneology of how the population came to be the focus of government, see Foucault (1991).
[46] Wright (1930) 229.
[47] On the emergence of development as an ideology, see Esteva (1992); on the emergence of development economics as an academic discipline and political practice, see Arndt (1989); Hirschman (1981); Sen (1983).

policy and culture.[48] As described by Alejandro Alvarez, the idealist Latin American international lawyer, in his dissenting opinion in the Advisory Opinion of the ICJ on the *International Status of South West Africa Case*, "because of these characteristics, the new international law is not of an exclusively juridical character. It has also political, economic, social and psychological characteristics."[49] As Anthony Anghie describes it, in the Mandate system "law asserted itself, not merely as a system of rules but as administration, as science."[50] This also coincided with the critique of nineteenth-century formalism by legal realists and nineteenth-century positivism by progressive internationalists. As the Permanent Court of International Justice pointed out in the *Mavrommatis Palestine Concessions Case*, "the Court, whose jurisdiction is international, is not bound to attach to matters of form the same degree of importance which they might attach in municipal law."[51]

This new turn in international law from a system of rules to a science of administration, was not without its tensions: in the PMC itself, there were extensive debates about whether to adopt a 'legal' or 'scientific' approach to their work.[52] Nor do I suggest that, by turning to the 'new' international law, the 'old' law was somehow transcended once and for all.[53] Rather, the two were blended to produce an international legal regime that remains essentially unchanged today.

Parallels with the work of the PMC can be found in the work of the BWIs, the WTO and the human rights bodies of the UN, with the same tensions between law and politics, politics and economics, and law and economics. There is no final resolution of these tensions nor are they meant to be resolved; rather, the process of producing these tensions had emerged as the process of governance (see next chapter). I then suggest that this new international law of administration is a clear precursor to the turn to pragmatism that is characteristic of post WWII international law.[54] In other words, though international law is believed to have turned to pragmatism, functionalism, and institutionalism only since WWII, I would suggest that crucial groundwork was laid for it in the Mandate system.

[48] Anghie (1995) 218. [49] ICJ Reports (1950) 176. [50] Anghie (1995) 218.
[51] *Mavrommatis Palestine Concessions Case*, PCIJ Series A, No.2, 34.
[52] Wright (1930) 227–28 and the contrasting approaches of PMC members, M. Van Rees and M. Yanaghita.
[53] For example, the *Lotus Case* was decided by the Permanent Court of International Justice in 1927 affirming a highly formalistic conception of state sovereignty.
[54] Kennedy (1987).

The establishment of 'standards': formula for institutional expansion

The flood of information relating to labor, land, health, and education that was reaching the League organs gave rise to the question of how the League should assess the information. In other words, what benchmarks of progress should be used? What standards would enable the League, especially the PMC, to determine if a mandatory was carrying out the purposes of article 22? This must be seen in the context of the legal obligation of all League members contained in article 23 of the League Covenant relating to the regulation by the League organs of standards in the areas of labor, treatment of natives, trafficking in women, children, drugs, and arms, the spread of disease, and freedom of communication and commerce.[55] This meant that the League organs must be able to supervise the activities of the member states and judge substantively when they violate international policy. This was no easy task, as supervision by an international institution of sovereign states was an unknown phenomenon until then. Indeed, being an international institution without sanctions, the League depended upon the voluntary cooperation of its members for its effectiveness.

Thus, the principal concern of the League, especially the PMC, was how to balance the necessity to maintain cooperation with States with the need to supervise their performance.[56] As the PMC put it classically, "the task of the Commission is one of supervision and co-operation . . . Supervision and co-operation are functions which, though neither incompatible nor in conflict with one another, may yet be accompanied with genuine difficulties when they have to be carried out simultaneously."[57] This concern was especially acute in the case of the mandates, as the League was explicitly charged with supervision in this area under article 23. As a result, the PMC tended to resolve the tension by inventing bureaucratic techniques that balanced both cooperation and supervision. Indeed, I would suggest that the PMC was so preoccupied with this tension that dealing with it became the guiding logic of its existence even at the cost of establishing objective standards in various technical fields. The lack of such technical standards is noted by Quincy Wright who concedes that "standards of colonial administration have been formulated to a very limited extent"

[55] Wright (1930) 592.

[56] This cooperation–supervision dichotomy, it can be readily observed, reproduces the age-old dichotomies in liberal internationalism, between autonomy and community. See Koskenniemi (1989); Carty (1986).

[57] PMC Min. VIII (1926), 200 quoted in Hall (1948) 207.

and consequently "judgments of the League organs have been to some extent based upon the rather imperfectly defined standards in the minds of the members of the Council and especially of the Commission."[58] He expresses the hope that in the future "the League's supervision will become a supervision of law rather than of men."[59]

This meant that in situations involving potential breaches of legal obligations by the mandatories – as when they act clearly contrary to the well-being of the natives by brutally suppressing legitimate dissent, – the PMC failed to exercise its supervisory role through criticism.[60] This did not mean that the PMC actually agreed with the questionable behavior of these mandatories or conspired with them secretly to legitimize their brutal rule. Such claims can be, and have been, made by those who attempt to explain away the entire mandate system as colonialism in (barely) a disguise.[61] Such criticisms are important in explaining the ideological bias of the international order. However, it should not be overlooked that the PMC was also strongly motivated – in failing to vigorously exercise its supervisory role – to simply define, reproduce, and defend a field of reality as its terrain of application. In other words, when confronted with the 'reality' of a legal violation through information from different sources, the PMC often chose to internalize the information in a series of bureaucratic maneuvers *whose main purpose was their very existence and reproduction, without any further exterior objective.* Such maneuvers included, for example, the appointment of rapporteurs and committees to study particular questions before the PMC, the consideration of on-the-spot visits, and draft resolutions for action by the Council. In other words, form, not substance, was key to supervision. This was not straightforward, but often involved a complicated series of adjustments between theory and practice, law and science, and bureaucracy and substance.

The net result of these maneuvers was that the PMC attempted to build an institutional identity for itself, which was technocratic, scientific, practical and cooperative, as opposed to legalistic, formalistic, substantive, and critical. As the Chair of the PMC put it, "the Commission was not a legal body having the duty of giving opinions for the use of the council on questions of interpretation before these questions had even arisen

[58] Wright (1930) 190. [59] Ibid.

[60] As in the French suppression of the 1925–26 Syrian insurrection or the South African suppression of the Bondelzwart insurrection of 1922. See Wright (1930) 197–98.

[61] For example, one commentator during the inter-war years, Salvador de Madariaga, said, "the old hag of colonization puts on a fig leaf and calls itself mandate." See Salvador de Madariaga, *The World's Design* (1938) 7, quoted in Claude, Jr. (1971) 321.

in practice. The Permanent mandates commission was a committee of control, whose duty it was to supervise the application of the provisions of the mandates.... It was important for the prestige of the commission that it should not engage in endless discussion concerning questions of theory."[62]

This self-generative and self-determinative aspect of the PMC's work, enabling it to determine its own field of reality has come to be, I suggest, a standard aspect of international institutions in general. In part this is due to the fact that these institutions are creatures of law and law in general displays a heuristic tendency whereby it needs to establish its own field of autonomy only by simplifying and excluding much of actual reality. As Philip Allot says, "actual reality, as it presents itself in human consciousness, is infinitely complex, uncertain, and dynamic. In order to make legal relations operationally effective, as instruments of social transformation, they must exclude much of actual reality."[63] This process is not easy or automatic; indeed, each time law comes into contact with 'reality,' it struggles to reflect it, even as it maintains its distance from it to show that as 'law,' it is different from the 'reality' and can therefore constrain it. A constant process, this is reflected in the self-image of the international lawyer.

This new technocratic image was to be the image of the 'new' international lawyer, as opposed to an 'old' lawyer with his/her focus on formal rules and reasoning alone. Thus, the PMC's members "must possess all knowledge – native law, native religion, native psychology, native customs, methods of combating disease and vice, understanding of climatic, geographical, and economic conditions, principles of colonial administration throughout the world from the beginning."[64] This was a new interdisciplinary image of the international lawyer, with an emphasis on the non-legal aspects of governance. This was a revolutionary move in international law, as it constituted a sharp break with the immediate nineteenth-century formalism and late Victorian liberalism, both of which remained within juro-centric frameworks. The formulation of this new professional identity was not achieved easily and indeed, the law–science tension, like the cooperation–supervision tension, was not meant to be resolved once and for all. Rather, the technique of governance was to find the facts and judge them for policy within the dynamic created by these tensions which closely paralleled each other. Thus, Wright moves effortlessly from his

[62] Wright (1930) 223. [63] Allot (1995).
[64] Hon. Ormsby-Gore, cited in Wright (1930) 137.

discussion of the cooperation–supervision tension faced by the PMC to the lawyer–scientist tension that is immanent in the self-image of the lawyer.[65]

Thus, the principal problem for the PMC was how to assess the voluminous data collected about the natives and decide if the objectives of article 22 were being fulfilled – viz., that the 'well-being and development' of the natives were being promoted by the mandatories. These problems arose from the plurality of the social, economic, and cultural aspects of the natives, as well as the absence of any objective 'indicators' that could enable judgments to be passed on the performance of mandatories.[66] In dealing with this, the PMC fashioned a new image for itself as an international institution, straddling the tensions between cooperation and supervision and law and science. But, more importantly, through these tensions, the PMC was able to avoid the political consequences of what it meant to supervise sovereign states and assure the well-being of natives, in the presence of often strong evidence that the natives were being exploited. As the PMC said regarding the French crackdown on the Syrian insurrections of 1925–26, "The procedure followed by the Commission and the character of the observations which it has the honor to submit to the council have been dictated by its desire to carry out, so far as the circumstances enable it to do so, this double mission of supervision and cooperation. As it is anxious not to make the task of France in Syria and the Lebanon impossible of performance, it does not in the present instance, recommend to the Council to set up a commission of inquiry independent of the mandatory Power. Nevertheless, recognizing its duty of supervision, it has not felt able to abstain from expressing certain criticisms."[67] This is what I have termed as the self-regenerative dynamic of international institutions, which are deeply deradicalizing in practice, as they oscillate between the desire to supervise and the need

[65] Wright (1930) 543: "while there has been an effort in the Council to direct the Commission's activity to judgment on things done rather than suggestion of things to do, and while the Commission has on the whole conformed to that view and has been cautious of generalization, yet the very limitations which the Council imposes upon its effective performance of a judicial task have led it to interpret its mission as one of cooperation with rather than criticism of the mandatories. That function requires the approach of the scientist rather than of the lawyer..." (Ibid).

[66] Thus Wright, after considering whether a judicial, technological, statistical, or historical method may best help in estimating the Mandate system, concludes that "because of the difficulties of statistical analysis and the presence of many imponderable factors, perhaps the subjective judgment of competent historians and observers in the areas is as reliable as the results of more refined methods" (Ibid. 549).

[67] Cited in Wright (1930) 197.

to cooperate. Overlooked in this dynamic are the larger issues of power, domination, and legitimacy, which fail to be questioned by international lawyers as they construct the world's governing edifice. As pointed out by Julius Stone, the reference in article 22(1) of the Covenant to peoples 'not yet able to stand by themselves under the strenuous conditions of the modern world' refers, without irony, to the conditions, which are the result of the rivalries of the colonial powers themselves and not due to the infirmities of the mandates' peoples.[68] The PMC, though designed with the best of intentions, simply served to obscure this reality.

Institutionalizing resistance: the petition process and supervision

Textbooks on international human rights law hail the invention of petition processes at the United Nations such as 1503 – whereby individuals complain about the violation of their rights to international institutions – as historical innovations that decidedly mark a shift in international law from states to individuals.[69] According to this progress narrative, international law never allowed sovereigns to be questioned about their actions towards their citizens until these innovations, which mark the beginning of a 'new international law' (see next chapter). In this narrative, as petitions are received, sovereignty retreats as law and institutions gain ground.

This narrative is decidedly ahistorical. Long before the 1503 or similar procedures, the League, through the PMC, had established a procedure for receiving petitions from the inhabitants of mandates. These petitions ranged from complaints about grievances in the application of the mandates to suggestions or information of a more general character. What is relevant here is not the mere fact that there was a historical precursor to 'modern' human rights procedures in the mandate system, though the neglect of this in the historiography of human rights law needs to be questioned for its political effect; rather, what interests me is the assortment of techniques through which the petition process made the Mandate system reap the benefits of appearing to be accountable even as the PMC deflected and contained the substance of the petitions. I suggest that the techniques that the PMC developed for dealing with the petitions essentially remain unchanged in the institutional practices of subsequent international petition processes, from UN human rights procedures to

[68] Cited in Weeramantry (1992) 89.
[69] Lillich and Hannum (1995) 342. A classic statement is Sohn (1982).

the recent World Bank Complaints Panel. These techniques were substantially the creation of the PMC. As acknowledged by William Rappard, a member of the PMC from 1925 to 1945, after the end of the war, the real contribution of the mandate system to human rights was in the 'methods of international supervision' that it devised which included the petition system prominently.[70]

Indeed, the petition system has been seen as one of the main and most interesting innovations of the mandate system. Though petitions formed an appreciable part of the Commission's work, they were not of great practical importance as they were mainly used by the residents of the 'A' mandates.[71] The peoples of the 'B' and 'C' mandates, from Africa and the Pacific, made little use of the petition system.[72] Nevertheless, the fact that the petition system could be set up without any textual basis in either the Covenant or the mandate agreement,[73] and despite its infrequent use by many residents, showed that the purpose of the petition as a tool of information for the PMC was more important than its purpose as a tool of grievance-redressal. In this, one can begin to see how the functionalist needs of international institutions determine their tasks, not sovereign consent or individual rights alone.

Under the procedure approved by the Council,[74] petitions from inhabitants of a mandated area could be received only if they are submitted through the Mandatory, which was requested to append its comments before sending it to the PMC. Petitions from other sources – such as investigators, writers, lawyers, travelers, humanitarian and other organizations – were to be sent to the Chair of the PMC who would decide to include them for consideration by the PMC.[75] In general, the attitude of the PMC was to attempt to treat the petition process, as much as possible, as a technocratic enterprise of obtaining information rather than legal determinations as a court of appeal. This was no doubt necessitated by the need to preserve the institutional identity of the PMC within the League

[70] Rappard (1946) 121.

[71] Hall (1948) 198. The Mandates were classified into A, B, and C, corresponding to paragraphs 4, 5, and 6 of article 22 of the League Covenant. The first included former Turkish territory, the second, Central African territory, and the third, Southwest Africa and Pacific islands. Wright (1930) 47.

[72] Hall (1948) 198.

[73] Ibid. It was Britain which suggested the petition system as a part of the toolkit of the PMC. Ibid. 199. On the other hand, article 87 (c) of the Covenant did authorize the League Council to accept petitions. For a description, see Chowdhuri (1955) 206.

[74] PMC Min. I, 28, cited in Wright (1930) 169. See also Hall (1948) 200.

[75] Wright (1930) 169; Hall (1948) 201.

system (see last section), vis-à-vis sovereign states, wherein it needed to balance cooperation with supervision. The net result of this policy was that the PMC adopted or was made to adopt by the council an attitude of containment towards the petitions, wherein the most serious allegations were either put off by bureaucratic techniques. Several examples could be cited. Thus, the PMC adopted a policy of refusing to consider petitions that opposed the mandate itself or its principles, as in the Arab protest against the Balfour declaration in the Palestine mandate.[76] Also, the question of oral hearing of petitioners was raised by the request of the Anti-Slavery and Aborigines Protective Society of London to be heard on behalf of the Bondelzwarts in the third session, but after much debate the PMC decided only to admit written information.[77] This was no doubt due to fears of political repercussions: as one member put it, oral hearings would enable petitioners "to confront the mandatory power and would give them in the minds of their fellow-countrymen a position of which they would not fail to make the greatest use in combating the local authority."[78] But it was also due to the fear that it would transform the PMC into a court of law, which would be inconsistent with the nature of the mandate system, as well as weaken the authority of the mandatory powers.[79]

All this does not mean that the PMC was engaged in camouflaging and covertly assisting the exploitation of the mandates. On the contrary, the PMC members took their institutional role seriously and sought to expand their powers, often to the exasperation of the mandatories. For instance, even though oral hearings of petitioners were opposed by the Mandatories, the PMC reached an understanding, as formulated by M. Rappard, that all members of the PMC could hear persons informally during personal interviews, but could not receive them officially.[80] This institutional independence of the PMC was assisted by the nature of its constitution. It was organized as a body of nine members, selected for their "personal merits and competence," the majority of whom "shall be nationals of non-Mandatory Powers."[81] They were prevented from holding any office, which made them dependent on their governments.[82] The

[76] Wright (1930) 171–72.

[77] Wright (1930) 173. This precedent was cited by the PMC as a ground for refusing to see delegates from Syria at its eighth session. Hall (1948) 202.

[78] M. Merlin, cited in Wright (1930) 175. [79] Hall (1948) 203. [80] Ibid.

[81] Constitution of PMC, cited in Wright (1930) 622.

[82] The information of all these from Wright (1930) 137–55; Hall (1948), chapter 12; Chowdhuri (1955), chapter 7.

PMC made its own rules of procedure and its members had a guaranteed salary. Clearly the parallel is strong with modern institutions such as the UN Sub-Commission on the Prevention of Discrimination and Protection of Minorities. However, the meetings were generally private, even though the rules provided for public hearings at the desire of the majority of the PMC. The PMC divided its work into general questions of law, procedure, and administration that arose from reports by a member of a Subcommittee; reports of the Mandatories which were scrutinized in the PMC meetings and which formed the basis of interrogations of representatives of Mandatories; and petitions which were similarly handled.

In performing these duties, the PMC was faced with four key issues: the independence of the PMC from the League; the PMC's power to suggest modifications to the Mandates that goes beyond the observance of the terms of the Mandates; the PMC's power to hear oral petitions and conduct on-site investigations; and the PMC's power to advise the Mandatories on the entire administration of mandates. In sum, on all these four issues, the PMC was considered by many Mandatories to be going too far and they sought to rein it in. For example, the question of PMC's competence arose in 1926 when Chamberlain of Great Britain objected to a questionnaire that the PMC wished the Mandatories to answer.[83] He declared, "this immense questionnaire was infinitely more detailed, infinitely more inquisitorial than that which had hitherto been in force with the sanction of the council – it raised the question of the true relative position of the mandatory governments in a mandated territory and the mandates commission which examined their report, and the council which took action as guardian under terms of the covenant."[84] Also, after much debate the PMC decided to publish petitions using its discretion, which also caused discomfiture to the Mandatories.

Thus, in the end, the institutional self-identity of the PMC compelled it to adopt a complex posture wherein it had to develop ways of dealing with petitions that juggled the demands of sovereign cooperation and its role of supervision, and in that process established a clear precedent which later international institutions have followed. The key aspect of the PMC, which is to be found in all latter petition mechanisms, is this: that, disputes/grievances from the mandate-inhabitants get converted into questions of institutional self-preservation and identity at the PMC.[85] In other words, the question of what to do with a petition

[83] Wright (1930) 151. [84] Ibid.
[85] Kennedy (1987) 982–983 (discussing the Gran Chaco case and institutional expansion).

could/can not be answered by looking at the severity of the 'violation' alone; rather, what mattered for the PMC was often what it could legitimately assert in its institutional role. This had a deeply deradicalizing effect on the petition process, as it ruled out vigorous PMC responses to the most serious allegations of abuses.

Conclusion

It has been argued here that the Mandate system contributed significantly, at least in the following ways, to mediating the contentious relationship between colonialism and development during the inter-war years: first, it legitimized the 'development and well-being of the natives' as an international principle, which marked the move from exploitative colonialism (imperialism) to cooperative colonialism (development); second, it created a new science of law and administration which was a clear precursor to post WWII development studies; third, it invented new techniques for the self-regeneration of the bureaucratic sphere by constantly inventing gaps between facts and standards and inventing techniques to bridge that gap; fourth, it had a highly problematic relationship to the 'local,' represented by the facts brought forth through petitions, which had the result of deradicalizing the content of those petitions. It is quite possible that this has remained true of all petition processes in international law so far.

The Mandate system ceased to exist along with the League. But it had contributed significantly to the process of transforming colonialism from a system of direct control to development, a new science that blended humanitarian motives, technology, and international bureaucracy. In that process, it had also fundamentally altered the conception of law in the international community from a formal conception of rules to a pragmatic conception of administration. International law would henceforth never be the same. Indeed, the Trusteeship system, which succeeded the Mandate system under the UN Charter, reflected the intellectual debt that it owed to the Mandate system.[86]

Despite these similarities and the continuance of colonialism in 1945, the perception of international institutions as mere instruments of great power politics had given way to a more nuanced and certainly uneasy understanding of them as players with their own internal dynamics, even as terrains of struggle between the colonial powers and the colonized peoples.

[86] For a synopsis of the similarities, see Claude (1971), chapter 16. On the Trusteeship system, see Haas, (1953) 1–21; Jacobson (1962) 37–56.

This is clearly borne out by the rather hostile response to the Trusteeship system from the colonial powers – if the Mandate system had been just a cloak for colonial hegemony, why would the colonial powers greet its successor with hostility? For example, at the Yalta Conference, Winston Churchill asserted hotly that "he did not agree with one single word of this report on trusteeships.... He said that under no circumstances would he ever consent to forty or fifty nations thrusting interfering fingers into the life's existence of the British Empire."[87]

Indeed in 1945, Third World mass politics had already entered international law. Colonial people and territories could no longer be disposed of by white Europeans and their descendants sitting in Geneva, London, and Paris. Many Third World countries had won independence – India, Pakistan, Iraq, and Syria – and they began radicalizing international institutions, especially the UN, in order to quickly annihilate the colonial system. They actively used the UN fora, including the Trusteeship Council, to put an end to colonialism. They looked upon these institutions as harbingers of progress, which would assist in the dismantling of colonialism and the economic and social progress of their peoples. This overlooked the more complicated fact that these institutions, starting with the Mandate system, had emerged as apparatuses that controlled and channeled the resistance from the Third World in the transition from colonialism to development.

[87] Claude (1971) 325. He was pacified by Secretary Stettinius that the proposed machinery would not deal with British possessions, but only with enemy territory. Ibid.

4

Radicalizing institutions and/or institutionalizing radicalism? UNCTAD and the NIEO debate

By the time of the First World War itself, there were elements of a 'universal' international society, but this was not consolidated and quickened until the Second World War. A real revolution was occurring in world affairs, as non-Christian states were admitted to the international 'community' for the first time in several centuries as a result of the revolt against the West.[1] As is well known, during the 1950s, 1960s, and 1970s, these new states took charge of the UN and its specialized agencies due to their numerical superiority, and attempted to transform international law through the use of UNGA resolutions, the establishment of new international institutions and the introduction of new elements into the doctrinal corpus of international law such as the doctrine of Permanent Sovereignty over Natural Resources (PSNR).[2] This was done under the umbrella of the NIEO, which broadly called for structural changes in the world economy that the new nations desired, in the interests of justice, world peace, and development.

This chapter provides an analysis of the important moments that characterized this Third World engagement with (what was still then) a European international law. My analysis differs, however, from the traditional historiographies of the NIEO,[3] which treat NIEO as a failure and attribute that failure to its radicalism and lack of realism. Instead, the NIEO constituted a moment of radical challenge to international law that resulted in transforming and expanding the reach of international law, but it was also inherently limited in the extent of its radicalism. In other words, neither was it a 'failure' as much as it is believed to be, nor was it as radical as it is commonly taken. In particular, the search for a Third World alternative to US capitalism and the Soviet command model, which characterized the Bandung Conference in 1955 and continued to be reflected in the NIEO proposals in 1974, were firmly premised on the need

[1] Bull (1984).

[2] See generally Anand (1987). On PSNR, see Hossain and Chowdhury (1984).

[3] Franck (1986) 82.

to *accelerate* the modernization process, and thereby essentially repeated the thinking that lay behind colonial and developmental discourses, viz., that the 'primitive' had to be morally and materially redeemed. The limitations inherent in such an approach can be seen, for example, in the concrete proposals that international lawyers put forth under the rubric of NIEO, which essentially revolved around the reform of the UN system. Fundamentally, these critiques were not aimed at challenging the categories of western modernity and rationality that were inherent in the economic and political systems that international law supported. In fact, they wanted more of it. More importantly, while the NIEO proposals radicalized and expanded the UN as an institution, the limited nature of those proposals also had the effect of institutionalizing the radicalism that was emerging from the Third World. In other words, the radical challenges to international law leveled by NIEO proponents had the paradoxical effect of expanding and strengthening international institution as the apparatuses of management of social reality in the Third World, and, thereby, of international law itself.

The spirit of Bandung

The Bandung Conference of 1955 was the first ever conference attended solely by Asian and African States, but it also came to symbolize the new spirit of solidarity of the Third World.[4] Twenty-nine countries (out of the then total world number of fifty-nine) attended the conference, featuring several prominent leaders such as Prime Minister Nehru, Prime Minister Zhou Enlai, Presidents Nasser and Sukarno, Princes Sihanouk and Faisal, nationalist leaders such as U Nu, Mohammed Ali, and Carlos Romulo. Despite several internal political tensions and contradictions, Bandung succeeded in two respects; first, it helped forge a common Third World consciousness that laid the basis for collective mobilizations by the Third World at the UN, through the Group of 77 (G-77) and the Non Aligned Movement (NAM).[5] Second, it underlined the two cardinal principles that would organize Third World politics in the coming decades: decolonization and economic development.[6]

Several themes emerged from this conference that formed the foundations of the NIEO proposals two decades later. The most important of these was a desire to articulate a 'third' way, a political position that

[4] Mortimer (1984) 6. On the Bandung Conference, see also Kahin (1956); Wright (1956); Republic of Indonesia, Ministry of Foreign Affairs (1956); Appadorai (1955); Romulo (1956).

[5] Mortimer (1984) 9. [6] Ibid.

would distinguish the Third World from the two Great Powers as well as, as it later turned out, China. This desire was manifested, for instance, in the famous diatribe of Ceylon's (as it then was) Sir John Kotelawala against Soviet colonialism. After observing that the delegates were well acquainted with colonialism in its "first and most obvious form" – western colonialism – he went on: "there is another form of colonialism, however, about which many of us represented here are perhaps less clear in our minds and to which some of us would perhaps not agree to apply the term colonialism at all. Think, for example, of those satellite states under Communist domination in Central and Eastern Europe – of Hungary, Rumania, Bulgaria, Albania, Czechoslovakia, Latvia, Lithuania and Poland. Are not these colonies as much as any of the colonial territories in Africa or Asia? And if we are united in our opposition to colonialism, should it not be our duty to openly declare our opposition to Soviet colonialism as much as to Western imperialism?"[7] This position was supported by many states including Pakistan, Iran, Iraq, Turkey, Japan, Lebanon, Libya, Liberia, the Philippines, and the Sudan, who then introduced a resolution providing for a condemnation of "all types of colonialism."[8] This reflected the reality that many of the states attending the conference were worried about incipient leftist/communist revolutions in their countries and wished to head them off.[9] Indeed, in many of these countries – such as Libya, Cambodia, and the Philippines – communist/leftist revolutions would sweep through in the coming decades. But the essential point to be noted here is that, contrary to popular and scholarly misunderstanding in the West, the attempt to articulate a Third World voice was genuine, and was not the extension of Soviet domination. This was evident, particularly in the realm of peace and security, where the neutralism of Nasser combined with those of India and Burma, led to the emergence of NAM in the following years.

The attempt to articulate a view of colonialism that would equally apply to the West and the Soviet regimes proved to be difficult in the conference, however. This was nowhere more true than in the economic sphere. In the absence of a viable alternative to US capitalism or Soviet communism, and being wedded to their modernization and nation-building ethos, the countries assembled in Bandung reiterated their commitment to promoting economic development, including through investment of foreign

[7] Cited in Kahin (1956) 19. [8] Ibid. 20.

[9] See Rajagopal (1998–99), for an analysis of Aijaz Ahmad, that Bandung should be seen in terms of the domestic political agendas of Nehru, Zhou Enlai, etc., rather than in terms of the international issues.

capital.[10] There was no call to preserve traditional ways of living or other ways of protecting cultural spaces, though colonialism and racism were condemned as means of cultural suppression.[11] While colonialism and racism were unequivocally condemned at the political level – particularly in the form of alien subjugation – there was no attempt to move away from the modernizing imperatives of nation-building. This was reflected not only in the functional and apolitical proposals relating to economic development, but also in the commitment to the Universal Declaration of Human Rights (UDHR), as common standards of achievement.[12] The latter is of special interest as it shows that in the 1950s, the Third World was hardly opposed to human rights though it had played very little part in drafting the UDHR.

This functional approach to modernization was seen in the proposals made to facilitate economic cooperation. These included foreign investment, technical cooperation, establishment of a Special UN Fund for Development, establishment of the International Finance Corporation (IFC) changes in the portfolio of the World Bank to favor the Third World, stabilizing commodity trade, and concerns about western dominance of shipping.[13] I do not deny that many of these were genuine concerns that were of great importance to the national survival of these countries. In a way these proposals were realized in the coming decades – the World Bank changed its portfolio allocation, IFC was established, etc. – and to that extent one could have an argument about whether the Third World initiative actually "failed" or "succeeded". But what is more interesting is the way in which radical criticisms of the international system (of finance, shipping, etc.) gets converted into institutional proliferation and practice. What is important, especially in retrospect, is the "instrument-effects", to quote Foucault,[14] of the critique: that is, effects that are at one and the same time instruments of what turns out to be an exercise of power. These effects which are unintended, have proved to be as important as the intended effects. Thus, commodity trade may not have been regularized in favor of the Third World yet, but it has surely produced a dense network of

[10] See Final Communiqué, cited in Kahin (1956) 76.

[11] Ibid. 79. [12] Ibid. 80. [13] Ibid. 76–78.

[14] Foucault (1979). Speaking of the prison, he suggests that instead of dwelling on the 'failure' of the prison, "one should reverse the problem and ask oneself what is served by the failure of the prison: what is the use of these different phenomena that are continually being criticized; the maintenance of delinquency, the encouragement of recidivism, the transformation of the occasional offender into a habitual delinquent, the organization of a closed milieu of delinquency" (272). I borrow this line of critique from Ferguson (1994), Part V.

international institutions, officials, practices, and knowledge-producing techniques that have proved to be resilient and important both for commodity trade and in their own right. These "instrument-effects" have driven the expansion of international law.

Traditional analyses of international institutions are different in two respects here: first, they pay very little attention to the role of Third World engagements (starting with Bandung), as an engine of growth of those institutions (indeed, they view Third World politics as a hindrance to the functioning of institutions); second, they pay scant attention to the "instrument-effects" of the Third World critique. I suggest that both are important: an increased attention to Third World engagements helps us move beyond the technocratic functionalism that characterizes the treatment of international institutions generally, to make visible 'forgotten' issues relating to power such as race or gender; on the other hand, looking at the "instrument-effects" of the Third World critique also helps us transcend the rather banal assessment of Third World engagements such as NIEO as "failures," to a more nuanced view that looks at the unintended consequences of the critique.

NIEO and the debate between incremental and fundamental reform

It is well known that the group of Third World States at the UN, led by OPEC, caused a system-wide international economic and political crisis, which is generally known as the attempt to establish an NIEO.[15] That period marked the first time the Third World emerged as a major actor in a system-wide international crisis. There were essentially three sources of impetus for the demand for the NIEO: the lessening of western aid; the disappointment with political independence in the Third World; and the success of OPEC as a primary commodity cartel.[16] The political, diplomatic, and economic offensive of the NIEO were launched on three fronts: the rise of oil prices by OPEC, acting for the first time as a coalition of producer states against western oil corporations; second, an oil embargo by OPEC against countries that supported Israel, including the US, its European allies and Japan; and third, the calling of the Sixth Special Session of the UNGA by Algeria which convened in April, 1974.[17] These were very significant events. Combined with the waves of nationalization

[15] On NIEO, see, Bedjaoui (1979); Sauvant (1981); Bhagwati (1977).

[16] Streeten (1981) 240. See also, Franck (1986).

[17] Mortimer (1984), chapter 4.

sweeping across the Third World from Algeria to Nigeria, it represented a fundamental challenge to the 'old' international economic order that rested on colonial relationships.

Yet, by the end of the 1970s, the NIEO had been judged a failure by many critics.[18] The West, led by the US, had blocked a fundamental reform of the international economic order, and cracks in Third World coalition began to appear. However, I would suggest that from the perspective of international law, this tendency to label the NIEO as a 'failure' is simplistic and ignores the radical and expansionary effect that the NIEO attempt had on international institutions, as well as norms. In other words, whatever be the 'success' or 'failure' of NIEO substantively, it had other unintended effects on international law that shaped it in important and continuing ways.

At the first level, the NIEO proposals were characterized from the beginning by a tension between those seeking incremental reforms versus those in favor of fundamental reforms.[19] Those in favor of incremental reforms interpreted the NIEO as a matter of rules and restraints, and stressed the need for increased debt relief, more concessionary aid, better access to capital markets, cheaper technology transfers, and non-reciprocal preferences for manufactured items. Those who preferred fundamental reforms saw the NIEO as a radical challenge to the rules, and a fundamental structural change to the international order in the form of new institutions, and changed power relations. The latter were inspired by the Dependency theorists who saw the post-colonial economic relations as essentially exploitative, between the western 'core' and the Third World 'periphery.'[20] Another way of characterizing this debate between incrementalism and radicalism is to think of it in terms of a tension between normative versus institutional approaches to international law, or simply, between sources and process.[21]

The Sixth Special Session of the UNGA and its aftermath

In reality, the incremental and radical approaches were simultaneously operative in the NIEO challenge, and interacted in complex ways to produce

[18] For criticisms see, Franck (1986); for an analysis of contradictions within NIEO from the perspective of international law, see Horn (1982); see also Bauer and Yamey (1977); Bauer (1976).

[19] For a nice overview, see Streeten (1981) 241.

[20] Literature on dependency theory includes Baran (1957); Amin (1976); Frank (1967, 1973).

[21] For a sophisticated analysis of the relation between sources and process debate and its impact on post World War II international law, see Kennedy (1994, 1995).

institutional changes. The Sixth Special Session of the UNGA in April, 1974 marked the radical moment in the emerging NIEO engagement. It was the first UNGA session specially devoted to development. Led by Algeria, and drawing inspiration from the NAM and G-77 texts adopted at the 1967 Algiers summit, the Special Session adopted two seminal resolutions that articulated the Third World claim to a right to economic development.[22] The first of these, the Declaration on the Establishment of a New International Economic Order,[23] called for an order "based on equity, sovereign equality, interdependence, common interest, and cooperation among all states irrespective of their economic and social systems which shall correct inequalities and redress existing injustices, and make it possible to eliminate the widening gap between the developed and the developing countries."[24] The major themes included both normative goals (creation of new doctrines such as PSNR, right to nationalization, regulation of MNCs (Multi-National Corporations), etc.), as well as institutional reforms (international monetary reform, facilitation of producer associations, etc.). The second of these resolutions, entitled Program of Action on the Establishment of a NIEO,[25] spelled out the policy implications of the principles set forth in the first declaration.

In many ways, these demands were quite radical. At the first level, as Robert Mortimer has pointed out, the very idea of the Sixth Session represented "a clash" between the voting power of the new Third World majority and US economic power.[26] Sovereignty was being used as a shield and a sword by weak states. At the second level, the NIEO proposals represented an attempt to shift the political balance in international law to the Third World by redesigning the architecture of international law. The momentum created at Bandung was resulting in concrete political contestations. Third, the NIEO also attempted to provide more leverage and power to Third World states against western corporations that had had a history of intervening in local politics.

Despite these, at another level these demands were neither new nor fundamentally radical. Many of the specific proposals of NIEO had been floated at least since the 1967 Algiers NAM declaration, whereas none of the proposals questioned the ethical and practical imperative of development itself, along with its modernizing ethos. The Third World states readily conceded the 'gap' that existed between the West and their 'backward' peoples and attempted to close it by copying the West. Besides, Bauer and Yamey as pointed out, the idea of a wealth or income gap between

[22] Mortimer (1984) 48–56. [23] United Nations (1974b). [24] Ibid.
[25] United Nations (1974c). [26] Mortimer (1984) 53.

the West and the Third World was a problematic concept, empirically and conceptually.[27] The very idea of a gap can exist only within a unified system, as pointed out by Douglas Lummis,[28] and to that extent constituted a watering down of the radical posturing of the Third World. Besides, the wealth gap *within* the Third World countries such as Brazil, which were sometimes as morally objectionable, was never raised as an issue in the NIEO. This was very much within the logic of mainstream development thinking. For example, as pointed out by H. Arndt, the 'trickle-down' theory was an international, not an intra-national, concept – that is, it never aimed at the reduction of inequality within countries.[29]

Even as the NIEO proposals were limited in some respects, they had a radical impact on the practice of international institutions, even though they were substantively blocked by the US. Thus, the twenty-ninth session of the UNGA which convened in 1974, adopted the seminal Charter on Economic Rights and Duties of States,[30] providing for normative standards on key issues such as nationalization, producer associations, and preferential trade arrangements. Outside the UN, the Third World offensive continued in many NAM and G-77 conferences, as well as attempts to establish international institutions such as UNIDO as specialized agencies that would be more favorable to the Third World.

This radicalization was generally overlooked by critics of the NIEO who see it as a failure because it failed to achieve its substantive goals, and not on its own terms. For example, Thomas Franck wrote a piece titled "Lessons of the Failure of NIEO," more than a decade after the NIEO debates had subsided.[31] In this piece, Franck exhibits a subtle appreciation of the importance of process over substantive outcome, in particular stressing the role of negotiations.[32] As he puts it, "there is no legislation in the contemporary international system. Only contract. And contract requires genuine *consensus ad idem*."[33] According to him, this was lacking in the Third World strategy towards the NIEO, since it was too confrontational, and made no attempt to reach out to public opinion in the West.[34] Indeed, he is entirely dismissive of such tactics which he says were wrongly based on "winning anti-colonial strategies" since "the campaign against colonialism, after all, had been won not in India and Algiers – except

[27] See Bauer and Yamey (1977). [28] See Lummis (1992). [29] Arndt (1983).

[30] United Nations (1974a). On the Charter, see American Society of International Law (1975), Rozental (1976).

[31] Franck (1986). [32] Ibid. at 100. [33] Ibid. 97.

[34] Ibid. 90–91. He draws a comparison between the confrontational Third World strategy and the black radicalism in the US in the 1960s.

in the a fortiori fiction of post-colonial nationalist mythology – but in London and Paris".[35] In this one sentence, Franck has simply written off the entire role played by mass resistance against colonialism. We know our history otherwise now. The subaltern collective on South Asia[36] and scholars such as Mahmoud Mamdani on Africa,[37] have done pioneering work to tell the history of the contributions made by ordinary people to anti-colonial movements, and thereby to dispute the elitist historiographies that have dominated so far. He also levels the criticism that no attempt was made by the Third World to concede the need for fundamental domestic changes: "it was all one-way guilt . . . it was not credible."[38] But this overlooks the fact that a confrontational strategy may have been part of the very formation of a common front, constituting an identity around which substantive discussions could be started with the West. As I have suggested, often the thrust of Third World offensive was first and foremost to constitute that common front and to hold it; it was only secondarily concerned with resolving substantive issues.

Institutionalizing radicalism: the seventh special session

Even as international institutions were converted into terrains of resistance by the Third World, its radicalism was gradually getting institutionalized and subdued. This was especially the case, for three reasons, in the Seventh Special Session of the UNGA which convened in September, 1975. First, after a prolonged period of leadership by a radical wing of Third World states led by Algeria, a more moderate wing came to dominate the Third World bloc.[39] Second, as a result of the sustained onslaught by a united Third World, the US had moderated its hard-line position and made a number of concrete proposals designed to respond to Third World demands.[40] The new US Ambassador, Daniel Patrick Moynihan, suggested the establishment of the expanded compensatory financing facility within the IMF, better access to western capital markets and technology, a pledge to give more resources to the IFC, commitments to negotiate tariff reductions, and other measures to promote Third World trade, programs to ensure global food supplies and augment agricultural production, creation of producer–consumer associations, World Bank support to raw

[35] Ibid. 86.

[36] The scholarship produced by these scholars, such as Ranajit Guha, Gayatri Chakravorti Spivak, Partha Chatterjee, and others, is vast. See the eight volumes of Subaltern Studies edited by Guha and others. See also Guha and Spivak (1988).

[37] See, e.g., Mamdani (1996). [38] Franck (1986) 91.

[39] Mortimer (1984) 67. [40] Ibid. 68.

materials production, and increased support to the poverty-related lending by IDA.[41] While conceding these, the US did not relent on other key demands such as a minimum 1% GNP development aid commitment or a link between development aid and the issuance of Special Drawing Rights or SDRs. The US also stressed that it did not accept the idea that the world was on a quest for a NIEO.[42]

Partly as a result of the US 'concessions' and partly due to the double-edged nature of solidarity – which compels radical factions to compromise in order to maintain unity – the Third World resistance had been largely contained at the Seventh Session without serious damage to western economic interests. But the fact remained that, whatever may be the demand and the concession, international institutions had gained significantly in their reach and power. More meetings and resolutions meant more analysis by legal academics, and more programs meant expanded activities for the IMF, World Bank, IFC, and International Development Agency (IDA). This dynamic – the "instrument-effects" – is key to the architecture of international institutions as apparatuses of management of social reality in the Third World.

UNCTAD: Third World politics as an engine of growth

In the Third World offensive during the 1960s and 1970s to change international law, several international institutions such as UNIDO, UNDP and UNCTAD were created by the UNGA. This institutional proliferation was part of a deliberate strategy of creating a level playing field with western economic power, by counterbalancing it with Third World voting power. As already noted, Third World lawyers looked upon this institutional proliferation as the means to bring about positive economic and social change in their countries. This desire – which was reflected in other areas such as the law of the sea as well – complemented the Third World attempt to remake international law at a normative level by focusing on sources of international law, by attacking custom, and promoting UNGA resolutions as sources of new norms.

The proliferation of institutions as well as their 'capture' by the Third World came under increasing criticism in the West.[43] Whatever may be

41 Ibid.

42 Ibid. 69. The US tried for eight hours to change "the" in the preamble of the proposed resolution referring to "the NIEO" to "a."

43 See, e.g., Finger (1976); Weintraub (1976). Some critics also saw proliferation of institutions as a good thing that would enable specialized issues to be disaggregated. See, e.g., Bergsten (1976).

the merit in these criticisms, it is undeniable, as the previous discussions show, that with the entry of the Third World in world politics, international institutions assumed an autonomous momentum towards expansion and multiplication. This momentum was made possible because of the 'politicization' of these institutions, as terrains of resistance and compromise. This, as I have noted earlier, is contrary to the neutral and apolitical way in which international institutions are presented in international law.[44] In this mainstream view, international institutions are presented as functional and apolitical organizations that have been established through forward-looking legal techniques that constantly push the frontier of international law towards a world community. Instead, I have suggested that the proliferation of institutions and the expansion of the international legal domain have been made possible because of the political "instrument-effects" of Third World resistance to the 'old' Eurocentric international law.

A classic example of this dynamic may be found in UNCTAD. Established in 1964 by the UNGA as a subsidiary organ of the UNGA,[45] UNCTAD played a prominent role in North–South relations as a policy-making and negotiating forum, at least until the end of the Cold War.[46] But more importantly, UNCTAD represents perhaps the clearest example of how radical conceptions of development – in this case dependency theory – that were a clear challenge to western liberal internationalism, were nevertheless limited in their radicalism through the acceptance of development as a process of western modernization. In the following, I shall examine the ambiguities, contradictions and opportunities in the formation and struggle over UNCTAD as a terrain of struggle.

Origins: the institutionalization of dependency theory

The origin of UNCTAD is to found in two factors: first, the entry of Third World states in international affairs, and second, the disappointment with the world trading regime, based on liberal trading principles, institutionalized in the form of General Agreement on Tariffs and Trade (GATT). Imbued with the 'spirit of Bandung,' the Asian, African, and, for the first time, Latin American countries coalesced together at a Conference on Problems of Developing Countries held in Cairo in 1962.[47] The Conference,

[44] See, e.g., Kirgis (1993).

[45] United Nations (1964). This is unlike a specialized agency, such as UNHCR, which was established through a constitutive treaty.

[46] On UNCTAD, see United Nations (1985); Rothstein (1979).

[47] United Nations (1985) 10.

UNCTAD I, which established it as a permanent institution under the UNGA in 1964, also marked the emergence of G-77 as a united Third World front in international relations.[48] From its beginning, UNCTAD was heavily influenced by dependency theorists such as Dr. Raul Prebisch, who became its first Secretary-General. Indeed, UNCTAD represented the institutional embodiment of dependency theory, as GATT represented the embodiment of modernization theory. As the History of UNCTAD puts it, "UNCTAD stresses the development approach, whereas GATT had been promoting a liberal international trading system."[49]

While dependency theory is generally considered to have offered a radical and powerful critique of international economic order, what is generally overlooked is the extent to which this critique influenced the formation and practices of international institutions. Indeed, international lawyers usually treat dependency critique as a powerful, yet esoteric and failed outsider critique and then go on to describe the workings of the liberal international order based on laissez faire principles. What is closer to truth is that aspects of dependency critique had a powerful and lasting influence on international economic order – in the justification of preferential trading arrangements, for example – that are routinely taken for granted as part of the 'liberal' international trading system. This was nowhere more true than in the case of UNCTAD.

This was made possible by the fact that theorists such as Raul Prebisch attempted to lay the groundwork for altering the rules of the liberal trading system that was codified in GATT which were based on symmetry between trading partners, a laissez faire conception.[50] But as Dr. Prebisch and others pointed out, this did not resemble reality, as developing countries were faced with a persistent external imbalance as a result of the disparity between the rate of growth of their primary exports and that of their import of industrial goods.[51] As a result, a number of external and internal changes were recommended. External measures included trade preferences, commodity agreements, debt adjustment, etc. Internal measures targeted economic and social measures within developing countries such as "land tenure, income concentration, ignorance of the masses and limited social mobility."[52]

As can clearly be seen, while the dependency critique was quite radical at the international level in demanding changes to liberal trading rules, it shared the colonialist mentality of reforming and redeeming the

[48] For the origins of UNCTAD, see Dell (1985) 10–32. [49] Ibid. 39.
[50] United Nations (1985) 11. [51] Ibid. [52] Ibid. 12.

"ignorant masses." The teleological imperative of catching-up, based on the superiority of the West, was never challenged. Indeed, in this respect, it was no different from modernization theory: as the History of UNCTAD puts it, "the universalist, developmental and comprehensive character of UNCTAD's philosophy will be evident" from its purposes.[53] UNCTAD, in this respect, was not different from GATT.

Law or politics? Contesting the institutional domain

The challenges to the liberal trading regime continued under UNCTAD through several conferences in the 1970s and 1980s and gradually led to the concretization of rules favoring special provisions in favor of developing countries, such as the Generalized System of Preferences (GSP). But it did not come easily. The western countries, which had been reluctant to support the formation of UNCTAD in the first place, proved to be even more reluctant to support its agenda, particularly in the Reagonesque 1980s. As a result, UNCTAD became a battlefield between the North and the South, with the latter represented through G-77. The most interesting aspects of this battle are to be found in two debates: first, whether UNCTAD should be an organ of the UNGA or ECOSOC; second, whether the Secretary-General of UNCTAD should be appointed by the UNGA or the UN Secretary General (UNSG).

At UNCTAD I, the western countries attempted to ensure that UNCTAD would be a subsidiary body of ECOSOC, whereas the developing countries insisted that UNCTAD should remain as a subsidiary body of the UNGA.[54] At issue was whether the formation of UNCTAD should follow a 'legal' interpretation of the UN Charter and therefore be coordinated by ECOSOC which is assigned such responsibility, or whether UNCTAD should be coordinated by the more political and more representative UNGA. The West supported the former whereas the Third World supported the latter. This western support for the 'legal' and the Third World preference for the 'political' could be seen not merely as a battleground between the North and the South over the institutional identity of UNCTAD, but as a broad engagement over the very nature of international institutions, or, indeed, of international law itself. As the History of UNCTAD puts it, the UNGA's consistent political and substantive support is "part of the continuing political process of democratization of international institutions, a process whereby newly independent and

[53] Ibid. 13. [54] Ibid. 37.

developing third world countries began to focus the attention and efforts of the international community on the all important problem of economic development."[55] Henceforth, international institutions would no longer be 'neutral' bodies that carried out collective sovereign wills, but a battleground for the very formation of collective wills. To say this is not to imply that international institutions were being radicalized in a unidirectional manner; as I have pointed out earlier, while certain strands of radical critiques were given institutional embodiment, several other strands were limited and contained due to their continuing commitment to the modernizing ethos.

A second example of the conflict over UNCTAD is the debate over the Secretary-General of UNCTAD, who is appointed by the UNSG subject to confirmation by the UNGA.[56] At UNCTAD I, western countries opposed the intervention of the UNGA in the appointment process on the ground that it would politicize the process, whereas the developing countries wished to provide political importance to the appointment by ratifying it.[57] This debate, which follows familiar debates in international law over the role of the UNSG – whether he/she is a 'leader' or a 'clerk'[58] – reflects the perennial tensions between law v. politics, and autonomy v. community. But it also reminds us of the "instrument-effects" of Third World resistance to international law, which resulted in the expansion of the ambit of the UNSG's responsibilities.

Institutionalizing radicalism: the art of maintaining unity in G-77

As I noted earlier, UNCTAD I also marked the beginning of the formation of a common Third World united front, the G-77. In the absence of a secretariat or a separate organizational structure, G-77 was entirely dependent upon UNCTAD for all its needs. As a result, the de facto headquarters of G-77 has been in Geneva, the seat of UNCTAD and its working members have been the delegations accredited to UNCTAD by developing countries.[59] As Robert Mortimer has noted, G-77's "very originality as an international actor has lain precisely in its lack of differentiation from the larger structures within which it has acted."[60] This identification between UNCTAD and G-77 had a politicizing effect on the activities of UNCTAD,

[55] Ibid.

[56] This *modus operandi* is also followed in the appointment of the heads of UNDP, UNIDO, and UNEP, following the UNCTAD example.

[57] United Nations (1985) 41–42.

[58] For this debate, see Gordenker (1972).

[59] Mortimer (1984) 75.

[60] Ibid. 78.

as a result of the internal tensions within G-77 and the ever-present need to maintain unity. The result was that UNCTAD became the institutional embodiment of the political compromises struck between moderate and radical positions within the Third World coalition, and thereby proved to be inherently moderate.

There were two kinds of challenges to the unity of Third World states in G-77. The first was the problem of differentiation between the members of G-77. This problem arose from the fact that certain Third World states were more 'developed,' or had greater economic stakes in particular negotiations with the industrialized world. Such states – such as India during the OPEC oil crisis – tended to adopt more conciliatory positions towards negotiations rather than adopt a hard-line confrontational position. This was compounded by the regional differences between the Asian, African, and Latin American groups within G-77. This greatly complicated the common stand of all Third World states and resulted, often, in radical demands being watered down.[61] This was not a one-sided outcome however. The proliferation and fragmentation of international institutions was also seen by some as a positive step towards the progressive reform of international institutions. For example, Fred Bergsten advocated decision-making in a series of concentric circles, with the inner core coming to an agreement and then broadening the agreement through general consultations with countries in outer loops.[62] Whatever may be the reasons for the tensions caused by the problem of differentiation between Third World states, UNCTAD, as the de facto secretariat of G-77, came to perform a dual role: on the one hand, only its existence made Third World unity and G-77 possible; on the other hand, to maintain that unity, it often had to adopt positions that reflected less radical, moderate positions. Combined with its continuing commitment to western modernizing ethos, UNCTAD could and did become deradicalized.

The second problem for Third World unity was the growing difficulties between NAM and G-77. The essential difference between G-77 and NAM was that Asian and Latin American alliance members (such as Mexico, the Philippines, or Pakistan) were allowed to be members of G-77 but not NAM. In addition to bilateral, intra-Third World disputes, the Cold War rivalries complicated the achievement of a common united front. This was becoming evident even by 1975–76.[63] While NAM had been eclipsed by G-77 from mid-1975 to mid-1976, it was more organized, with its own

[61] Ibid. 70. [62] See Bergsten (1976). [63] Mortimer (1984) 84.

Bureau and a more explicit political position. Yet, at the Fifth NAM meeting in Colombo, an existential angst was expressed in the Political Declaration: 'it is incontestable that there is an integral connection between politics and economics, and it is erroneous to approach economic affairs in isolation from politics...The importance given to economic affairs does not diminish the importance given to political affairs at Nonaligned meetings."[64] While this observation can be understood as a defense of the continuing political relevance of NAM in relation to G-77,[65] it also indicated that NAM wished to lay claim to a political and economic raison d'être of its own vis-à-vis G-77. This assertion had its reaction: at the subsequent G-77 Conference at Mexico City, a small group of states led by Pakistan, Mexico, and the Philippines, led a campaign for a G-77 summit meeting and a separate and permanent secretariat for G-77. This was, as noted by Robert Mortimer, nothing short of a thinly veiled challenge to the political authority of NAM.[66] It also inscribed the political challenges between G-77 and NAM into UNCTAD, as the institutional apparatus of G-77. Thus, even though UNCTAD was the result of radicalism of the dependistas, its actual practice was circumscribed and contained in multifarious ways.

The most important 'lesson' that should be learned from the UNCTAD example is that international institutions should no longer be thought of merely in terms of whether they successfully carry out the functions that they have been assigned, but rather they should be thought of in their own terms of occupying and politicizing the space of international law. In this mode of analysis, it is less important that UNCTAD did not 'succeed' in its functions; what is important is the very establishment of it as an embodiment of Third World identity as well as the creation of information and knowledge within its own domain. As the *History of UNCTAD* puts it, "there is little doubt that in terms of specific policy proposals and targets UNCTAD's accomplishments fall far short of its founder's expectations and of the aspirations of the NIEO. And yet it would be somewhat simplistic to pose the question in terms of success and failure. UNCTAD's contribution to the recognition of the interdependence of the world economy and of the development consensus by the international community is not in doubt; nor is its role in the evolution of the world's political economy and of the third world."[67] UNCTAD stands as a quintessential example of the constitution of the domain of international institutions as terrains of resistance and struggle and of its essential limitations.

[64] Cited in Mortimer (1984) 87. [65] Mortimer (1984). [66] Ibid. 91. [67] Ibid. 48.

The NIEO and the fetishism of institutions – Mohammed Bedjaoui

As noted already, the NIEO was a radical challenge to the 'old' European international law of the pre-War period. But, as I have argued, it was also limited in its radicalism by its commitment to the peculiar form of western modernity, with its belief in the idea of scientific progress of the natives from their backward state, that was encapsulated in international institutions. Third World lawyers, while being critical of the 'old' international law, shared its underlying civilizing commitment. This was nowhere more reflected, as I have argued earlier, than in their belief in the beneficent character of international institutions. That was quite understandable, since institutions provided a terrain – perhaps the only one – on which they could struggle against western hegemony through the affirmative use of their numerical superiority based on the principle of sovereign equality. But this also had the effect of deradicalizing many of their claims about 'old' international law since international institutions were not value-free instruments that could faithfully carry out their sovereign wills, but simply yet another terrain of political and ideological struggle. In effect, this meant that there was a certain fetishism of institutions that prevented the most radical claims from being translated into reality. As an example of this phenomenon, in the following pages I analyze Mohammed Bedjaoui's acclaimed critique in his book, *Towards a New International Economic Order*.[68]

Mohammed Bedjaoui, a famous Algerian international lawyer and diplomat, and an ex-President of the ICJ, wrote this book in the immediate aftermath of the NIEO debate at the UNGA. In his capacity as the Algerian Ambassador to the UN, he played an active role in the formation of the Third World coalition and the politics of the NIEO, including as the Chair of G-77 in 1981.[69]

His book is a scathing indictment of 'old' international law which he labels international law of 'indifference.'[70] This indifference was found in its laissez-faire principle of non-intervention, which favored plunder and exploitation of the Third World under colonialism.[71] This has resulted in what he calls the "poverty of the international order" in which international law is derived from the "laws of the capitalist economy and the

[68] Bedjaoui (1979).

[69] Mortimer (1984) 177, f.n. 48. In fact he became the first to direct a newly approved mini-secretariat of G-77 (Ibid).

[70] Bedjaoui (1979) 49. [71] Ibid.

liberal political system."[72] This international law "thus consisted of a set of rules with a geographical basis (it was a European law), a religious-ethical inspiration (it was a Christian law), an economic motivation (it was a mercantilist law), and political aims (it was an imperialist law)."[73] He notes that until decolonization started, "there was no perceptible change in this law as a backing for imperialism."[74] It is clear that Bedjaoui's aim is far reaching; it is to condemn received international law in its entirety and to argue for the creation of a new structure of law and institutions that will enable the reversal of the "international order of poverty." Indeed, the radical nature of his critique becomes more evident when we turn to his analysis of development, in its relationship to international law.

He begins by attacking Rostowian modernization theory which reduced underdevelopment to a mere question of 'backwardness.' The crux of this form of theorizing is the reduction of 'development' to a "single, undifferentiated phenomenon."[75] These authors "reduce the problem of underdevelopment to backwardness vis-à-vis Western civilization, and the problem of development to a mere effort to become part of the 'civilization of power,' the horsepower civilization, as Bertrand de Jouvenal has called it."[76] This understanding of development is wrong not only because of its bias towards a western progressivism, but also because of its linear nature. As he says, on this point "even the Darwinians and the school of Marx and Hegel are in agreement."[77] In this, Bedjaoui shows that his critique is not simply a Marxist one; in fact, he targets Marxism too, along with capitalism.[78] His critique is what we would today call a postcolonial one.

He correctly deduces from this that the logical corollary of this ideology of development is "a need for international cooperation in order to spread progress ... this being so, the notions of development and cooperation have become linked, the first being impossible without the second, and the second having no other aim but the generalization of the first."[79] He rejects this in favor of a "development of another kind ... which will restore their peoples' dignity and put an end to their domination by imperialism."[80]

It is clear from this critique that Bedjaoui's aims are far more radical than is evident at a first glance. His attempt to build a new international economic order, as he puts it, "involves choices between different kinds of society."[81] No other international lawyer from the Third World had, until

[72] Ibid. 49. [73] Ibid. 50. [74] Ibid. [75] Ibid. 67. [76] Ibid. [77] Ibid. 69.

[78] He quotes George Corm: "Marxism is a protest within the Western system, but not a protest against it" (Ibid).

[79] Bedjaoui (1979) 69. [80] Ibid. 71. [81] Ibid.

Bedjaoui, taken aim at the very nature of development and its linearity and progressivism.[82] Despite such radicalism, it is clear that Bedjaoui is apparently not entirely familiar with the depth of popular disaffection with development in the 1970s and the burgeoning literature that it had spawned.[83]

But far more importantly, the limits of his radicalism begin to be revealed when he moves from critique of 'old' international law to a discussion of the Third World's impact on international law. Though he had condemned international law as the law of 'indifference,' now he affirms that "just like the developing countries, international law is also a 'developing' law."[84] The key issue for this new international law is development, because "the real equality of States depends on their development."[85] Though he had celebrated the right of the Third World to think of another kind of development that would provide it with the choice of different societies – in other words, acknowledging the rightfulness of the existence of material, cultural and other differences between societies in international law – now he is concerned with the objective of "reducing and, if possible, even of eradicating the gap that exists between a minority of rich nations and a majority of poor nations"[86] – in other words, eradicating difference.

This is surely a far cry from a radical critique of development. What Bedjaoui fails to grasp here is that the very creation of the 'gap' between the West and the Third World is intelligible only if one adopts a western notion of what 'development' means. In order to declare some societies and lifestyles 'deficient' or 'backward', a standard is needed to judge them, and it is the western standard that is used. Despite his earlier radicalism, Bedjaoui adopts this standard by treating the Third World as a lump that is 'lagging behind' the West, and by his prescription that it needs to reduce the 'gap,' that is, 'catch-up' with the West. This can be done only by adopting the western model of development, since only that will enable the level of mass consumption that marks a nation as 'advanced.'

What explains this apparent volte-face? How can the call to 'reduce the gap' between nations be reconciled with the critique of the very idea

[82] It is not surprising since Algeria had always represented the more radical factions within the Third World, which advocated, at the extreme, a 'delinking' of Southern economies from the North. See Mortimer (1984) 90–94. A softer version of this was the South–South cooperation model advocated chiefly by NAM (Ibid). The classic statement on delinking from a political economy perspective is, of course, by Amin (1990).

[83] He cites Ivan Illich, but not anyone else.

[84] Bedjaoui (1979) 125.

[85] Ibid.

[86] Ibid. 127.

of 'development'? I suggest that the answer is to be found in a double identity that is common among Third World lawyers in the postcolonial era. On the one hand, he/she is a political activist who is interested in social transformation and in that capacity he/she develops a radical critique of the entire edifice of the 'old' law and the economic system that it sustains. On the other hand, he/she is also a postcolonial lawyer who identifies himself with building his/her 'nation,' and in this capacity he/she needs to use law to achieve the best possible conditions for the emergence of his/her 'nation' as a respected power. At bottom this is a conflict that emerges from the very nature of law, between change and stability. Indeed, Bedjaoui himself speculates on the nature of law, though not in the context which I have drawn here, but which is nevertheless pertinent: "at such a time, one is conscious of the amazing yet fruitful contradiction contained in the law, the contradiction between its true nature and its real function. It seems to be evolutionary by nature, yet conservative in function. On the one hand, it reflects a social reality which is changing and which it is obliged to try to keep up with, though there is bound to be some discrepancy and lag. In this, it appears as something evolutionary. On the other hand, by being the expression of social relations, it fixes or stabilizes the social milieu of which it is the product. It thus reinforces and protects established practices, rejecting any change which might threaten them, and in this respect its function is conservative. Movement and inertia, change and conservatism are the two factors permanently activating what it is and what it is becoming."[87]

Bedjaoui's tapering radicalism finds its zenith (or nadir) in his institutional proposals for a new international economic order. It is here that we see how international institutions, by virtue of being the product of the sovereign wills of states, create their own internal dynamic for the pace and direction of change in international social life. That dynamic, as I have suggested before, is inherently conservative even as it constitutes institutions as the apparatuses of management of social reality in the Third World. Bedjaoui begins by displaying an ambivalence towards the UN that tries to grapple with the fact that it is the tool of great powers even while recognizing the reality that, for the Third World, the UN is the only arena that provides an opportunity for challenging western hegemony.[88]

[87] Ibid. 112.

[88] As he puts it: "the Third World exposes the weakness of the United Nations system while still bearing a real affection for it, and this is not the result of some strange fickleness. The developing or non-aligned countries do not challenge the United Nations' existence, which they value, so much as its conditioning by the great powers, which they refuse to accept" (Ibid. 195).

If one had concluded, after reading his earlier condemnation of international law that he wished to do away with it all, that is quickly dispelled. Now international law becomes a tool of achieving development through the NIEO, and the UN would play the principal role in that process. As he puts it, "the new international economic order is the new name for development... It is the United Nations system and it alone that, through its democratization, could accomplish this task of prime importance."[89]

This was to be achieved by specific proposals for UN reform which include:[90]

a. *short term action*: internal restructuring, strengthening the role of UNGA and ECOSOC in development, establishing regional 'outposts' of the UN system, appointment of a new assistant UNSG with the title of Director General for Development and International Economic Cooperation and other programming and budgetary reform;
b. *medium term action*: revision of the UN Charter to expand the powers of ECOSOC and the establishment of a new Council on Science and Technology, creation of other specialized institutions such as a new organization for trade, and the creation of directly operational international bodies such as the WHO (World Health Organization) or Asian Development Bank.

These constitute the entire gamut of institutional reforms advocated by Bedjaoui in his book. It is well known that almost all of his proposals have now been implemented in the UN (though not entirely due to his urging), but that has not led to the establishment of the NIEO. However, what is striking for my purposes is the way his proposals – fairly uncontroversial as they are – seek to expand and reproduce the UN system and the general arena of international institutions. There is no apparent anxiety that proliferating the space of institutions will not also prove to be a mirage of sought-after social change, given that according to his own critique the UN has been prevented from doing just that. There is the beneficent sensibility here which looks upon international institutions as positive instruments of social change in the Third World.[91] Thus, one witnesses a gradual deradicalization from his earlier critique of 'development' to programmatic proposals concerning international institutions. The end

[89] Ibid. 197. [90] Ibid. 200–20.

[91] The purpose of this analysis is not to dismiss Bedjaoui's critique as unimportant; on the contrary, I have only the highest regard for his critique and have personally been inspired by it. However, my analysis is an attempt to deconstruct his arguments internally in order to think about the possibilities for radical politics through international law.

result is that institutions have gained in their space and activities, while the radical claims that generated them have been contained.

Conclusion

This chapter has advanced the view that Third World engagements with international institutions have had a double character: on the one hand, they have radicalized these institutions by converting them into arenas of political and ideological struggle over issues of power, distribution and justice; on the other hand, the most radical strands of Third World critique have also been tamed by being centered on the reform of international institutions. This has had the consequence of expanding the space of international institutions as autonomous actors in the "legal field,"[92] and thereby of international law itself. Looked at this way, it matters less that the NIEO was a 'failure'; rather, the NIEO assumes its own importance due to the "instrument-effects" that it has had on international institutions. Ultimately the dynamic of international institutions and international law are to be explained through this internal ability to generate a momentum for its own reproduction, to construct its own "field of reality", to quote Philip Allot,[93] rather than exclusively through a functionalist or policy-oriented analysis.

[92] Bourdieu (1987). [93] Allot (1995).

5

From resistance to renewal: Bretton Woods institutions and the emergence of the "new" development agenda

International lawyers who focus upon international economic law as well as international institutions readily concede the importance of the BWIs to the success of their respective disciplines.[1] While the GATT/WTO mechanisms constitute an important segment of the institutional framework of international economic law, the BWIs are better known and have historically wielded much more influence over the economic and financial policies of Third World countries. In particular, due to their enormous resources, considerable intellectual power, and the resultant influence they have over the national policies of developing countries, they are also more "sexy" and constitute favorite targets of media and academic critiques.[2] Indeed, for many Third World states, their historical relationships to the BWIs have been not only more significant, but also more problematic than their relationships with other organizations. This is partly due to the role of these institutions as gate-keepers to the international economic system, including access to western capital. It is also due to the far-reaching power of these institutions that extends into most domains of human activity in

[1] As a leading textbook on international economic law states, "to a great extent, contemporary international economic interdependence can be attributed to the success of the institutions put in place just after World War II, what we call in this book the Bretton Woods System." See Jackson, Davey, and Sykes (1995) 1. By BWIs, I mean the World Bank group of institutions and the IMF. The World Bank group consists of: the International Bank for Reconstruction and Development (IBRD), the International Finance Corporation (IFC), International Development Association (IDA), the Multilateral Investment Guarantee Agency (MIGA), and the International Center for the Settlement of Investment Disputes (ICSID).

[2] Indeed, there has been a veritable explosion of literature on the World Bank, while the IMF has received somewhat less attention. The following works are merely a sample of this wide-ranging phenomenon: Cornia, Jolly, and Stewart (1987); Broad (1988); Caufield (1996); Hildyard (1997); Killick (1984); Nelson (1995); Payer (1974); Payer (1982). Part of the reason for this explosion is that the BWIs have released much more information about their internal workings – never full or adequate information, but some information, nevertheless – than the more secretive GATT/WTO, or, most importantly, the private financial enterprises behind the BWIs. I thank Devesh Kapur for illuminating conversations on this topic.

the Third World, including economic and social policy, urban and rural development, and even the very structure of the state. Furthermore, due to their focus on issues of justice – mainly anti-poverty programs – the BWIs figure inevitably in radical Third World critiques of the international economic order.[3]

Yet, it is not automatically obvious why or how these institutions became so important and powerful. Their origins do not reveal much concern with either development in the Third World[4] or the overriding concern with sustainability and equitability that characterizes them now.[5] The World Bank Articles of Agreement, for example, do not refer to poverty, equity, or the environment, and the IMF traditionally concerned itself only with balance of payments deficits – and still does to a large degree.[6] How then did these institutions acquire a "new" character, a character that has made them all-powerful and yet vulnerable to critique and response?

This chapter suggests that the BWIs have acquired these "new concerns" in the course of their interaction with the Third World, especially since the 1970s. Still, as indicated earlier, the character of this interaction is different from their interaction – however limited – with the Third World states in the 1950s and 1960s. Unlike then, the "Third World" that these institutions encountered in the 1970s was not just an agglomeration of states at the United Nations, but an effervescent and troublesome cauldron of peasants, women, environmentalists, human-rights activists, indigenous people, religious activists, and other individuals that challenged the political and economic orders of the time. In particular, the late 1960s and 1970s witnessed a series of popular movements – both in the traditional Marxist sense and in the sense of "new social movements" – that put the issues of equity and justice squarely on the political agendas of ruling elites.[7] Both along the lines of class (Marxist) and identity (environment, ethnicity, feminist, and radical low-caste), BWIs engaged with popular resistance by employing a series of measures that contributed to those movements' agendas.

[3] See generally, Bedjaoui (1979); Chimni (1993, 1999).

[4] On the origins, see Dam (1982); Kapur, Lewis, and Webb (1997).

[5] "Operational Directive 4.15: Poverty Reduction" (1992), compiled in The World Bank Operational Manual 2 (December 1992), cited in Kapur, Lewis, and Webb (1997) 51. It states that "sustainable poverty reduction is the Bank's overarching objective."

[6] See, article I(v) and article V(3) (a) of IMF (1945). See also, IMF (1991) (interpreting IMF articles to mean that authority to use its resources is limited to giving temporary assistance in financing balance of payments deficits on a member country's current account for monetary stabilization operations).

[7] For a discussion, see Omvedt (1993); Calderón, Piseitelli, and Reyna (1998).

Unlike the modernizing nationalist elites of the immediate post World War II period, the activists and ordinary people who participated in popular organizing in the 1970s were concerned about the social and human costs of "development" that had been unleashed in the Third World, because they themselves were the victims of that process. In their view, the root of misery in the Third World was not the failure to deliver development; rather, it was the very process of delivering development that made them miserable.[8] I suggest that the BWIs' new "turn" to poverty, environment, and equity in the 1970s, which continues with much more vigor today, was necessitated by a complex and ambivalent alliance with and in opposition to these popular movements.[9] In other words, the BWIs did not come to occupy the positions that they do today either as a result of a functionalist logic to solve "problems" or as a result of a gradual learning process, but as a consequence of a historically contingent and complex interaction with popular resistance to "development" in the Third World. It is in this interaction that these institutions have invented and reinvented themselves as apparatuses of the management of social reality in the Third World.

Beyond benevolent liberalism and denunciatory radicalism

There have been basically two kinds of critiques of the BWIs. The first of these, which may be termed "liberal," essentially admits the beneficent character of development and the role of these institutions in the development process, which is defined as the collective effort to eradicate poverty and raise standards of living.[10] The writers adopting this position may concede that sometimes these institutions do not achieve their objectives, but that is all the more reason to "reform" them and to make them work better. Using a domestic analogy, the problem for these writers is similar to the "capture" of the state by reactionary interests: the BWIs remain "undemocratic" and unrepresentative since they have been captured by

[8] For an extended discussion of this point and the impact this has on how we "read" First World and Third World engagements with international law, see chapter 2.

[9] There may be many factors that made it particularly easy for such an "alliance" to work. One could mention the Cold War imperative to design a security policy that would encompass social development as a safety measure, as in the Alliance for Progress in Latin America. One could also examine the role played by charismatic leaders such as Robert McNamara at the World Bank during the 1970s. I focus here only on the gradual process by which the BWIs began relating to grassroots movements and thereby acquired their "new character."

[10] Much of the literature supports this view. See generally Bedjaoui (1979); Myrdal (1957, 1970); Schachter (1976).

only western interests. To the extent that the purpose of this critique is to make these institutions perform better, much of this literature is policy oriented and prescriptive.

A second line of critique of BWIs draws from radical neo-Marxist and dependency theories.[11] According to this critique, capitalism is a reactionary force in the Third World and therefore the *cause* of poverty, not a cure for it. Given this premise, these critics see the BWIs as mechanisms that enable the exploitation of the "periphery" by the "core." Thus, these critics see the development interventions launched by BWIs as the result of the "logic of capital" and therefore condemn them.

Both of these critiques have served important purposes; still, they appear to lack explanatory power. The "liberal" critique is politically naive since it assumes that the development interventions by BWIs occur in a class-neutral manner – in other words, in their interventions class relations are simply reproduced and not made worse. However, this does not explain either the popular resistance to these interventions (if they are so beneficent, why do they get opposed so much) or the consistent 'failure' to achieve their goals (such as reduction of poverty). On the other hand, the dependency critique assumes too much: that every intervention by BWIs is a core–periphery relation that mechanically reproduces unjust capitalistic relations between the West and the Third World. This overkill leads dependency-critiques to a policy paralysis[12] as well as a homogenizing tendency that ignores the actual process of resistance to development by different actors such as women or indigenous people (since the class character of the struggle has been assumed already) and the resultant heterogeneity of "voices." Neither approach seems satisfactory for these, and other, reasons.[13]

[11] See Williams (1981); Payer (1982). For an incisive deployment of dependency theory critique to western law, see Greenberg (1980). A classic statement of dependency theory is Frank (1973).

[12] Though I should note that even these critiques never abandon the faith in the idea of international institutions – just not BWIs.

[13] Other reasons include at least two types of critiques; first, a postcolonial legitimacy critique that insists on the historical continuity between colonial and development interventions and sees BWIs as essential elements in that continuity, and therefore illegitimate. See Escobar (1995). I liberally rely on the insights of this critique in this chapter. Second, a democratic deficit critique, from the left and the right, that challenges the BWIs (and now the WTO as well) not simply because they are tools of capitalist domination, but because of their unaccountability to the people (however that term is defined). See Commission on Global Governance (1995) 14–16 (proposing a right of petition to civil society members). See the websites of Public Citizen's Global Trade Watch (www.tradewatch.org), International Forum on Globalization (www.ifg.org), and Alliance for Democracy (www.afd-online.org). The most extensive treatment of legitimacy of

The approach I adopt in this chapter will differ from both of these critiques. Instead of assuming that the BWIs are basically "good" or "bad," or asking if they "succeeded" or "failed" in reducing poverty, I am interested in exploring the interaction between the development interventions of the BWIs and the resistance such interaction provoked in the Third World. It is my suggestion that this process of resistance (from the Third World) and response (by institutions) is an essential part of the way in which these institutions have become the apparatuses of management and control of social reality in the Third World. In this analysis, it matters less that these institutions are "successes" or "failures"; rather, what is important is that such an apparatus may, as James Ferguson elegantly puts it, "do what it does, not at the bidding of some knowing and powerful subject who is making it all happen, but behind the backs of or against the wills of even the most powerful actors."[14] As argued in the last chapter, the outcomes of their interventions are "instrument-effects" that were not intended or even recognized, but are nevertheless effective for being "subjectless."[15] These "authorless strategies," in a Foucaultian sense,[16] reproduce the discursive terrain on which these institutions operate in their interactions with the Third World.

Cold War and the "other" Third World resistance

I begin with the role the BWIs played in furthering the Cold War objective of containing Third World mass radicalism, since it is essential for understanding the later emergence of poverty alleviation programs. It is often forgotten that during the few years after the establishment of the BWIs, their lending focus was substantially on "developed" countries such as Japan and Australia (Table 5.1 below). Thus, from January, 1949 to the approval of the first IDA credit in April, 1961, the World Bank lent these countries $1.7 billion, or one-third of a total $5.1 billion. Australia ($317 million by June, 1961), Japan ($447 million), Norway ($120 million), Austria ($101 million), Finland ($102 million), France ($168 million) and Italy ($229 million) all received World Bank funding for reconstruction and development.[17] This situation continued until the establishment of the IDA in 1961, even though several large loans had been made to India and Latin America.[18] At the end of this key period of 1947–61, which

international law and institutions is in the original and important work of Thomas Franck. See Franck (1993); Franck (1990); Franck (1988).

[14] Ferguson (1994). [15] Ibid. 19. [16] See generally Foucault (1979, 1980).

[17] Kapur, Lewis, and Webb (1997) 93. [18] Ibid.

also witnessed the height of the Cold War, it was becoming obvious to the West that it was "losing the poor," and that explicit programs had to be invented that would contain the rebellion from the bottom.[19] This Cold War imperative had a major impact on the evolution of the BWIs, for now there was a security rationale to their developmental work.[20] In particular, the World Bank moved from its "reconstruction" phase to its "development" phase as the Cold War intensified. As Bank President Eugene Black characterized it while speaking before the Annual General Meeting in 1956, though "originally concerned solely as a financial institution," the Bank "has evolved into a development agency which uses its financial resources as but one means of helping its members."[21]

This technique of combining security and development was not entirely new; colonial regimes had perfected it in their handling of anti-colonial nationalist movements by designing welfare schemes for the protesting natives. The "dual mandate," articulated by colonial administrators like Sir Frederic Lugard was based on the idea that the native had to be cared for, not simply exploited.[22] As one colonial governor said as early as 1937, "*the exploitation theory... is dead, and the development theory has taken its place.*"[23] In this view, caring for the welfare of the natives was a crucial aspect of colonial dominance. Welfare spending was becoming necessary to achieve the dual purposes of sustaining production by fully constituting the *homo oeconomicus* in the Third World, and containing dissatisfaction and rebellion from the masses. The Cold War reinforced this historically crucial link between security and development, and had a major impact on the evolution and expansion of BWIs, especially the World Bank. Looked at this way, these international institutions are neither simply benevolent vehicles for "development" (whatever that means), nor ineluctably exploitative mechanisms of global capitalism, but, rather, a terrain on which multiple ideological and other forces intersected, thus producing the expansion and reproduction of these very institutions.

The Cold-War-generated link between security and development was borne out by the Superpower rivalry over the Third World for political and economic allegiance. The American Secretary of State, John Foster Dulles,

[19] This led to an invention of 'social development' as a substitute for economic development in UN practice. For a discussion, see Esteva (1992) 13.

[20] I refer here only to the international aspects of the security dimension; development, of course, also had a domestic security dimension.

[21] Cited in Kapur, Lewis, and Webb (1997) 88.

[22] See Lugard (1922).

[23] Bernard Bourdillon, *The African Producer in Nigeria, West Africa*, January 30, 1937, 75, cited in Kapur, Lewis, and Webb (1997) 96 (emphasis added).

Table 5.1 *World Bank development lending before IDA*

Recipient	(billions of US dollars) Gross commitments		Net lending
	1948–61	1956–61	1948–61
Total development loans	5.1	2.8	3.9
More developed countries	1.7	0.9	1.1
Colonies	0.5	0.3	0.4
Less developed countries	2.9	1.7	2.3
Power and transportation	2.4	1.4	2.0
Agriculture and irrigation	0.1	0.1	0.1

Source: World Bank, *Annual Report 1961, cited in* Kapur, Lewis, and Webb (1997) 86.

S, stated in 1956 that there was "a contest in the field of development of underdeveloped countries.... Defeat... could be as disastrous as defeat in the arms race."[24] This was based on the evolution of events since the 1955 Bandung Conference, which had itself thrown the notion of "containment" of communism out of focus by offering a "third" identity, beyond the East and the West, for the non-western world.[25] Nationalist and leftist coups occurred during the 1950s in Syria, Egypt, and Iraq, and, with the take-over of Cuba by Fidel Castro in 1959, the western world, led by the United States, undertook frenzied efforts to contain communism. This had an immediate impact on how "development" was conceived and deployed in the Third World. For instance, the United States, in order to justify its new foreign assistance (and therefore security) rationale with respect to Latin America, demoted and reclassified the region from its pre-War status as a region with "advanced" economies to an "underdeveloped area."[26] High US bilateral assistance during the period from 1949–61 reflected this priority: it averaged $1.8 billion on "soft" terms, some four to five times that of World Bank lending during the same time.[27]

[24] Cited in Daniel (1992).

[25] On the Bandung Conference, see Appadorai (1955); Kahin (1956); Romulo (1956); Wright (1956). See also chapter 4.

[26] Kapur, Lewis, and Webb (1997) 143.

[27] Ibid. 90–91. The security-development alignment was more readily conceded in bilateral assistance. As Robert Packenham notes: "[a]t no time was all economic and technical assistance principally used for developmental ends; during... most of the fifties and the latter half of [the] sixties... security ends were dominant" Robert Packenham, *Liberal America and the Third World* (1973) xix, cited in Kapur, Lewis, and Webb (1997) 149.

This marriage of security and development was reflected in the academic discourse as well as the practice of the BWIs. The academic discourse, constituting the mainstay of "development," acknowledged its Cold War origins openly. As a university textbook on development economics began, "the Cold War is not going very well for the western world. Soviet or Chinese influence is infiltrating into many of the undeveloped countries, in Asia, Africa, and Latin America."[28] Barbara Ward, arguing for more development assistance, pointed out that "we should realize soberly that the world-wide struggle is not necessarily 'going our way.'"[29] The loci of production of academic discourses were also equally caught up in the logic of the Cold War. The MIT Center for International Studies pioneered much of the development thinking under Paul Rosenstein-Rodan and received financing from the CIA, and Harvard scientists were deeply involved in Pakistan.[30]

In the practice of the World Bank, the security dimension of development began to have a major impact. Thus, Nicaragua, a nation of one million inhabitants, received ten World Bank loans between 1951 and 1960 because of the close connection between the US military and covert operations in the region, and the ruling Somoza family.[31] By contrast, Guatemala, with three times the population, did not receive a loan until the overthrow of its "communist" regime in 1955.[32] This coincided with the then US preference for "hard" regimes over "liberal" ones. As George Kennan said in 1950, "it is better to have a strong regime in power than a liberal government if it is indulgent and relaxed and penetrated by communists."[33]

In addition to being used to fund anticommunist actions in the Third World, the Bank was also deeply affected in its internal workings by the political strategies that were adopted by the United States to fight the Cold War. This is evident on at least two important fronts. First, under political influence, the lending portfolio of the Bank began to shift from a legalistic, cautious, and Wall Street oriented approach to project lending, to a more political and ad hoc approach to program lending.[34] The quasi-official

[28] Enke (1963) vii, cited in Kapur, Lewis, and Webb (1997) 144.

[29] Ward (1962), cited in Kapur, Lewis, and Webb (1997) 144.

[30] Kapur, Lewis, and Webb (1997) 148. President Kennedy drew on both Harvard and MIT to create his foreign policy staff.

[31] Ibid. 103. [32] Ibid.

[33] Quoted in Chace (1984), cited in Kapur, Lewis, and Webb (1997) 103.

[34] This meant for example, that the Bank could fund a specific project such as the construction of a road, while it could not fund broad social or economic programs dealing with health or education. The World Bank's Articles of Agreement originally committed it to lend primarily for specific projects in order to convince Wall Street that the Bank's

history of the World Bank traces the shift from project lending to program lending quite well.[35] With the establishment of the IDA in 1961, and the expansion of the Bank's lending to poverty alleviation in the 1970s, the shift from project to program lending became complete, thereby expanding the reach and scope of the Bank's activities immeasurably. The next section will analyze this shift and the corresponding expansion.

The second level at which the Bank was internally affected by the political necessities of the Cold War was in its sectoral allocation. As can be seen from Table 5.1, a very large part of the lending until 1961 for developing countries was for power and transportation projects. Agriculture and social sector activities, such as health and education, were neglected. This lending portfolio was based on a biased understanding of "development" as capital accumulation and physical modernization, as opposed to human development. This not only reflected the dominant thinking towards development at that time, which emphasized investment in infrastructure rather than human beings, but it also followed from the Bank's status as a conservative institution, dependent upon Wall Street for its financing, which placed it in a much harder position to justify "unproductive" or fuzzy investments like education or even urban water supply.[36] Agriculture fared worse: only 3% of all development lending to developing countries through 1961 was for agriculture.[37] This was mainly due to the Bank's wish to remain attractive to Wall Street financing. In the end, with the establishment of the IDA and the expansion into poverty alleviation, the Bank's sectoral allocation expanded dramatically to embrace health, education, rural development, and agriculture. While this changed focus has not actually reduced poverty, improved health, or made

investment would be responsible and could be monitored easily through hard evidence of project fulfillment. See International Bank for Reconstruction and Development, Articles of Agreement, article III(4) (vii) ("Loans made or guaranteed by the Bank shall, except in special circumstances, be for the purpose of specific projects of reconstruction or development"). For a discussion of the Wall Street connection to the project approach to lending, see Kapur, Lewis, and Webb (1997) 88–90, 120–21.

[35] Kapur, Lewis, and Webb (1997) 85–214.

[36] For a discussion, see Ibid. 109–11. In addition, a certain teleology also crept in that judged projects by whether they were appropriate for a particular country at its given scale of "development," when compared with western countries at similar stages of development. Thus, the President of the World Bank, then Robert Garner, questioned the need for urban water supply in developing countries: "when I was brought up in Mississippi . . . we didn't have water in our house." Interview by David Sommers with Robert Garner, President of the World Bank (July 18, 1985), cited in ibid. 110–11.

[37] In taking this path, the Bank differed from US bilateral assistance during the same period, which focused on agriculture, health, and education, presumably free of Wall Street financing compulsions (Kapur, Lewis, and Webb (1997) 112).

agriculture more efficient as much as had been intended,[38] the "instrumental effects"[39] of the change have involved a dramatic expansion of the BWIs into every conceivable sphere of human activity in the Third World. Quite apart from whether they actually achieve their intended goals, the interventions carried out by BWIs acquire an internal logic in their own right. This expansion in the domain of their activities could not have occurred without the security dimension provided by the Cold War as a response to the mass peasant and anti-colonial movements in the Third World. However, this obvious trend receives scant acknowledgement in historiographies of BWIs in international law.

The "discovery" of poverty and the establishment of the IDA: rejuvenating the BWIs

As already noted, the Articles of Agreement of the BWIs do not refer to poverty or justice explicitly. Yet, in 1991, the World Bank declared in an Operational Directive that "sustainable poverty reduction is the Bank's overarching objective."[40] This new faith was not the result of a smooth evolution towards rational objectives that resulted from a learning process, though the Bank itself has recently portrayed it as such.

> In the 1960s, the Bank focused on economic growth as the key to poverty reduction. During the 1970s attention shifted first to *redistribution with growth* and later to satisfaction of *basic human needs.* In the early 1980s policy-based adjustment lending overshadowed the Bank's poverty reduction objectives . . . [This] eventually enabled the Bank to address more effectively the relationship between poverty and the policy environment. In 1987 and 1988, the primacy of the Bank's poverty reduction objective was reemphasized in task force reports . . . [The importance of poverty reduction was bolstered by later reports that] contributed to a further reaffirmation of the Bank's commitment to poverty reduction as its fundamental objective.[41]

This account is, of course, antiseptic and neat. In contrast, as can be seen from the discussion in the previous section, the Bank's mandate was

[38] As an official publication of the UN conceded a decade after the establishment of the IDA, "the fact that development either leaves behind, or in some ways even creates, large areas of poverty, stagnation, marginality and actual exclusion from social and economic progress is too obvious and too urgent to be overlooked." See United Nations (1971). For an analysis of how poverty and exclusion remain enormous obstacles despite development interventions, especially in the context of globalization and the East Asian economic crisis, see UNDP (1999).

[39] See above for discussion. [40] The World Bank (1992). [41] Ibid. 51–52.

an explicitly political one that was gradually crafted in complex struggles: between the two Cold War power blocs, between the Third World and the West, between leftist and reactionary politics, between peasant rebellions and authoritarian governments, between mass movements and elite manipulation, between colonial and anticolonial forces, and between multiple conceptions of "development." Still, it is important to focus on the process by which poverty came to constitute the governing logic of the *episteme* of development: the BWIs. This is because it is in the course of "discovering" poverty that the BWIs, particularly the Bank, discovered themselves as international institutions. *In other words, if the Cold War provided a security dimension to the constitution of BWIs as "development" institutions, the objective of poverty reduction provided the moral, the humanitarian dimension.*

"Discovering" poverty: engaging with the "poor, dark, masses"

In order to grasp the process that led to the crowning of BWIs as poverty-reducers, one must analyze the establishment of the IDA in 1961, for it was the first major international institutional milestone in the turn to poverty as an international objective, and to the "dark, poor and hungry masses" of the Third World as the target group of international interventions. There were several factors which were responsible for this turn. First, there was a realization that in the Cold-War-driven competition for allegiance of regimes, it was essential to promote intra-country redistribution to pacify the "masses" that were becoming restive due to rising anticolonialism and nationalism. Indeed, it was a commonplace in development thinking in the late 1950s and early 1960s that poor countries would succumb to communism if they were not rescued from poverty.[42] Aid began to be seen as a way of achieving that goal. The importance of redistribution as a policy goal of foreign assistance in order to pacify the masses was clearly spelled out, for example, by Undersecretary of State Douglas Dillon in the aftermath of Fidel Castro's victory while speaking to the Senate Foreign Relations Committee of the United States: "while there has been a steady rise in national incomes throughout [Latin America], millions of underprivileged have not benefited."[43]

[42] See Escobar (1995) 34.

[43] Milton S. Eisenhower (1965) 249, cited in Kapur, Lewis, and Webb (1997) 142 (Kapur, Lewis, and Webb paranthesis). As President Kennedy's Secretary of the Treasury between 1961 to 1965, Dillon had a major impact on the creation of the IDA.

Second, there was also an awareness that traditional foreign lending was too focused on accumulation of capital (mainly through infrastructure and power projects) and too little on "social lending." This was true not only due to the fact that the Wall Street financiers considered social lending to be unproductive and fuzzy,[44] but also because social lending seemed too political and therefore violative of the principle of non-intervention in international law and relations. The BWIs provided a way around this impasse. This rationale was articulated by President Eisenhower with regard to the establishment of the Inter-American Development Bank in 1959:

> Traditional unilateral aid was sustaining a prevailing social order which was unjust to the masses of the people, but we could do nothing directly about this without violating the policy of non-intervention in the internal affairs of other nations. The creation of the new bank changed this, for now the Americas had a multinational instrument, secure against control by any one country, for bettering the life of people throughout the Americas; *if this instrument insisted upon social reform as a condition of extending development credit, it could scarcely be charged with "intervention."*[45]

The expansion of the BWIs into poverty-focused lending fit perfectly with this reasoning.

Third – and connected to the first two – the World Bank itself was clearly realizing the politically quiescent effect that its loans were having on Third World "masses." Though this could not be articulated as an economic rationale to justify social lending, the Bank was nevertheless widely aware of this angle and was influenced by this in lending to Third World countries. Thus, in discussing a proposed IDA loan to Ecuador in June 1961, a member of the Loan Committee stated: "Colonialism is certainly bad in Ecuador . . . even . . . worse than in the Far East. Something violent is going to happen . . . *I think that our projects do serve to relieve internal pressures . . . I agree that we might consider more IDA money because of these political risks.*"[46]

Fourth, the discovery of "underdevelopment" as a domain of intervention in the 1950s had put poverty squarely on the international agenda. Before World War II, the poverty of the natives was taken as natural

[44] For a discussion, see above.

[45] Dwight D. Eisenhower (1965) 516, quoted in Kapur, Lewis, and Webb 155 (emphasis mine).

[46] Mr. Aldewereld in Rough Notes of Staff Loan Committee Meeting 1–4, IBRD Doc. SLC/M/6124 (June 14, 1961), cited in Kapur, Lewis, and Webb (1997) 166 (emphasis mine).

because they were seen to lack the capacity for science and technology and the will to economic progress.[47] On the other hand, the poor in the West had been subjected to a series of "poor laws" since the medieval period, but more intensely since the nineteenth century.[48] In this new conception, the poor were seen to lack in particular social domains which called for technical interventions in education, health, hygiene, morality, savings, and so on. Relying on a negative conception of "deficiency," this new approach to the poor defined them in terms of *what they were not*, instead of simply describing them for *what they really were*. This negative conception enabled the initial deployment of an economic sense of poverty to all social domains, but it soon transformed into a cultural, political, and psychological sense of poverty as well: the native was seen pathologically lacking in simply all social domains.[49]

Consequently, the discourse of poverty became a series of interventions that acquired multiple dimensions – medical, economic, social, legal, and political. The ensemble of interventions to manage the poor has been termed as the domain of the "social" by scholars.[50] This new approach to the poor differed from older western approaches that celebrated the honor of voluntary poverty – e.g., medieval Franciscan orders – and paralleled many non-western approaches to the poor, such as in India.[51]

This process of "discovering" poverty intensified during the troubled inter-War period, particularly in Britain and the United States, due to Keynesianism and the New Deal respectively. These processes – reflected in the discovery of both the "social," by US and French legal realists,[52] and the "new international law," by inter-war lawyers such as Alejandro Alvarez[53] – prepared the groundwork for a more intense engagement with the poor masses. Finally, a very important factor responsible for the evolution of the poverty discourse with its focus upon the Third World masses was the inter-war experience of colonialism and the Mandate system of the League of Nations, both of which attempted to construct a new

[47] See Escobar (1995) 22.

[48] For an analysis of poverty generally, see Rahnema with Bawtree (1991). For a brilliant analysis of the poverty idea, see Sachs (1990).

[49] Escobar (1995) 21–24. [50] Ibid. 23.

[51] For an interesting discussion of the comparative dimensions of poverty across cultures, see Rahnema (1992). In India, the Gandhian tradition managed to maintain this holistic approach throughout the twentieth century.

[52] For an excellent account of US–French comparative legal experiences with legal realism, see Belleau (1994). For a sophisticated discussion of the use of the "social" in Egyptian private law and its relationship to US–French private law theory, see Shalakany (2000).

[53] See Alvarez (1929).

"humanitarian" approach to the rule of natives, moving away (rhetorically at least) from exploitative colonialism.[54] This experience provided institutional continuity to the "rule of the natives" after the Second World War when many colonial administrators joined the World Bank.[55]

However, the internationalization of the "social" domain did not occur in a true sense until after the Second World War, following the establishment of BWIs. The World Bank, for example, invented "per capita income" as a tool to compare countries in 1948. As a result, they magically converted almost two-thirds of the world's population into the "poor" because their annual per capita income was less than $100.[56] Along with the invention of the notion of 'Third World' as a terrain of intervention in the 1950s,[57] the discovery of poverty emerged as a working principle of the process whereby the domain of interaction between the West and the non-West was defined.[58] The institutional grid that made this process possible was the complex network of international institutions exemplified by the BWIs, but including the economic, political, and security institutions of the post World War II era. These institutions, beginning with the Mandate system of the League, had begun adopting the poverty and welfare discourse well before the much-touted turn of the World Bank towards poverty-alleviation in the 1970s,[59] which had the effect of consolidating and quickening the internationalization of the 'social' domain.

As a result, it must be recognized that contrary to popular wisdom, the BWIs were neither benevolent do-gooders nor mechanistic tools in the hands of global capital opposed to social justice and equity. Rather, they constituted a complex space in which power and justice and security and humanitarianism functioned in contradictory and complementary ways. Indeed, these phenomena could not exist without each other. As Karl Polanyi has perceptively remarked with regard to the rise of capitalism in the West, "[p]auperism, political economy, and the discovery of society were closely interwoven."[60] By analogy, I have suggested that poverty, political economy, and the discovery of international institutions as sites where relations between the West and the non-West are constructed, are inseparable.

[54] For an extensive discussion of the Mandate system, see chapter 3.

[55] Kapur, Lewis, and Webb (1997) 54.

[56] Ibid. 83. See also Escobar (1995) 23–24 (noting that comparative statistical operations had been carried out only since 1940).

[57] See generally Rajagopal (1998–99). [58] See Escobar (1995) 31.

[59] The most famous event that marked this turn was Bank President McNamara's speech to the Board of Governors of the Bank in Nairobi on September 24, 1973.

[60] See Polanyi (1944).

Institutionalizing poverty discourse: the IDA and the development apparatus

The invention of poverty discourse during the first decade following World War II began to have a tangible impact on international institutions. This was inevitable, because the moral justification provided by the poverty discourse and the security justification provided by the Cold War created a powerful momentum towards greater international institutionalization. These forces became evident as new institutions were rapidly established in the late 1950s and early 1960s. In addition, the changed focus of international institutions began to generate new conceptual apparatuses in many disciplines, including international law, which attempted to take account of their new "social" character.[61] The BWIs were inevitably affected by these processes.

The establishment of the IDA in 1961 marked the most significant moment in the institutional expansion of the BWIs towards a "poverty" focused approach. As discussed earlier, the Bank resisted turning directly to "social" lending because it sought to preserve its commitment to project-based lending and thus its financial image to its Wall Street financiers. As a result, upon the initiative of the United States, a new institution, the IDA, was established under the umbrella of the Bank with the explicit mandate of assisting the "less developed countries."[62] This marked a decisive turn in the ongoing relationship of development and intervention between the BWIs and Third World masses in at least two ways, both of which had a significant impact on international institutions. First development would henceforth acquire a "morally discriminatory sense" whereby it would equal poverty alleviation in developing countries.[63] As a result, international economic institutions began to acquire an aura of legitimacy, which continues to this day, that derived from their supposed beneficent contribution to poverty-alleviation. Second, the formation of the IDA also coincided with and led to the establishment of dozens of additional development institutions, both multilateral and domestic, that today constitute the institutional framework of international economic relations.

The establishment of the IDA had profound effects on the character of the Bank as an institution on several levels. This was nowhere more evident

[61] See generally Rajagopal (1999a).

[62] See generally Kapur, Lewis, and Webb (1997), chapters 4, 17. This purpose distinguished the IDA from the terms of the IBRD Articles of Agreement, which treated all member States as equals.

[63] See Ibid. 140.

Table 5.2 *IBRD and IDA lending, 1961–69*

	(millions of US dollars)			
Borrower	Number of borrowers	IDA	IBRD	Total
Total	93	2,217	7,219	9,436
High income	16	15	1,644	1,659
Middle and low income	77	2,201	5,575	7,776
Middle income	43	354	4,113	4,467
Low income	34	1,847	1,462	3,309
India	1	1,044	405	1,449
Pakistan	1	413	375	788
Power and transportation	68	852	3,593	4,445
Agriculture, education, and water	49	604	941	1,545

Source: World Bank data, *cited in* Kapur, Lewis, and Webb (1997) 140 table 4–1.

than in its "new" character as a First World institution lending primarily to poor Third World countries. As shown in Table 5.2 total Bank lending to high-income countries such as Australia or Japan "dropped from 43 percent of commitments in the 1950s to 21 percent over 1961–69, and to only 7 percent during 1968 and 1969."[64] By contrast, one third of all lending during the 1960s was allocated to India and Pakistan, two of the world's poorest countries.[65] In addition, the number of low-income borrowers ballooned following decolonization in Africa. Henceforth, the Bank would truly become an "international" institution, one that mediates the contentious relationship between the West and the non-West while occupying its own (expanding) space. Furthermore, the Bank also began to diversify its sectoral allocation to include agriculture, education, and other "social" sectors. For example, loans to agriculture rose from 2% of pre-IDA lending to 11% during the 1960s and reached 20% during the last two years of the decade.[66]

However, the establishment of the IDA and the turn to "social" lending was not easy. As a BWI, the IDA was still bound to restrict funding to specific projects "except in special circumstances."[67] Except for the window provided by such circumstances, the Accompanying Report of the Executive Directors, which was used to interpret the Articles of Agreement of the IDA, stated that "specific projects" must include "a railway program,

[64] Ibid. 139. [65] Ibid.
[66] See below Table 2. See also Kapur, Lewis, and Webb (1997) 141.
[67] See Kapur, Lewis, and Webb (1997) 159.

an agricultural credit program, or a group of related projects forming part of a developmental program."[68] While this expanded definition of "specific projects" enabled the Bank to lend for social projects and further weakened the distinction between project and program lending, it also carefully avoided mentioning "social" projects by name, for fear of tarnishing its Wall Street-friendly image.[69]

As expected, the new course charted by the Bank after the IDA's establishment was intricately bound with the Cold War strategy of the United States of containing Third World communism. The IDA made several loans to "friendly" regimes that were clearly motivated by the desire to contain irate domestic populations and render them quiescent. For instance, a loan was approved for a water supply project for King Hussein's Jordan in October 1960 even before the IDA had opened for business to save his regime from leftist and nationalist forces.[70] In the aftermath of Fidel Castro's revolution, several loans were also made available for projects in Latin American countries such as Chile, Honduras, Nicaragua, Colombia, Costa Rica, and Paraguay.[71] President Eisenhower even claimed after the Latin American revolts that "constantly before us was the question of what could be done about the revolutionary ferment in the world.... We needed new policies that would reach the seat of the trouble, the seething unrest of the people."[72]

These new policies were beginning to have a global impact independent of expanded Bank funding. This manifested itself concretely through the creation of a large number of development institutions – multilateral, regional, and domestic. The first wave of institution-building occurred between 1945 and 1950 and included the BWIs, most UN agencies (such as UNESCO [UN Educational, Scientific, and Cultural Organization], FAO [Food and Agriculture Organization], UNICEF [UN Children's Fund], WHO [World Health Organization], ESCAP [Economic Commission for Asia and the Pacific] and ECLA [Economic Commission for Latin America]) and bilateral aid agencies in the United States, Britain, and France.[73] The second wave occurred between 1958 and 1962 and included bilateral development agencies (such as The Canadian International Development Association [CIDA], Ministries of Cooperation in France

[68] IDA, Articles of Agreement and Accompanying Report of the Executive Directors of the International Bank for Reconstruction and Development, Article V(1) (b)¶ ¶ 13–15 (1960), cited in Kapur, Lewis, and Webb (1997) 159.

[69] See Kapur, Lewis, and Webb (1997) 159.

[70] Ibid. 162.

[71] Ibid. 163.

[72] D. Eisenhower (1965) 530, 537.

[73] See Kapur, Lewis, Webb (1997) 150–51. The United States had the largest aid program, which was administered through agencies such as the AID and the Export-Import Bank. See Ibid.

and Germany, and development agencies in Japan, Switzerland, Belgium, Denmark, and Norway), regional agencies (such as the European Investment Bank, including its European Development Fund, the Organization for Economic Cooperation and Development [OECD] with its Development Assistance Committee, The Inter-American Development Bank [IADB], the Alliance for Progress, African Development Bank in 1964 and the Asian Development Bank in 1966), multilateral agencies (such as the UN Economic Commission for Africa [ECA], the Special UN Fund for Economic Development [SUNFED], the IDA, and the International Finance Corporation [IFC] in 1956), and country-specific aid efforts such as the India Aid Consortium.[74] With the birth of UNCTAD (UN Conference on Trade and Development), UNDP (UN Development Program), and UNCLOS (UN Conference on Law of the Sea) in the 1960s and 1970s and MIGA (Multilateral Investment Guarantee Agency) in the 1980s, the international institutionalization of the 'social' domain was complete.[75] Without the moral, security, and material opportunities provided by Third World masses, this institutionalization could never have been completed.

In the coming decades, these international institutions gradually formed the grid for the smooth operation of the world economic and political system, based on the idea of "development." This idea of "development," as we have seen, was not merely a rational response to the problems of the Third World but a specific exercise of power that was constituted in the complex struggle between the West and the non-West, and whose most concrete manifestations were to be found in international institutions such as the BWIs. The "instrument-effect" of this specific exercise of power was, I have argued, the expansion of the BWIs. In this view, the development apparatus is not a machine for the elimination of poverty, which incidentally leads to increasing international bureaucracy; rather, development is principally a machine for expanding the bureaucratization of the international sphere, which takes 'poverty' as its incidental point of entry.[76] As Arturo Escobar states concerning development discourse, "the forms of power that have appeared act not so much by repression but by normalization; not by ignorance but by controlled knowledge; not by humanitarian concern but by the bureaucratization of social action."[77] The BWIs, especially the Bank, exemplified this form of power.

[74] Ibid. 152. [75] Ibid. 2, 13–14, 26.
[76] In this, I echo Ferguson (1994) 255. [77] Escobar (1995) 53.

"Greening the Bank"[78] – a new frontier for expansion

As the BWIs entered the 1970s, a whole new discourse was taking shape in the international arena: the discourse of environmentally sustainable development. This discourse had emerged after decades of grassroots activism in the West, beginning with the protests against big dams in the United States in the 1950s, the pollution resulting from industrial and urban expansion in the 1960s, and Malthusian fears of a "population bomb" in the 1970s.[79] The earliest concrete expression of this trend was the "limits to growth" theory advanced by the Club of Rome in 1972,[80] which questioned the basic postulate of development: that economic growth could be infinite. In its place, the Club postulated that due to the finite resources available in an interdependent world, economic growth, and therefore development, had certain limits that could never be exceeded. The momentum provided by the western environmental movements led to the 1972 Stockholm Conference, which marked the birth of the modern environmental legal framework.[81] Since then, sustainable development has firmly anchored itself in development discourse and has led to a virtual explosion of legal and political texts for the protection of the environment and the biosphere, including the Rio Declaration in 1992.[82] More importantly, the environment has emerged as perhaps the "hottest" terrain in the complex struggles between the BWIs and the Third World, with the former being accused of causing environmental disasters in the latter.[83]

The BWIs were at the intellectual forefront of the new environmental movement, starting from the appointment of an environmental advisor to the World Bank in 1970 to the gradual recognition of environmental sustainability as a core objective for lending in addition to the usual objectives of economic growth and poverty reduction.[84] The BWIs themselves portray their turn to environment as the result of a rational learning, in which these new objectives were integrated into development. As the former

[78] Wade (1997) 611.
[79] "[A]rticles on the environment in the *New York Times* skyrocket[ed] from about 150 in 1960 to about 1,700 [in] 1970." See Sachs (1992b) 27.
[80] See generally Meadows and Meadows (1972).
[81] It was in Stockholm that NGOs first staged their own counter-conference on alternative paths to development. See Sachs (1992b) 28. See generally Wade (1997).
[82] On the Rio declaration see generally Porras (1994).
[83] See generally Rich (1994).
[84] See generally Wade (1997). The Bank was the first development agency to appoint an environmental adviser. See ibid.

Bank general counsel Ibrahim Shihata notes, the change is the result of the staff's and management's own "increasing understanding of the relationship between environmental protection and development."[85] But the reality was far more complex. Two distinct phenomena need to be understood in order to fully appreciate the complex interaction between the growth of environmental consciousness, including grassroots activism in the First and Third Worlds, and the BWIs' own institutional evolution.

The first of these phenomena concerns the political economy of the sustainable development discourse and the impact it had on the new orientation of the BWIs. In this section I suggest that the discourse of sustainable development discourse provided a new set of justifications for the BWIs to expand their reach and power over the "poor, dark and hungry masses" of the Third World. The second phenomenon relates to the smooth, progressivist narrative that the BWIs themselves offer to explain their turn to the environment, exemplified by Shihata's remarks above. Here I suggest that whatever changes have occurred in the BWIs in the field of environment have occurred mostly through an intense and ambivalent engagement by the BWIs with the grassroots political pressure applied by different social movements in the West and the Third World. In other words, the constitution of a new discourse of sustainable development and the concomitant expansion of BWIs was not a one-sided process; rather, it was actively promoted and resisted by many grassroots movements around the world. I focus on and briefly discuss two key moments in this evolution. Before that, a brief account must be given of the factors that were responsible for the constitution of the environment as a terrain of intervention by the BWIs.

The birth of the new discourse and the reaction of the BWIs

Several factors were responsible for the discovery of the "environment" as a new domain for social intervention in the Third World. First, in development discourse, the focus on agriculture as part of an overall Cold War strategy of containing mass peasant radicalism had already led to new discursive strategies such as the Green Revolution and Integrated Rural Development.[86] The discovery of the environment as a new domain of intervention fit this pattern of evolution. Second, by 1970, it was becoming obvious that development was running out of legitimacy due

[85] Shihata (1995) 183, 184.
[86] See Escobar (1995), chapter 5.

to its high social, human, and environmental costs. A new justification was needed to recover "the moral initiative" of international governance, as Wilfred Jenks put it in a different but related context.[87] The sphere of the environment perfectly suited that need. Further, by treating environmental problems as technical ones that should be managed by professionals, the environmental discourse revived the necessity for regional and sectoral planning, which had become discredited along with its sibling, development.[88] Third, by 1970, many western countries had also suffered an internal "legitimation crisis"[89] that sprang from spontaneous grassroots challenges to the legitimacy of the post-industrial state. These challenges ranged from civil rights and feminist movements in the United States, to student movements in France, to environmental movements in West Germany. For many of these activists, the discourse of environment provided a new grammar of politics, a new way of understanding the world, that would not be bound by the limitations of liberalism or the excesses of Marxist-Leninism.[90] Fourth, by the early 1970s, in many Third World countries, such as India and Brazil, many had similarly become disenchanted with the supposed beneficent effects of both development and nation-building.[91] These sensibilities were beginning to become apparent in grassroots environmental movements such as the Chipko movement in Northern India.[92] This birth of the process of imagining alternatives to the postcolonial state found the realm of the environment to be fertile ground for the articulation of these alternatives.

As a result of the conjunction of these factors, environmental discourse began to have an early impact on the practices of the BWIs.[93] First, Bank President Robert McNamara created the post of environmental adviser in the Bank in 1970,[94] making it the first development institution,

[87] See Jenks (1958) 246–48 (describing how the need to incorporate welfare aspects into international law is needed to recover the moral initiative lost by the West due to colonial rule). For a discussion of Wilfred Jenks' scholarship in terms of how post-War international lawyers 'received' development discourse, chapter 2.

[88] See Sachs (1992b) 26. The 1987 Brundtland Commission Report stated in its opening paragraph: "This new reality, from which there is no escape, must be recognized – *and managed*" (World Commission on Environment and Development [1987] 1 [emphasis added]).

[89] Habermas (1971). See also Habermas (1981).

[90] See, e.g., Habermas (1981).

[91] See, e.g., Kothari (1993); Sethi (1993). See also Mamdani et al. (1993).

[92] For a discussion, see Omvedt (1993), chapter 6; see also Sethi (1993).

[93] The environment discourse had a direct effect on the proliferation of other international institutions, starting with UNEP and continuing with the various treaty monitoring mechanisms and the Global Environmental Facility.

[94] See Wade (1997).

multilateral or bilateral, to create such a post. Second, the Bank played a crucial role in the 1972 Stockholm Conference. The environmental advisor of the Bank, James Lee, was a key figure in the preparatory meetings. A senior Bank official, Mahbub ul Haq,[95] was the author of the Founex report, which became the basis for the Declaration, Principles, and Recommendations of the Conference. Ul Haq also played a key role in persuading developing countries not to withdraw from the conference. Finally, McNamara also established the intellectual leadership of the Bank through key speeches at the Conference, though he focused more on developed countries. He stated with passion that "[t]he evidence is now overwhelming that roughly a century of rapid economic expansion has gradually contributed to a *cumulatively monstrous assault on the quality of life in the developed countries.*"[96]

Still, these changes were cosmetic and the BWIs remained oblivious to environmental concerns until the mid-1980s. For example, only one annual report between 1974 and 1985 had a separate section on the Bank's environmental work.[97] The question naturally arises: why did the Bank show such indifference and why did it begin changing after 1985? The reasons for this are complex, but they can be broadly reduced to two sets of factors. First, despite the early rhetoric, the Bank never took environmental concerns seriously except as a public relations tactic to "'turn around' external criticisms."[98] This occurred because the continuing and unresolved contradictions between the logic of development and the logic of environment persisted and were not "resolved" until the 1987 Brundtland Commission report. Second, the Bank began changing only after encountering grassroots resistance from many environmental and social movements in the West and the Third World during the 1980s. These factors must be examined in detail.

First, contradictions between environment and development continued to persist at several levels throughout the 1970s and mid-1980s. The one critical contradiction was between the logic of economic growth, which is based on infinite economic exploitation of both labor and resources, and the logic of environment, which is premised on inherent limits to growth. Although the language of "sustainability" made a valiant effort to resolve this contradiction, it has never quite succeeded in theory

[95] Mahbub ul Haq went on to become a major intellectual force behind the reshaping of the UN's development thinking, specifically behind the Human Development Reports of the UNDP.

[96] McNamara (1981), cited in Wade (1997) 620.

[97] See Wade (1997) 624.

[98] Ibid. 621.

or practice. A second contradiction could be found in the relationship between environment and poverty alleviation. Throughout the 1970s, developing countries assumed that the environment was inimical to the alleviation of poverty, which provided the moral leitmotif for the post-colonial state.[99] The most notable example of this attitude was Prime Minister Indira Gandhi's remark at the 1972 Stockholm Conference that poverty was the world's worst polluter.[100] This idea was built upon the notion that environmental concerns, such as pollution, related to quality of life were appropriate only in wealthy western societies, and therefore poor industrializing societies could not afford such luxuries. This attitude was reflected among international lawyers as well, such as R. P. Anand,[101] who favored developmental concerns over environmental ones.

This contradiction was significantly resolved at a rhetorical level by the Brundtland Commission Report in 1987 which stated: "Poverty reduces people's capacity to use resources in a sustainable manner; it intensifies pressure on the environment... A necessary but not sufficient condition for the elimination of absolute poverty is a relatively rapid rise in per capita incomes in the Third World."[102] Thus, the contradiction was resolved in favor of development by preserving the need for economic growth so long as it was sustainable. The net effect of this report was the consolidation of the discourse of sustainability, which provided yet another lease of life for "development." Indeed, the discourse of sustainability provided a new, more intrusive set of reasons for managing the "dark, poor and hungry masses" of the Third World. The logic of the discourse was the following: (a) the poor, not the rich alone, can damage the environment due to their unsustainable practices, and therefore poverty is environmentally unsustainable; (b) for this reason, they need to be managed to ensure that their practices are sustainable; (c) since the ultimate way to reduce unsustainable practices of the poor is to make the poor richer, the heart of the strategy must be economic growth. Thus, the development rhetoric completed a full cycle, and practices that had been discredited became resuscitated under the new banner of "sustainable development."

[99] Sachs (1992b) 29.

[100] For an account of the views of various developing countries at the Stockholm Conference, see Sohn (1973). As the UN General Assembly declared prior to the Conference, "no environmental policy should affect the present or future development possibilities of the developing countries." See, United Nations (1972), 70.

[101] See, e.g., Anand (1980).

[102] *World Commission on Environment and Development* (1987) 49–50.

Indeed, the Brundtland report marked the beginning of the rise of a global "ecocracy," which had adroitly resolved the tension between continuous development and environment that formed the core of the more radical 1970s critique of "limits to growth."[103] The ecodevelopmentalist vision that was expressed in the Report reproduced central aspects of the development discourse, including basic needs, population, resources, technology, and food security. More importantly, the Report articulated a notion of sustainable development that began to view poverty as an environmental problem and the poor as irrational peasant masses who destroy their forests and indulge in "unsustainable" practices like swidden agriculture.[104] This shifted the visibility and blame away from the large industrial polluters in both the West and the Third World as well as the exploitative and predatory aspects of developmentalist ideology. Even more importantly, this analysis enabled the reconstitution and expansion of the BWIs with special reference to and invocation of the 'irrational' masses of the Third World. This 'Other' had simply become indispensable to the very definition and existence of the international sphere.

The end result of this shift is that ecology and economics are now seen as closely related (as they are etymologically), and that "sound ecology is good economics," as World Bank President Barber Conable put it.[105] Ecology has become a higher form of efficiency and environmental planning has come to occupy a central place in development. However, the old tensions and contradictions continue to persist and can be seen in the 1992 Rio Declaration, between the "right to development" (principle 3) and "sustainable development" (principle 4), or in defining poverty alleviation as a requirement of sustainable development (principle 5).[106]

Grassroots resistance and the expansion of BWIs

Since the mid-1980s the Bank has grown exponentially in the field of environment (see Table 5.3). The number of environmental specialists employed by the Bank grew from just five in the mid-1980s to 300 a decade later.[107] Budgetary resources for the environment rose at 90% a year in the same period while agriculture and forestry resources shrank at 1% a year.[108] After 1987, environmental clearance procedures became mandatory and a new portfolio of environmental projects was begun.[109]

[103] See Escobar (1995) 193. [104] Ibid. 195. [105] Cited in ibid. 197.

[106] See *Rio Declaration on Environment and Development*, U.N. Doc. A/Conf.151/5/Rev.1, 1992.

[107] See Wade (1997) 611–12. [108] Ibid. [109] Ibid. 611–612.

Table 5.3 *Indicators of the Bank's environmental work, 1975–95*

Indicator	1975	1980	1985	1990	1995
Staff	2	3	5	106	162
				(270)	(300)
Lending (in million $)	n.s.	n.s.	15	180	990
Bank reports					
Environment	13	46	57	196	408
Poverty	16	57	16	95	210
Total	635	968	1,238	1,593	1,760

Source: Wade (1997) 612 table 13–1.

This tremendous increase in size and activity from the mid-1980s was not accidental. It coincided with perhaps the most intense engagement between grassroots groups and any international organization. From the late 1970s and accelerating through the mid-1980s, many western and Third World environmental and social movements began targeting the World Bank as an egregious violator of the environment and destroyer of livelihoods.

The impact of outside grassroots pressure on internal reform of the Bank was rarely conceded openly, lest it be thought that the Bank was giving in to "political" or other extra-financial demands by non-state actors with whom it did not traditionally deal. But the activism from below was beginning to have an impact. For instance, the Bank's environmental adviser stated with respect to the formulation of a tribal rights policy in the early 1980s: "There were a number of outside groups who were quite vociferous... in bringing this to our attention... groups like Amnesty International, the Harvard group of Cultural Survival... and others. They were quick to chastise us and rightly so. And so... my office moved out in front on this and... began to fashion... a tribal policy for the Bank."[110]

As a result, the Bank adopted several important measures before the mid-1980s, such as a policy for involuntary resettlement of project-affected persons in 1980, a policy on the treatment of indigenous peoples in 1982, and a new Operational Manual Statement setting out guidelines for the environmental review of projects in 1984.[111] Nevertheless, it was

[110] Interview with James Lee, public health specialist and environmental advisor, in World Bank Oral History Program 3–4 (April 4, 1985), cited in ibid. 630.

[111] Wade (1997) 630, 634.

not until the engagement with grassroots resistance in the Third World that the Bank began to reorient itself and expand in new directions. There were two such key moments of engagement between grassroots resistance and the Bank that had a decisive impact on its evolution towards the discourse of sustainable development.

Polonoroeste

The first of these moments arose from the Polonoroeste project in Brazil between 1979 and 1989. The principal objective of this project was to pave a 1,500-kilometer highway from Brazil's densely populated south-central region into the sparsely populated northwest Amazon.[112] The project was a mammoth and comprehensive effort at regional planning with plans for feeder roads, new settlements, provision for health care, and the creation of ecological and Amerindian reserves.[113] The affected area was as large as California or Great Britain. The World Bank, which was the only non-Brazilian source of finance, approved five loans for this project, totaling $457 million, between 1981 and 1983.[114]

Despite some reservations held by insiders at the Bank, this project was fully supported because the Bank under McNamara saw it as an historic project that not only conquered the "world's last frontier" but also had poverty alleviation as its principle rationale.[115] Nevertheless, the Bank was aware all along that given the sensitivity of the issues involved, such as the protection of Amerindians, "control would be difficult and bad publicity unavoidable. This would remain a high-risk project, but one worth doing."[116] For whom it was "worth doing" and who was to bear the "high risks" was, of course, never explicitly discussed, because everyone knew that the real risks would be taken by the victims of the project and not by the Bank. While the construction of the highway was actually completed, the remaining parts of the project lagged far behind scheduled completion. There were additional problems created by the influx of new settlers and the consequent threat to the ecology and the Amerindians in the areas.[117] As the environmental and human costs of the project mounted, the Bank attempted to evaluate and deal with the project internally, but it was hampered by its bureaucracy, which misled the Board with false assurances of satisfactory implementation of the project.[118]

[112] Ibid. 637. [113] Ibid. [114] Ibid. [115] Ibid. 638–39. [116] Cited in ibid. 644.

[117] On the problems created by the project, see Maybury-Lewis, (1981); Brunelli (1986).

[118] Wade (1997) 649–50. The Bank also suspended a disbursement after a critical mid-term review in 1985.

In the meantime, the real pressures were mounting, not only from NGO accounts of the catastrophic impact of the project on ecology and Amerindians,[119] but also from increasing attention from the environment-friendly members of the US Congress.[120] Surely, the latter were not solely motivated by the plight of Amerindians to criticize the World Bank – domestic political considerations were inseparable from their actions. This created novel legal problems for the Bank, because it was thought that it was constitutionally bound by its Articles of Agreement to deal only with finance ministries of executive branches, and not with legislative branches or with NGOs.[121] For example, in one instance, after receiving a critical report from US-based NGOs about the project in 1984, the Bank responded with a rather dismissive letter. Upon receipt of the letter, Senator Robert Kasten, Jr., a conservative Republican senator from Wisconsin and the Chair of the Senate Appropriations Subcommittee on Foreign Operations, challenged the Bank. This situation introduced the question of whether the Bank should legally respond to an individual legislator from one of its member countries or insist on dealing only with the Treasury department, which represents the executive. Ibrahim Shihata, the Bank's general counsel, advised the Bank's President, Clausen, that the Bank should refuse to deal directly with individual legislators, as its Articles of Agreement expressly dictated relations solely with executive agencies of member states.[122] This episode reveals the explanatory limitations of the extreme anti-imperialistic critiques of the BWIs, which say that they are simply tools of capitalist domination, as well as liberal critiques who decry the capture of BWIs by the West. In this instance, the Bank resisted the pressure from the US senator, but for reasons that came across to NGOs as unaccountable. More importantly, western interventions intersected in complex ways with the local politics of Third World social movements and the global politics of western NGOs, which often adroitly exploited these interventions strategically to promote their own objectives. Dismissing these interventions under the banner of sovereignty, and dismissing Third World social movements for not being authentic enough, resulted – and continues to result – in the silencing of heterogeneous voices emerging from the Third World.

In the end, the concerted efforts carried out against the Polonoroeste project in the US media, US Congress and by NGOs worldwide forced the

[119] See Lutzenberger (1985); Rich, Stoel, and Brambe et al. (1985); Aufderheide and Rich (1985); Eckholm (1984).

[120] Wade (1997) 652.

[121] IBRD Articles of Agreement Article III, § 2.

[122] Wade (1997) 665.

Bank to respond.[123] The concrete result was the expansion of the Bank. A new Central Environmental Department and four regional environmental divisions were created, and environmental clearance procedures became mandatory for all projects.[124] This did not mean, however, that the Bank was departing from its traditional role as a development institution. As President Barber Conable remarked, "the added staff will help define policy and develop initiatives to *promote growth and environmental protection together*. They will work to ensure that environmental awareness is integral to all the Bank's activities."[125] Thus, grappling with the resistance generated by a broad coalition of western NGOs and Amerindians resulted in expanding the sphere of activities of the Bank into the new arena of sustainable development as part of the broader process of problematization of global survival.[126]

Narmada

The second key moment in the institutional evolution of the BWIs in the area of sustainable development concerns the Narmada Valley Project.[127] As a result of the political momentum created by the NGO and public opposition to this project, the Bank was transformed as an institution at three levels. First, the Bank appointed a quasi-independent inspection panel in September 1993,[128] in effect the first such institutional body created to allow individuals to bring legal actions against an international institution, to which project-affected persons could complain about the Bank's noncompliance with its own operational policies. Second, the Bank both completed the mainstreaming of the environment into its development

[123] Other political developments provided additional leverage. In Brazil, the first civilian government in twenty years had taken over in 1985 and had a more flexible attitude toward the project. Furthermore, due to the so-called Baker Plan to respond to the Latin American debt crisis, the US Congress had to approve any increase in capital contribution by the United States to the IBRD. This provided a strong incentive for the Bank to compromise with the US Congress, which saw the Bank in dire need of an environmental reform. See ibid. 668.

[124] Wade (1997) 674. [125] Ibid. 673–4 (emphasis added). [126] See Escobar (1995) 194.

[127] On the controversies surrounding the Narmada Valley project, see Fisher (1995); Baviskar (1995); Alvares and Ramesh Billorey (1988); Special Issue on Dams on the River Narmada (1991).

[128] World Bank, The World Bank Inspection Panel, Resolution 93–10, International Bank for Reconstruction and Development, Resolution 93–6, International Development Association, September 22, 1993. The Panel consists of three semi-independent commissioners and has received twenty-three complaints since its establishment relating to the violations of World Bank's own policies. For a discussion, see Shihata (2000); Bradlow (1993); Bradlow and Schlemmer-Schulte (1994).

discourse, which was exemplified by its 1992 annual report on Environment and Development and its role in the 1992 UNCED (UN Conference on Environment and Development) Earth Summit and the subsequent establishment of the GEF (Global Environmental Facility), and ironed out its problematic relationship with NGOs, who henceforth became partners in development. Third, through participation in the World Commission on Dams during the duration of the Narmada Project,[129] the Bank has shown its ability to weather radical criticisms through time-tested bureaucratic devices, though the impact of the Commission's findings remains highly unpredictable and contingent on the complex interaction between mass resistance, member States, financial interests and the Bank.[130]

The Narmada Valley project is a development scheme to harness the Narmada river, one of the longest and most unexploited in India, for hydropower, drinking water, and irrigation. According to original plans, some 30 major, 135 medium and about 3,000 minor dams and thousands of smaller dams would be built along the river, which runs through three states in central and western India.[131] Of truly gargantuan proportions, the largest dam, Sardar Sarovar, would alone potentially affect 25–40 million people, whereas the canal to be built would have displaced 68,000 households.[132] This human casualty would compound the already considerable environmental costs to a fertile valley boasting a wide variety of fauna and flora. Given the large number of people affected by the project, resettlement rather than environment became the focal point of the national and international campaigns against the project. Conceived in the spirit of post-independence nation-building, the Narmada dams were

[129] On the World Commission on Dams, see its Web site at www.dams.org. Established in 1998, the Commission consisted of twelve members drawn from international institutions, the private sector, NGOs and social movements. It submitted its final report in November 2000 on the ecological, financial, operational, human, and social viability of large dams. This was expected to have a major impact on the World Bank Group's funding of the construction of large dams in developing countries, which has become the lightning rod for broad-based resistance movements against development in such countries, exemplified by the anti-Narmada movement. This was also expected to have a large impact on how the World Bank and other major development actors went about their business. While the report has had some impact on the funding of large dams by the Bank, it has largely failed to have a significant impact on traditional development practice, due to the fierce resistance of most countries to the report's recommendations. See also the Symposium Issue (2001).

[130] See World Commission on Dams (2000); Dubash et al. (2001).

[131] See Wade (1997) 687–88. See also Fisher (1995).

[132] Wade (1995) 688. It also promised to irrigate 1.8 million hectares in Gujarat plus 75,000 in Rajasthan, to generate power for three states, providing irrigation to 2.5 million villagers and drinking water to 29.5 million. See Omvedt (1993) 267–68.

truly imagined as "temples of India," as Nehru described dams. Several factors ensured that Narmada would become a *cause célèbre* that would play a crucial role in the evolution of the Bank as a BWI, as well as in the evolution of sustainable development discourse.

First, a rising environmental consciousness among India's discontented urban middle classes and lower rural classes, which had been coalescing together in social movements throughout the country since the early 1970s, made Narmada a symbolic struggle that raised basic questions about India's political and economic structures and the place of the most vulnerable persons within them. This consciousness was reflected in several vigorous social movements with a strong environmental focus throughout India in the 1970s, such as the Jharkhand Mukti Morcha (in the forested hilly areas of South Bihar), the Chipko movement (in the Himalayan foothills of Uttar Pradesh), the National Fishworkers' Federation (in Kerela), the Silent Valley movement (in Kerela) and the peoples' science movements (in Kerela, Uttar Pradesh, and Tamil Nadu), and in the establishment of NGOs devoted to environmental issues such as the Center for Science and Environment in New Delhi.[133] The remarkable aspect of these movements was that they cut right across class lines, and included a broad coalition of peasants, tribals, women, farmers, middle-class consumers, and radical intellectuals.[134] The struggle over Narmada thus tapped into an impressive national environmental movement. Second, for the international NGOs, the struggle over the Polonoroeste project had begun tapering off by 1987, and they gladly latched onto the Narmada project struggle to continue their campaign against the BWIs' social and environmental record.[135] As Lori Udall has put it (for these activists) "Narmada had become a symbol of a highly destructive development model and the 'test case' of the Bank's willingness and capacity to address the environmental and social impacts of its projects."[136] Third, the US Congress and

[133] For a detailed discussion of the emergence of environmental movements in India, see Omvedt (1993), chapter 6, 127–49.

[134] Wade (1997) 146–49.

[135] The role played by western NGOs is an important factor in the success or failure (however they are defined) of many 'local' social movements. A social movement perspective focuses on the intersections between these cross-cultural mobilizations, in terms of how the objectives of different actors in a movement are achieved in the politico-cultural spaces produced by their interactions. This has the advantage of not treating the entire West as being incapable of moral solidarity with 'local' social movements. Such a morally righteous approach simply fails in explanatory power. For an example of the kind of social movement theorizing indicated here, see Esteva and Prakash (1998) (especially chapter 2).

[136] Udall (1995) 202.

several legislatures of western countries began to show a large interest in environmental issues and the Narmada struggle was the perfect opportunity to engage in a low-risk environmental struggle in the Third World. Fourth, as the environment went mainstream, the Bank, like academia and governments around the world, gradually altered its attitude towards the environment.

In addition to the human and environmental costs of the project, there were other complicating factors that threatened the design and implementation of the project. For instance, the project stretched over three states, Maharashtra, Madhya Pradesh, and Gujarat, all of which had different political and economic stakes in the project and therefore were unwilling to work together for most of the duration of the project. Gujarat had the maximum interest in the project because of its potential to provide irrigation and a drinking water supply to its dry inland territory. Madhya Pradesh had scant interest in the project because it stood to gain little, but most of the project-affected people – more than 80% of the 245 villages to be flooded – resided in Madhya Pradesh. Similarly, Maharashtra had very little interest in the project.[137] Since these states had authority over water resources under India's federal constitutional structure, the central government could not exercise much influence over the states, thereby complicating the World Bank's job. Moreover, since 1987 the Bank itself was in the middle of a serious internal restructuring and was thus internally paralyzed with respect to the project. The high turnover of managers meant that project personnel had little time to familiarize themselves with the project before they moved on to other projects.[138]

India approached the World Bank for help in 1978, though the scheme had been on the table of the national planners for decades. The Bank prepared the first-stage project in 1979–83, appraised it in 1983–84 and approved a loan and credit for the project in 1985 for $450 million. As the project evolved, grassroots opposition to it also increased beginning in the late 1970s and accelerating in the 1980s, assisted by the liberal democratic processes of India including a free press, civil liberties and an independent judiciary. The opposition was led by several groups,[139] the most prominent of which was the Narmada Bachao Andolan (NBA), or Save the Narmada, (a national coalition of human rights and environmental groups, project-affected people, academics, and scientists), at the local level and the Environmental Defense Fund (EDF), an NGO in

[137] Wade (1997) 688–89. [138] Ibid. 697–98.

[139] There were/are groups and NGOs that do not oppose the dams as such, but work to obtain better rehabilitation packages for the oustees. Prominent among them is Arch-Vahini, an NGO in Gujarat. See Fisher (1995) 21–26, Patel (1995).

Washington, DC.[140] When the Bank in 1992 compiled an Independent Review under the chairmanship of Bradford Morse, known as the Morse Commission, the Narmada project had acquired a reputation as perhaps the most notorious of Bank-financed ecological and human disasters. The report of the Review[141] found that the Bank's own directives on resettlement and environment had not been followed, and it recommended that the Bank "step back" from the project. The Indian government subsequently requested that disbursements be stopped for the project in March 1993 – when it became clear that the Bank would in fact cancel further disbursements anyway. The Bank pulled out of the project. The construction of the dams continues with government and private sector funding, and the grassroots opposition also continues through intense civil disobedience despite intense government repression, public apathy, and even loss of judicial support.[142]

Nevertheless, the Narmada project has had a lasting impact on the Bank – the Inspection Panel was created in 1993, and a new information policy was approved in August 1993, making the publication of Bank documents easier and thus the Bank more accessible.[143]

The massive public resistance to the Bank that has emerged in the last two decades has been unprecedented. No other international institution – with the very recent exception of the WTO after the collapse of the Seattle talks in 1999 – has had to grapple directly with such an intense popular resistance in recent years, though as I have suggested, engagement with Third World masses is a fairly constant feature of the evolution of international institutions since the Mandate system. The engagement with the "dark, poor and hungry masses" of the Third World has been key to the expansion and proliferation of these institutions and has occurred by converting the substance of criticisms leveled by social movements into opportunities for the construction and deployment of knowledge in general. I have argued that such engagement is a fairly standard character of international institutions.[144] As Foucault said about the clinic, "[s]ince disease can be cured only if others intervene with their knowledge, their resources, their pity, since a patient can be cured only in society, it is just that the illnesses of some should be transformed into the experience of others... [w]hat is benevolence towards the poor is transformed into knowledge

[140] See Fisher (1995) 43 (f.n. 24). [141] Morse and Berger (1992).

[142] The Indian Supreme Court has, through a notoriously partisan judgment, branded the movement as an anti-dam one and allowed the construction to proceed despite non-compliance with many previous commitments and legal awards. See *Narmada Bachao Andolan v. Union of India*, Supreme Court (Judgment dated October 18, 2000).

[143] See Wade (1997) 727. [144] Kennedy (1987).

that is applicable to the rich."[145] The BWIs reveal, as few international institutions do, how "benevolence towards the poor" is transformed into knowledge and self-proliferation of the "international."

Conditionality and the transformation of the IMF

Despite the fact that one associates words like surveillance, structural adjustment, and conditionality with the International Monetary Fund (IMF), these words have only existed in the vocabulary of the IMF since the late 1970s and early 1980s.[146] In fact, for a substantial part of its existence, the IMF had little significant involvement in the Third World. During its first two decades, the IMF used more than half of its resources to deal with the balance-of-payments difficulties of industrialized countries.[147] For instance, the conclusion of the General Agreements to Borrow (GAB) in 1962 anticipated possible large scale IMF assistance to the United States, which would not have been allowed under the regular quotas.[148] Indeed, as late as November 1978, even the US drew on its reserve tranche in the IMF as part of a stabilization exercise.[149] In short, the IMF is legally and functionally empowered to lend to all member States, unlike the World Bank, which focuses upon developing and transitional countries.

Yet, in the decade between 1978 (when the second amendment of its Articles was adopted) and 1989 (when the debt crisis had been weathered), the IMF fashioned a new identity for itself.[150] First, the IMF has

[145] Foucault (1963).

[146] See De Vries (1986); Guitián (1992); Hooke, (1982); Barnett, (1993). On the IMF and the developing countries, see Gold (1971). Indeed, most of the recent literature on the IMF is in the context of its relations with the Third World, especially in regard to the debt crisis of the 1980s and the subsequent structural adjustment programs (SAPs), conditionalities, and their social and political impact. A sample would include: Cornia, Jolly, and Stewart (1987); Broad (1988); Guitián (1981); Gold (1979); Williamson (1983); Payer (1974); Conrad (1989); James (1998); Pastor (1987). For an earlier critique of the IMF that touches on many of the themes developed in this chapter, see Rajagopal (1993). See also Bradlow (1996).

[147] See Polak (1991). [148] Ibid. [149] Ibid.

[150] This new identity was also crucially shaped by the decision of the US to remove itself from the Gold Standard in 1971, the emergence of international capital markets in the 1970s and the subsequent loss of role for the IMF as a clearing house of western finance, and the debt crisis of Latin American and African countries in the 1980s. I do not discuss these factors at length here due to lack of space, but I shall note that these factors do not detract from my overall thesis about the new institutional identity of the IMF. Even if the IMF was looking for new pastures after the 'loss' of the West in the 1970s, it does not explain the intensity and the direction of its growth. For such an explanation, I suggest that we need to look at the IMF's embrace of the popular energy unleashed by Third World social movements.

become a lender to the Third World primarily, leaving the West to the capital markets and regional regulatory arrangements. The IMF has thus come to occupy a crucial position in the production and reproduction of power relations between the West and the Third World. Second, economic growth is now recognized as an objective of the IMF even though it is not mentioned in its Articles as a purpose.[151] It is clearly not accidental that growth became accepted as one of the IMF's purposes at exactly the same moment that the Third World emerged as its main clientele; rather, this resulted from an intense political engagement with the Third World. Third, the IMF's surveillance role under article 4 of its Articles of Agreement dramatically expanded through new policy tools of intervention in the form of conditionality, which were/are implemented through the Structural Adjustment Facility (SAF), Enhanced Structural Adjustment Facility (ESAF) and now through High Impact Adjustment Lending (HIAL).[152] In this new capacity, structural adjustment and conditionality have come to be seen as poverty alleviation tools,[153] though the IMF is not legally required to promote this latter objective. Indeed – and fourth – the IMF has now completely embraced the poverty alleviation discourse like the World Bank, and has renamed the ESAF as the new Poverty Reduction and Growth Facility (PRGF).[154] This effort, as the IMF puts it, "aims at making poverty reduction efforts among low-income members a key and more explicit element of a renewed growth-oriented economic strategy."[155] This discovery of poverty as a domain of intervention by the IMF coincides with a new focus of debt-relief, for example in the Highly Indebted Poor Countries Initiative (HIPC),[156] to enable eligible countries to reduce their external debt burden to levels that "will comfortably enable them to service their debt through export earnings, aid, and capital inflows."[157] Thus, the IMF has also come to engage with the "poor, dark and hungry masses" of the Third World in the process of expanding its domain of activities. Fifth, the IMF has

[151] Ibid. at 17.

[152] These facilities are in addition to the others such as the Oil Financing Facility, the Compensatory Financing Facility, the Supplementary Financing Facility and the Extended Fund Facility. See Rajagopal (1993) 91.

[153] For example, see Landell-Mills (1988).

[154] See Communiqué of the Interim Committee of the Board of Governors of the International Monetary Fund, September 26, 1999 (available at www.imf.org). The changes to the ESAF Trust Instrument to rename the facility and redefine its purpose were agreed by the Board on October 21, 1999, and became effective on November 22, 1999. See IMF (1999a) and Supplement 1 (11/22/99).

[155] See World Bank (1999). [156] See Andrews et al. (2000). [157] See IMF (1999b).

come to embrace so-called non-economic concerns such as poverty alleviation, income distribution, environmental protection, reduction of military expenditure and anti-corruption, though it rationalizes them in terms of their impact on balance of payments.[158] The catch-all phrase that has been used to denote this tectonic shift has been that of "good governance."[159]

This sea-change in the institutional identity of the IMF has not occurred automatically as a result of a smooth learning process, nor has it connoted the IMF's complete embracing of non-economic concerns in any real way in its policies and programs. *However, the very real changes in its institutional practices in the last two decades have occurred only because the IMF has embraced the political, the non-economic, and the social concerns.*[160] As the IMF Executive Board instructed in its new 1997 guidelines to the Bank staff, it is now "legitimate to seek information about the political situation in member countries as an essential element in judging the prospects for policy implementation."[161] Despite frequent avowal that it is excluded from considering political and other non-economic considerations under its Articles,[162] the IMF has nevertheless formed a complex and ambivalent alliance with the forces that generate such concerns in the Third World, expanding its own institutional domain in the process. The IMF does not encounter popular movements at the local level because of its mode of financing, which focuses on policy-financing rather than project-lending like the World Bank; nevertheless, it has not been prevented from evoking the "social" as a central part of its policy intervention. The forces that generate the "social" are primarily the Third World countries that were flexing their new economic and political muscle in the United Nations in the 1970s in the form of the demands for a NIEO, grassroots poor people's agitations against the IMF-imposed SAPs in the 1980s, and the environmental and human rights movements of the late 1980s and 1990s. At each of these stages, the IMF has acquired new words in its vocabulary that have gradually transformed its character and expanded the range and magnitude of its power vis-à-vis the Third World.

[158] See Polak (1991) 24–33.
[159] IMF (1997c); OECD (1995); UNDP (1997b); World Bank (1994). See also, Gathii (1999a).
[160] For discussion, see below. [161] James (1998) 46.
[162] In its August 1997 guidelines to staff, the IMF Executive Board indicated that the IMF's judgments should not be influenced "by the nature of the political regime of a country" and that "the IMF should not act on behalf of a member country in influencing another country's political orientation or behavior" (ibid.). This schizophrenia about politics has become quite usual in functional organizations such as the IMF.

Engaging with the third world: towards 'development'

The IMF's transformation from a short-term monetary institution to a long-term financial/development institution over the last two decades has been the most significant and visible aspect of the changing nature of its relations with the Third World.[163] The principal purpose of the IMF under its Articles is to provide short-term financial assistance to member states who experience balance of payments deficits.[164] This emphasis on short-term financing and balance of payments deficits originally distinguished the IMF from the World Bank, which was to provide medium- to long-term financing for development.[165] The single-minded attack on balance of payments deficits also meant that the IMF did not have to pay attention to economic growth and could advocate deflationary, anti-populist policies that had a serious impact on the poor through the elimination of food subsidies and welfare services.[166] This narrow monetarist approach, which made the attack on balance of payments an end in itself, was subject to much criticism as it was seen to neglect other objectives of the IMF.[167] As Sidney Dell noted, "this is a distortion of IMF priorities, of the priorities of article 55 of the UN Charter, and of the International Development Strategy drawn up under that Charter."[168]

The IMF chose to treat such critiques as directed towards growth issues as opposed to the IMF itself.[169] It sought to mitigate the critiques by providing resources over a longer period of time with lower conditionalities and by arguing that its programs do not slow down growth.[170] However, this mitigation has proved insufficient and over time the IMF has conceded that growth is in fact at the heart of its purposes. As Michel Camdessus, the Managing Director of the IMF in 1990, stated, "Our prime objective is growth. In my view, there is no longer any ambiguity about this. It is toward growth that our programs and their Conditionality are aimed. It is with a view toward growth that we carry out our special responsibility of helping to correct balance of payments disequilibria."[171] This convergence to growth has expanded in recent years to include non-monetary dimensions that reveal the IMF's new domain of power. As Camdessus went on to explain, what he had in mind was "high quality growth rather than flash-in-the-pan growth fueled by inflation and

[163] See Pastor (1987) 251. See also Rajagopal (1993) 91. [164] See IMF (1945), article 1(V).
[165] See Gold (1979) 18. [166] See Rajagopal (1993) 90.
[167] For different strands of the critique, see Pastor (1987) 250–54.
[168] See Dell (1983) 18. [169] See Pastor (1987) 251.
[170] Ibid. 251. [171] Quoted in Polak (1991) 19.

excessive borrowing, or growth at the expense of the poor or the environment, or growth run by the state."[172] Thus, the IMF has come around to accepting a notion of growth that bears great resemblance to the World Bank's notion of development. While significant differences continue to remain between the two institutions in regard to institutional philosophy, objectives, and tactics, it is undeniable that the IMF has acquired its new identity as a result of its engagement with the issues generated substantially by the same social movements of "poor, dark and hungry masses" of the Third World that have profoundly impacted the World Bank. These issues have spurred the IMF to embrace the "social" as a new discursive terrain of development represented as growth.

The new face of conditionality

The main policy tool that has been developed by the IMF to carry out its new mandate is conditionality. Quite simply conditionality means that the resources provided by the IMF will be conditioned on certain policy measures that the member state must carry out as part of the IMF-approved stabilization program.[173] Originally, conditionalities related mostly to appropriate macro-economic reforms and policy measures necessary to stabilize the economy. In the last decade or so, the rise of development, human rights, environmental NGOs and social movements has triggered the debate as to the appropriate attitude to be adopted concerning IMF-imposed conditionalities. Should they be opposed or supported? Should the conditionalities target morally or socially just goals such as basic needs, environmental protection or even human rights?[174] How can the IMF impose such conditionalities without violating its Articles, which prevent it from considering non-economic factors in its decisions? At what level of commitment will a member state have to carry out these non-economic conditionalities, and to what extent is it realistic to expect such reforms to work even if the ruling elites actually express commitment? The debate about conditionality therefore lies at the fault line between many opposing dualities: between a financial and a social or political approach; between project and policy lending; and between national ownership and

[172] Ibid.

[173] See Gold (1979); Guitian (1981). Not all IMF resources are conditional on stabilization programs; a country can normally use IMF resources unconditionally up to its own quota. See IMF (1945) articles V(6), XXX(c).

[174] On basic needs conditionality, see Gerster (1982). On human-rights conditionality, see Rajagopal (1993) 104–06. On the evolution of IMF conditionality, see James (1998).

international responsibility. These dualities have framed the terms under which the debate about conditionality is conducted and have thereby determined the outer limits of the politics of knowledge production by the IMF.

Concrete results of this debate with respect to the BWIs may be found at several levels. First, though it is fairly readily conceded that conditionalities fail more often than they succeed, the BWIs and several NGOs continue to insist on the value of conditionalities. For instance, both the World Bank and the IMF have in recent studies determined that using conditionality to induce policy changes is extremely difficult.[175] Nevertheless, both the BWIs and the NGOs cannot do without conditionalities – the former need them to justify the loans and the continuing allocation from member states, that is, to justify their very existence, while the latter need them to influence the behavior of Third World states that are usually the targets of their benevolent interventions. As has been recently suggested, "since the mid-eighties, lending has often been justified in terms of the benefits of the policies adopted as the result of conditionality clauses. The policies have become the projects, with investment in economic infrastructure replacing investment in physical infrastructure. *Loans are justified by the policy changes instead of vice versa.*"[176] Conditionality, then, has emerged as a crucial element in the expansion and proliferation of the BWIs.

Second, the tensions between the failures of conditionalities on the one hand and the pressures to make them more "social" on the other have provided the BWIs with the opportunity to generate new terms in the discourse of development that signify the changing aspects of their relationship with the Third World. Two terms are of particular importance – "ownership" and "selectivity."[177] Ownership is derived from the idea that conditionalities cannot succeed unless they are "owned" by the target government, such that recipient ownership of programs becomes an important factor in their implementation.[178] The new notion of 'ownership' evokes powerful images of property and democracy. It is nevertheless a meaningless concept in the end because the real question concerns whose ownership is involved – that of the state or the local community? Given the IMF's focus on either the state or the market, it is extremely unlikely that the concept of 'ownership' will be interpreted in a broad manner to enable the most vulnerable people to defend their life spaces under this

[175] Wood (1999). [176] Ibid. 4 (emphasis added).
[177] See Wood (1999), passim. [178] Ibid. 21.

banner. However, as long as these questions remain unresolved, the social costs that are exacted in the name of conditionality will continue to be resisted by those who lose out.

Selectivity is based on the idea that donors should be more discriminating about the governments that they are willing to support.[179] The criteria for such discrimination are by no means self-evident but are supposed to include a good policy environment and a "clean" government that has not engaged in massive repression, such as the Burmese Junta.[180] These criteria are in the end self-contradictory or self-defeating. It is the absence of good policy that leads to the financial crisis that calls for conditionality-based intervention in the first place; therefore, a good policy environment could not be a criterion for positive discrimination. Besides, this criterion fixes the threshold for positive discrimination at an unreasonably low level, by suggesting that only the Burmese Junta-like regimes should not be supported. In fact, there are several levels of different kinds of repression that matter equally to those who are being repressed, for example the repression of labor movements in the East Asian Tiger economies. By delegitimizing one level of repression, this criterion allows the normalization of supposedly lesser forms of repression. Thus, the invention of these new terms of discourse ultimately has resulted in the reconstitution of the terrain of intervention that has itself remained the same – the Third World, with its poor, hungry, dark, and repressed masses. Conditionality has become the discursive terrain for the deployment of all the "authorless strategies" by the BWIs for constituting and reconstituting the Third World and in that process, themselves.

Conclusion

This chapter has outlined an understanding of the BWIs as Foucaultian "complete and austere institutions" that have had a complex relationship with Third World resistance. This resistance has been exhibited in environmental and various other social movements during the 1960s, 1970s, and 1980s. The basic contention has been that it is the processes by which the BWIs have dealt with that resistance and not so much the resistance itself that have revealed the centrality of the resistance to the formation of the BWIs' changing institutional agendas. In particular, the invention of poverty and the environment as terrains of intervention show how the resistance of the Third World feeds the proliferation and expansion of the

[179] Ibid. 22. [180] Ibid. 34.

BWIs and how, simultaneously in that process, Third World resistance itself gets moderated and acted upon. This dialectic between resistance and institutional change is hardly acknowledged by the BWIs, who see their evolution as being governed purely by the laws of economics, finance, or their Articles of Agreement. From the vantage point that is advocated here, it matters less that poverty alleviation programs never alleviate poverty or that conditionalities never achieve their policy goals. Rather, these specific interventions have their "instrument-effects" that redound to the authority and expansion of international institutions.

6

Completing a full circle: democracy and the discontent of development

The post Cold War era has witnessed an unprecedented and far-reaching transformation in the normative corpus and the institutional architecture of international law.[1] This fundamental transformation in international relations could be seen for instance, in the emergence of a new political culture of legitimacy in the form of human rights, a new private law regime in the areas of trade and finance that has tremendous implications for notions of sovereignty and autonomy, new notions of sustainability and resource-use, and a vast network of new international institutions including those that involve civil society actors and even the private sector in addition to states. Indeed, there has been a veritable legalization of international relations. Legal scholars have exhaustively commented upon these developments during the 1990s and tried to offer theoretical frameworks within which a 'new' international law could be formulated.[2] This chapter seeks to examine a key theme that has come to dominate the legal and political landscape of the post-Cold-War era: democratization. In particular, I am interested in examining and explaining certain questions such as: What are the social, political, and economic forces that drive democratization and who are the most important actors? What is the relationship between the drive towards democratization and the drive towards marketization in the Third World, which has been the target of massive international interventions since the so-called end of the Cold War? What are the institutional consequences for international law of embracing democratization as an important goal?

The argument in this chapter is that democratization has supplanted modernization as the discourse of social transformation in the Third World and, therefore, as the driving ideology behind international law as the law that governs the relations between the West and the Third World,[3]

[1] For a thoughtful and balanced assessment, see Kennedy (1999).

[2] See, e.g., Franck (1995); Higgins (1994); Falk (1998).

[3] By this, I do not mean to offer a definition of international law, but simply point out that it provides the normative framework for regulating relations between not just states, but also

and provides a principal explanation for its expansion through institutionalization. If modernization theory was based on the idea of the economic backwardness of the Third World, democratization theory is based on its political backwardness, which, it suggests, may contribute to its economic backwardness as well. This turn towards democratization in international relations is not occurring in a vacuum, but as the distinct and concrete result of an attempt to contain and channel the mass resistance of social movements since the 1980s. Just as in the 1950s and 1960s, international institutions are experiencing an unprecedented growth and reach, due largely to an intense interaction with the democratic mass movements in the Third World. I offer a detailed examination of how this has occurred through a critical mapping of UN peace operations that have focused on promoting democracy, and more recent international development thinking that has begun to embrace democratization. These institutional developments are juxtaposed against the mobilization of Third World social movements for democracy and against development. Viewed this way, is becomes clear that the tremendous expansion in the domain of international law and institutions in the last two decades cannot be understood without a proper appreciation of its relationship to the resistance from Third World mass movements. This resistance–renewal dialectic, it would appear, is a core aspect of 'modern' international law.[4]

One must begin with a set of theoretical clarifications about what we mean by democratization. A wave of political and social movements has occurred in the Third World (including in Eastern Europe and the former Soviet Union) since the early 1980s, culminating in the end of the Cold War and the subsequent 'triumph' of democracy. This has been greeted by many with naked triumphalism,[5] or studied optimism.[6] Whatever we

cultures. See Anghie (1999) (also citing his earlier works positing 'a dynamic of difference' that governs international law). See also Berman (1999). Of course, international law also regulates the relations *inter se* within the West or the Third World. See, e.g., Alexandrowicz (1967). Also, for an extensive analysis of the complex connection between international law and modernization and dependency theories in the post World War II period, see Rajagopal (1999a).

[4] I trace this dialectic in a systematic manner in Rajagopal (1999a). This dialectic could also be understood as one between the 'international' and the 'local,' which is a familiar, if overlooked, aspect of modern international law dating to, at least, the inter-war period. For pioneering scholarship that establishes the centrality of this aspect, see Berman (1992, 1993); Kennedy (1987). See also Kennedy (2000). For an examination of how this local–international interaction evolved during the colonial period, see Berman (2000).

[5] The most notorious of this reaction is Fukuyama (1992).

[6] The chief proponent of the wave theory of democracy has been Huntington (1991). In this book, he discusses a third wave of democracy that has swept the globe since 1974.

may think of such reactions, these enormous mass mobilizations have led to two momentous events in the contentious relationship between the West and the non-West. The first of those is the final configuration of a new identity for the native: that of *homo politicus*. If the Mandate system of the League of Nations launched the process of constructing the *homo oeconomicus*, and subsequent institutional interventions solidified it, the native has begun now to be seen as a peculiar political animal who is capable of dealing with the cultural, political, and economic contradictions of modernity unleashed on him/her by the development encounter.[7] It is now not enough for the native to be able to produce for the economy; he/she has to be able to participate in polity as well. This has meant significant transformations in international law and in the matrix of international institutions in at least two major ways.

At the first level, a discourse of democracy – interpreted mostly in human rights terms[8] – has attempted to constitute itself as the 'approved' discourse of liberation and resistance. As a result, there has been a tremendous proliferation of international institutions to achieve social transformation in the Third World, mainly under the rubric of democratization and peace maintenance. Whatever may be the immediate purpose in establishing peace operations – such as a desire to secure a cease fire or to enable the transition to a post-war phase – the net result of these operations has seen the most intense management of popular resistance, the wholesale 'modernization' (read westernization) of political and economic structures in the Third World and a tremendous expansion in the size and power of international institutions. The articulation of an intricate nexus between peace, democracy, and development has become a central feature of international interventions in the Third World, where peace operations contribute as much to the building of a 'modern' market economy and 'democratic' political institutions as they do to the maintenance of peace. In other words, instead of understanding post-Cold-War peace operations and the turn to democratization as merely functional responses to a chaotic post-Cold-War world, I suggest that it might be more useful to understand them from a perspective of political economy as interventions that aim to incorporate the Third World into the 'modern'

Among international lawyers, the best statement of the triumph of western-style democracy (though with much more nuance and sophistication than Huntington) is Franck (1992). See also Fox and Nolte (1995).

[7] For an argument outlining the process and consequences of constituting the natives as *homo oeconomicus*, see Rajagopal (1999a).

[8] For an incisive argument that this is indeed the case, see Mutua (1996a).

world. In this sense, they merely continue the violent transformations begun with colonialism and the Mandate system of the League of Nations.

The second major result of the complex relationship between Third World democratic mass movements and international institutions in the last decade is the invention of a whole new ensemble of practices and discourses that resignify the meaning of development as a value-based, culturally particular discourse. The effect of these new practices has been to add another layer to the existing layer of meanings attributed to development: now development is not merely poverty alleviating, environmentally sustainable, or gender equalizing, it is also democracy dependent, democracy enhancing and peace building. As a result, the institutions and processes of development – from multilateral institutions to bilateral donors – have embraced democratization as a crucial component of their interventions in the Third World. I examine this by analyzing the new discourse emerging from the World Bank and certain bilateral donors.

But I also argue that these apparent moves towards democracy remain only at the surface level. In particular, the international economic institutions such as the BWIs and the WTO remain entirely outside genuine democratic accountability.[9] Indeed, the last decade has seen a tremendous concentration of power at the hands of international civil servants, at the expense of the ordinary people in the Third World. For mainstream international lawyers, this greater institutionalization of international law represents a much-needed strengthening of multilateralism and a retreat of sovereignty, thus overlooking the democratic legitimacy crisis of multilateral institutions themselves.[10] This gradual erosion of sovereignty and democratic control is true of multilateral institutions such as the WTO and, to a varying degree, in regional institutions such as the EU.[11] This is reflected, for example, in the debate over the concept of "subsidiarity," whereby member states of the EU have attempted to retain democratic control over some responsibilities.[12] In the US, the accession to NAFTA (North American Free Trade Agreement) and then to the 1994 GATT Uruguay Round has raised fundamental questions about US sovereignty, democracy, and constitutional law.[13]

[9] For a trenchant analysis of how social movements have challenged this democratic deficit, see O'Brien et al. (2000). On BWIs and social movement dialectic, see Rajagopal (2000a).

[10] See the symposium, 'Unilateralism in international law' in EJIL (vols.1 and 2, 2000). See also the perceptive critique of international lawyers' 'messianic multilateral agenda' in Alvarez (2000).

[11] For thoughtful analyses, see Kingsbury (1998); Schachter (1997).

[12] On subsidiarity, see Bermann (1994); Cass (1992).

[13] See, e.g., Jackson (1997); Ackerman and Golove (1995); Vagts (1997).

Social and political movements around the world have recognized this fact and have rallied together against these institutions. Indeed, for the first time in the history of international law, there is a strong cosmopolitan sentiment and popular energy, against certain international economic institutions such as WTO and the economic and cultural aspects of globalization that they represent. Despite this, the praxis of these movements is not visible in the recent scholarship that celebrates the triumph of democracy and the arrival of civil society, or in the scholarship on international economic law. To qualify as an 'authentic' democratic movement, it seems that certain lines – such as the articulation of a place-based knowledge system as a real alternative to space-based 'development' – should never be crossed. However, the popular energy behind these movements can not be ignored for long without some serious rethinking of the ethical, cultural, normative, and institutional foundations of the current international order and a correspondent change in worldviews.

The last stage of modernization and development: peace operations

With the end of the Cold War, peace-keeping by the UN increased dramatically in scope and size. As the UNSG's *An Agenda For Peace* pointed out in 1995, thirteen peace-keeping operations were established between 1945 and 1987, whereas thirteen others had been organized as of 1995.[14] These new operations had been enabled by the brief period of optimism and cooperation at the Security Council in the immediate post Cold War period. These operations differed from traditional peace-keeping operations – with their emphasis on consent of the parties, neutrality, and impartiality between parties, defensive rules of engagement, and a narrow scope of just keeping the peace – in such a stark manner that a new term was coined to denote them: 'multidimensional peace operations.'[15] These new operations were complex, expensive endeavors that focused on several areas such as refugee repatriation, economic rehabilitation and reconstruction, human rights and rule of law, electoral assistance, civilian police training, demobilization of the military, and so on.[16]

[14] United Nations (1995a) 57.

[15] See, e.g., United Nations (1995b). See also Doyle, Johnstone, and Orr (1997). For useful surveys of earlier peace-keeping, see United Nations (1990b); Higgins (1969–81).

[16] The first example of this new generation of peace operations is the Cambodian one, United Nations Transitional Authority in Cambodia (UNTAC), which was delegated extensive powers by the Cambodians for an interim period in 1992–93, in order to conduct

This called for dramatic changes in the organizational requirements of international institutions such as the UN. As the Secretary General put it, "increasingly peace-keeping requires that civilian political officers, human rights monitors, electoral officials, refugee and humanitarian aid specialists and police play as central a role as the military."[17] This has had a tremendous effect on international institutions in at least two ways: first, the size and reach of international institutions have expanded to unprecedented levels. More areas of the Third World and the lives of the natives have been opened up for technical 'interventions' by 'experts' ranging from anthropologists, lawyers, economists, geologists, engineers, biologists, and so on. A telling example of this expansion can be seen in the fact that in 1993 – when peace operations peaked – the peace keeping costs stood at $3.6 billion a year whereas an estimated 528,000 military, police and civilian personnel had served under the UN flag.[18] Of the fifty-four operations set up since 1948, two thirds (thirty-six) have been established since 1991 until 2000, whereas 38,000 police and military personnel and around 3,500 civilian officers were serving in peace-keeping missions of the UN at the end of 2000.[19] This represents a huge apparatus of administration over 'troubled' or 'failed' Third World states.

At the second level, the nature of international institutional presence in the Third World underwent a radical change. Until the end of the Cold War, international institutions occupied a 'global' space, distant from the Third World that they administered, mostly in western capitals and making occasional visits to the 'field' as necessary. Now in the post Cold War period, international institutions have gone 'local,' establishing 'field' presence in the Third World countries where they are active. This applies not only to the classic development agencies such as Food and Agriculture Organisation (FAO) and (United Nations Children's Emergency Fund) UNICEF (which had been present in the 'field' for many years already), but to the mainstream UN and even the BWIs. For example, the World Bank has over 100 field offices now whereas the IMF has around seventy resident representatives in sixty-four countries. Until the end of the Cold War, both had very little field presence. This new field-based approach was

the election and serve as the mechanism for the 'transition' to the post-election phase. On Cambodian peace agreements, see Ratner (1993). On the post-election transition to 'democracy,' see Jeldres (1993). See also the annual reports of the Special Representative of the Secretary-General for Human Rights in Cambodia, to the General Assembly and the Commission on Human Rights, e.g., United Nations (1998b).

[17] United Nations (1995a) 59–60. [18] Ibid. 58. Also from the UN website, below.

[19] Information obtained from the UN at http://www.un.org/Depts/dpko/dpko/pub/pko.htm.

justified by the reasoning that a more intensive, hands-on management of social reality in the Third World was necessary to effect 'development'. As the Secretary-General put it in the *Agenda for Peace:*

> The social stability needed for productive growth is nurtured by conditions in which people can readily express their will. For this, strong domestic institutions of participation are essential. Promoting such institutions means promoting the empowerment of the unorganized, the poor, and the marginalized. *To this end, the focus of the United Nations should be on the "field," the locations where economic, social and political decisions take effect.* In furtherance of this I am taking steps to rationalize and in certain cases integrate the various programmes and agencies of the United Nations within specific countries.[20]

Different terminologies were invented in international relations to give urgency and potency to this new type of peace-keeping operations as instruments of the last stage of modernization and development in the Third World. Chief among them was the idea of "saving failed states" such as Somalia, Liberia, Afghanistan, and even Cambodia.[21] Based on openly patronizing and racist attitudes towards the Third World, these saviors of "failed states" advocated restoring UN trusteeships and even recolonization[22] on the purported basis that these states had "collapsed." A second idea that worked closely with the first was that of promoting democratization in "new" or "restored" democracies or countries that are "in transition" towards democracy. This has been the main basis for the new development paradigm, combining elements of peace-keeping, democracy promotion, electoral assistance, institution building and rule of law. However, through it all the pretense was maintained that the UN does not promote any specific form of government or ideology as it would contradict articles 2(4) and 2(7) of the UN Charter.[23] As the Secretary-General put it, "the United Nations system, in assisting and supporting the efforts of Governments to promote and consolidate new or restored democracies, does not endorse or promote any specific form of government....

[20] United Nations (1995a) 70–71 (emphasis mine).

[21] For a critical review of this idea, see Gordon (1997).

[22] Helman and Ratner (1992). Indeed, the advocates have included even Third World radical intellectuals. See Mazrui (1994) 18. For a softer version based on the same idea but advocating the redrawing of colonial boundaries to restore pre-colonial ones, see Mutua (1995b).

[23] Article 2(4) prevents the violation of the territorial integrity or the political independence of states and article 2(7) prevents the UN from interfering in matters that are within the domestic jurisdiction of states.

That is why, in the present report, I do not attempt to define democracy but refer to democratization."[24] Conceived this way, democratization becomes disaggregated into a series of bureaucratic steps taken by the UN solely in response to the wishes of the countries requesting assistance, and therefore in conformity with sovereignty. As the International Court of Justice affirmed in the *Nicaragua* decision concerning the commitments made by the Sandinista government to abide by democratic electoral standards, that it "can not discover, within the range of subjects open to international agreement, any obstacle or provision to hinder a State from making a commitment of this kind. A State, which is free to decide upon the principles and methods of popular consultation within its domestic order, is sovereign for the purpose of accepting a limitation of its sovereignty in this field."[25] In this way, international law self-defines itself as neutral and apolitical even as it enables the UN to engage in promoting democracy in transitional countries, a task that is overtly political.

It is in fact through large-scale UN interventions in "new" democracies, many of which had been battlegrounds in the Cold War, that most rebel armed movements were transformed into political parties and in that process much of their revolutionary rhetoric was moderated and contained. Recent UN operations where such transformations have taken place include Mozambique,[26] Cambodia,[27] and El Salvador.[28] Despite this rather extensive role in transforming the internal political structures of these countries, the UN continues to make a feeble attempt to portray itself as apolitical and neutral, mentioning for example that training for political party members is "better" carried out by NGOs rather than the UN.[29]

[24] United Nations (1996), paragraph 5 (emphasis mine).

[25] *Military and Paramilitary Activities in and against Nicaragua (Nicaragua v. U.S.)*, Merits, ICJ Reports (1986), 14, 131.

[26] United Nations ((1996)), paragraph 19. In Mozambique, the UN operation, ONUMOZ, played a significant role in transforming the opposition movement RENAMO into a political party (ibid).

[27] In Cambodia, the de facto ruling party (CPP) was itself the 'opposition' party as it remained unrecognized by the UN. The UN operation, UNTAC, played a major role in legitimizing the CPP as a ruling party and transforming its socialist rhetoric into a pro-market one. The UN operation also actively delegitimized the Khmer Rouge, a radical and unpalatable part of the UN-recognized 'government' as a political actor.

[28] In El Salvador, the UN mission, ONUSAL, assisted the FMLN's transformation into a political party (United Nations [1996] paragraph 21).

[29] Ibid. paragraph 22. The report mentions as an example, the training provided to Cambodian political parties by the US "NGOs", the National Democratic Institute and the International Republican Institute. These organizations are affiliated with the two major US political parties, and were perceived to be heavily biased against the CPP, the ruling

Whatever may have been the intentions behind the establishment of these 'multidimensional peace operations' that focus on democratization efforts, an unambiguous result has been the proliferation in the number and size of international institutions as well as in their reach. The space of the domain of the 'international' itself has been reconfigured in a way that makes it much more powerful and contested than was ever the case in previous decades, precisely because the 'international' and the 'local' are no longer separated by clear boundaries. This was made possible because of the marriage between development, democracy, and peace. In this sense, the complex interactions between these different discursive strategies have had a defining impact on the production and reproduction of social reality in the Third World.

The holy trinity: development, peace, and democracy

The most significant and visible aspect of the new strategies can be found in the linking of three independent concepts that had hitherto remained unrelated: that of development, peace, and democracy. The reasoning behind the relationship between these three concepts goes something like this. Peace is essential for the functioning of the basic mechanisms of democracy as well as development, whereas a culture of democracy is likely to lead to peace, both intra-nationally by defusing discontent and tensions, and internationally by enabling democratic states to trust each other more, due to their openness. The relationship between development and democracy, while more problematic, is also seen as positive: democracy enables development to succeed through its participatory methods, whereas development encourages the stakes that a community has in defending its autonomy. The doctrinal basis for this holy trinity of development, peace, and democracy, is to be found in the three reports issued by the UNSG, Boutros Boutros-Ghali, between 1992 and 1997.[30]

While his first report, *An Agenda for Peace*, issued in 1992, is much better known in academic and policy literature, less known are the other two reports that followed it on the subjects of democracy and development. I shall focus on one of them, the *Agenda for Democratization*, to substantiate my argument that democratization discourse in the 1990s is doing to

party. In addition, some of their "NGO" trainers were alleged to be disreputable characters such as one individual, a former American intelligence operative who had trained death squads in Latin America. I draw on my years of work in Cambodia to make these comments.

[30] See United Nations (1995a 1996, 1997a).

international law/institutions what modernization discourse did to it in the 1950s–70s.

The report itself is fairly slender, and written in the bureaucratic language of UN reports, but the report does not miss the historic moment of the topic and its relation to the Third World. Thus, it begins by firmly positioning the UN's role in democratization as a natural successor to decolonization. After mentioning the Declaration on the Granting of Independence to Colonial Countries and Peoples[31] as one of the doctrinal/ legal bases for the UN's role in democratization, the report continues: "Just as newly independent States turned to the United Nations for support during the era of decolonization, so today, following another wave of accessions to statehood and political independence, Member States are turning to the United Nations for support in democratization."[32] Just as decolonization was the political precursor to modernization of the Third World, democratization could then be the precursor to neoliberal globalization. In this progress narrative, the United Nations is there for Third World states to "turn to" at transformative moments, whereas it could be argued that the UN was itself *constituted* to a significant extent because of the Third World, as I have argued in chapter 4. In other words, there was nothing to "turn to" before the Third World arrived on the international plane. The political effect of this subtle repositioning of the UN vis-à-vis decolonization and democratization should not be missed: whatever is the result of this new wave of democratization, the UN has gained by positioning itself as the organization that member states "turn to"; after judging what qualified as "genuine" anti-colonialism,[33] the UN, as the voice of the 'international community,' was now moving to evaluate "genuine" democratization.

Continuing this progress narrative, the report makes the claim that the Cold War had "thus interrupted the project of democratic international organization begun by the founders."[34] In this view, the failure of the UN to support democratization in the Third World since its founding is not due to fundamental faults in the founders' vision or institutional design, but due to 'aberrations' such as the Cold War. An encounter with the 'historic' opportunity provided by Third World democratization

[31] United Nations 1960.

[32] United Nations (1996) 2. It adds that nearly a third of all member states – more than sixty – had requested electoral assistance since 1989.

[33] For an excellent analysis of the politics of anticolonial nationalism under the British rule and its deradicalizing effect on Third World politics, see Furedi (1994).

[34] United Nations (1996) 13.

is thus converted into an *internal argument* of institutional pedigree/ legitimation.

At the next level, the report turns to the relationship between democratization and development, making it clear that modernization and development have found a successor paradigm. As the report states, "...a culture of democracy... helps to foster a culture of development."[35] After noting that "United Nations' activities and responsibilities in the area of democratization thus parallel and complement those in development,"[36] the report explains the nature of the "assistance" that it provides for democratization: "traditionally technical assistance has been provided in the context of economic and social development...; assistance in governance beyond that was made virtually impossible by the political climate throughout most of the United Nations history. While the United Nations still provides technical assistance in those areas, the wave of economic and political transitions witnessed in the post Cold War period has led Member States to reorient their requests for technical assistance towards areas more relevant to democratization, broadly defined."[37] This emphasis on 'technical' assistance for democratization nicely dovetails with the nature of development interventions, not only because it is the common vocabulary of development discourse, but also because these interventions are carried out within the terms of "good governance," a cornerstone of development ideology in the 1990s.[38]

Reading through it all, it is hard to avoid the conclusion that the project here is not a forthright support for democratization, but rather a support for the revival of the ideologies of development and modernization. Implicit in it is also an overriding concern with the institutional role of the UN, much more than with democratization per se. Thus, the report mentions how following the first and second International Conferences of New or Restored Democracies, held at Manila in June 1988 (with thirteen states participating) and at Managua in July 1994 (seventy-four states participating), the UN has expanded to meet the needs of technical assistance requests: a new Electoral Assistance Division has been created within the Department of Political Affairs, various trust funds have been established for electoral assistance, and a global electoral assistance information network has been created with NGO participation, coordinated by the EAD.[39]

[35] Ibid. 9. [36] Ibid. 9–10. [37] Ibid. 5.

[38] Ibid. 9–10. The report makes the claim that "... democratic processes contribute to the effectiveness of State policies and development strategies ...". On good governance, see generally Tendler (1997); Quashigah and Okafor (1999); Gathii (1999a).

[39] Ibid. 16.

Indeed, the kind of explosive growth of international institutions seen in the post Cold War era has occurred once before – at the height of modernization and development in the late 1950s and early 1960s.[40] Now democratization has provided the perfect rationale for a similar expansion.

Through it all lurks the shadow of the third element in the holy trinity: peace. Asserting that "a culture of democracy is fundamentally a culture of peace,"[41] the report discusses how the explosion of peace operations in the post Cold war period has enabled the UN to push for democratization most effectively. These peace operations have been the primary vehicles for the increased "developmentalization" of the Third World, by deploying the language of "transition" and "peace-building"[42] and by opening them up to fundamental economic and political restructuring. While there are certainly differences, the democratization experiment of the 1990s bears far too many historical and disciplinary similarities to modernization efforts of the 1950s and 1960s. As then, international institutions have now emerged as the crucial variable as well as a site of resistance and domination in the relationship between the West and the non-West, between mass democratic movements and elite politics.

Participation rhetoric, democracy and the Comprehensive Development Framework

If the first conceptual axis for the expansion of international institutions in the post-Cold-War period is the nexus between democracy and peace, the second axis is the nexus between democracy and development. Though the relationship between political freedoms and markets has puzzled and animated thinkers in the West for centuries – starting with at least the Scottish enlightenment thinkers – mainstream development discourse did not usually concern itself with democracy in the beginning. Only recently has it increasingly come to rely heavily on the rhetoric of participation, empowerment, human rights, and democracy as essential aspects of supposedly authentic 'development.' The most recent manifestation of this new face of the apparatus of development is the discourse emerging from the World Bank under the umbrella of the Comprehensive Development Framework (CDF).[43] This has not, of course, happened automatically as a result of a gradual process of learning or a benign coincidence, though

[40] See chapter 4.

[41] United Nations (1996) 7.

[42] See the section on post-conflict peace building in United Nations (1995a) 61–62.

[43] See Wolfensohn (1999).

this is how international institutions tell the story retroactively. As a recent opinion piece by the World Bank's President James D.Wolfensohn and Professor Amartya Sen puts it, "the end of the Cold War has been accompanied by a growing recognition of the importance of political, social, and economic participation, by widespread demands for human rights and gender equity, and by an emerging globalized economy. This offers an unprecedented opportunity to make development work."[44] Several questions remain unanswered here: how did the end of the Cold War come to be "accompanied" by all these processes? Is that a mere coincidence, a new phenomenon or an old discourse that has been newly baptized? Was the Cold War holding back all these forces? Just for whom is development supposed to "work"? Just why/how is it that more participation would make development work?

In order to tease out some issues raised by these questions, and the impact of these issues on the expansion of international institutions as well as Third World mass resistance in the post Cold War period, it is important to outline the major ways in which development discourse has engaged with democracy and participation rhetoric in the last fifty years. Crudely put, there were always at least two strands of theories concerning this relationship. The first of these was dominated by political development theorists (such as Daniel Lerner, Samuel Huntington, and Sidney Verba) and classical economists (such as Paul Samuelson) who argued that there was an essential trade-off between democracy and economic growth. Basing themselves on the empirical 'evidence' of the Soviet (and later the Asian Tigers') experience which saw a rapid increase in economic growth at high human costs through a harsh, top–down model, they argued that rapid economic growth could be jeopardized by democracy since those regimes could enact populist measures such as land reforms and redistributive schemes (taxes), that are inimical to such rapid economic growth. Political development theorists such as Samuel Huntington also argued that increased political participation was an obstacle to economic growth, and that calculations of equity reduced the total economic benefits to everyone in society.[45] Many of these political development theorists were influenced in their analyses by a fear of mass society, and had a deep suspicion of mass politics in the context of the Cold War when anti-imperialistic (read anti-US) politics was at its strongest among the peasant 'masses.'[46] In this they were assisted by elitist political

[44] See Sen and Wolfensohn (1999) 3. [45] Huntington and Nelson (1976).

[46] For an insightful analysis of the intellectual and political climate in which political development theories were worked out in the US, see Gendzier (1985).

and democratic theorists starting from Joseph Schumpeter, and including Robert Dahl and other post-War theorists, who also saw the 'people' as less important than institutions and mechanisms of democracy – in other words, the *process* as more important than outcomes.[47] If at all economic growth was to contribute to democracy, it was going to be in an indirect way, by expanding people's choices and with the growth of a middle class. Roughly put, all these groups of scholars understood 'development' in an economistic sense, accorded the economic aspect priority over the political aspect of social life and saw democracy as a 'luxury' good that only the rich could afford, and even then only in processual, not substantive terms.

A second strand, which has much older intellectual roots in the West, consisted of political theorists starting from at least the Scottish enlightenment thinkers such as Adam Ferguson,[48] and social theorists from Karl Marx,[49] P. J. Proudhon,[50] and continuing with Karl Polanyi[51] and others who believed that the forces of capitalism are essentially inimical to democracy by destroying the civic culture and the sense of community that makes a society possible. After the Second World War, this group declined in influence, though one could see this line of critique living on through the work of radical social theorists (Ernesto Laclau,[52] Bowles and Gintis,[53] Charles Tilly[54]), economists (Schumacher,[55] radical dependency critiques), political and democratic theorists (the entire social movements critique consisting of European, American, Asian, and Latin American scholars such as Claus Offe,[56] Jurguen Habermas,[57] Frances Fox Piven,[58] Eric Hobsbawm,[59] Rajni Kothari,[60] etc.). This group saw the process of economic growth as a violent appropriation of peoples' resources, autonomy, and space, and treated democracy as an end that could not be sacrificed for other ends. Summarily put, this group also saw development in economistic terms, but accorded the political aspects of social life priority over economic aspects, and treated democracy in substantive terms.

The current discourse about democracy and development continues to reflect both these trends. The first 'trade-off' trend continues to be visible in the discourse of economists such as Robert Barro, who stated recently in the *Wall Street Journal*: "theoretically the effect of more democracy on growth is ambiguous. . . . Democracy is not the key to economic growth

[47] Schumpeter (1942); Dahl (1956). [48] Ferguson (1767). [49] Marx (1978).
[50] Proudhon (1876). [51] Polanyi (1944). [52] Laclau and Mouffe (1985).
[53] Bowles and Gintis (1986). [54] Tilly (1975). [55] Schumacher (1973).
[56] Offe (1984). [57] Habermas (1975, 1996). [58] Fox Piven and Cloward (1977).
[59] Hobsbawm (1959). [60] Kothari (1989).

and political freedoms tend to erode over time if they are out of line with a country's standard of living."[61] But this type of argument is increasingly becoming rare in development discourse, which has come to accommodate many of the criticisms made by the second strand of scholars. Essentially, the accommodation has taken the form of a 'modernist' one, whereby the very meaning of development – and indeed growth – is being reconfigured to include democratic elements such as participation.[62] As the UN Secretary-General Boutros Boutros-Ghali put it after assessing the failures of development without democracy, "there can be no flowering of development without the parallel advance of another key concept: democratization. Peace is a prerequisite to development; democracy is essential if development is to succeed over the long term. The real development of a State must be based on the participation of its population; this requires human rights and democracy."[63]

This new turn is best represented by the development discourse emerging from the World Bank, exemplified in the Comprehensive Development Framework (CDF). Drafted by its President, James Wolfensohn, the policy document attempts to redefine development by expanding its meaning from an anthropocentric, economistic one to a comprehensive one that includes ecological and human aspects. As it describes the 'new' vision of development:

> The Comprehensive Development Framework I am proposing highlights a more inclusive picture of development. We cannot adopt a system in which the macroeconomic and financial is considered apart from the structural, social and human aspects, and vice versa. Integration of each of these subjects is imperative at the national level and among the global players.[64]

The key to this 'more inclusive picture of development' is participation. The CFD document itself does not discuss democracy or participation

[61] Barro (1994).

[62] Of course, I do not mean that this is the first time that the rhetoric of participation is being used in development discourse. Indeed, from the beginning development discourse has attempted to legitimize itself by pointing to its positive impact on the welfare of the 'masses,' through poverty alleviation programs. Reflective of this was the early use of participation discourse in community development projects in the 1950s in India. Several subsequent paradigms of development continued to reflect this surface-level concern with the people and social justice from the early 1970s through the 1980s and 1990s: 'growth with equity,' 'growth with redistribution,' 'basic needs approach,' 'adjustment with a human face,' 'right to development,' 'participatory development,' 'human rights and development,' and now 'social capital' are some examples. Due to lack of space, I can not offer a detailed chronology of these stages.

[63] United Nations (1993). [64] Wolfensohn (1999) 7.

much, but instead makes the case for greater civil society involvement in projects and local 'ownership'. A clearer idea of the CDF's relationship to participation can be obtained by examining recent speeches of Joseph Stiglitz, the former Chief Economist of the World Bank. In a recent speech entitled "Participation and Development: Perspectives from the Comprehensive Development Paradigm," Stiglitz argues that broadly participatory processes, such as 'voice,' openness, or transparency promote truly successful long-term development.[65] He starts from the premise that CDF sees development as a "transformative moment" which involves a "movement from traditional relations, traditional ways of thinking, traditional ways of dealing with health and education, traditional methods of production, to more 'modern' ways.'[66] In this Manichean world of tradition versus modernity, tradition is synonymous with backwardness, lack of technology, stagnancy, oppressive human-rights conditions, and every aspect of life found in the Third World; whereas the 'modern' is seen as progressive, embracing change, and ensuring rising living standards through better technology as in the West. In constructing this world, Stiglitz is no different from the apostles of modernization theory in the 1950s such as Arthur Lewis.[67] The only significant operational difference is that the concept of the 'dual economy' has been abandoned.[68]

Having set himself up for an analysis of development within the dichotomy of 'tradition v. modernity,' Stiglitz makes the case that broadly participatory processes make the transition from tradition to modernity that development entails, effectively painless and acceptable. This emphasis on participation makes sense because in this new view of development, the transition from tradition to modernity essentially involves a change in mindset.[69] That change in mindset can not be forced from the outside or the top, but can only be gradually internalized from below. In this view, the transition itself is not questioned nor is the inevitable epistemological superiority of the 'modern' over the 'tradition.' Instead, it is assumed that the resistance to change is because of information deficit, or lack of adequate stake, which can be corrected by getting the population to 'participate.' The possibility that after full 'participation,' the 'traditional' may be preferred by the people over the 'modern,' is not entertained here.

Even with this caveat, Stiglitz's analysis goes much farther than any of the available theories of development, though it continues to share some

[65] Stiglitz (1999). [66] Ibid. 3 (citing his 1998 Prebisch lecture). [67] Lewis (1955).

[68] As Stiglitz states, "a dual economy is not a developed economy" (Stiglitz, 1999, 3).

[69] Quoting Luther to J. S. Mill to Albert Hirschman, Stiglitz puts the emphasis heavily on the acculturation process that is central to modernity (Ibid. 4).

commonalities with received political development paradigms. Those commonalities include: a continued emphasis on process rather than substance as the heart of participation; and a continued faith in the beneficent effects of economic development, though he acknowledges that it often "undermines social development."[70] The major departures include the following elements.

First, Stiglitz defines participation as a broad process that goes beyond a Schumpeterian definition of "voting as democracy" that was a standard in political development theories. In this new definition, based much on Albert Hirschman's concept of 'voice,'[71] participatory processes include not just government decisions, but also those at local and provincial levels, in the workplace, and in capital markets.[72] He explicitly recognizes that concentrations of economic power can occur in various ways and different strategies – including redistributive taxation and antitrust laws – are needed to combat them, lest they become a threat to participatory processes.[73] Second, as a result of this broad understanding of participation, he emphasizes the importance of making corporations accountable, by extending participatory processes to corporate governance.[74] This goes farther than any definition of participation advanced so far and clearly borrows from the more radical second strand of critiques that I mentioned above. Third, he cites studies to argue that grassroots level participation enhances the effectiveness of development projects. While the older models have mostly assumed that this was the case, the recent studies provide 'evidence.' One of the studies cited, for example, by Lant Pritchett and Daniel Kaufmann, makes the argument that there is a "strong and consistent link between measures of the extent of civil liberties in a country and the performance of World Bank-supported projects."[75] Studies like this continue to have serious drawbacks: their data sets are constructed from 'tainted' information provided by politically biased NGOs such as Freedom House; and they continue to suffer from the problem that participation, voice, and civil liberties are seen in instrumental terms as simply tools that make projects more 'efficient' and not in their own terms. Nevertheless, it can not be denied that a more nuanced understanding must

[70] Ibid. 17. [71] Hirschman (1970). [72] Stiglitz (1999) 5.

[73] Ibid. 7. As he puts it, "the temporary gains in efficiency may, I suggest, be more than offset by the inefficiencies introduced by excessive market power – and even if that were not the case, one should raise questions about the potential adverse effects on participation and openness."

[74] Ibid. 8–9. He quotes James Wolfensohn: "free markets can not work behind closed doors."

[75] Pritchett and Kaufmann (1998) 27. The larger version of this study is Isham, Kaufmann, and Pritchett (1997).

take into account their role in expanding the political space for resisting orthodox economic interventions.

More interestingly, Stiglitz also exhibits a nuanced understanding of the political and ideological impact of participation discourse on mass politics and radical opposition. First, he recognizes that given the fundamental changes in mindset that development calls for, there will be resistance. The best way to deal with this resistance is not to suppress it, but through participatory processes because they "ensure that these concerns are not only heard, but also addressed; *as a result, these processes dissipate much of the resistance to change.*"[76] The impact of mass resistance on the production of discourse and institutional practice is thus readily acknowledged. Second, he makes the argument that participation by the affected people in a democratic decision-making process ensures that the changes effected will be politically sustainable.[77] He cites India's economic reforms as an example of such internally generated process that has been sustained through various changes in governments. This strategy of letting resistance run its course, is a time-tested strategy deriving from old British colonial rule, parallels of which may readily be traced.

This new Stiglitz vision of development is largely based on the scholarship of Amartya Sen and Albert Hirschman. In particular, Sen's work has inspired CDF. As acknowledged by Sen and Wolfensohn themselves, "some of the ideas underpinning this framework are also found in a forthcoming book by one of us (Mr Sen), *Development as Freedom*, which argues that development can be seen as a process of expanding the real freedoms that people enjoy."[78] Over a period of more than two decades, Sen and Hirschman have contributed substantially to the expansion of the meaning and purpose of development, to make it less economistic and more ethical. Nevertheless, it is Sen's more recent scholarship on 'rights' discourse which seeks to use the moral potency of that discourse to supply legitimacy to a new concept of development, that has had maximum value for the CDF and the general turn towards participation and democracy. This new turn is beginning to be supported by recent economic research that attempts to show the impact of democracy and decentralization at the micro-level, and more loosely in the emerging literature on new institutional economics and social capital.[79] Examples include

[76] Stiglitz (1999) 9 (emphasis mine). [77] Ibid. 14–15.
[78] Sen and Wolfensohn (1999) 2. See also Sen (1999a).
[79] On new institutional economics and democracy, see Haggard (1997); Ostrom (1997); Picciotto (1997). On social capital, see Fukuyama (2000); Putnam (1993). For a nuanced analysis of democracy and capitalism, see Pierson (1992).

a study on the positive correlation between participation and project effectiveness[80] and another showing a robust association between the extent of democracy and the level of manufacturing wages in a country.[81] The unmistakable impression one gains from all this proliferating literature and policy discourse is that democratization is being anointed as the central discourse of social and economic transformation in the Third World.

New institutional actors in democratization

As mentioned above, the turn to democratization in the 1990s has witnessed an explosive proliferation of international institutions similar to the first wave of proliferation in the 1950s and 1960s that accompanied modernization. While governments of western countries remain the most vigorous promoters of democracy, they have been joined by a host of NGOs and IGOs.

State agencies The largest democracy assistance program today in terms of both scope and funding is that of the USAID (US Agency for International Development). With the announcement of its "Democracy Initiative" in December 1990, USAID spent, by one estimate, some $400 million in 1994 for democracy promotion[82] and in 1999 and 2000 this remained between $350 to $495 million.[83] This is an entirely new turn, since until 1990, USAID funding focused mainly on social and economic development. For example, USAID democracy promotion funding for Africa increased from $5.3 million in 1990 to $119 million in fiscal year 1994.[84] Other US agencies such as the US Information agency, and even the US Defense Department have turned to democracy promotion. This turn to democracy is also evident among the European Union, and various bilateral agencies such as SIDA (Swedish International Development Agency), DANIDA (Danish Agency for Development Assistance), NOVIB (Netherlands Organization for International Development Cooperation), CIDA and the International Japanese Aid Agency.

[80] See Pritchett and Kaufmann (1998). [81] Rodrik (1998).

[82] Diamond (1995) 13. The subsequent discussion is based on information contained therein. See also, Carothers (1999) for a comprehensive assessment of democracy promotion efforts by the US. For a nuanced critique of this book, see Alford (2000).

[83] See http://www.usaIbid.gov/pubs/account/fy_2000/ 2000_accountability_report_part_b.pdf (visited on July 12, 2001).

[84] Diamond (1995) 14.

International and regional institutions In addition to UN peacekeeping/peace-building efforts that have been discussed above, other UN agencies have also considerably expanded their democracy focus. The UNDP for example, devotes a full third of its funding to good governance projects.[85] In addition, the High Commissioner for Human Rights in Geneva has tremendously expanded its size, reach, and focus through the opening of twenty-seven field offices around the world (from almost no offices in the early 1990s), and by providing project assistance to countries.[86] In addition to these, among regional organizations, the EU, OSCE, and Council of Europe have taken a very proactive role in promoting democracy as a precondition for economic assistance to Eastern European states, or as a precondition to admission to EU. Through the creation of EBRD (European Bank for Reconstruction and Development), which has the promotion of democracy as a founding purpose, the EU has played an aggressive role in promoting democracy in Eastern Europe. The OAU (Organization of American States) has established a Democracy unit "to provide program support for democratic development" and its Permanent Council has adopted a resolution in 1991 calling for the "promotion and defense of representative democracy."[87]

NGOs The most prominent democracy promoting NGOs are the German Freidrich Naumann Foundation, the Konrad Adenauer Foundation, the Freidrich Ebert Foundation, and the Hans Seidel Foundation, and the American National Endowment for Democracy (NED), the International Foundation for Election Systems (IFES), and the Asia Foundation.[88] These NGOs occupy very important positions in the new development discourse, through their resources and the resulting influence. For example, the German Friedrich Ebert foundation disbursed DM 88.5 million (about $55 million) in sixty-seven Third World countries, with the assistance of ninety-seven German experts and 500 local personnel. The NED, IFES, and Asia Foundation have also provided millions of dollars of democratic aid, and constituted themselves as important parts of the development architecture.

This extensive proliferation of international, regional, and local institutions reveals the important place democracy promotion has come

[85] Interview with senior UNDP official. During 1994–97, 28% of resources were allocated to good governance. See http://magnet.undp.org/about_us/Mdgdbro_htm#2.Management (visited on July 12, 2001).

[86] See http://www.unhchr.ch/html/menu2/5/field.htm (visited on June 24, 2001).

[87] Diamond (1995) 36–37. [88] Ibid. 15–19.

to occupy in the development discourse and in the progressive expansion of the domain of international law. This expansion has not occurred innocently simply to promote democracy any more than the reason international institutions proliferated in the 1950s and 1960s was to fund rural development schemes or to 'alleviate poverty.' Rather, I have suggested that this institutional expansion must be seen in a complex dialectic with the mass democratic movements in the Third World since the 1980s. As mass radical movements have increasingly emerged around the claims for human rights and democratic entitlement, a host of international organizations have emerged to program this new area. The power to program implies the power to select the voices that constitute 'legitimate' democratic ones in the Third World, including for funding, just as the rural development and poverty alleviation programs targeted 'authentic' Third World elites. This process has the consequence of containing and deradicalizing mass resistance in the Third World, as Jospeh Stiglitz has so clearly recognized. It is through the process of containing and channeling this mass resistance that international relations and law have expanded their institutional reach and turned to democracy. To paraphrase James Ferguson,[89] the "democratization apparatus" is not a mechanism for promoting participatory development or peace building that is giving rise to the incidental expansion of international institutions; rather, it is primarily a mechanism for the expansion and consolidation of international institutions, which takes democratization as its point of entry. In this, it resembles the way international law and institutions took modernization as their point of entry for consolidating and expanding their reach over the Third World.

Democracy against development:[90] cultural dimensions of grassroots resistance

This bureaucratization of democratic resistance is not a one-sided process; it is actively resisted through counter-hegemonic coalitions in the Third World. Indeed, the 1980s and 1990s have also seen the emergence of a 'new cosmopolitanism': selective anti-internationalism. Consisting mainly of an eclectic coalition of deprofessionalized intellectuals,[91] grassroots movements, NGOs, mainly from the Third World but increasingly supported by a sophisticated and diverse network of scholars and activists

[89] See Ferguson (1994) 255.
[90] I have borrowed this title, in reverse, from Gendzier (1985).
[91] I have borrowed this term from Gustavo Esteva who refers to himself this way.

in the West, this new cosmopolitanism differs substantially from the more traditional cosmopolitanism that has characterized international law during the twentieth century.

First, unlike the traditional variety, this new cosmopolitanism does not see increasing internationalization as essentially a good thing. It is highly critical of the economic and institutional dimensions of the international project, while being supportive of the political and emancipatory ideals inherent in its liberal tendencies. In particular, it is highly critical of the global economic and financial institutions, such as the WTO, BWIs, and TNCs (Transnational Corporations) due to their enormous and unaccountable power and the resultant weakening of democratic structures in the Third World.[92] Second, the new cosmopolitanism also differs from the old one in preferring local democracy and decentralization-based strategies rather than rights-based ones.[93] Animating this new sensibility is a commitment to increasing people's space,[94] a post-liberal strategy for preserving the autonomy of communities in ways that differ from the 1970s'-style communist autarky symbolized best in the rule of the Khmer Rouge. The move away from an uncritical celebration of human-rights discourse is characteristic of this new cosmopolitanism.[95] This does not, however, mean that human rights discourse is not part of the action repertoire of the new cosmopolitan social movements. Far from it, they actively use it to promote their goals and objectives, to the extent that it is compatible. This fact has been noted by political scientists writing about the way transnational advocacy coalitions have used human rights in recent years.[96] Third, the new cosmopolitanism is favorably disposed towards a culture-based local resistance strategy against the global culture of economic and cultural imperialism of the West. In this new view of culture, it is a defense against the expanding power of globalization, but in a non-exclusive and cosmopolitan way that enables engagement with selected aspects of other cultures.[97]

[92] See, e.g., Mander and Goldsmith (1996); Korten (1995); Esteva and Prakash (1998).

[93] Mainstream liberal political theory has traditionally seen democracy in rights terms. See, e.g., Dworkin (1978). For a recent (unsuccessful) attempt to articulate a political theory of rights that can bridge liberal and non-liberal peoples, see Rawls (1999) (drawing a distinction between human rights and rights of citizens in liberal democracies).

[94] See Esteva (1987).

[95] For such a critique of human-rights, see Esteva and Prakash (1998) 382.

[96] The most prominent examples are Keck and Sikkink (1998); Risse, Ropp, and Sikkink (1999). See also, Falk (2000). For detailed case studies of transnational social movements in diverse areas including peace and security and environment, see Smith, Chatfield, and Pagnucco (1997).

[97] At a theoretical level, I follow the insights of postcolonial theory here. See, e.g., Guha and Spivak (1988).

Several factors have aided the emergence of this new cosmopolitanism. First, the very real shift in power that has occurred or is occurring from national to international level, most visibly in the case of the EU, has led to serious concerns about people's ability to maintain democratic control over vital social and natural resources. As already noted, in the EU this has taken the form of the "subsidiarity" debate, a compromise that attempts to preserve some local autonomy within a pluralistic legal regime.

Second, highly visible symbols of the hegemonic nature of global capital, such as the WTO and the debate over the Multilateral Agreement on Investment (MAI), have aided an effective mobilization of public opinion. The MAI, which was being secretly negotiated by a coalition of twenty-nine rich countries, was opposed and finally stalled by an effective coalition of grassroots organizations and cosmopolitan individuals in 1998. One of the principal arguments used against MAI was that it was antidemocratic, and that it would remove crucial decision-making powers from local communities and national governments to international bureaucrats.[98] Here is a clear example of the how the 'democracy wave' can also work against the proliferation of international institutions and norms. Other examples of the global democracy working against global economy include the very visible public demonstrations against the WTO and the BWIs, beginning with the 1999 Seattle battle to the recent skirmishes in Quebec over the Free Trade Area of the Americas (FTAA).

Third, the array of organizations that have engaged in this democratic struggle against selective aspects of the 'international,' have consisted of unusual capabilities. Such organization include:

NGOs like International Rivers Network (IRN) Established in 1985 as an NGO dedicated to the preservation of rivers and watersheds as living systems, IRN has played a significant role in many transnational campaigns including the anti-Narmada dam campaign, and has an ongoing International Finance Campaign that tracks and lobbies against major development and aid agencies.[99]

Think tanks like International Forum against Globalization (IFG) Established in 1994, it works to "reverse the globalization trend," especially in its economic and institutional manifestation, and to "redirect action toward revitalizing local economies."[100] It explicitly opposes the increasing internationalization of economies through the WTO, NAFTA and BWIs, and the paradigm of unlimited economic growth, and supports the revitalization of local communities. It played a critical role in the campaign

[98] Barlow and Clark (1998). For other criticisms, see Third World Network (1997).

[99] See its website, www.irn.org.

[100] See its website, www.ifg.org.

against the MAI including through a well-coordinated media campaign in the West.

Platforms of people's movements such as People's Global Action (PGA) The only one of its kind so far, the PGA is a global platform of peoples' movements from all continents that was launched in February 1998 against "free trade" and the WTO. The alliance is founded on "a very clear rejection of the WTO and other trade liberalization agreements," "a confrontational attitude," "a call to non-violent civil disobedience," and "an organizational philosophy based on decentralization and autonomy."[101] The alliance is organized as an instrument for coordination, and therefore explicitly has no membership, or juridical personality. Yet, it has staged several impressive demonstrations against the WTO and the MAI (Multilateral Agreement on Investment). Indeed, the visibility generated by this coalition of the depth of popular sentiment against economic globalization has unnerved the ruling elites and prompted them to take police action against it or to avoid the activists completely (as in the WTO's decision to hold a ministerial meeting in Doha, Qatar). At the "Geneva Business Dialogue" organized by the International Chamber of Commerce on September 23–24, 1998, the PGA had planned to mobilize popular peaceful demonstrations. However, the Swiss police raided a seminar on globalization held by the PGA, arrested everyone present, questioned and expelled several foreigners, openly admitting that their action was "preventive" with respect to the International Chamber of Commerce (ICC) organized Business Dialogue.[102] The police also raided the homes and offices of the organizers, interrogated six people, seized eight computers, more than a hundred diskettes and PGA documentation. This violence against the PGA has not managed to come to the attention of human-rights groups such as Amnesty International yet, and is certainly unlikely to be reflected in the discussion of the WTO by international economic law scholars. The final declaration of the ICC-organized "Business Dialogue" mentioned that markets need "strong and efficient" (i.e. lean) governments, one of whose four functions is the control of "activist pressure groups". This paranoia, while out of proportion, tells us something about the growing influence of groups that seek to challenge the 'international' through democracy.

Indeed, this new sensibility has grown influential enough that it has found supporters within the UN. The UN Sub-Commission on the Promotion and Protection of Human Rights has recently adopted resolutions

101 See its website, www.pga.org.

102 See Alert! United Nations sold out to MAI and the TNCs? (Press release, PGA, October 1, 1998).

calling for mechanisms to defend economic, social, and cultural rights in the face of globalization, and the resultant inequality and erosion of popular sovereignty. In August 1998, the UN Sub-Commission adopted a resolution calling for a close scrutiny of the MAI, "which might limit the capacity of States to take proactive steps to ensure the enjoyment of economic, social and cultural rights by all people, creating benefits for a small, privileged minority at the expense of an increasingly disenfranchised majority"[103] and in 2000, it issued a major report on the impact of globalization on human rights.[104] Indeed, the latter report has been deemed to be so critical that the WTO has taken the unusual step of protesting against the report to the then UN High Commissioner for Human Rights, Mary Robinson.[105] This suggests that even within the statist international organizations, there is political space for building counter-hegemonic alliances.

As the UNSG's report, "Agenda for Democratization," stressed, "democratization within states may fail to take root unless democratization extends to the international arena" because "unrepresentative decisions on global issues can run counter to democratization within a state and undermine a people's commitment to it."[106] This glaring disparity between the advocacy of democracy within states while keeping the increasingly powerful international domain entirely undemocratic, has been noted by scholars,[107] but it remains true today. In the meantime, new forms of democratic struggles are emerging that challenge the old axioms that to be an internationalist is to be unreservedly in favor of "free trade," and for a shift in power from the 'national' to the "international." The new internationalist sensibility crafted in the struggles of these groups calls for a more eclectic identity that resists hegemonic and undemocratic aspects of the 'international,' partly through the space provided by the 'international' itself but sometimes through a defense of the national and the local. In this sense, it stands contrasted with the very different way in which the 'international' relates to the 'democratic,' wherein the province of the 'international' expands in relation to the resistance from the Third World. This relationship is, as can be seen now, profoundly ambiguous and two-sided.[108] This ambiguity is increasingly well-captured in the works of recent international legal[109] and

[103] United Nations (1998a). [104] United Nations (2000). See also United Nations (2001b).
[105] See Singh (2000). [106] United Nations (1996) 27. [107] See Crawford (1994).
[108] For an elegant statement that captures this ambiguity, see Koskenniemi (1999).
[109] See, e.g., the works of Nathaniel Berman (1999), Anthony Anghie, and David Kennedy (1999a). See also, Falk (1998).

international relations[110] scholarship, which provide a foundation for rethinking the role of international law in the twenty-first century.

Conclusion

This chapter has argued that democratization has replaced modernization as the discourse of social transformation in the Third World. It also traced the consequences this transformation has for international law and institutions. Modernization theory provided the framework for the integration of the newly independent Third World into the international economy, and now democratization theory is providing the terms on which the Third World would be incorporated into the global economy. International law and institutions underwent a profound expansion during their encounter with the Third World during the heyday of modernization discourse,[111] and are again undergoing a profound expansion during an encounter with Third World social movements when the discourse of democratization has assumed primacy in key areas of international relations from peace and security to economic relations. The export of particular economic policies – including neoliberal ones – from the West must be seen through the prism of democratization, for that is what provides legitimacy to it. At another level, the discourse of democratization has provided a means for the intensification of the management of social reality in the Third World by international institutions, thus expanding their reach and scope. International institutions have proliferated and expanded their power and reach in the post-Cold-War period, due, among others, to peace operations and participatory development projects. These projects/operations have had as their primary impetus, the various democratic and people's movements in the Third World. As resistance encountered from these movements has mounted, international institutions have responded by embracing the democratic moment, just as they embraced the nationalistic moment at the time of decolonization. As a consequence, democratization discourse has come to succeed modernization discourse.

[110] In international relations, this scholarship has mostly fallen into the critical postmodern tradition focusing on the role of culture, but has its precursors. For an example of the latter, see Bull and Watson (1984). For more recent works, see Walker (1990, 1993); Mazrui (1990); Paolini (1999) (a postcolonial and postmodern critique).

[111] For a classic statement of the challenge of the Third World to western dominance and the impact on international law and relations, see Bull and Watson (1984).

It has also been argued that the 'arrival' of democratization as the language of social transformation in the Third World was necessitated and propelled by the increasing resistance of Third World social movements to development. As social movements resist more, international law and institutions renew and grow more. This resistance–renewal, I have suggested, is a central aspect of 'modern' international law.

This proliferation/expansion of international institutions has been enabled by the emergence of a new discourse of development that seeks to recast the political basis of individual and social life in the Third World, through peace operations to save "failed states" and through "comprehensive development" paradigms. Understanding the role of this new discourse provides a better grip on the explanations for the growth of international law through its institutions, since it is now exposed as ideological and in complex interaction with Third World mass resistance – two aspects that are ignored in explaining the newly expanding domain of international law.

Production of this new discourse has consequences not only for international law or development: it also affords space for resistance. Indeed, it is inevitable that the production of a discourse would have these multiple dimensions. If discourse is the process through which social reality comes into being – as I understand it[112] – then it is inevitable that such a process will be a contested one. Democratic spaces are used by several grassroots movements to struggle against the dominant discourse of development, even as their struggles are imbricated and made a part of the production of that discourse itself. It is this dialectic – of resistance and renovation – that I have suggested explains the political economy of international law through its institutions.

[112] As Foucault said, to analyze something as a discourse is "to show that to speak is to do something – something other than to express what one thinks; . . . to show that to add a statement to a pre-existing series of statements is to perform a complicated and costly gesture." See Foucault (1972) 209.

PART III

Decolonizing resistance: human rights and the challenge of social movements

"Civilization must, unfortunately, have its victims"[1]

Part II offered an analysis of how the disciplines of international law and international institutions shaped and were shaped by Third World resistance to the deployment of 'development' beginning with the Mandate system and accelerating during the post-War period – in short, how development was 'received' – and how this process has generated the apparatuses of international law and development. This Part proposes to describe and analyze how development, as an ensemble of practices and discourses of a particular form of western modernity, has been 'resisted' by the Third World through international law, and what the limitations of that resistance has been. Specifically, I am interested in investigating the constitution of the modern human-rights discourse as the sole approved discourse of resistance, and the peculiar blind spots and biases towards the violence of development that this resulted in. The limitations to the human-rights discourse as a complete liberatory and emancipatory discourse that could tame the violence of development has been reflected in the range of resistance encountered by development in the Third World. Much of this resistance has been in the form of popular movements against the cultural, economic and political effects of modernization and development since the 1970s in the Third World. Despite this, these "other" forms of resistance to development are not cognizable within the apparatuses and discourse of human rights, even though they form an increasingly important source of identity formation for individuals and communities, and have begun to have significant influence on the making of states and the practices of international organizations.

Unlike the national liberation movements, which saw themselves and were seen mainly in political and economic terms, these 'new' movements have embraced culture as a terrain of resistance and struggle. This 'turn

[1] Lord Cromer (1913) 44.

to culture' among mass movements in the Third World during the last two decades has emphasized rights to identity, territory, some form of autonomy and most importantly, alternative conceptions of modernity and development. As Fernando Calderón puts it, these movements pose the question of how to be both modern and different.[2] They "mobilize constructions of individuals, rights, economies, and social conditions that cannot be strictly defined within standard paradigms of Western modernity,"[3] and certainly not within that most prominent paradigm of Western modernity, viz., human rights.

However, this is precisely how international lawyers have attempted to deal with democratic challenges in the Third World. Their strategy involves a double move of appropriation and invisibility: at one level, the resistance of mass movements is appropriated as empirical evidence of the triumph of the human-rights discourse, that finally a 'western' style democratic revolution is sweeping the world;[4] at another level, the praxis of these movements is largely ignored – in other words, the substance of their democratic agitations is not taken seriously as constituting alternative conceptions of territory, autonomy, rights, or identity.[5] This homogenizing, universalizing tendency of international law towards Third World mass resistance is in fact not an aberration, but a central aspect of its history.[6] After all, international law has never been concerned primarily with mass movements, save in the context of self-determination and formation of states.[7] As argued in Part I, even in this context, international law leaves the terrain as long as the political situation is murky, and 'returns' only to welcome the victor to the club of states.[8] It has treated all other popular protests and movements as 'outside' the state, and therefore illegitimate and unruly. This division has been based on a liberal conception of politics, which sharply distinguishes between routine institutional politics and other extra-institutional forms of protest.[9] According to this model of politics, all forms of protest expressed outside the 'recognized' public arenas of politics is 'private,' or 'simply social' or just 'illegitimate.'

[2] Quoted in Alvarez, Dagnino, and Escobar (1998) 9. [3] Ibid.

[4] The best statement of this is Franck (1992). See also Huntington (1991).

[5] For such an attempt, see Rahnema (1997).

[6] As David Kennedy pointed out in an early piece, a standard feature of international law is the predictability of form and the incoherence of substance. See Kennedy (1980).

[7] Cassesse (1995); Crawford (1979); Quaye (1991).

[8] Berman (1988); "Aaland Island Question Report," *Official Journal of the League of Nations*, Special Supp.No.3, October (1920). For an analysis, see Rajagopal (1992).

[9] Bright and Harding (1984) 5.

Whatever be the appellation used to describe these forms of protest, they remain invisible. While aspects of the human-rights discourse gives the appearance of having moved international law beyond this liberal conception of politics, it nevertheless remains invisible to several forms of collective resistance that challenge received notions of modernity, specifically those underlying the development discourse.

I analyze these forms of resistance under the rubric of social movements. As examples of these movements, I offer a case study and numerous other examples. The case study concerns the Working Women's Forum (WWF), the largest women's movement in India, and is concerned with the analysis of the relationships between the processes of identity formation for the members of the movement as feminists and working women, the processes of state formations as responses, the particular configurations of the market in the 'informal' sector where the women made their living, the discourses of development and human rights, and India's economic reforms driven by neoliberalism. The basic contention here is that the international legal discourse is inadequate in meeting the actual purposes for which these women organize, or in explaining their complex interactions with the state structures, or in exposing the ideological framework within which such identity formations resist and sometimes assist the neoliberal project. The study argues that the WWF is simply incapable of being represented solely as a 'women's movement' or an NGO or a trade union, thereby defeating the liberal categories currently in vogue. In fact, it is the very heterogeneity of its multiple forms that gives the WWF its unique character as a social movement. Consequently, the liberal discourse of human rights, based on its conception of the unity of the social actor, and the sharp divide between public and private, cannot accommodate the praxis of the WWF as 'human rights'.

Numerous factors suggest that this analysis is germane and timely. First, despite its nominal counter-sovereign rhetoric, modern international law does not ordinarily concede mass movements and local struggles as makers of legal change. Instead, it continues to explain international legal change through either of two theories, both of which remain elitist: voluntarism (legal change occurs because the states have accepted them) and functionalism (legal change results from the tendency of law to reflect social reality or to respond to social needs).[10] In both, there is no indication of whether and how legal norms could be generated from the praxis

[10] I owe an inspiration to Gordon (1984), especially 70–71.

of social movements. Rather, both theories accord the role of the agent of legal transformation to a small group of elite policy makers.

The idea that law could result from the actions of mass movements is not fanciful at least in international law.[11] Debates about how "practice" could build law have been central to sources doctrine, dealing, for example, with customary international law. As the Restatement (Third) says about the definition of customary international law, "each element in attempted definitions has raised difficulties. There have been philosophical debates about the very basis of the definition: how can practice build law?"[12] While such debates have raged, they have not moved beyond either formalism or functionalism, as they remain committed to the idea that ordinary people can't make law, only state elites may.

Second, human-rights discourse has achieved an unparalleled moral and political status around the world.[13] More importantly, human-rights discourse has become the language of progressive politics in the Third World, replacing old left strategies of revolution and socialism.[14] Indeed, now it is not only the language of resistance, but also that of governance, thus decisively shaping policies in divergent areas of institutional reform, economic and social policy, and political reform. In its range and ambition (if not its depth), the human rights discourse has come to take the place of modernization theory, as the grand ensemble of practices and ideas that will drive social change in the Third World. In one sense, the emergence of numerous popular movements – from ecological, human rights, feminist, peasant, urban, and others – could be seen as the empirical confirmation of this rights revolution. Indeed, this is how they have been seen in recent scholarship in international relations that celebrates the emergence of a "global civil society." The question then becomes: is this in fact what is happening? Given the fact that the "human rights movement" – strictly defined in the legal and organizational terms of lawyers – is ordinarily

[11] This doesn't mean that in domestic law (at least American) there has been no attempt to think about the role of "practice" in generating theory. See, e.g., Bourdieu (1977); Simon (1984); Kennedy (1993).

[12] Restatement (Reporter's notes to section 102). Section 102, clause 2 defines custom as follows: "Customary international law results from a general and consistent practice of states followed by them from a sense of legal obligation." Cited in Steiner and Alston (1996) 28–29.

[13] For example, the doyen of the human rights field, Louis Henkin, states: "Ours is the age of rights. Human rights is the idea of our time, the only political-moral idea that has received universal acceptance." See Henkin (1990) ix.

[14] As put by Santos: "It is as if human rights were called upon to reconstitute the language of emancipation." See Santos (1997) 1.

only a small subset of popular movements for social change in most Third World societies, is it justified to interpret all social movements as evidence of a rights revolution? Unpacking the different assumptions of these issues may shed light on the ambiguities and contradictions that come to the surface when analyzing social movements as well as the uses and limitations of rights discourse vis-à-vis development.

Third, in most Third World countries, there is currently a crisis of governance and a search for political and economic models that go beyond the market and the state. This search for a "third way" is characteristic of Third World societies in the post Cold War era, but is currently fashionable even in industrial democracies.[15] The 'end-of-history' triumphalistic spirit of the immediate post Cold War era having quickly dissipated, many countries are now facing the hard realities of economic and political transformations that reveal the limitations of the liberal theories of politics and economy. This task is especially difficult because of the general loss of faith in the moral possibilities of the state as the agent of social change in the Third World. The question for progressives then becomes: is it possible to articulate a progressive politics that does not fall back on the state, but is nevertheless free of the market and rights fetishism of Washington Consensus? In this search for models, it is important to understand the place-based practices of various social movements to ascertain whether they offer alternative visions and programs for social change that are not based on the human rights discourse alone. In other words, a legal and regulatory architecture for a post-Cold-War era could be based not only from the space-based 'universal' discourses of globalization, marketization, democracy, and rights, but also from the concrete and place-based cultural and political practices of social movements.

Fourth, the emergence of social movements in the Third World has substantially contributed to the debates about the nature of citizenship in a world of globalization and multiculturalism.[16] While Third World societies debate reform of the state, crucial issues concerning the nature of their societies, the place of cultural difference in their national communities, the role of individual and group rights, and the overall relationship between identities, culture, and democracy have come to the fore. It is

[15] Dahrendorff (1999). Indeed, the search for a 'Third Way' must reject the very phrase "post-Cold-War era" as it is symptomatic of a narrow vision of history which takes the Cold War as the most era-defining event of world history during the second half of the twentieth century. It could easily be argued instead, that the end of formal colonialism is easily the most significant such moment.

[16] For a sample of the debates, see Beiner (1995); Sarat and Kearns (1995); Franck (1996).

important for international lawyers to understand the praxis of social movements in order to engage these debates, since international law for a post-realist, post-liberal world must de-elitize itself and remain primarily grounded in the actual struggles of the people. Instead of being seen as an aberration, popular resistance must be written into the very 'text' of international law. The purpose of this rewriting/rethinking of human rights in international law by studying it in concrete contexts of social movements is not to argue for or against rights per se. While such arguments about 'rights' as a universal category have proved to be valuable in themselves – as among critical legal theorists and critical race theorists, for example – they appear to eschew the significance of historical timing, cultural, economic, and political context and global power in evaluating the emancipatory value of the rights discourse. Indeed, by paying attention to these factors in concrete settings of social movements, I hope to offer an understanding of how place-based, concrete strategies for survival of individuals and communities in the Third World often constitute another kind of human rights, aimed at building radical alternatives to the received models of markets and democracy.

In chapter 7, I offer an analysis of the main themes that have characterized the ambiguous and sometimes contradictory relationship between the Third World and human rights discourse. The purpose of this chapter is to outline the limitations of the mainstream human-rights discourse in coming to grips with the violence of development in the Third World. In chapter 8, I offer an analysis of the different forms of Third World resistance that are ignored or are not captured by the mainstream international legal (and human rights) discourse, by introducing the category of social movements. These forms of everyday resistance and their cultural politics, I maintain, offer several radical challenges to the mainstream international law discourse, but they are not without internal inconsistencies and contradictions. I focus on four of those challenges: the ambiguous role of institutions (including the state) in resistance; the role of civil society in organizing democratic spaces; the debate about local control over property resources (paralleling and drawing from the older debates about 'permanent sovereignty over natural resources' in international law); and the problematic role of globalization. In chapter 9, I offer the case study on the WWF mentioned above.

7

Human rights and the Third World: constituting the discourse of resistance

Human rights and the Third World have always had a troubled and uneasy relationship ever since they were invented as epistemological categories at the end of the Second World War. Human-rights discourse has generally treated the Third World as object, as a domain or terrain of deployment of its universal imperatives. Indeed, the very term "human rights violation" evokes images of Third World violence – dictators, ethnic violence, and female genital mutilations – whereas First World violence is commonly referred to as "civil rights" violations. At least in this sense, "human rights" have traditionally never been universal. On the other hand, the Third World – at least that which is represented by its governments – has looked upon human rights as 'luxury goods' that they could ill afford in their march towards development and modernization or as tools of cultural imperialism intended to disrupt the 'traditional' cultures of their societies. Indeed, many non-western societies do not have words that are synonymous with human rights. In many of these societies, for ordinary people, the words "human rights" often evoke images of thieves, robbers, and criminals rather than political prisoners, torture victims, or hungry children.

While this basic disjuncture and asynchrony continue to pervade the relationship between human rights and the Third World, a new sensibility has emerged. In this new sensibility, the idea of human rights has emerged as the language of progressive politics and resistance in the Third World, *as seen by the West*. Earlier modes of postcolonial resistance to colonialism, through nationalism, non-alignment, the NIEO, Marxism and revolution appear to have faded. No other discourse, except perhaps anticolonial nationalism, has had such a stranglehold on both the imagination of progressive intellectuals as well as mass mobilization in the Third World. As Louis Henkin has termed it, we are now in an "Age of Rights."[1] This "common language of humanity"[2] is seen as the script for the spiritual and

[1] Henkin (1990). [2] As termed by Secretary-General Boutros Boutros-Ghali (1993).

material deliverance of the Third World from all of its current problems of bad governance, corruption, and all manner of violence (both public and private). In other words, for many in the West, human-rights discourse has emerged as the sole language of resistance to oppression and emancipation in the Third World.

This is a startling and remarkable turnaround. This is nowhere more evident than in the waves of social movements that have swept across the Third World – Latin America, Asia, and Eastern Europe, and to a lesser extent, Africa – at least since the 1970s.[3] These movements have not only revolved around 'traditional' identities such as class, nation, or ethnicity, they have also been organized around the 'new identities' of woman, gay and the environment. This has been noted by international law and international relations scholars who have interpreted these grassroots awakenings as evidence of the triumph of human-rights discourse and western liberal democracy. Before investigating the theoretical and practical challenges posed by these mass movements to international normative structure, I wish to begin by investigating more broadly the important themes that have traditionally characterized the relationship between the Third World and human-rights discourse. This is important in order to understand the similarities and differences between human-rights discourse and the praxis of these social movements. I do not claim that these are the only themes that have been significant in their contentious relationship. But, to the extent that generations of human-rights and international law scholars, and international institutions have pondered over, argued about, and disagreed over them, these themes provide a good entry point into an investigation of mass movements of more recent years in the Third World.

- First, there is the question of the politics of production of knowledge about human rights and the place of the Third World in it. Here I am concerned with the paradox that though the Third World is the principal arena of deployment of human-rights law, it doesn't figure at all in the origin and evolution of human-rights discourse in the mainstream tellings of the story. This "logic of exclusion and inclusion"

[3] Admittedly, traditional international lawyers do not look at social movements for evidence of legal/normative change, but, instead, focus on the proliferation of norms and institutions as "proof" that a legal revolution is occurring. Hence, this statement is intended not as an expression of how traditional international lawyers have reacted to these movements, but as an indication of how social scientists and progressive international lawyers have. For an analysis of how different categories of lawyers interpret social events in their relation to law, see Gordon (1984). With regard to international law, see Kennedy (1995).

as Professor Upendra Baxi has referred to it,[4] is a theme that needs to be traced if we are to understand the political consequences of constituting the human-rights discourse as the sole discourse of resistance.

- Second, the role of the state in human-rights discourse needs to be clarified if we are to appreciate why even many Third World governments have, over time, taken the position that all resistance (if it exists at all) must be expressed in human-rights terms to be legitimate. In particular, I am interested in investigating how human-rights discourse assisted nation-building through a process of etatization though it is commonly seen as a counter-sovereignty discourse.
- Third, the fundamental relationship between violence and human-rights discourse must be explored to figure out which types of violence are recognized as 'violations' by the human-rights discourse and which are not and why. In other words, I ask if human-rights discourse has a theory of violence and how that theory relates to development.
- Fourth, the tension between universality and cultural relativism in human-rights discourse that has become an acute arena of controversy in the last decade or so needs to be investigated more broadly. In particular, I am interested in the political economy of the relativism debate and its relationship to the East Asian 'miracle' debate, and what the consequences of accepting human-rights discourse as the sole discourse of resistance are for questioning received development practices.
- Finally, I trace the last – and so far the only – attempt made by international lawyers, to compel human-rights law to take the violence of development seriously. This, in the form of the emerging relationship between human rights and development and the well-known 'right to development,' is a story that needs to be analyzed in order to figure out if those normative aspirations would have achieved their objectives, and if not, why not.

By addressing these themes, it is hoped to expose some of the limitations of constituting human-rights discourse as the only language of moral currency and resistance for the oppressed 'social majorities' of the world. However, this does not mean that I dismiss the psychological importance of the discourse of rights for oppressed majorities or the value of deploying the rights language strategically in specific social struggles. The objective here is only to investigate and expose the risks of relying entirely on human rights as the next grand discourse of emancipation and liberation.

[4] Baxi (1998) 133.

A historiography of exclusion: colonialism and (in)visibility of the discourse

In the mainstream historiography of the human-rights discourse, the Third World's 'contribution' is seen as minimal. In this view, human-rights discourse is the result of benevolent responses by Euro-American States to the atrocities committed during the Second World War, through the framing of principles (such as Nuremberg principles), treaties and other legal documents (such as the International Bill of Rights[5] and the various Conventions relating to human rights) and institutions (such as the United Nations Commission on Human Rights and its various bodies, the European Commission and Court on Human Rights, etc.). The historiography also acknowledges, especially in recent years, the contributions made by NGOs[6] but these are usually restricted to 'Third World watchers' located in the First World such as Human Rights Watch or Amnesty International. The distinguishing character of this historiography is its emphasis on the actions taken by the states or intergovernmental organizations consisting of states such as the UN. For example, a leading text book[7] on international human-rights law deals almost entirely with the UN and says almost nothing about what happens inside different countries. So, according to this element in the historiography, international human rights resulted from the wisdom and the benevolence of Euro-American States. In essence, as Ranajit Guha has called it, this is an "elitist historiography"[8] in which the *agency* of rights-transformation is the state or statist forms such as international organizations and the *direction* of rights-transformation is ineluctably from the 'traditional' to a (Eurocentric) 'modern'. Excluded from this historiography is the role that ordinary individuals and social movements may have played.

There are at least two ways in which the Third World is displaced by the West and is made invisible in this historiography. The first (weak) version, which could be labeled liberal processualism, is offered by scholars such as Louis Sohn, Louis Henkin, and Oscar Schachter.[9] This version consists of two somewhat contradictory strands: first, whatever may have been the

[5] The International Bill of Rights includes the Universal Declaration of Human Rights, the International Covenant on Civil and Political Rights and the International Covenant on Economic, Social, and Cultural Rights.

[6] Steiner (1991); Welch (1995); Forsythe (1977, 1980). A recent comprehensive attempt is Charnowitz (1997).

[7] Lillich and Hannum (1995).

[8] See Guha (1988) 37–44.

[9] See, e.g., Sohn (1982); Henkin (1990); Schachter (1991) chapter XV.

origins of human rights, they exist because states of all political stripes have ratified them; second, nevertheless the political idea of rights derives from western natural rights theory of Locke.[10] These scholars, being mostly of an activist/pragmatist orientation, balance uneasily between their desire to root human rights in universal sovereign consent (process), and their wish to retain a genealogy that is traced back to the West.

The second (strong) version, which could be called liberal substantivism, is exemplified by scholars such as Maurice Cranston, Jack Donnelly, and Rhoda Howard.[11] According to their view, the idea of international human rights is entirely western in origin and indeed, the non-western societies had no conception of human rights whatsoever. The more sophisticated version of this argument is put forward by Jack Donnelly, who suggests that the notion of human rights was lacking in all pre-modern societies including western ones, and that they gradually evolved in response to the problems generated by the modern market and the state. As he puts it, "human rights represent a distinctive set of social practices, tied to particular notions of human dignity, that initially arose in the modern west in response to the social and political changes produced by modern states and modern capitalist market economies."[12]

As if to drive home the point, the Third World is not only seen as having contributed very little to the idea of rights, it is seen as incapable of realizing and sometimes even of banishing the very idea of rights from political practice. In the 1980s, this took the form of the argument that the new Third World bloc at the UN was "biased" against the West, against political and civil rights, and against enforcement,[13] whereas in the 1990s it took the form of cultural relativism. Notwithstanding the factual accuracy of these criticisms,[14] it reinforced extant understandings of the Third World as an anti-human-rights camp.

In both strands of this historiography, the human-rights discourse is 'untainted' not only by the Third World, it remains free of any relationship to or influence by colonialism. This complete indifference to, indeed the erasure of, colonialism in the historiography is built on the idea that the

[10] For example, Louis Henkin states: "international human rights derive from natural rights theories and systems, harking back through English, American and French constitutionalism to John Locke et al., and earlier natural rights and natural law theory" (Henkin [1990] 6).

[11] See, e.g., Cranston (1973); Donnelly (1989); Howard (1995).

[12] Donnelly (1989) 50.

[13] See Donnelly (1988); for a critique, see Rajagopal (1991).

[14] Rajagopal (1991).

'new' international law of human rights had decisively transcended the 'old' international law of sovereignty which had been tainted by, among others, colonialism.[15] Through this stratagem, human-rights discourse is offered as an emancipatory discourse of empowerment for the masses in Third World states *on the assumption that the realization of human rights will not reproduce any of the power structures related to colonialism.* To say the least, this is a problematic assumption that proves, I suggest, to be unfounded. In fact, far from being untainted by colonialism, human-rights discourse retains many elements which are directly descended from colonial ideology and practices. If this is indeed the case, constituting human-rights discourse as the sole discourse of resistance may run the risk of reproducing many of the assumptions and biases of colonial governance. One should then ask if it makes sense to allow human rights to be constituted as the only language of resistance. As examples of the colonial origins of human-rights discourse, I proffer two: the doctrine of emergency, and the rule prohibiting torture.

The doctrine of emergency and governance 'colonial style'

The ICCPR provides in article 4 that the rights mentioned in the Covenant may be suspended in a situation of national emergency, with the exception of certain 'non-derogable' rights.[16] Since the ICCPR entered into force, the doctrine of emergency has turned out to be the Achilles' heel of the human rights doctrinal corpus. International lawyers have lamented the wide latitude that this doctrine provides to authoritarian and violent regimes to commit atrocities against their citizens. Indeed, the problem is by no means restricted to some isolated countries. As the report of the UN Special Rapporteur, Mr. Leandro Despouy, put it:

> (as of 1997) some 100 States or territories – in other words, over half the Member States of the United Nations – have at some point been de jure or de facto under a state of emergency. The fact that during the same period

[15] See, e.g., Sohn (1982).

[16] Article 4 states: "1. In time of public emergency which threatens the life of the nation and the existence of which is officially proclaimed, the States Parties to the present Covenant may take measures derogating from their obligations under the present Covenant to the extent strictly required by the exigencies of the situation, provided that such measures are not inconsistent with their obligations under international law and do not involve discrimination solely on the ground of race, colour, sex, language, religion or social origin; 2. No derogation from articles 6, 7, 8 (paragraphs 1 and 2), 11, 15, 16 and 18 may be made under this provision."

> many have extended emergency measures or lifted and then reintroduced them, shows that states of emergency have been proclaimed, extended or maintained in some form much more frequently in the past dozen years or so. . . . If the list of countries which have proclaimed, extended or terminated a state of emergency in the last 12 years, as indicated in this report, were to be projected onto a map of the world, we would note with concern that the resulting area would cover nearly three-quarters of the Earth's surface and leave no geographical region unaffected. We would also note that in countries so geographically far removed, with such dissimilar legal systems, as the United States and China, or located at such polar extremes as the Russian Federation and Argentina, including such intensely conflictual regions as the Middle East, the former Yugoslavia and certain African countries, in all cases, Governments have chosen to adopt de facto (in the case of the latter countries) or de jure (in the case of the former) emergency measures in order to cope with their successive crises.[17]

These emergencies have become a standard coercive tool in the repertoire of states to maintain "law and order." These were particularly useful during the Cold War, when ideological opponents, real and imagined, were hunted down in countless regimes around the world using the pretext of the 'national security doctrine.'[18] In many of these countries, emergencies simply continued and legitimized pre-existing repressive measures and laws such as the Internal Security Act which is a standard tool in the coercive apparatuses of states, for example, in South and Southeast Asia such as India, Pakistan, Sri Lanka, Malaysia, Indonesia, and Singapore. These countries have had to live with the concrete legacies of colonialism, but very few are as violent and disruptive in their effects as the idea of emergency. Indeed, emergencies, both conceptually and practically, have prevented the realization of basic human rights to millions of people in countries around the world.

The draft article that eventually became article 4 in the ICCPR was introduced by Great Britain at the drafting stage.[19] This naturally raises the question of how and from where Britain obtained this notion of emergency. Suspension of fundamental rights in the interests of public order, national security, public health, and other matters of public interest had certainly been a standard feature of many western regimes and had been incorporated in several national constitutions. Wholesale suspension of civil liberties, occasioned by riots, war, or other public disturbances was

[17] United Nations (1997b) paragraphs 180–81.
[18] Ibid., paragraphs 3–5. [19] Nowak (1993) 76–77.

also not unknown. But it is my suggestion here that the particular concept of emergency that is brought into the human rights corpus through article 4, essentially drew its character from Britain's anticolonial wars since the 1940s and 1950s.[20] These wars, euphemistically self-styled as 'emergencies,' were conducted by the British in many of its colonies from Malaya to the Gold Coast to suppress radical anticolonial nationalist movements and to promote more moderate ones. In particular, the emergencies played a central role in the management of anticolonial nationalism in general and the role of the masses in it, in particular. The particular techniques that were developed by the British to deal with mass resistance and the concerns that drove the formulation of such techniques bear striking similarities with those adopted by Third World regimes to deal with mass resistance in their own countries using emergencies. To appreciate this, a brief discussion of at least two factors that led Britain to adopt emergency as a form of 'total rule' is necessary.

The first factor was their fear of the masses. By the 1940s, various anticolonial nationalist movements had begun attracting the support of the poor, peasants, the working class, and other deprived sections of society. This worried the colonial administrators. Though publicly proclaiming their commitment to advance the colonies to self-government, the increased participation of the masses in political activities was dismissed often as irrational and dangerous outbursts of 'nationalism.' Indeed, the very term nationalism came to acquire a pejorative connotation after the entry of the masses into politics, whereas Third World nationalism had been lauded by the progressives when it remained an indigenous-elite affair. This schizophrenia towards Third World nationalism – appreciating it as a general concept, but deriding it when it is applied against imperial rule – remained at the heart of colonial rule and could be clearly witnessed in the implementation of emergencies.

Thus, writing about the Mau Mau revolt in Kenya in December 1952, the commissioner of police in Kenya, M. S. O'Rourke initially commented positively that "it is becoming increasingly evident that a spirit of African nationalism has been born in Kenya."[21] But four months later when the colonial forces were forced onto a defensive by the Mau Mau, O'Rourke's assessment of Mau Mau had become derisive: "underlying all is a rapid

[20] My discussion here is based on the brilliant treatment of the subject by Furedi (1994). I have borrowed his thesis to develop my critique. I am also heavily influenced by Ranajit Guha's original treatment of peasant insurgencies. See Guha, "The Prose of Counter-Insurgency" in Guha and Spivak (1988) 45–88.

[21] Quoted in Furedi (1994) 111.

return to the savage and primitive which there is good reason to believe is the heart of the whole movement."[22] This fear of the 'savage' became the dominant theme in evaluating anticolonial nationalism in the Third World. Coinciding with the fear of nationalism that fascism had provoked, Third World nationalism became everything that western nationalism was not.[23] Thus, a new East–West dichotomy was invented to dismiss the fundamentally 'irrational' Third World nationalism as opposed to the 'rational' western nationalism. Thus, Hans Kohn's classic text on nationalism of the 1940s praised western nationalism as a "rational and universal concept of political liberty", "while dismissing Eastern nationalism as one that was" "basically founded on history, on monuments, on graveyards, even harking back to the mysteries of ancient times and of tribal solidarity."[24] Essentializing the atavistic nature of the natives' nationalism was crucial to colonial rule, as it enabled them to dismiss or play down the seriousness and the widespread nature of the threat their rule faced from the masses. This essentialization was expressed in a series of dualities meant to capture the differences between the East and the West that rendered Eastern masses so irrational. As Evans-Pritchard wrote in 1965:

> we are rational, primitive peoples prelogical, living in a world of dreams and make believe, of mystery and awe; we are capitalist, they are communists; we are monogamous, they are promiscuous; we are monotheists, they are fetishists, animists, pre-animists or what have you and so on.[25]

This fear and distrust of the masses was not an aberration found only in the colonial practices of the British. Rather, it reflected the intellectual dispositions in Anglo-American social sciences as well, at least from the late nineteenth century. Combined with the racist ideology of colonialism and the pragmatic need to discredit Third World resistance and prevent their labeling as 'nationalist,' this fear of the masses served as the central reason for the imposition of emergencies in the colonies.

The second factor responsible for the adoption of emergency as a policy measure by Britain in its colonies was the need to establish control over a rapidly deteriorating situation so that it could be managed and possibly

[22] Quoted in ibid.

[23] In addition to Furedi, I am also drawing on Nathaniel Berman's analysis of modernism and nationalism, as well as Edward Said here. See, e.g., Berman (1992, 1993); Said (1978).

[24] Hans Kohn, *The Idea of Nationalism* (1946) 543, quoted in Furedi (1994) 117.

[25] Evans-Pritchard (1965) 105, quoted in Furedi (1994) 120.

converted to the advantage of Britain.[26] Nationalist resistance had broken against the Empire all over the globe and the British had to deal with the challenge to their authority. They may or may not have achieved it through sheer brutality, but they chose not to rely on force alone. In this view, emergencies were not crude instruments of force that were used to preserve naked imperial power; rather, it was recognized that "force could not conserve, but it could be used to influence the outcome of change in Britain's interest."[27] The most important aspect was to present the use of force against nationalism under emergency as having very little to do with imperialism, but only with "law and order." As a major policy document of the British Colonial Office, "The problem of nationalism in the colonies" put it in July 1952:

> *Provided that we have the forces necessary*, it is well arguable that there are circumstances in which we should use them, but it is an indispensable condition of that use that it should not be for the preservation of any advantage which can be reasonably presented as imperialistic.[28]

The practice of Third World states in the postcolonial period clearly reveals the legacy of these two colonial concerns. On the one hand, the alienation of the masses from the post-independence leadership, the weakening of moral authority of the state and the necessity to tighten control of the people for developmental and national security interests, have interacted to maintain a deep suspicion of the masses. On the other hand, Third World regimes have clearly revealed their appreciation of the use of emergency measures as political tools to manage and control resistance, not simply to use it to crush dissent. For example, in countries like Sri Lanka, emergency measures have been continuously in effect for years, enabling the government to navigate its way through internal political challenges like the JVP (Janata Vimukti Peramuna) movement, in addition to the LTTE (Liberation Tigers of Tamil Eelam). At least in this sense, very little has changed since colonial times. Thus the claim of human-rights discourse to be the 'new discourse,' the sole language of resistance, has to be cautiously received with all its historical and ideological baggage.

[26] Of course, this is not how imperial – and even popular – historiography of the end of Empire interprets the events. According to that historiography, decolonization was not the result of political pressure generated by nationalist movements, but rather, the goodwill of the British. I am not discussing this here. For an extended discussion, critique, and refutation, see Furedi (1994), particularly chapter 2.

[27] Furedi (1994) 144.

[28] Written by Harold Ingrams, quoted in Furedi (1994) 143 (italics in the original).

More must be said about the political and legal effect of using the term 'emergency' as opposed to 'civil war' or 'liberation movements.' Politically the effect of using the term 'emergency' is to characterize the situation as one of 'law and order' rather than a political challenge to the regime concerned – in effect, a public relations tool.[29] Legally, the effect is to create a legal void, wherein neither the rules relating to the conduct of war (*jus in bello*) nor human rights are applicable.[30] This is because, while human rights are supposed to apply only during times of peace, and humanitarian law only during times of international or civil wars, emergencies were *sui generis*: very few, if any, international legal rules applied during those periods. Thus, while at least some legal protections may apply during civil wars – such as those mentioned in (common) article 3 of the 1949 Geneva Conventions – emergencies essentially provide a *carte blanche* to governments to violate the rights of their citizens. The appellation 'national liberation movements' has also been reserved only to the colonial contexts. Avoiding that appellation was crucial to the imperial strategy of defeating legitimate claims of independence.

This is in fact what the British aimed for when they began announcing emergencies in their colonies starting with Malaya in 1948. Their purpose was to use force to put down and (later) guide anticolonial mass movements, while keeping their violence out of international legal scrutiny. During the 1950s and early 1960s – the years of the formal dismantling of the Empire – few international legal rules applied in the colonies to protect the rights of the 'natives'. Chapter XI of the UN Charter applied only to Trust territories, not colonies. Human-rights doctrine did not apply to colonial areas or even to mandated territories.[31] As William Rappard acknowledged, the Mandate system, "it should be recalled, was not set up primarily for the protection of human rights, but for the settlement of rival political claims." The question of application of human rights had become a contested issue between the Soviets and the British during the drafting of the UDHR,[32] and due to the support received from India and several other developing country delegates, the UDHR was made applicable to member states and to "the peoples of territories under their jurisdiction," a euphemism for colonies.[33] The human-rights corpus remained pretty much in this weak form, unable/unwilling to treat

[29] Furedi (1994) 1. [30] For a discussion, see United Nations (1997b) paragraphs 7–8.
[31] Rappard (1946) 119. [32] For a fascinating account, see Morsink (1999) chapter 3.
[33] See UDHR, preamble. At the drafting stage, the Working Group also replaced "citizen" with the word "everyone" in article 21 of the UDHR to draw in the peoples living in the colonies. See Morsink (1999) 98.

colonialism as a human-rights issue, until the entry of Third World states into the UN Commission on Human Rights starting in 1967.[34] Thus, in effect, describing a situation as an emergency took it out of the ambit of law, indeed the very international sphere. Thus understood, emergencies provided Britain the interregnum necessary to 'normalize' governance, and to carry out political and economic reforms without being bothered by laws. As Sir Arthur Young, one of Britain's most senior colonial policemen with direct counter-insurgency experience in Palestine, the Gold Coast, Malaya, and Kenya, put it with regard to the Mau Mau rebellion in Kenya, "most authorities in Kenya now accept my view that the best which the Police and the Military can hope for is that they may prevent the situation getting worse and *to hold the emergency until political reforms and development can take place.*"[35]

The point is not just that the concept of emergency is illegitimate because it was 'tainted' by colonialism at its origins. Rather, the form in which Britain deployed it to combat anticolonialism has proved to be particularly enduring among postcolonial regimes in the Third World, but more perniciously, we do not even notice it anymore; colonial policies that were invented as ad hoc responses to mass resistance, have thus been made a 'natural' part of the international legal corpus. Indeed, this culture of emergency is so 'naturalized', so deeply rooted among the governing elites that it is hard to see it being shaken fundamentally anytime soon. One must then ask if the present human-rights corpus, which incorporates the concept of emergency, is fatally flawed because it perpetuates the same fear, contempt, and loathing of the masses, the same legal void that enables governments to take extreme measures without sanction, and uses the same binaries – politics v. law, national v. international – that allows it to overlook legitimate 'other' political challenges.

The prohibition of torture and the 'normalization' of pain

The second example of a legal concept that reproduces colonial structures of power and culture, is the prohibition of torture in international law, principally under article 5 of the UDHR and the Covenant against Torture and Other Inhuman or Degrading Treatment or Punishment (which reproduces and expands the UDHR definition). I shall rely on Talal Asad's

[34] I am not discussing this complex story here. For an account of the UN Commission's various stages of transformation, see Alston (1992); Alston and Crawford (2000).

[35] Furedi (1994) 144 (my italics).

recent discussion of torture[36] and Upendra Baxi's concept of 'human suffering,'[37] in elaborating on this issue. Prohibition of torture is one of the core elements of the human rights corpus, a non-derogable right, even a *jus cogens*.[38] It is also one of those rules whose normative content is seen as mostly beyond subjective disagreement – who could deny that torture is morally wrong, and culturally indefensible? In this sense, it is one of those human rights which is more 'universal' than the other rights. However, a closer look at the actual meanings that are attributed to 'torture' in human rights discourse makes it somewhat questionable if the definition of torture is indeed universal and beyond subjective disagreements, and raises the possibility that it retains a culturally–biased core of meaning that derives its substance from the colonial-era mission to civilize the natives. In addition, it also reveals the various exclusions that render the meaning of 'torture' fairly narrow and meaningless.

First, the history of the definition of torture shows that the concept is based on a colonial schizophrenia between the dual need to allow 'necessary suffering' and to outlaw 'unnecessary suffering.'[39] In this view, the colonial authorities remained outside the moral universe of suffering so that they could draw the boundaries between 'necessary' and 'unnecessary' suffering. Both these types of suffering consisted of a 'private' and a 'public' aspect. 'Necessary suffering' was usually taken to include not only acts of private individuals against themselves or each other (private), but also the violence inflicted upon the natives in the name of development and modernity, for example by forcibly conscripting the natives for war or massive development projects or by destroying local ways of life (public). 'Unnecessary suffering' included local community practices especially in the area of religion wherein individuals often inflicted mental or physical injuries upon themselves (private), as well as the standard excesses of the modern state's coercive apparatus (public). While the colonial apparatus gave undue prominence to the private aspect of 'unnecessary suffering' by outlawing it, it maintained silence towards the violence that inflicted 'necessary suffering.' Banning 'unnecessary suffering' had a dual effect: on the one hand, it stigmatized local cultural practices as 'torture,' and on

[36] Asad (1997) 111–33.
[37] Baxi (1998). See also, Baxi (1988).
[38] See article 4 of the ICCPR which mentions the prohibition against torture under article 7 as one of the non-derogable rights. See also common article 3 of the 1949 Geneva Conventions which mentions torture as one of the acts that remain prohibited 'at any time and in any place whatsoever.'
[39] I have borrowed this distinction from Baxi (1998) 132.

the other hand, it reinforced the centrality of the modern state by counterposing it to the local 'bad' practices. This stigmatization of local practices did not happen automatically but through a complicated maneuver. The colonial regimes first conceded the application of local customary law to judge such local practices, subject to some restriction based on a test of repugnancy to 'justice or morality'.[40] Then they proceeded to outlaw such practices based either on the argument that the customary law itself outlawed it, or that in any case it offended 'justice or morality'. This technique was perfected especially by the British in India (in Acts condemning Sati, Prohibition of Widows' Remarriage) and other colonies.

Striking parallels exist in the human-rights discourse, with this technique. For example, article 63 (3) of the European Convention on Human Rights provides a ground for derogation from human-rights norms on the basis of culture, which states that "(t)he provisions of this Convention shall be applied in (colonial territories) with due regard, however, to local requirements." Interpreting this, the European Court of Human Rights has held in the *Tyrer* case that corporal punishment is violative of the Convention, despite local acceptance in the Isle of Man.[41] One can readily see the colonial techniques at work here.[42]

Second, the actual meaning of torture has a serious statist bias that makes it clear that certain types of violence committed by the state are more easily tolerated by the human-rights discourse, even as it expands the meaning of 'torture' to include mental pain and other types of injuries. It is now well known, after feminist critiques, that the definition of torture is built on the public–private divide in that it recognizes only acts by public officials in their official capacity as torture, and not those by private individuals against each other, such as domestic violence.[43] This statist bias in the definition of torture makes the definition less important than who's being tortured, for what purpose and who's in charge of the state. This is important as many acts of violence that may qualify as 'torture' – such as repeated denial of food and water to vulnerable populations,

[40] Talal Asad cites James Read: "... customary laws could hardly be repugnant to the traditional sense of justice or morality of the community which still accepted them, and it is therefore clear that the justice or morality of the colonial power was to provide the standard to be applied" Asad (1997) 118.

[41] *Tyrer v. United Kingdom*, E.C.H.R., Series A, No.26 (1978).

[42] For a discussion of this, see Rajagopal (1998).

[43] See MacKinnon (1993) 21. For a reverse argument that the 'private' may provide women refuge and protection from the state, see Engle (1993) 143. See also Abu-Odeh (1992).

causing malnutrition, diseases, and sometimes death – escape the normative embrace simply because they are 'private' (that is, there is no 'right') or because they are 'necessary suffering'. Indeed, at least since 'torture' entered the western political vocabulary two centuries ago, it has been recognized that outlawing 'torture' would not outlaw all suffering, and prevent the state from applying necessary force for carrying out its 'legitimate' functions, whether they be law enforcement or forcible displacement of populations for development. As a US State Department Report on Human Rights put it with respect to Israel's notorious policy of using force on Palestinian detainees: "torture is forbidden by Israeli law ... In 1987 the Landau Judicial Commission specifically condemned 'torture' but allowed for 'moderate physical and psychological pressure' to be used to secure confessions and to obtain information."[44] This distinction, between causing grievous injury and 'moderate physical and psychological pressure' persists in the imagination of international lawyers and activists themselves.

Given the ubiquity of the recourse to extra-legal violence by state agents in many Third World countries – to obtain confessions, to maintain discipline in prisons, or simply out of sadism – this is a recipe for disaster. This statist bias in defining torture reveals clearly that the violence of development against the poor, the violence against women or other 'invisible' groups, does not count as torture, thus rendering the meaning of torture too narrow.

Third, the language in article 5 of the UDHR and article 7 of the ICCPR essentially reproduces the language from the US Constitution.[45] While this in itself does not take away the 'universal' quality of the norm in question, it does raise questions about what sort of interpretive tools are used in construing 'torture,' who is doing the interpretation, and whether subjective notions and cultural biases enter the human-rights discourse through those interpretive acts. Given the predominance of US-based scholarship in setting the contours of human-rights discourse, the possibility that torture may be interpreted more in accordance with American cultural norms can not be ruled out.

[44] US Department of State, Country Reports on Human Rights Practices for 1993 at 1204, quoted in Asad (1997) 120–21. The notorious practice of 'shaking' by Israeli security forces during interrogations, has been recently held by the Israeli Supreme Court to be unconstitutional. See "Israel Court Bans Most Use of Force in Interrogations," September 7, 1999, Tuesday, Section A, Page 1, Column 6, *New York Times*.

[45] US Constitution, Amendment VIII.

The purpose of defining 'torture' is not to include every conceivable pain and suffering. There are many types of pain – for sexual pleasure, sports, religion, etc. – that are not thought of as 'torture.' Nevertheless, while defining torture, care must be taken not to exclude significant sources of pain and suffering, since 'torture' will then be nothing more than a partial, fragmented concept with limited appeal. For the ordinary people, and various excluded groups in the Third World who are victims of the violence committed by the state in the name of modernization and development, it is not a consolation to be told that their suffering and injuries cannot constitute a violation of a 'non-derogable right.' My purpose here has been to show, through these examples, that there are some basic problems in constituting the human-rights discourse as the sole discourse of resistance in the Third World, because it remains caught up in the discursive formations of colonialism that makes it blind to many types of violence. In this sense, at least, there is no 'break' from an old international law of states to a new international law of individuals.

The political consequences of (in)visibility

What are the consequences of the invisibility of many types of violence? In addition to the obvious practical consequence that unrecognized forms of violence are in effect 'authorized' to continue, at the level of the production of the human-rights discourse, there are serious political consequences. A principal factor behind this must be recognized at the outset: the leading role given to the state in the realization of human rights inside states. An example would be the 1993 Vienna Declaration on human rights at the World Conference on Human Rights, which states that the promotion and protection of human rights is the "first responsibility of Governments." Or the International Bill of Rights which states in article 2 that "each State party... undertakes to respect and to ensure to all individuals within its territory and subject to its jurisdiction the rights recognized in the present covenant..." It is axiomatic in human-rights theory that the state is the primary duty-holder against its citizens who are the primary rights-holders. This suffers from two serious flaws. First, this notion is built on the moral possibilities of the state.[46] Given the bloody history of almost all states in the area of treatment of their own citizens, this is a naive, if not a dangerous hope. Despite a plausible argument that the above notion is based on a respect for autonomy and independence, there is no

[46] I discuss and critique this in the next section.

reason why the line had to drawn around the idea of the state; it could, for example, have been drawn around local communities, whether national, ethnic, or issue-based.

The second flaw in the notion of the centrality of the state is the immediate association this idea has had with the doctrine of sovereignty. Given the colonial origins of the doctrine of sovereignty, this itself was a problematic move, especially for postcolonial societies.[47] But this also had the effect of reducing international human-rights activism to reactive, negative, and symbolic actions such as lodging of protests instead of forging genuine and meaningful links with like-minded actors in other countries. As a result, a critical weakness of the received historiography of human rights is the predominant role given to the state where it is looked upon not only as the source of the normative framework, but also as the implementer of that framework. This has enabled it to ignore the existence of protest or resistance movements inside societies that could themselves have constituted the source of the normative framework. So, despite its nominal anti-sovereignty posture, human rights discourse as it exists today, is a state-centered one.

This elitist and statist historiography ignores the existence of human rights activities and movements inside various countries, either in the form of social movements in the nineteenth and early twentieth centuries, or the various independence movements in colonized societies since the nineteenth century. Indeed, no human-rights textbook discusses these movements, including even the antiapartheid movement in South Africa or the civil-rights movement in the US. For example, leading textbooks on human-rights law[48] do not offer readings on major social movements and the role of law and courts in those movements, but, instead, focus solely on the pronouncements of the UN and intergovernmental bodies. Even as the human-rights discourse ignores the role played by anticolonial movements, mainstream international lawyers rarely discuss colonialism and its attendant abuses anymore. It is well worth noting that while countries have apologized for the Holocaust, and reparations are being paid for past abuses to Jewish communities and Korean 'comfort' women, no country has apologized for slavery, colonialism, or racism, nor has any mention of reparations been made. The President of the UNGA has drawn

[47] Anghie (1996).

[48] Lillich and Hannum (1995). Even a progressive textbook such as Steiner and Alston (1996) represents human rights discourse as principally institutional, with almost no mention of anticolonial resistance as human rights praxis.

attention to this recently.[49] Of course, the European countries formally apologized for slave trade at the Durban antiracism summit in September 2001 whereas the dialogue about reparations for slavery has now culminated in a range of law suits against US corporations, and taken on new dimensions including Third World debt and globalization.[50]

Another consequence of the elitist historiography at the level of production of knowledge is a certain racist ideal-type of what constitutes a valid human-rights 'voice.' In essence, this means that a valid human-rights 'voice' – one that can authoritatively comment on and criticize human-rights problems – is implicitly taken to be 'western,' and 'white.' Third World 'voices,' in this view, do not command the authority to speak. In my own personal experience as a human-rights activist, this reality has confronted me frequently. A common version of this 'voice-constituting' is found in media attributions to 'western observers' in stories that deal with Third World human-rights problems. These media reports cite local or non-western human rights activists only if they cannot find a western 'voice.' Even when they do cite a non-westerner, those voices are sometimes miraculously transformed into 'western' voices. I have, for example, been cited as a 'western observer.' Having 'lived in the west' (in my case for less than two years then) gave me a moral standing to be a human-rights activist, according to the former Director of the UNCOHCHR.[51] Other manifestations of this racism include ignoring the presence of or comments made by local or non-western individuals in meetings, a phenomenon similar to sexist practices of ignoring women's voices in meetings. These phenomena, while mostly invisible and at an individual level, have serious consequences on who gets to speak for human rights, and consequently what gets spoken about as human rights. The systematic discrediting of a non-western contribution to human rights is one of the major reasons for this latter phenomenon. Given this, the present fetishism of human rights and constituting it as the sole discourse of resistance in the Third World, appears highly problematic unless (and

[49] Slavery: UN Leader Wants Apology To Africa, UN Wire, UN Foundation, September 16, 1999. He expressed the view that descendants of slave traders and colonists should apologize to African nations, and that African treasures and artifacts that were looted must be returned. See also BBC On-line, September 15, 1999.

[50] See United Nations (2001a). On lawsuits against US corporations for slave trade, see "Companies are Sued for Slave Reparations," *New York Times* (March 27, 2002).

[51] I base these examples on my professional experience with the United Nations in Combodia between 1992–97.

until) the process of production of human-rights discourse overcomes these problems.

Human rights and etatization: floundering on the moral possibilities of the state

The second theme that needs to be analyzed to determine the benefits and risks of constituting the human rights discourse as the sole discourse of resistance in the Third World, is the role of the state in the realization of human-rights. There is perhaps no other issue that is more discussed and less understood than this issue of the role of the state in human-rights discourse. A cobweb of myths and half-truths continues to complicate the debate in this area, partly due to the lack of agreement between human-rights scholars as to what constitute human rights – for example, are economic and social rights really rights? – and partly due to disagreements among economists and policy makers over the role of the state in the economy – should the state be a minimalist 'market-friendly' state, or an expansionist welfare state? While these debates are important, they suffer from a common schizophrenia and ambivalence: a deep suspicion of sovereignty and state on the one hand (conflating them in that process), and a total reliance on the moral possibilities of the state on the other. That is, while the human-rights discourse celebrates the retreat of the state, the realization of human rights is predicated on the expansion of the state. This is nowhere more evident than in the debate over which set of rights – political and civil or economic, social, and cultural, – takes precedence. Before tracing the contours of that debate, a central myth concerning the role of the state in human rights discourse must be dispelled.

The biggest such myth is that human rights is an anti-state discourse. According to this minimalist version – of the kind offered by the likes of Robert Nozick and Friedrich Hayek – since a state must abstain from interfering with the pre-political rights of individuals such as property, more rights must necessarily mean less state. While this view of human rights is common in popular imagination and policy analyses, mainstream human-rights scholars do not support such a view. Louis Henkin, Jack Donnelly, and Philip Alston, for example, expressly recognize that a welfare state providing worker benefits is as important as freedom of assembly. These scholars expressly or implicitly consider human rights discourse to be based on a theory of justice – such as that of John

Rawls' – that compels the state to protect the human rights of all its citizens including economic and social rights.

For example, Henkin states: "Inevitably, international human rights also implicate the purposes for which governments are created, but they surely do not imply a commitment to government for limited purposes only. Born after various forms of socialism were established and spreading, and commitment to welfare economics and the welfare state was nearly universal, international human rights implied rather a conception of government as designed for all purposes and seasons. The rights deemed to be fundamental included not only limitations precluding government from invading civil and political rights, but positive obligations for government to promote economic and social well-being, implying government that is activist, intervening, planning, committed to economic-social programs for the society that would translate into economic-social rights for the individual."[52] Similarly, Jack Donnelly, after analyzing the division of human rights into two sets of rights, states: "The categorical moral arguments against economic and social rights simply do not stand up to scrutiny. And with the rejection of such arguments, the conventional dichotomy also falls, for I am aware of no other positive arguments for it."[53]

Thus, the frequent misunderstanding that mainstream human-rights discourse is somehow opposed in principle to the acceptance of economic, social, and cultural rights must be put to rest. It is not that the latter rights are equally 'respected' in practice, or that more could not be done to protect them. But it must be recognized that at the level of discourse, it is not accurate to charge, as some critics continue to do, that the mainstream neglects one set of rights or treats them as inferior.[54] Contrary to that, the buzzword in mainstream rights discourse is "interdependence and indivisibility" of rights, and it has been evolving towards that position at least since the 1970s.[55]

The belief that more rights must mean less state confuses – and conflates – the concept of state with the concept of sovereignty. Whether it is an exaggeration to say, as Henkin claims, that "the move from state values to human values, from a liberal state system to a welfare system . . . is undeniable, irresistible, irreversible," it must be conceded that

[52] Henkin (1990) 6–7. [53] Donnelly (1989) 34. [54] Kausikan (1993), Sunstein (1997).

[55] See, UNGA Res.32/130, and then a long list of UNGA resolutions, starting at the 41st GA as a separate agenda item.

a half-century ago, what most states did to their citizens was their own business. In that sense, the ability to cordon off "internal affairs" of states from external scrutiny – a central aspect of sovereignty – has eroded. It is not true, however, that the state and its mechanisms that wield sovereign power internally have also eroded. On the contrary, the last half-century has witnessed a certain 'etatization' of the world, viz., the proliferation of state functionaries, the bureaucracy (what Hannah Arendt calls "the rule by Nobody") intended to create and thereby constrain rights. The development of human-rights discourse has been central to this 'etatization' of our social lives. A strong and vigorous state is not only seen as a prerequisite to the protection of civil and political rights – such as right to fair trial – it is also seen as essential to protect economic and social rights – such as the right to be free from hunger. The importance of 'public action' to protect human rights[56] is, in this view, translated into a formula for the expansion of states and the ruling class. More importantly, the last fifty years have seen the emergence of an enormous international bureaucracy that has significant power over the lives of global citizenry, without any democratic accountability.

This confusion between the concepts of state and sovereignty can be tackled if sovereignty is understood in a Foucaultian sense to mean governmentality, that is, the ability to govern.[57] Human-rights discourse very much rests on this understanding of sovereignty, and its corollary, an expansionary state. Understood in this way, it becomes clearer why Third World states have generally not objected to human-rights discourse at a conceptual level (though they did object at an ideological level), except in the context of East Asia, after the success of their economies made them believe that a 'Third way' was possible.[58] In other words, contrary to popular wisdom, Third World states were not the obstinate opponents of human rights from the beginning, that were dragged kicking and screaming by western states to embrace human rights, as is commonly believed. Rather, through much of the post-WWII history, Third World states have embraced human rights as the sole discourse of resistance in their countries, as seen through their posture at the international level. This was mainly due to the fact that the

[56] On public action, see Dreze and Sen (1989).

[57] As Foucault puts it, distinguishing between sovereignty and government: "To govern, then, means to govern things." See Foucault (1991) 94.

[58] I expand on this theme, the relationship between cultural relativism and the East Asian miracle, in the following sections.

human rights discourse enables the expansion of the state and the sphere of governance.

For example, if we take the much-discussed division between civil and political versus economic, social, and cultural rights, it transpires that through much of the post-WWII period, the western and Third World states have agreed on the essential logic behind the division between these sets of rights, as well as the vision of the state that lay behind such division. In this aspect, the differences between them were not due to some cultural division based on, for example, the greater compatibility between Asian values of community and the obligation-based economic and social rights. As Farroukh Jhabvala points out, no delegation deprecated the importance of economic, social, and cultural rights at the drafting stage of the International Covenant on Economic, Social and Cultural Rights (ICESCR) and in fact many Western countries such as UK, France, and Canada declared that both sets of rights were equally important.[59] This was hardly surprising since the vision of the welfare state that is implicit in human-rights theory was attractive to all states, especially the newly independent ones which saw nation-building in terms of strengthening of the state. Nonetheless, all these delegations favored two covenants because the implementation of economic and social rights was seen to require positive state action whereas the implementation of civil and political rights was thought to require only legislative and administrative measures that could be readily enacted. But, as Jhabvala and Henry Shue have convincingly shown, protection of both sets of rights requires vigorous public action by the state organs.[60] In this sense, guaranteeing the right to a fair trial may take as much state intervention and may be as costly as the elimination of hunger. On the other hand, guaranteeing a 'positive' right such as freedom from hunger may sometimes entail only a 'negative' obligation of the state, for example by not compelling farmers to substitute cash crops for subsistence crops.

As I suggest later, this division into two sets of rights was inevitable given the fact that the human-rights ideology was based on a fully participating *homo oeconomicus* who had to be accommodated into both capitalist and communist economic systems. The only common ground of agreement between western and Third World states, then, was etatization. A concrete result of this is that the implementation of social and economic rights, no less than civil and political rights, creates, in the first instance, the apparatus of modernity, viz., the bureaucracy, that rations freedom

[59] See Jhabvala (1987) 296. [60] Ibid. passim. See also Shue (1996).

as largesse to the "poor" and the "illiterate." For instance, implementing right to health puts the focus on an increase in the number of medical staff rather than on the processes of actual healing itself, for example by strengthening traditional systems. In this sense, human-rights discourse simply becomes a point of insertion for new state programs and interventions that expand the power of governmentality, in a Foucaultian sense. Human-rights discourse is, in this sense, yet another part of the continuing etatization of social life. As Dutkiewicz and Shenton put it in the African context with respect to etatization in Africa:

> ... like corruption, inefficiency in establishing and managing state enterprises, financial institutions, import and exchange rate policies, and development projects, rather than preventing the social reproduction of this ruling group, was an absolute prerequisite for it ... The completion, or, in a rational capitalistic sense, the efficient operation of such parastatals or development projects, would have obviated the need to generate further plans and projects to achieve the ends which their predecessors failed to do. *In this sense, inefficiency was "efficient," efficient for the expanded reproduction of the ruling group.* One result of this was the geometric expansion of a poorly skilled and corrupt lower level bureaucracy incapable of fulfilling even its few professional obligations, itself fuelled by academics and others who saw the solution to every problem in the creation of yet another position or agency to deal with it and to employ more of their own number.[61]

This means that mainstream human-rights discourse is incapable of understanding a claim for liberty that is not cognizable within this apparatus of modernity. The moral possibilities of the state then, in this view, function to constrain the range of human rights that can actually be realized. This view suffers from an over-reliance on the state as the essential instrument of social change, especially in the context of the present Third World where there is a general loss of faith in the state as a moral and political agent.

This is not an easy dilemma. On the one hand, it is undeniable that public action of some kind is essential to establish respect for many basic rights – from eliminating hunger to providing personal security. On the other hand, emphasizing the predominant role of the state in the realization of human rights simply reproduces the same structures that have prevented the realization of those rights in the first place. The challenge

[61] See Dutkiewicz and Shenton (1986) 111 (emphasis added).

for us then is to imagine futures in which human rights can be protected through mechanisms and structures that do not replicate and increase etatization. In other words, is it possible to think of public action that does not depend entirely on traditional state structures to be carried out?

Human rights and the economic model of violence

The third theme in the constitution of human-rights discourse as the sole discourse of resistance in the Third World is its relationship to violence. Here I am interested in investigating whether human rights discourse has a comprehensive theory of violence that provides remedies to victims that would justify its constitution as the sole discourse of resistance. If there are forms of violence that are not 'visible' to human-rights discourse, then it may not be advisable to rely on it as the only discourse of resistance. To begin, it must be noted at the outset that the term violence is not known to international law or politics, as Louis Henkin has put it.[62] While traditional international law dealt primarily with inter-state conflict through the law of war, the law of peace traditionally dealt with the cooperative aspect of relations between states. After the establishment of the UN and the emergence of human-rights discourse in the post-WWII period, international law has begun regulating other types of violence, including violence in the 'public sphere' (state violence against its own citizens), and, recently, violence in the 'private sphere' (such as mass rape, domestic violence, etc.). The impetus for the latter type of regulation has come from women scholars and activists, strengthened by the emergence of a feminist approach to international law.[63] These scholars have criticized the public–private divide that enabled traditional international law to treat certain forms of violence against women as private and therefore beyond the reach of international law and within the domestic jurisdictions of states.[64]

While the types of violence that are regulated by international law have expanded, human-rights discourse – under whose banner this expansion has occurred – maintains a highly ambivalent relationship to the use of violence in general. First, though it is commonly (mis)understood to

[62] Henkin (1997).

[63] Ibid. 576. On feminist approaches to international law, see Charlesworth et al. (1991).

[64] For feminist critiques of the public–private divide, see Romany (1993); Charlesworth (1992).

be a pacifist philosophy, under the human rights discourse it is clearly legitimate for the state to use violence to protect the rights of its citizens. Indeed, human rights discourse imposes obligations upon the state to use violence in order to secure basic rights – such as rights to life, personal liberty, physical security, equality, freedom of religion, or 'compulsory' education. As Upendra Baxi aptly puts it, "the discourse about rights is in this sense always, and everywhere, the discourse concerning justified violence."[65]

It is then imperative to recognize – contrary to popular misconceptions – that human-rights discourse is not based on a theory of non-violence. Rather, it approves certain forms of violence and disapproves certain other forms. For example, the mass deportation of 1.5 million people from Phnom Penh by the Khmer Rouge in 1975 is argued to be a crime against humanity, while the mass eviction/deportation of 33 million development refugees from their homes due to development projects such as dams, by the Indian Government, is simply seen as the 'social cost' (if at all) of development.[66] It is unfortunately true that violence committed in the name of development remains 'invisible' to the human-rights discourse. The question then becomes: does human-rights discourse have a theory that justifies, or provides the basis for this selective approval of some forms of violence?

The answer is that human-rights discourse does not really have a theory that justifies this selective seclusion of some forms of violence, even though it relies upon the familiar division between the two sets of rights to justify treating some rights as more important. *This is because the division of two sets of rights is not itself based on a theory that is internal to the human-rights discourse*, but, rather, reflects the dominant understandings of the role of the state in the economy which are derived from the development discourse. According to one strand of this understanding, the state – as the motor of economic development – needs to engage in repression of political and civil rights in order to guarantee economic and social rights or simply, development. This so-called 'trade-off thesis' justifies "developmental repression" as Jack Donnelly has termed it.[67] The other strand of this understanding would instead allow a narrowly formulated set of political and civil rights while ignoring structural factors such as income inequality, skewed distribution of land, and intense poverty. While I will discuss this in detail in the last section of this chapter, I should draw

[65] Baxi (1991) 163.
[66] The figure of 33 million comes from Roy (1999).
[67] Donnelly (1989) 188.

an important conclusion of my analysis here: human-rights discourse can ignore/condone certain forms of violence, not because it is justified by the division of rights or the principle of 'progressive realization' in ICESCR;[68] rather, it can do so because it is pathologically wedded to the two models of the state in the economy that are reflected in the human-rights discourse. Both are derived from the development discourse.

In addition, though human-rights discourse now appears to have expanded to embrace 'private' forms of violence in the family for instance, it remains aloof from the 'private' violence of the market on individuals and communities. This tendency has become more pronounced in an era of globalization and privatization wherein the march of the market is celebrated unreservedly. This is not new – after all, use of the criminal process and violence to maintain rights to private property has always been legitimate in human-rights law, even if the interference that caused such violence was occasioned by extreme deprivations of food or shelter.[69]

Examples of the blindness of the human-rights discourse to the violence of the market abound. Thus, the Bhopal gas tragedy in 1984 in India was never treated as a human-rights issue by the UN or human-rights NGOs though thousands of innocent civilians lost their lives and thousands more were affected by the gas leak from the Union Carbide plant. Indeed, even now, as the case winds its way through American courts again, the human-rights community is hardly engaged on ensuring delivery of justice to victims. Second, although the International Law Commission's original draft articles on international crimes mentioned dumping of toxic wastes as an international crime, the recent discourse on international criminal law appears to have conveniently 'overlooked' this. From the perspective of those who are affected by the dumping of toxic wastes – who are mostly poor, marginalized communities in the Third World or racial minorities in the First World – it is inconceivable how this mass crime differs from the other mass crimes that are becoming the staple of international criminal law. In essence, economic violence – that is, violence caused by the market – is treated as out of bounds of human-rights law, even as it attempts to assert itself as the sole liberatory discourse in the Third World.

[68] The principle of 'progressive realization' in ICESCR is the fuzzy legal yardstick by which the states agree to be monitored in their respect of the rights mentioned in that covenant. This should be contrasted to the 'immediate' and binding commitments made by states under the ICCPR.

[69] Baxi (1998) 164.

Explaining the economic model of violence in international law: homo oeconomicus *and the principle of scarcity*

These disciplinary blind spots in international human-rights discourse to the violence of development and the market must be explained from a broader perspective, in particular, from the perspective of international law of which it is a part. I begin by asking: why was/is international law oblivious to the violence of development and what does it tell us about the relationship between law and violence as well as between law and resistance?[70]

There were at least three reasons why international law was/is oblivious to the violence of development. The first reason had to do with the very nature of law in the international society and its relationship to violence. International law has always been under the shadow of violence and, in fact, under the danger of being overwhelmed by it. This is not unusual, since as Hannah Arendt points out, the very substance of violent action is ruled by the means–end category where the end is always in danger of being overwhelmed by the means that is needed to reach it.[71] This is particularly so with regard to international law where the doctrine of sovereignty, understood in the Austinian sense of that repository of organized force, has been the fundamental organizing principle. This gives rise to a paradoxical situation whereby the exercise of violence by the sovereign, whether internally or externally, is an essential attribute of its very definition on the one hand; but on the other hand, every exercise of that act of violence undermines the end of establishing a community based on values of mutual respect and accommodation. This is nothing but a retelling of that old problem in international law: how to establish order in a world of sovereign states. But at a deeper level, this is a problem faced by law in general: on the one hand law needs to constitute itself as the "other" of violence to be legitimate;[72] on the other hand, it needs to use violence instrumentally to preserve power. The contradictions created by this paradox become part of the constant crises of law. It hardly needs to be emphasized that in development, as in international law, the means are always in danger of overwhelming the ends.

Second, the emphasis on political order and state-building in Third World countries in the 1950s and 1960s meant that any resistance to

[70] This section is drawn from Rajagopal (1999a). [71] Arendt (1970) 4.

[72] This is partly because it takes confrontation outside the law to make law itself, as pointed out by David Apter. See Apter (1997) 3.

the state or its developmental activities was seen as anti-national. This inevitably followed from the establishment of development as the *raison d'etat* of newly independent countries. As Ashis Nandy puts it, "when after decolonization, the indigenous elites acquired control over the state apparatus, they quickly learnt to seek legitimacy in a native version of the civilizing mission and sought to establish a similar colonial relationship between state and society. They found excellent justification for this in the various theories of modernization floating around in the post World War II period."[73] This constituted a shift in international law from resolving the problems created by bad nationalism (Versailles model) through a focus on self-determination and democratic peace to the opportunities created by good nationalism (International Economic Institutions model) through a focus on nation-building and development.

This was aided in the anticolonial climate of that period by the radical writings by Franz Fanon, Jean-Paul Sartre, and others who began to glorify the role of violence in the cause of anti-imperialism and radical Third World nationalism which encouraged violence against suspected internal class enemies. As Sartre said in the preface to *The Wretched of the Earth*, "in order to fight against us the former colony must fight against itself; or rather, the two struggles form part of a whole. In the heat of battle, all internal barriers break down; the puppet bourgeoisie of businessmen and shopkeepers, the urban proletariat, which is always in a privileged position, the *lumpenproletariat* of the shanty towns – all fall into line with the stand made by the rural masses, that veritable reservoir of a national revolutionary army; for in those countries where colonialism has deliberately held up development, the peasantry when it rises, quickly stands out as the revolutionary class. For it knows naked oppression, and suffers far more from it than the workers in the towns, and in order not to die of hunger, it demands no less than a complete demolishing of all existing structures."[74]

In the context of many Marxist revolutions in Indo-China and Latin America in the 1970s where all existing structures were 'smashed,' the role of violence gained in reputation in domestic affairs among the Left, even as it was becoming dubious in international relations.[75] According to this view, the violence of the revolution was intended to get rid of imperialism and provide the basis for nation-building through development, based on the model of state-led growth. Therefore, for the Third World elites, the battle against underdevelopment – including that waged within

[73] Nandy (1992) 269. [74] See Fanon (1963) 11. [75] A point made by Arendt (1970) 11.

the parameters of leftist dependency theory – justified high human and social costs. This convergence of development, the nationalist project, and the violence of the state proved devastating for the populations of the Third World countries who were the targets of revolutions and then development.

The effects of this convergence of the ideologies of national liberation, state-building, and development could be seen on several fronts in international law; the confinement of the principle of self-determination to the colonial context and its external aspect; the doctrine of *uti possidetis*, especially in Africa, which enabled international law to ignore all movements for cultural/territorial autonomy; the doctrine of Permanent Sovereignty over Natural Resources (PSNR) which focused attention on the issue of source of control over exploitation of resources, rather than on how just the exploitation itself was; the distinction in humanitarian law between 'refugees' and 'displaced persons,' that denies legal protection to development refugees and condones massive population displacements; and finally – as discussed above – the exclusion of economic violence carried out under the banner of modernization and development from the human-rights discourse.

The third reason why international law has remained oblivious to the violence of the development encounter is because of the inherent limitations of what I have called the market or economic model of resistance that international law sanctions through the doctrine of human rights. In particular, I have suggested that the "human" in human rights is the *homo oeconomicus*, the modern market being who is possessed of full rationality, and whose attempt to realize his/her full potentialities are confined within the moral possibilities of the state and the material conditions of the global market. Therefore, certain forms of resistance to the dominance of the modern market or the state are inherently incapable of being subsumed under the banner of human rights. Further, I also suggest that the idea of *homo oeconomicus* is based on the idea of scarcity, which is used to legitimize a particular and dominant role of the state in the economy. The result of this is the infliction of myriad forms of violence on individuals and communities which remain out of the bounds of the human-rights discourse which treats those forms of violence as 'normal' and 'necessary' to the task of governance.

The most visible aspect of this marketization of freedom is the division between the two sets of rights – civil and political versus economic, social, and cultural – that is codified in the form of two covenants, the ICCPR and the ICESCR. This much discussed North–South division between the two sets of rights was not due to some cultural division based on, for example, the greater compatibility between Asian values of community and the obligation-based economic and social rights. Nor was it because of some inherent opposition to economic and social rights from Western countries or to political and civil rights from the Third World countries. Rather, it was because of a conception of human rights, shared equally by Western and Third World countries, in which the state was seen as the active provider of the "goods" that constituted the core of economic and social rights.

Indeed this division into two sets of rights was inevitable given the fact that the human-rights ideology was based on a fully participating *homo oeconomicus* who had to be accommodated into both capitalist and communist economic systems, faithfully reflected in the division between the two sets of rights. The only common ground of agreement then, was etatization as already noted. As such, certain economic functions of the state began to be seen as natural – provision of law and order, creation and extension of infrastructure, etc. – and if substantial violence needed to be used to perform those functions, human-rights discourse did not oppose it. Indeed, far from opposing it, it was built on the expectation that 'necessary' forms of violence needed to be perpetrated by the state on some to secure human rights for some others.

This means that mainstream human-rights discourse is incapable of understanding a claim for liberty that is not cognizable within this apparatus of modernity, viz., the bureaucracy. Such claims are periodically made by cultural revivalist and anti-modern movements that seek to realize, for example, their own rights to health and education, as well as dispute resolution mechanisms that are not based on the hospital, the school, and the court. Within the human-rights universe, there is no space for such pluriverse.[76]

A crucial reason for this is the economic thinking that underlies our political discourse of rights.[77] The basic concept of this economic thinking is that of scarcity, which means "the technical assumption that man's wants are great, not to say infinite, whereas his means are limited though improvable. The assumption implies choices over the allocation of means (resources). This 'fact' defines the 'economic problem' par excellence, whose 'solution' is proposed by economists through the market or the

[76] I have borrowed the term 'pluriverse,' from Esteva and Prakash (1998).
[77] See Bowles and Gintis (1986).

plan."[78] The concept of scarcity is at the heart of development even though it has been shown by Marshall Sahlins, among others, to be absent in cultures wherein non-economic assumptions govern lives.[79]

This concept of scarcity also firmly governs the human-rights discourse, through rights such as the 'right to a better standard of living' or the 'right to employment'. The 'right to a better standard of living' is not only located within a dynamic of a perpetual "catching-up" by the Third World with the West (because it is based on the consumption of modern goods such as roads, telephones, faxes, etc., by the World Bank and other gate-keepers of global standards), it also makes it legitimate for the state to increase its size in order to implement that right. The 'right to employment' is similarly predicated on participation in a modern formal economy, as it refuses to recognize the value of labor in the informal economy or the family. Agitating simply for a 'right to employment,' then, creates the moral and material basis for absorption into the institutional structures of the state and the market and could therefore hardly constitute progressive politics for Third World lawyers in the context of early twenty-first-century global capitalism. The point is not that better living standards should be opposed or that right to employment is a bad idea; rather, I suggest that the questions we should be asking are: what sort of living standards are being talked about, whose living standards are they and what are they measured against? Who has the responsibility to define and realize those standards? What should the role of public policy be? Are constantly rising living standards sustainable environmentally? Raising these questions will inevitably focus attention on the nature of the social changes that are intended by these rights, and the role of the state, international institutions, and the market in securing those changes. Instead of this, the present human-rights discourse is based on a limited and somewhat outdated concept of scarcity that serves only one result: it strengthens the role of the state, makes particular roles of the state, the market and international institutions seem "natural" in the development process and legitimizes the use of violence by the state to secure certain preconceived ends.

If many economic and social rights, such as employment, are based on the concepts of civilization and scarcity, and are explicitly seen to warrant and legitimize particular configurations of international institutions, national authorities, and the market, civil and political rights are no better. Many of those rights – such as rights to assemble, organize, fair

[78] See Esteva (1992) 19. [79] Sahlins (1972).

trial, freedom of information, freedom from arbitrary detention, etc. – are based on the existence of state officials from police and prison officials to judges, prosecutors and defenders, thus justifying a substantial level of etatization, which makes the extension of the market to the remotest areas possible.[80]

Reversing the ambivalent and contradictory relationship between the human-rights discourse and violence is a long and complex task. But a process of disciplinary introspection must begin by asking and answering several key questions: should human-rights discourse have a theory of violence and what principles should that theory be based on? What sorts of violence are visible to the discourse and what sorts of violence are not visible? If some types of violence are less visible, is this due to a 'class bias' against poor and marginalized communities? In particular, why is the violence of development, which has claimed and has continued to claim millions of 'victims,' never as visible as some other types of violence? Can human-rights discourse go on relying on the state as the guarantor of economic and social rights which may simply legitimize the role of the state in development? How can human rights discourse come to terms with the fact that *it is the process of bringing development that has caused serious human-rights violations* among the deprived sections of Third World peoples? Instead of asking these critical questions, mainstream human-rights discourse labels itself progressive for a facile support of a 'welfare' state in an age of market fetishism and globalization. If one is not careful, this may simply end up relegitimizing violent forms of state interventions in many Third World societies.

Developmentalization and the turn to culture

The most fierce debates in human-rights law today are, as Makau Mutua has noted, over culture.[81] From the Chinese "White Paper"[82] to the Bangkok Declaration of Asian governments prior to the 1993 Vienna Conference[83] to the Cairo declaration of human rights in 1990 by the OIC,[84] governments of various political stripes and religious persuasions have declared their dissatisfaction with the universalist language of

[80] For the argument that the market system emerged as a result of deliberate and often violent interventions by the state, see Polanyi (1944).

[81] Mutua (1996a).

[82] See Human Rights in China, Information Office of State Council, Beijing, 1991, cited in Steiner and Alston (1996) 233.

[83] Reprinted in Davies (1995).

[84] For a discussion, see Mayer (1994).

human-rights discourse. The most potent and visible part of this debate has been with regard to Asian values: the argument made principally by several East Asian and Southeast Asian leaders and government spokespersons that culturally their societies have notions of human rights that differ from the 'universal' human rights found in UDHR and other international instruments. This assertion of Asian values reached its peak during the late 1980s to mid-1990s, the same period when the 'East Asian Miracle' report of the World Bank[85] heralded the emergence of a possible 'Third Way' of development. This temporal coincidence must be explored at length to figure out if there were any possible connections between these two Asia-centered debates. Indeed, historically cultural relativism was not a political or a legal stance of newly independent countries during either the drafting of the UDHR (when there were only a few of them), or the two human rights covenants. It is essentially a recent debate that has its origins in the mid-to-late 1970s, specifically in the context of the failure of Third World redistributist claims in UN forums, and the success of the so-called Tiger economies of East Asia. By linking the debate about cultural relativism and human rights with the debate about Asian development, some of the perils of constituting human-rights discourse as the sole discourse of resistance may be exposed. Specifically, it is suggested that the debate between universality and cultural relativism is better understood as a debate about development, rather than about human rights, and, in particular, about the proper role of the state in the economy. The 'developmentalization' of human-rights discourse has, in my view, caused this turn to culture.

Tracking the discourse on "culture": human rights v. other discourses

Before outlining the various strands of recent relativist critiques, some brief remarks are warranted about the role of culture in human-rights scholarship in order to figure out what different strands of it mean in relativist critique. One must first clarify what this scholarship consists of – whether it consists of only 'legal' writings on the corpus of human rights, or whether it includes writings on human rights in anthropology, sociology, political theory, and other social-science disciplines. Traditionally 'legal' human-rights scholarship did not concern itself with culture and the doctrine did not, with one exception,[86] allow any derogations from universal rights on the ground of culture. Traditional human-rights

[85] World Bank (1993). [86] Article 63(3) of the ECHR makes an exception for colonies.

scholarship – being almost entirely dominated by lawyers in the US – did not concern itself with culture and this was reflected in leading textbooks.[87] This reflected an assumption that culture was something that was "out there," while universality was the normal language of international law which was beyond culture. Even as human rights began increasingly to be on the global agenda from the mid-1970s, leading international lawyers did not engage with the issue of culture. The closest was Oscar Schachter's 1983 piece on human dignity, which attempted to canonize 'dignity' as a normative concept, as a partial response to emerging Third World engagements with human rights at the UN.[88] Indeed, until today, most leading human-rights scholars have not written any major articles or books where they have engaged with the challenge of cultural relativism.

For example, Henkin's celebrated *Age of Rights*, does not devote a chapter to cultural relativism.[89] This was even truer in the case of state practice of non-western states. In their pronouncements at the UN and elsewhere, the non-western states rallied behind human rights in their struggle against apartheid, while critiquing the 'bourgeois' nature of western human-rights rhetoric. But rarely, if ever, did they object to human-rights discourse on the ground of cultural difference, until the late-1970s and 1980s.

The situation is somewhat different in social science writings on human rights. Despite the well-known critiques of human rights emerging from political and social theory – Bentham's "nonsense on stilts," Marx's critique of 'egoistic' rights in *On the Jewish Question*, and Alasdair MacIntyre's critique of rights that "belief in them is one with belief in witches and unicorns,"[90] to name a few prominent examples – it is anthropology that has supplied long-standing critiques of human rights from the perspective of culture.[91] Indeed, this suited the colonial division of social sciences in the post-WWII period, where anthropology, which dealt with the non-western peoples, was concerned with 'culture,' while the other social sciences dealt with 'universal' categories. Thus, the celebrated American Anthropological Society's (AAA) Executive Board's statement on cultural relativism, drafted by Melville Herskovits, declared that "standards and values are relative to the culture from which they

[87] For example, see Lillich and Hannum (1995).
[88] Schachter (1983). This was not surprising, as he was among a handful of progressive liberal international lawyers who paid attention to Third World concerns.
[89] Henkin (1990). [90] MacIntyre (1981) 67.
[91] For an excellent collection of essays on anthropology and human rights, see Wilson (1997).

derive so that any attempt to formulate postulates that grow out of the beliefs or moral codes of one culture must to that extent detract from the applicability of any Declaration of Human Rights to mankind as a whole."[92] Despite this initial engagement with the global discourse of human rights, anthropology remained fairly removed from North–South and East–West debates, until the early 1990s when it again begun engaging with human rights. Thus, in 1994, the AAA convened on the theme of human rights.

The other disciplines had already begun, at least by the 1970s, to engage with the issue of culture due to the influence of several new areas of inquiry – cultural studies, feminist studies, postcolonial theory, etc. – and the necessity to understand a world of hybridization and creolization. But even earlier, the discipline of development studies had decisively engaged with the issue of culture, starting in the 1950s, after Arthur Lewis' 'dual economy' thesis[93] and Gunnar Myrdal's *Asian Drama* [94] had been published.[95] This engagement with culture had been made necessary by the fact that it was development studies that formed a "bridge" between the developed and developing world, and provided the disciplinary means for the transformation of 'traditional' areas of the Third World into 'modern' ones, culturally, politically, and economically – the crux of modernization theory.

Indeed, reflecting the changes underway, the journal "Economic Development and Cultural Change" was started in the University of Chicago in 1956. This concern with 'tradition' and 'culture' continued in various disciplinary disguises in development studies through the 1960s, 1970s, and 1980s, taking such forms as political development studies, rural development, and social role of knowledge. In the 1990s, this concern with culture continues unabated in development discourse. For instance, Joseph Stiglitz, the Chief Economist of the World Bank, recently described development as a "transformative moment" which involves a "movement from traditional relations, traditional ways of thinking, traditional ways of dealing with health and education, traditional methods of production,

[92] Cited in Steiner and Alston (1996) 199.

[93] Although the term 'dualism' was coined by the Dutch economist J. H. Boeke, and may have been articulated in the writings of colonial economists like J. S. Furnivall, it was Arthur Lewis who put it in the context of economic theory. See Lewis, "Economic Development with Unlimited Supplies of Labor," Manchester School (May) 22/2, 131–91 (1954), cited in Banuri (1990).

[94] Myrdal (1968).

[95] For a superb analysis of the evolution of development studies, see Banuri (1990). See also Hirschman (1981); Sen (1983).

to more 'modern' ways."[96] This constant juxtaposition of 'tradition' and 'modern' is by now entirely familiar in development discourse.

Similarities exist between development and human rights discourses, with respect to their attitude towards culture. Human-rights discourse constitutes itself in opposition to and in a complex tension with culture, by contrasting its universal space of "science of law" to the particular place of culture.[97] In this view, law is to culture what rights are to violations: both need each other, even as they attempt to transcend each other. Similarly, development discourse constitutes itself in opposition to and in a complex tension with culture, by contrasting its universal space of merit-based scientific bureaucratism of economics, with the particular place of culture. Here culture is seen as an obstacle to be overcome as it is held to be responsible for economic, political, and social ills – for example, 'extended families,' or 'communal landholdings,' or 'patron-client relationships' – and thus for the failure of development or democracy. On the other hand, development discourse also needs culture, as it can not self-define the 'ideal' or the 'standard' market or state without contrasting it to something else. Thus, both discourses acknowledge culture even as they attempt to transcend it.[98] In both discourses, the universal is the self-representation of the metropole while the cultural is the description of the periphery.

Yet, there are significant differences between human rights and other discourses in their attitudes towards culture. Human-rights discourse presents itself as neutral, apolitical, legal, and non-ideological, and therefore does not express itself on whether 'traditional' or 'modern' is preferable. Indeed, human-rights corpus even entertains a right of minorities to their own culture in article 27 of the ICCPR. In this view, human rights are compatible with modern and traditional societies, because the basic rights are beyond culture. As Henkin says, "The justification of human rights is rhetorical, not philosophical... Human rights are universal: they belong to every human being in every human society. They do not differ with geography or history, culture or ideology, political or economic system, or stage of societal development."[99] Whereas, as noted above, development discourse makes it clear that its project is to enable the transition from 'tradition' to 'modern' because the latter is better and more efficient.

[96] Stiglitz (1999) 3 (citing his 1998 Prebisch lecture) (available on-line at http://www.worldbank.org/html/extdr/extme/js-022799/index.htm).

[97] See the collection of essays in chapter 2, Alston (1996). For a critique, see Rajagopal (1998).

[98] As the President of the World Bank Group, James D. Wolfensohn, puts it, "... we do not believe that you can move forward unless you have a recognition of the base and the past from which we have come." See Wolfensohn (1998).

[99] Henkin (1990) 2.

Though at first glance this agnostic stance taken by human-rights discourse towards 'culture' seems puzzling, it must be remembered that it is part of an effort to remain 'legal' and therefore above the fray of ideological and cultural contestation. Indeed, human-rights discourse is constantly positioning itself as 'law,' though, as it is conceded by a leading textbook, the "struggle for rights... (is) a political struggle in which courts may at best be marginal actors."[100] This essential difference must be borne in mind to understand the contrasts between the 'legal' and other disciplinary strands within the relativist critique. A template of binaries, drawn below, could be useful in further clarifying and comparing the various strands of the critique that is outlined.

Universality v. cultural relativism: a conceptual template

Law	Other disciplines
Formalism	Antiformalism
Adjudication (courts)	Agitation (streets)
Law	Politics
International	Comparative
Universality	Culture
Norms	Institutions
Theory	Activism

It is not by accident that almost all the relativist critiques have come from outside 'law,' from philosophy, political theory, anthropology, and feminist studies. Legal writings have, by and large, maintained the universalist chorus. This is due to the fact that human-rights lawyers – as most lawyers – tend to be generally inward-looking and emphasize normative, theoretical, and adjudicative aspects of human rights which end up on the side of universality. Anthropologists, political scientists, and other disciplinarians who work in the field of human rights tend to stress the agitational and political aspects of rights struggles. Lawyers look for harmony and synthesis for general principles, while other professionals focus upon difference and concreteness.

These differences proved to be important when, in the 1970s, the debate on development and the NIEO began to 'take over' human-rights discourse. As the NIEO strategy was failing, many Third World intellectuals were looking to human rights as the last available tool to counter western

[100] Steiner and Alston (1996) vi.

economic and political hegemony.[101] Thus African scholars such as Keba M'baye articulated the right to development, Mohammed Bedjoui wrote about the right to solidarity, and sympathetic left-wing intellectuals in the West such as Richard Falk and Reńe Dupuy wrote applauding the value of socialism for human rights.[102] It was clear that development debate had arrived at the doorstep of human-rights discourse, that the developmentalization of human rights discourse was well on its way. Western scholars began to publish articles on 'third generation human rights' and the UN Secretary-General issued his first report on the right to development in 1980[103] – it was becoming clear that the Third World had 'arrived' in the intellectual arena of human rights. From then on, it was only logical and inevitable that human-rights discourse would increasingly grapple with 'culture.' In other words, before the Third World intellectuals and states began appropriating human-rights discourse in the 1970s for the development debate, it was a fairly marginal discourse with little relevance to the political and social lives of most peoples in the world. After such appropriation, human-rights discourse became part of a larger discourse of development, thus becoming a terrain of conflict and struggle over culture, resources, forms of violence and justice between the West and the non-West. In consequence, it must be stressed that the so-called tension between universality and culture in the arena of human rights is not the timeless phenomenon that it is made out to be, but, rather, a historically specific and contingent debate that emerged fairly recently in the context of ongoing debate over development.

From redistribution to culture? Relativism and development

This parallelism between human-rights discourse and development discourse – the progressive 'capture' of the former by the latter – becomes visible when we view the temporal sequencing of various strands of cultural relativist critiques. Almost all the writings on relativism date from the early 1980s, starting with Panikkar's 1982 article.[104] That same period was, it may be recalled, marked by a reorientation in Third World politics at the UN after the failure of NIEO proposals, the rise of Reagan

[101] I thank Mohan Gopal at the World Bank for discussions on this point.

[102] Falk (1981); Dupuy (1980).

[103] Marks (1981); United Nations (1979).

[104] I do not mean that there were no writings on cultural relativism before the 1980s, but merely assert that such writings did not explicitly address themselves in relation to universal human-rights discourse, but, rather, in relation to other categories. For a sample of early literature, see the bibliography cited in Renteln (1990). I describe the various strands of the relativist critique below.

and Thatcher, and the rise of neoclassical economic paradigms – neoliberalism – celebrating the market. Consequently, human-rights discourse came to occupy the new terrain on which the meaning, and the nature of 'development' was fought between the West and the Third World. In other words, as noted earlier, the failure of Third World redistributist claims at UN forums led the Third World to turn to human-rights discourse as the new arena of struggle over development. Former redistributist claims were now presented in terms of 'rights' – such as the right to development – while the West attempted to counter it by recourse to 'rights' as well – narrowly tailored individual rights that refused to consider obligations and social relations. The expansion of the UNHRC in 1979, by the inclusion of a large number of Third World states, also contributed to this contestation over the meaning of human rights.

Relativist critiques that emerged in the early 1980s, did so in the context of this struggle over human rights within the broader relationship to development. More broadly, the relativist critiques were concerned about the nature of modernity that was sought to be transmitted by 'universal' rights discourse. This was nothing but an old conundrum faced by development discourse, about the appropriate relationship its 'modernity' ought to have with 'culture' and 'tradition.' On the one hand, some sort of 'modernity' was seen as necessary by Third World intellectuals, in order to engage in progressive social reform and continued nation-building. On the other hand, 'tradition' and 'culture' provided the specific context within which the 'universal' claims could be actually realized. Juxtaposing modernity and culture was then a standard tool in the repertoire of colonial and postcolonial governance.

Among the relativists, this tension between a desire for universal standards and a hope of preserving particular contexts persisted. Most relativists have resolved this tension by positioning themselves in opposition to the *particular kind of universality that is embedded in the rights discourse, but not to the idea of universality per se.* In this sense, most relativist critique is 'weak relativism' as opposed to 'strong relativism.'[105] The object of the critique here is the narrowness of 'universalism,' with a call to expand the cultural bases of rights discourse. The result then is a commitment to normativity, to the idea of a universal set of rights that are "culturally

[105] Weak relativism is used to describe those who concede the conceptual possibility of a universal set of rights, but argue that their realization depends on cultural context; strong relativists hold that culture is the principal source of rights and, therefore, no transcultural rights are possible by definition in a world of pluralism. See, e.g., Steiner and Alston (1996) 192–93. See also Alston (1996), Part II, introduction. Jack Donnelly uses three categories – radical, strong, and weak. See Donnelly (1989) 109–10.

correct." In other words, with a few exceptions, most relativist critiques concede the conceptual necessity of universality, even as they critique the cultural bias inherent in the extant version of universal rights. In this sense, it is quite wrong to see relativism and universality in Manichean terms, since both are necessary elements in the rights discourse, just as 'tradition' and 'modernity' are in development discourse.

This becomes evident through a quick glance at the various strands of relativist critiques. Crudely simplifying, I divide this critique into four categories:[106]

(a) *Culture-as-community*: equates culture with community. Influenced by Marxist critique of rights, it views mainstream human-rights discourse as individual-oriented, and therefore incapable of being relevant to community-based cultures of non-western societies in Africa and Asia. Examples include the 1947 American Anthropological Association's Statement,[107] Panikkar,[108] Kothari,[109] and Kausikan.[110]
(b) *Culture-as-nation*: equates culture with the nation-state. Mainly articulated by government spokespersons from the Third World. Examples include Teson[111] and Kausikan.
(c) *Culture-as-universality*: believes that universal values can and should be deduced only within each culture. Sees multiculturalism and diversity as prerequisites to the generation of universal rights. Examples include An-Na'im,[112] Renteln,[113] Mutua,[114] Santos,[115] Baxi,[116] and Peerenboom.[117]
(d) *Universality-as-culture*: views extant universal rights discourse as the product of a particular cultural tradition, viz., the West. Skeptical about the possibility of a universal discourse ever transcending culture. Examples include AAA statement, Donnelly,[118] Panikkar[119], Kothari[120] , Ghai[121] , Kausikan[122], Shivji,[123] Esteva,[124] Otto,[125] and Engle.[126]

[106] I borrow these categories from Rajagopal (1998). These categories are not water-tight – as can be seen, some authors who fall into one category, are also found in others. For a different categorization and discussion, see Mutua (1996b).
[107] For the text, see Steiner and Alston (1996) 198. The AAA has recently issued a new statement on human rights. For a critical review of the AAA's position, see Engle (2001) 536–59.
[108] Panikkar (1982). [109] Kothari (1987). [110] Kausikan (1993). [111] Teson (1985).
[112] An-Na'im (1990). [113] Renteln (1990). [114] Mutua (1995a).
[115] Santos (1997). [116] Baxi (1998). [117] Peerenboom (1993).
[118] Donnelly (1989). [119] Pannikar (1982). [120] Kothari (1987). [121] Ghai (1994).
[122] Kausikan (1993). [123] Shivji (1989); Shivji (1995).
[124] Esteva and Prakash (1998). [125] Otto (1997a, 1997b). [126] Engle (1992b).

The positions of these authors differ considerably within these categories. For example, within the culture-as community position, though all the authors cited share that starting point, they differ considerably in their results: the AAA Statement and Panikkar do not reject universality of human rights, Kothari is ambivalent, whereas Kausikan does reject universality. In other words, their approaches towards the meaning of culture do not appear to be dispositive of their attitudes towards the normative regime of human rights and the end-use for which it should be put.

Similarly, though Teson and Kausikan appear to understand culture as nation, they reach opposite conclusions: Teson, a strong supporter of universality and Kausikan, an articulate destroyer of it. Teson reveals his understanding of culture as nation through his unproblematic analysis of whether cultural diversity is recognized as a justification for violation of human rights under positive international law. Since positive international law is a product of state behavior actualized through treaty or custom, his analysis can proceed only by equating the boundaries of culture with nation-states. That is precisely what he does. Thus, he states that "nothing in the human rights conventions... acknowledge[s] any right of governments to avoid compliance by alleging the priority of local traditions" (page 125).

An-Na'im, Renteln, and Peerenboom conceive of culture as universality in the sense that they do not reject the idea of universality per se, but argue that such universality must be attained within cultures, rather than be imposed from outside. To An-Na'im it must be attained within the Sharia, for Renteln it must be based on the principle of *lex talionis*, and for Peerenboom, the Confucian values provide the framework. To some extent this view is also shared by Panikkar and Kothari, who stress the Hindu culture/Indian culture respectively. A slightly different strand of this argument is adopted by Santos, Baxi, and Mutua, who argue for a universality that *reflects* cultural values.[127] But despite this simultaneity in approach to culture, they all seem to have different attitudes towards the normative framework of human rights. While An-Na'im appears to assume the pre-existence of a coherent 'international' normative framework quite unproblematically (though he never quite explicitly states it) and discusses the compliance of Shariat with it, Peerenboom seems to be quite self-conscious about the normative status of human rights and

[127] For a sophisticated formulation of a 'multicultural' approach, see Santos (1997). See also Mutua (1995a).

avoids making any assessments about the compliance of Chinese practices with it. Renteln also thinks that a cross-cultural universality is possible, whereas Santos, Baxi, and Mutua quite explicitly acknowledge the necessity of a universal normative framework.

Finally, the AAA Statement, Donnelly, Panikkar, Kothari, Ghai, Kausikan, Shivji, Otto, and Engle appear to have an understanding of universality itself as culture. Thus all of them argue, to varying degrees, that the human-rights tradition is a western one, though none of them reaches similar conclusions towards the normative framework of human rights. Donnelly argues unreservedly for universality, Panikkar, Shivji, and Ghai are qualified, Kothari is ambivalent, Kausikan rejects universality, and Engle and Otto are agnostic. Thus, once again, one sees the problem of divergence between attitudes towards culture/universality and attitudes towards the normative framework of the discipline.

This finding is important because it shows that contrary to the standard division of the authors into two camps – those who argue for cultural sensitivity and those who reject human rights – there are in fact many complex positions among them, which make it impossible to predict what their attitude towards the normative structure is likely to be. In other words, one cannot simply assume that there are those who 'support' universality and others who don't. In reality, it seems far more complicated. But more importantly, a closer reading of many of the authors makes it clear that discussions of the culture–universality dialectic is also at bottom a discussion of the tradition–modernity dialectic that lies at the heart of development discourse. This similarity between human rights and development discourses in their relation to culture is lost when one sees universality and relativism as totalizingly opposed to each other. As I have suggested, it is better to see these categories as part of the constitutive process of human-rights discourse, just as tradition and modernity are at the heart of the constitutive process of development discourse.

Two debates or one? Tracing Asian values and the East Asian miracle debates

The dialectic between the Asian values debate in human rights and the East Asian miracle debate in development is a clear example of this constitutive process. First begun in the mid-1980s with the publication of a volume,[128] the Asian values debate reflected some years of debates within

[128] Hsiung (1986).

rapidly growing East Asian economies about the relationship between economic growth and equity and economic and political freedoms. More than just a passing fad, it has now come to occupy an important position in the literature of human-rights theory and practice.[129] The key element of the Asian values critique of human rights, as articulated by leading intellectuals and politicians in East Asia,[130] is as follows: the communitarian and obligation-oriented cultures of East Asia generate particular Asian values that are incompatible with western, individualistic human-rights notions, and in fact generate different conceptions of justice, solidarity, and governance that 'work' as effectively as (if not better than) those found in the West. A powerful empirical proof of how successful these Asian values are in protecting basic human rights of the people, they maintain, is provided by the performance of East Asian economies – the East Asian miracle – such as South Korea, Japan, and Malaysia – that have maintained high growth rates, maintained relative equality through land reform, and provided strong and efficient governments that deliver public goods to all citizens.

On the other hand, the key element of the East Asian miracle debate in development has made the following claim:[131] that the incredible success of several East Asian countries since the 1970s in promoting high growth rates while assuring equity and sound human development has been made possible due to the interventionary role played by the governments of these countries in their economies, and not due to market forces alone. Promoted aggressively inside the World Bank by Japan, the report is in many ways an ambivalent document due to its attempt to walk the tight rope between its traditional commitment to the superiority of markets – made more central due to neoliberalism – and the irrefutable proof of the success of interventionism. As Robert Wade puts it, the World Bank's report shows how the classic art of "paradigm maintenance" works.[132]

As can be readily seen, both debates share several commonalities. First, temporally, both debates arose more or less together in the early 1990s, as the end of the Cold War opened up the ideological debate on a possible 'Third Way' in development, referring to the economic success of East Asia. Before then, neither the G-77, nor the ASEAN (Association

[129] Recently there has been a flood of literature on the Asian values debate in human rights. See, e.g., Bauer and Bell (1999); de Bary (1998).

[130] See China White Paper, cited in Steiner and Alston (1996) 233. The classic statement is Kausikan (1993). See also Zakaria (1994).

[131] World Bank (1993). [132] Wade (1996).

of SouthEast Asian Nations) had leveled such cultural/regional critiques of the 'universal' human-rights regime or the extant models of development. Of course, the Third World states at the UN had pushed for the primacy of development over rights in the UN, during the 1980s' debate on the right to development. But that debate was not conducted primarily in cultural terms, nor was it hinged on the economic successes of these states. Therefore, the temporal coincidence of these debates has much to tell us about how intertwined both of them really are.

Second, both debates arose from within the top echelons of governments: Japan in the case of the East Asian miracle, and Singapore and Malaysia in the case of the human-rights debate. This showed that these debates were driven primarily by the dictates of governance, and not by the interests of human-rights victims. This is important, as it is often forgotten in the West that the proponents of both of these Asia-centered debates do not represent either the totality of Asia or even the multiple voices of their own societies. As Yash Ghai and Amartya Sen have convincingly argued, there can neither be a single 'Asian' perspective given the diversity of the cultures, polities, and economies of the region, nor can the ruling elites' perspective be taken to represent the views of their societies.[133] Indeed, even as these government spokesmen articulated their 'Asian' perspective, several Asian human-rights NGOs advanced their own 'Asian' perspectives.[134] Which one then qualifies as representative (given the undemocratic nature of many of the East Asian governments)?

Third, both debates were defenses of a particular conception of the role of the state in the economy, leveled from two different directions. Specifically, both debates attempted to support an expansionary role of the state in the economy, as a counter-measure to the pro-market liberalization agenda of neoliberalism. The proponents of the Asian values debate explicitly argued that economic development – reduction of poverty, increase in living standards, decrease in unemployment, etc. – should take precedence over civil and political rights, and therefore, by definition, the governments should be more or less free to implement development goals despite human and social costs. As Bilahari Kausikan put it, the experience of East and Southeast Asian governments "sees order and stability as preconditions for economic growth, and growth as the necessary

[133] Ghai (1994) 5; Sen (1997, 1999a, chapter 10, 1999b).

[134] This tension was clearly seen in the case of the Bangkok Governmental Declaration versus the Bangkok NGO Declaration before the 1993 Vienna World Conference on Human Rights. Both are cited in Steiner and Alston (1996) 235.

foundation of any political order that claims to advance human dignity."[135] This argument complemented the East Asian miracle debate, which also argued for a vigorous, interventionary government in financial, trade, and social sectors.

There is a serious concern with the merging of these two debates, in addition to the ones I have noted above. The convergence of these debates has the inevitable consequence of legitimizing and reinforcing the state as the primary framework for the moral and material advancement of the people in East Asia. The proponents of Asian values achieve this in two ways: first, by conflating the 'community' and the state in their 'communitarian' critiques of human rights;[136] and second, by stressing economic, social, and cultural rights, which require the state to provide public goods such as education, health, social services, etc. Given the violent and predatory nature of state power and its general inability to deal effectively with the violence of development so far, this does not augur well for the most vulnerable people in these countries. The moral crisis of, and the loss of faith in, the state in many of these countries is real, from the perspective of the most vulnerable, which is hardly reflected in these two debates. It is not my argument that the state must be dispensed with and human rights must be achieved through the operation of the market: wholly to the contrary, I firmly believe in the use of public power to protect human rights. I am only against reinstating the old structures and practices of the state under new banners. Instead, a serious attempt must be made to reconceive the very notion of the state and the spatial dimensions for the exercise of public power as such. The two Asia-centered debates do not help this process.

The experience of the two Asia-centered debates shows how the political economy of human rights functions, hand-in-hand with that of development. But this is hardly how the two debates are received in international law. Instead, the Asian values debate is engaged with, if at all, only at the cultural level, while the East Asian miracle debate is hardly ever engaged. As my argument shows, however, the material and the cultural are intricately connected in these two debates, and the "material forces

[135] Kausikan (1993). As the Chinese White Paper on Human Rights put it, "to the people in the developing countries, the most urgent human rights are still the right to subsistence and the right to economic, social and cultural development. Therefore, attention should first be given to the right to development . . ." See China White Paper, cited in Steiner and Alston (1996) 233.

[136] Ghai (1994) 5.

represented by the state and the economy are decisive for the ideology and practice of rights."[137]

Human rights and development: ambivalences and contradictions

There are two key issues here: first, the problematic and contradictory relationship between human rights and development in the light of the gradual 'capture' of the former by the latter discourse – what I have called 'developmentalization of rights.' Here, I am mostly concerned with the coherence of policy-oriented explanations, which dominate practice in this area. A second concern is with the theoretical and pragmatic crisis posed by the right to development to the human rights corpus.

Modern human-rights and development discourses were born almost simultaneously after the Second World War.[138] Despite this temporal coincidence, there is no apparent substantive thread that ran through them until recently. Traditional conceptions of human rights meant only civil and political rights, despite the acceptance of economic, social, and cultural rights and the concept of duties in the Universal Declaration of Human Rights. Development, on the other hand, meant primarily economic growth to which human-rights concerns were marginal, if not irrelevant. Lawyers remained the high priests of human-rights discourse, while economists ruled the development field. These divisions were manifested in the UN system, where different institutions were established to deal with human rights and development, with almost no mechanisms for coordination.[139]

These divisions were consolidated by the Cold War, with the two blocs each supporting one set of rights, and also by the nation-building efforts of the newly independent developing countries, which put development before rights. However, this situation began changing with the entry of developing countries into the UN Commission on Human Rights and the politicization of the UNGA from the 1960s. The developing countries aggressively used human-rights discourse to counter racism and

[137] Ghai (1999) 252.

[138] Ideas relating to human rights are no doubt quite old in the western liberal tradition, dating back at least to the Enlightenment. Nevertheless, as I have argued, the ideological character and the architectural framework of the modern human-rights movement is a distinctly post World War II phenomenon, in part because it is so tied to the entry of non-western states into the international system. For a work that takes the entry of non-western states to the international system seriously, see Bull and Watson (1984).

[139] For a review of these aspects, see Alston (1988).

colonialism – especially apartheid – but focused most of their energy on the achievement of equitable and just economic conditions under the rubric of the New International Economic Order (NIEO). By the mid-1970s, it was becoming apparent that the NIEO initiatives were failing and that achieving the optimum international environment for promoting development was going to be very difficult. In the changed atmosphere, the developing countries began turning to the human-rights discourse to continue their quest for a just and equitable international economic order, shorn of imperialism and capable of promoting rapid economic development. The key steps in this process include the Declaration of Teheran (1967), and the articulation of the right to development by Judge Keba M'baye of Senegal in the early 1970s.[140] By 1977, the UNGA had affirmed for the first time that all human rights were equal, indivisible, and interdependent, thus putting an end to the hierarchization of rights.[141] Other UN agencies such as UNESCO played a key role in promoting a 'third generation' of rights including solidarity, development, and peace from the late 1970s. The stage was set for the birth of the right to development in the 1980s. Since then, human-rights discourse has rapidly expanded normatively and institutionally and gained in reputation as a uniquely powerful discourse of legitimacy. Indeed, as Louis Henkin has put it, we are now in "an age of rights."[142] More significantly, in the 1980s and 1990s, human-rights discourse has been thoroughly 'localized,' appropriated in struggles and peoples' movements around the world to challenge the violence of development. What the developing countries could not win at the UN in the 1970s, grassroots movements are attempting to win locally in the 1990s.

Meanwhile, development discourse had undergone several radical changes.[143] After the 'failure' of the economistic stages-of-growth and trickle-down theories in the 1950s, development institutions began emphasizing rural development and agricultural sectors in the 1960s, as they responded to grassroots pressure and a felt need to alleviate poverty and human suffering.[144] In the early 1970s, this had emerged as the 'redistribution with growth' model, which made it clear that not all social objectives

[140] Ibid.

[141] United Nations December 16, 1977. For an earlier affirmation of the equality of human rights and social justice, see Declaration on Social Progress and Development, UNGA Res. 2542 (XXIV).

[142] Henkin (1990) ix. [143] For a review, see Esteva (1992); see also Banuri (1990).

[144] See Escobar (1995). For a description in relation to the Bretton Woods Institutions, see chapter 5 above.

could be sacrificed to achieve growth. Meanwhile, the Club of Rome's 'limits to growth' thesis, combined with the 1972 Stockholm Conference on Environment, began having a profound impact on development discourse, by focusing attention on the social and environmental costs of development. By the end of the 1970s, the poverty alleviation agenda had become the principal task of development agencies, under the 'basic needs' approach.[145] Thus, if human-rights discourse turned gradually from pure law and politics towards economics, development turned from pure economics towards some politics and ethics. Still the gap between the two discourses remained. In the 1980s, under the influence of Reagan and Thatcher, the rise of neoliberalism, and the debt crisis in the developing world, the 'new' development agenda with a human focus suffered a setback. Thus, when the UNGA proclaimed the right to development in 1986, development discourse was in an ideological crisis. Since then, it has attempted to capitalize on the unique legitimacy of human-rights discourse in the post-Cold-War era, by adopting the discourse of 'good governance,' 'rule of law,' and, finally, through a 'human rights approach' to development planning.[146] Indeed, this 'developmentalization' of human rights has given rise to concerns among activists and scholars that a narrow, market-oriented version of human rights is being used to promote economic liberalization and globalization around the world.[147]

Before elaborating on the right to development, some unresolved issues in the area of human rights and development need to be mentioned. The first of them concerns the old question of the legal status of economic, social, and cultural rights. As noted already, human-rights discourse has traditionally been dominated by an overemphasis of civil and political rights, partly due to the dominance of western scholars and NGOs. This bias is built into the normative corpus of human rights. Thus, the International Covenant on Civil and Political Rights contains rights, such as the right to be free from torture, which are immediately implementable through national mechanisms, while the International Covenant on Economic, Social, and Cultural Rights subjects the realization of rights such as health or education to a legal standard of "progressive realization."[148] The legal status of this formulation has been subject to much debate

[145] For a description of the evolution of development thinking, see Banuri (1990); see also Streeten (1981). On basic needs approach, see Galtung (1980); Muchlinski (1987).

[146] On governance, see World Bank (1994); OECD (1995); UNDP (1997). On human rights and development, see World Bank (1998); see also UNDP (1998a).

[147] See, e.g., Baxi (1998); Oloka-Onyango (1999); Shivji (1995).

[148] ICESCR, article 2.

and criticism from scholars, but the fact remains that economic, social, and cultural rights are still sidelined in national constitutions and international human-rights-enforcement mechanisms.[149] This has a direct bearing on which human rights are likely to be more promoted by development agencies.

Second, the belief that there is a legitimate 'trade-off' between development and human rights lives on among policy-makers. This belief, dating from the political development literature of the 1960s, continues to see human rights in narrow, political terms, while understanding development to be economic growth.[150] Recently, the trade-off theory has resurfaced in the form of the so-called Asian values debate, wherein it is asserted by rulers of China, Singapore, and Malaysia that, culturally, Asians do not care much for political liberties, but, rather, they do care for rapid economic improvement. This belief lies behind public policy arguments for large dams, for example, which assert that the benefits provided by these dams are more important than the costs. It must be noted that this belief contradicts existing human-rights doctrine, which declares, as noted already, that all human rights are now accepted as a matter of international law, to be equal, interdependent, and indivisible.

The third issue that must be noted here is related to but different from the second: the continuing appeal of the 'basic needs' idea, especially among international development agencies. This issue is recirculated by arguing that since resources for social programs are limited, one should prioritize and focus on the 'core rights.' A sophisticated version of this argument is that since governance is about choosing between priorities, we should accept such prioritization. This argument is a slippery slope and offers no credible legal or policy guidelines for choosing which rights should qualify as 'basic needs.' Crudely put, the danger here is that this argument will become an excuse for wholesale denial of a whole set of rights which is not permitted under the human-rights corpus.

Right to development as framework: problems and prospects

The UNGA's adoption of the Declaration on the Right to Development (DRD) in 1986 was a major milestone that brought development and

[149] For an overview of the debate and issues involved, see Steiner and Alston (1996) chapters 5 and 16.

[150] The literature on this is huge. For a sample, see Trubek (1973); Goodin (1979); Hewlett (1979).

human-rights discourses together. It is now being relied upon by development agencies, such as UNDP, as the legal framework for integrating human-rights and development discourses. To what extent is this concept appropriate as a framework? My assessment is that while the DRD must be approached cautiously given the meaning it has acquired as a right of (developing) states, it provides important elements that may legitimize the alternative development practices of social movements. But I am skeptical about whether this is what the development agencies intend to use the DRD for.

As noted earlier, the right to development debate emerged at a time of the eclipse of developing countries' redistributist claims under the NIEO and the ascendance of neoliberalism and Reaganomics. As a result, the debate acquired a polarized North–South character, evidenced by a division between western and non-western states at the drafting and adoption of the DRD in 1986.

In a nutshell, for developing countries, the right to development means the right to expand their economies rapidly, irrespective of environmental and social costs. In this sense then, right to development becomes simply a right of states to pollute rivers, displace people, and create development refugees. For developed countries, the right to development is simply not a 'right,' but only a goal or a claim – that is, it is not an entitlement that can be enforced in courts by individuals. Scholarly opinion on the legal status of this right is divided, with western scholars opposing the right and non-western scholars supporting it in general.[151] The UNGA and the UN Commission on Human Rights have affirmed the existence of the right several times in their resolutions, but the concrete meaning of this right remains unclarified.

The views of both developing and developed countries seem inconsistent with the DRD. At issue are the very meaning of 'development,' and the question of rights and duty-holders. In other words: development of what, of whom, and at whose expense? In the DRD, the right to development means "an inalienable human right by virtue of which every human person and all peoples are entitled to participate in, contribute to, and

[151] The literature on right to development is vast. See, e.g., Marks (1981); Dupuy (1980); Rich (1983); Alston (1988); United Nations (1990a). Of course, some western scholars, notably Philip Alston, have supported the right to development (indeed, he has played a pioneering role), but it remains true that the western mainstream international law position does not take "third generation rights," such as the right to development, seriously. Even the casebook edited by Philip Alston himself, with Henry Steiner, does not contain a chapter on third generation rights such as the right to development, the right to peace, or the right to environment, thus showing the limits of what mainstream human-rights scholars will consider acceptable. See Steiner and Alston (2000).

enjoy economic, social, cultural and political development, in which all human rights and fundamental freedoms can be fully realized." The DRD makes it clear that this implies the full realization of the right of peoples to self-determination and "their inalienable right to full sovereignty over all their natural wealth and resources." It is then clear that social movements, local communities, and individuals, not states, have the right to development. Indeed, the DRD articulates just such a definition.

This definition had the potential to destabilize not only the human rights discourse but the entire international order, which is based on the unequal and lop-sided system of relations between the West and the Third World, codified and administered through the development discourse. First, by articulating the Gandhian notion that human beings have personalities that they alone can be in charge of fulfilling, it created an epistemological crisis for international law, which relies on states to make decisions about who will live within their borders and how they will live. Second, it powerfully introduced the right of communities into the human-rights corpus, which remained focused on individuals. This had an immediate resonance among grassroots movements in the Third World, as it enabled them to use the human-rights language to protest against violence against their communities. Third, it opened up the entire meaning of development, which had heretofore meant mainly economic growth, national development, and individual entitlements. Now, communities could define what kind of development they wanted – whether they wished to retain traditional medicinal practices instead of adopting western medicine, for example. This would have had the consequence of fundamentally disrupting the capitalistic basis of the international order, which relies on rapid exploitation of resources for profit by replacing traditional practices with modern ones. This is bolstered by the recognition of the right to permanent sovereignty over natural resources which strengthens the positions of communities, for example, versus dam builders and governments. Such a definition would indeed destabilize the statist paradigms of human-rights and development discourses, for example, in the areas of police powers and eminent domain doctrines.

There is also the issue of rights and duty-holders. The DRD vests the right in peoples and individuals and imposes obligations to respect the right upon the international community, private actors, states, and individuals. Clearly, such a vast scope leaves the right fuzzy and difficult to enforce. Nevertheless, I believe that the duties it imposes on the international community, individuals, and private actors to respect human rights is unique, and could constitute a potential source of normative obligations. This is essential because a human-rights approach to development demands a fundamental transformation of the way in which international institutions 'do development' or private actors do business. There is no other human-rights norm that can offer this advantage.

Yet, despite these potential challenges, the DRD petered out as a political challenge in the late 1980s, due to a combination of factors. The first among them was the end of the Cold War and the consequent weakening of the Third World coalition. Second, the rise of neoliberalism and the Reagan administration's hard line policy on opposing economic and social rights and the right to development had a morale-weakening impact on the Third World coalition. Third, the leading definition of the right was formulated by the Third World states as the right of states to development and this had the consequence of weakening its moral legitimacy. Fourth, most importantly, the very meaning of 'development' in the right to development, with its 'catching-up' rationale, was not challenged by Third World states, who wished to continue the exploitative and violent way of doing development. However, as my argument shows, there is a different 'Third World' in the form of social movements, which has actively put forward alternative conceptions of development, relying quite liberally on the DRD itself.

A meaningful human-rights praxis could, then, be built only by questioning the developmental ideology of the State as well as by rooting such a praxis in the actual struggles of peoples, not in the conservative confines of the counter-sovereignty liberal-rights rhetoric.

An assessment of recent global trends in the developmentalization of human rights

Some recent global trends in the 'developmentalization' of human rights may now be described and the problems and prospects associated with them may be considered. The suggestion in this section is that while these new forms of policy interventions hold out some promise in overcoming the limitations of classic convergence proponents (who advocate a merger of development and human rights discourses), they still fall far short of what they promise: a fundamental change in the way development is done. In the 1990s, some substantial strides have been made to merge development and human rights, and three key areas are focused on below.

Integrating human rights with sustainable human development

Experience in integrating human rights with development is limited, though attempts towards this end have been made since the 1970s by

UN agencies.[152] This has now emerged as a primary area of policy intervention by development agencies around the world, in the form of an enormous number of projects in the Third World.[153] These projects range from poverty alleviation, women's rights, environmental protection, and an umbrella category of good governance. A rights-based approach to development assumes that rights can be defined and operationalized in ways that facilitate planning and programming for their realization. This has been encouraged by the revived popularity of right to development as a broad umbrella concept. However, this is not self-evident. How, for example, would one define freedom of speech and access to information in the context of a development project or program? Or the right to participation in decision-making? Should this be a process-based right that simply recognizes the right of project-affected people to express their 'voice,' or does it give them a substantive right of veto over the projects themselves? Indeed, the World Bank see-sawed between a veto-right and a process right approach to indigenous peoples' authority to approve infrastructure projects, finally choosing the narrower process right in its operational directive in 1991.[154]

When it comes to economic, social, and cultural rights the situation becomes even more complex. Does the right to health mean freedom from all major illnesses or just access to health services, or entitlement to all health services required to restore health? Does the right to education involve a right to 'modern' education through nine years of primary school or will 'religious' education do? And once such rights have been defined and integrated in development, do they then become enforceable through the courts, if not realized? There are no simple answers to these questions. Yet the proponents of the convergence thesis often sound as if integrating human rights with development is a smooth and technical process, and eschew any discussion of potential problems, conflicts, or contradictions that may arise in the effort.

To take one example, the UNDP's (United Nations Development Program) 1998 policy document on Integrating Human Rights with Sustainable Human Development talks about 'mainstreaming' human rights in its activities, and recites a list of rights such as participation, work, food, health, education, land, equality, environmental protection, due process, and of children, workers, minorities, and indigenous peoples. Mere recitation is not, however, dispositive of the various meanings of these rights in

[152] For discussion, see Paul (1989); United Nations (1986).

[153] See, e.g., UNDP (1998a, 2000). [154] I thank Eva Thorne for pointing this out.

particular local contexts, and more significantly, it hides the real conflicts that exist between various rights themselves. To take an obvious example, the right to equality may very well conflict with the rights of women, or indigenous peoples. How a country wishes to resolve a problem of inequality in gender relations – for example through affirmative action – will decide if there will be a conflict between rights. In other words, it is often the design of government programs that determine the content of actually existing rights, not the other way around. There are no abstract rights that pre-exist public interventions. Rather, the content of various rights is formulated in the conflict between social, political, and ideological forces, and the confluence of public actions and private initiatives. In other words, the content of rights are to be found in the praxis of social movements, not in the abstract legal formulations of international lawyers.

Clearly then, these issues need to be resolved in specific country contexts, even when elaborate global guidelines through treaties have been developed. Perhaps what is more important is the operational consequence of this strategy for the development discourse itself. How would development institutions change their own practices to be consistent with the objective of integrating and realizing human rights in development? A human-rights approach means, for example, taking self-determination and cultural rights seriously, but development practices often seek to displace traditional practices with more modern, efficient ones. Indeed, the former World Bank Chief Economist Joseph Stiglitz defines development as the replacement of everything 'traditional' with everything 'modern.'[155] How can we reconcile localizing human rights with globalizing development? The extant analyses of human rights in development do not consider these issues sufficiently. For example, the 1998 UNDP report referred to above has almost nothing to say about the cultural–institutional implications of a human-rights approach to development, in terms of the extent to which alternative development practices must be recognized or the extent to which it has to modify its own practices.

Supporting the strengthening of human-rights institutions

The second strand in the recent 'developmentalization' of human rights is the increasing attention bestowed on the strengthening of human-rights institutions. This has emerged primarily from the neoliberal turn towards 'good governance,' 'rule of law,' and the demands for the reform of developing countries' state/governance structures including Parliamentary,

[155] Stiglitz (1999).

executive, and judicial branches, NGOs, educational institutions, and the media. Human-rights discourse has assisted this drive by insisting on the establishment of 'national institutions' for promotion and protection of human rights, such as Human Rights Commissions and Ombudspersons, in addition to supporting the institutional reforms, which also form the core of neoliberal demands. The UNHCHR (United Nations High Commissioner for Human Rights) has a special advisor on this topic, and has recently provided technical assistance to numerous countries for establishment of these national institutions. The UNDP has been very active in supporting this idea in several countries, as part of its Country Cooperation Framework. Bilateral aid, especially from countries that have national institutions on human rights, is not difficult to obtain, though it often comes 'tied' to the specific model that the donor wishes to promote. Thus aid from Nordic countries is often tied to the adoption of an Ombudsperson model, while aid from Anglo-Saxon countries (such as Australia) is often tied to the adoption of Human Rights Commissions.

This fetishism of human-rights institutions overlooks the importance of well-functioning regular state institutions for ensuring protection of human rights. Indeed, since the human-rights violations relating to development stem largely from dysfunctional state structures including democratic ones, they can not be remedied simply by establishing a new institution. The establishment of any new institution should go hand in hand with the reform and strengthening of existing institutions. This is often lost in the drive to establish national human-rights institutions.

Does the establishment of national institutions strengthen the convergence between human rights and development? While I do not focus on this issue here, available evidence suggests that extant models of national institutions narrowly focus on promoting a narrow set of civil and political rights to the comparative neglect of economic, social, and cultural rights. This has been the experience in India, Australia, the Philippines, and a host of other Asian countries. There are several other design weaknesses that continue to bedevil the national-institution model (including): they are quasi-governmental agencies that do not have meaningful links with civil society groups, they tend to investigate abuses committed only by government agencies to the neglect of private corporations and they suffer from lack of coordination with other government agencies which often look at them with suspicion. Nevertheless, the convergence proponents continue to advocate the establishment of national institutions as a general requirement. It is safe to say, however, that extant models of such institutions do not offer the hope of transforming the way development is done now.

Preparing national plans on human rights

The third, and perhaps the most prominent area in which human rights is being gradually 'developmentalized' is in the drafting of National Action Plans on Human Rights (NAPHR) by a number of countries. The 1993 Vienna Conference on Human Rights called on states to develop such plans in order to set concrete national priorities and the process for achieving them. Since then, the UNHCHR has been active in promoting this idea and has held a number of regional workshops to develop guidelines for principles and processes. Two prominent workshops in Asia, attended by representatives of governments, recently adopted a series of guidelines after affirming the "desirability of developing national human rights plans of action."[156] A number of countries such as Latvia, Bolivia, Ecuador, Brazil, Mexico, Indonesia, the Philippines, Australia, Thailand, Malawi, and South Africa, have adopted such national plans since then, and many other countries are in the process of adopting them. This effort is being financially supported by the governments concerned, supplemented by development assistance from agencies such as UNDP, which has a special joint-agency project called HURIST (Human Rights Strengthening) with the UNHCHR. Under this project, operational activities towards national action plans on human rights are being initiated or carried out currently in almost twenty-eight countries in Asia, Africa, Arab states, Latin America, and the Caribbean, and Eastern Europe/CIS.

The national plans adopted by these countries differ considerably. Nevertheless, some common elements can be identified among them[157]:

1. Coverage of a broad range of rights including all internationally recognized human rights. This marks a considerable improvement from 'pure' human-rights interventions that focus only on civil and political rights, or traditional development programs that are conceived only in economic terms.

[156] Conclusions of the Inter-Sessional Workshop on the Development of National Plans of Action for the Promotion and Protection of Human Rights in the Asia-Pacific Region, Bangkok, Thailand, July 5–7, 1999; Eighth Workshop on Regional Cooperation for the Promotion and Protection of Human Rights in the Asia-Pacific Region, Beijing, China, March 1–3, 2000.

[157] The following discussion draws upon UNDP and UNHCHR internal materials, and also Muntarbhorn (1999).

2. Targeting vulnerable groups such as women, children, the elderly, those with disability and the indigenous peoples. Such a group-targeting strategy, while no stranger to development discourse, is new to human rights.
3. Normative linkage between national and international human-rights standards. This is entirely new to the development planning, which was neither traditionally grounded normatively nor measured against global legal standards.
4. An emphasis on legal reform to improve human-rights performance. This feature is nothing new to the development area, which has witnessed an array of law and development projects since the 1950s.
5. Support for national institutions to protect human rights, such as Human Rights Commissions.
6. Partnership with key government agencies to implement the NHRP. This is a radically new component in human rights, which is traditionally a counter-sovereignty discourse, not willing to cooperate with the government on most matters.
7. Capacity building of specific powerful groups such as the police, the judiciary, and bureaucrats, to respect human rights. This is also not new in the area of development.
8. Involvement of civil society (meaning NGOs) in the implementation of the plan. This element clearly owed more to the existing practices in the area of development (as in the poverty alleviation plans), which involve NGOs in implementation. Human rights discourse does not accommodate civil society in its normative framework, as noted above.
9. Allocation of resources to implement the plan.
10. Identifying a national monitoring mechanism to follow up the implementation of the plan. This is a new component in development where administrative, rather than independent, monitoring of plan implementation has been the norm.

As can be seen, the concept of a NHRP poses some significant challenges to the way human-rights work has been done so far, in an accusatory, counter-sovereignty mode. Rather, the NHRP mode calls for a more symbiotic relationship between government action, NGO services, social movement action, and international advocacy and funding. To that extent, the NAPHR may constitute a challenge to the way human rights are currently implemented. But the impact of the NHRP on development practices is far more ambiguous. With the clear exception of a normative link with international standards (element 3), many of the components of NHRPs appear to simply reproduce existing practices of development. This finding sits uncomfortably with the proponents of the convergence thesis, who claim that by converging with human rights, development will be fundamentally transformed. I fail to see such transformation.

This becomes more evident when one looks at the main issues that have been addressed in these countries mentioned during the preparation of the NHRP. These issues are the process leading to the preparation of the plan, the form and content of the plan, implementation, and monitoring. While it is too early to judge the implementation and follow-up of NHRPs (as they have been adopted only within the last four to five years in most countries mentioned), the overall impression that one obtains is that of an overwhelming emphasis on the process of preparation of the plan, with a comparative neglect of the substantive aspects of the plan. While I acknowledge the potentially empowering aspect of a really democratic and participatory process involving NGOs and other actors, I do suggest that substantive outcomes are equally, if not more, important. Indeed, it is the failure to achieve substantive outcomes that has led to a legitimacy crisis for development. Most of the funds allocated are spent on the process, thus leaving little for actual implementation. Such a process-fetishizing, proceduralist approach belies the promise held out in the convergence thesis: that development would be transformed for good.

As noted, the most significant departure that is heralded by the planning approach to human rights is that it seeks to provide a normative basis for development interventions. Hitherto, development was a political, economic, social, and, even, an ideological project. By grounding the planning for development in human rights, an attempt is being made now to make development into a legal project. The motive for this move to escape ideology, and ground development normatively, comes from two sources. First, it comes out of a sense of a crisis of legitimacy and an impasse in action that development has been facing for years, as it has failed to bring about the economic and social transformations that it promised to poor people around the world. Human rights discourse is seen to provide an injection of legitimacy into development. Second, it also comes from a belief in law as a neutral, trans-ideological, meta-cultural terrain that is beyond contestation. By grounding development in such (an international) law of human rights, the development profession is hoping that the normative basis of the discourse will decrease contestation over its interventions. As I have suggested, however, this is unlikely to happen as the very normative terrain that is being relied upon to escape contestation is itself the product of ideological, political, and cultural struggles.

The NAPHR concept is the most definite example of the developmentalization of human rights. The whole idea of planning, which is foreign to the area of human rights, has been borrowed from development. On the one hand, this is criticized by many NGOs as an unfortunate occurrence, as the state is accorded the central role in planning and the 'experts' assume their role as the gatekeepers of human rights. On the other hand, if done properly, the NAPHR also has the potential to achieve two things, which may assist the reform of the development apparatus and ensure concrete implementation of human rights. First, by 'projectizing' human rights, it may bring much-needed resources for social programs that have been cut under neoliberalism and Washington-consensus. One of the key problem for human-rights enforcement has always been the lack of resources, which may improve considerably because of this factor. Second, the NAPHR may also compel policy-makers to take human rights more seriously as an essential component of development planning, programming, and implementation, rather than treating them as afterthoughts. But what it does not appear to offer, as the proponents of the convergence thesis argue, is a fundamental change in the way development has been done so far.

Problems in 'developmentalizing' human rights

A whole set of further problems render the task of doing human-rights planning, programming, and policy within the boundaries of the development discourse extraordinarily difficult. Some such problems may be discussed here. First, there are no objective indicators or benchmarks that measure all human rights. For the purpose of this chapter, 'objective' is the absence of any ideological, cultural, political, or other bias towards one or more of possible outcomes. This makes it impossible to do programming, implementation, and monitoring in a technical manner (if that's at all possible). Indicators on political and civil rights are most problematic due to their political bias, such as the Freedom House Index. Despite this, economists freely rely upon them in measuring, for example, the relationship between democracy and wages,[158] or between civil liberties and the performance of government-funded projects.[159] Indicators on economic, social, and cultural rights are more developed, such as the Human Development Index, but they are not free of bias in using criteria that favor 'modern' over 'traditional' ways of living. For example, in computing quantitative measurements of how many cubic meters

[158] Rodrik (1998). [159] Pritchet and Kaufman (1998).

of space is a minimum requirement in the right to housing, traditional forms of housing as a Mongolian Ger or a Tamil kudisai are not used to set the standard; rather, the standard is derived from 'modern' housing. This is not to make the case that 'indigenous' forms of life are superior to 'modern' ones. Rather, it is merely to point out the inconsistency in measurements that purport to be 'objective' but end up favoring one over the other.

The second problem in integrating human rights into sustainable human development is that the normative framework for imposing responsibilities on development institutions is underdeveloped. As I suggested, adopting a human-rights approach to development often means changing the way development has been done before. This entails legal responsibilities on international institutions and the private sector and there is very little normative framework except the DRD, which aims at this. Other efforts to establish the normative basis for realizing a human-rights approach to development are blocked or frustrated easily. For example, the International Law Commission's Draft Articles on International Crimes included dumping of toxic wastes as an international crime. Given that a substantial amount of toxic-waste dumping is done by private companies in developing countries, this was a sensible proposal. However, this proposal has disappeared from view, especially in the final draft of the Rome Charter that established the International Criminal Court in 1998.

The third problem in integrating human rights into development is the central role accorded to the state in the realization of human rights under international law. As discussed earlier, this is a very complex problem with no easy answers. On the one hand, the crisis over development in many countries has arisen largely because of the failure of the state to 'do development' in a socially and environmentally responsible manner. It would then be problematic to 'return' to the state under the rubric of human rights, when it stands thoroughly discredited in the eyes of civil society in many developing countries. On the other hand, relying entirely on the market means simply caving in to neoliberalism. The key challenge here is to try to identify modalities for doing development that do not replicate, but go beyond both the traditional state and the market models, perhaps by reinventing the very idea of public action.

Conclusion

This chapter has argued against the progressive constitution of the human-rights discourse as the sole discourse of resistance in the Third World.

I offered analyses of several themes to illustrate the perils of focusing exclusively on the human-rights discourse and ignoring forms of resistance that are not 'representable' within its logic. These themes included the following, among others. First, the problematic relationship between colonialism and human-rights discourse has imbedded a series of representative practices within the latter, which produce a double effect: dismissal of the 'Third World' as a site of epistemological production of human rights, while rendering several forms of violence, such as that generated by development, invisible to the discourse. Constituting human-rights discourse as the sole discourse of resistance may continue to re-enact these colonial representative practices. Second, human-rights discourse is based on the creation of an apparatus of modernity mainly through a process of 'etatization,' since the realization of rights is predicated on the moral possibilities of the state and the material possibilities of the market. I suggested that unless the forms of public action can be reconceived in terms that move away from traditional statist models, focusing only on human-rights discourse may simply tend to reproduce discredited state structures. Third, I examined the internal structure of human-rights discourse to figure out if it has a theory of violence, and made the argument that forms of economic violence remain invisible to human-rights discourse due to its commitment to transform human beings into economic agents. This blindness has a serious consequence for attempts to constitute human-rights discourse as the sole discourse of resistance. Fourth, the normative consequences of the gradual appropriation of human-rights discourse by the development discourse was analyzed and it was argued that this developmentalization has led to the emergence of debates about culture in human-rights discourse. In particular, I suggested that the emergence of 'culture' as a terrain of engagement in human-rights discourse, in the form of the Asian Values debate, coincides with the East Asian miracle debate in development discourse. This political economy of the human-rights discourse makes it less likely to be neutral or impartial in countering the violence of development. Finally, some recent moves in international institutional practice to merge human rights and development discourses were examined, in the light of the historical relationship between the two and the right to development debate. I suggested that while a more radical interpretation of the DRD could have changed development as it has so far been done, it has been frustrated because, among others, the DRD did not question the very model of development that it was purportedly promoting as a right. This problem continues to beset the most recent policy interventions that seek to merge development and human-rights discourses.

While I do not dismiss the value of human rights as a tool of strategy and mobilization for oppressed groups – as Patricia Williams reminded us[160] – I remain deeply skeptical of current tendencies to constitute it as the sole language of resistance and emancipation in the Third World. Given its colonial legacy, statist and anti-tradition bias, economistic method, and deep imbrication with the development discourse, human-rights discourse remains, at best, a partial, fragmentary, and a sometimes-useful tool of mobilization – not by any means a sole language of resistance and emancipation for oppressed social majorities around the world.

[160] Williams (1991).

8

Recoding resistance: social movements and the challenge to international law

> A focus on social movements with restructuring agendas itself incorporates a political judgment on how drastic global reform can best be achieved at this stage of history.[1]

Lawyers generally do not concern themselves with mass politics or popular resistance. By professional training, intellectual orientation, political and class alignment, and tradition, lawyers focus on institutions of various kinds, whether governmental or private. As such, they tend to ask different sets of questions about social change and the role of law in it. For instance, in domestic law, they examine the 'contribution' of courts to the civil rights movement in the US by studying landmark cases such as *Brown v. Board of Education*. Such 'technical' or 'legal' discussions result in distilling the contribution of the masses out of historical transformations, and they highlight only the role played by judges and lawyers. In this rather clinical reduction of facts, the 'case' becomes the historical event itself, so that legal history is reduced to a cataloguing of factually abstracted episodes that bear little relation to each other.

This tendency in western domestic law to ignore the contribution of the masses has been subjected to criticism from at least two directions in recent years. First, in the US, an assortment of critical race theorists, feminists, gay-lesbian-queer theorists, have subjected this decontextualized, technocratic-rational model of law and legal history to criticism on the grounds that it ignores the role that law plays in everyday life and empowerment and also the role played by ordinary people as agents of legal transformation. To them, the liberal legal model that has remained dominant in the US so far, is fatally flawed due to these, among other, blind spots and needs to be fundamentally rethought. Nevertheless, though some of these writings allude to social movements, much of this literature does not explicitly engage with social movement literature,

[1] Falk (1987) 173.

with the recent exception of some scholars such as Kimberle Crenshaw, Lucy White, and Janet Halley.[2] These draw inspiration, inter alia, from the legal theoretical work of Robert Cover, positing the notion of "interpretive communities"[3] that create law and give it meaning through their own lived action.

Second, a small number of socio-legal theorists and comparativists from the US and Europe, and several constitutional scholars from non-western countries, have engaged in pioneering critiques of liberal theories of rights, justice, and democracy, by explicitly engaging with social movements literature. This includes the works of Joel Handler on civil rights, welfare and other movements in the US,[4] Austin Sarat on identity and rights,[5] Jurgen Habermas on democracy and rights,[6] Alan Hunt and Neil Stammers on human rights,[7] Sousa Santos on legal theory and human rights,[8] Upendra Baxi on democracy, rights, and justice,[9] and, more recently, Diane Otto on human rights and postcolonial theory[10] and Julie Mertus on transnational civil society.[11] These critiques have pointed out the elitist bias of extant rights theories and conceptions of democracy and have attempted to formulate general conceptions of law that could accommodate the role of subaltern communities and individuals.

A central aspect of these two streams of literature has been the interrogation of the role that law plays in regulating power in everyday life, and, in turn, the impact of everyday practices on the law itself.[12] This study of the dynamic between the institutional and extra-institutional aspects of social life, and the importance of extra-institutional mobilization for the success/failure of institutions, has injected new elements into an understanding of law. Indeed, one of the main distinguishing characteristics of the social movements literature was this emphasis on the interconnectedness between everyday forms of power struggle and institutional politics, including at the national and global levels.[13] To put it differently, a social movement perspective emphasizes the importance of extra-institutional

[2] Crenshaw (1988); White and Handler (1999); White (1997); White (1993); Halley (1998).
[3] Cover (1983) 40.
[4] Handler (1978). His more recent work has focused on welfare and poverty law. See, e.g., Handler and Hasenfeld (1997).
[5] Sarat and Kearns (1995). [6] Habermas (1996).
[7] Hunt (1990); Stammers (1999). [8] Santos (1995). [9] Baxi (1998).
[10] Otto (1997b); Otto (1996a); Otto (1996b). [11] Mertus (1999).
[12] This is the understanding of power that Michel Foucault has put forward, that power is not confined to the institutional, political arenas, but 'circulates' through all spheres of life as a relational phenomenon. See Foucault (1980).
[13] See, e.g., Falk (1987).

forms of mobilization for the 'success' or 'failure' of institutional forms.[14] In this sense, these extra-institutional forms of mobilization constitute important arenas of resistance that remain beyond the cognitive boundaries of international law's sole, approved discourse of resistance, viz., human rights.

Very little of this has yet percolated international law, however. International law remains trapped in a version of politics that is narrowly focused on institutional practice, and an understanding of the 'social' that takes the unity of the agent as given. This has given international law an artificially narrow outlook. Leading scholars are aware of this, and have attempted to construct a broader approach to international law, mainly by identifying non-state actors as 'international' actors,[15] and by arguing for a right to personal identity that would allow international law to accommodate the plurality of social agents (on the basis of class, gender, race, ethnicity, and so on).[16] Despite this, much of what happens in the extra-institutional spaces in the Third World remains invisible to international law. Indeed, I shall argue that it is partly due to the limitations of the liberal categories such as rights, employed to represent social movements, that such blind spots continue to exist.

In this chapter, I discuss the emergence of various social movements in the extra-institutional space, in the form of religious movements, peasant movements, environmental movements, indigenous peoples' movements, workers' movements, farmers' movements, urban squatters' movements, feminist and women's movements, and gay and lesbian movements in the Third World and their relationship to international law. The main argument put forward in this chapter has two components: first, it is suggested that the praxis of these social movements pose radical theoretical and epistemological challenges to international law – both the mainstream and the critical – to the extent that they articulate alternative conceptions of modernity and development that can not be sufficiently captured by

[14] This is what Claus Offe calls 'noninstitutional politics,' and Rajni Kothari calls non-party political formations.' Offe (1985); Kothari (1993).

[15] This has a rich pedigree. The first wave of scholarship argued for the recognition of international institutions, and MNCs as legal actors. See Corbett (1924); Jenks (1958); Friedman (1964); Jessup (1956). A second wave argued for recognition of individuals, peoples and liberation movements as legal actors. Lauterpacht (1950); Sohn (1982); Quaye (1991). A third wave has now been arguing for recognition of NGOs as international legal actors. See Spiro (1995); Charnowitz (1997). Richard Falk has been calling for a post-Westphalian world order based on the emergence of a 'globalization from below.' See Falk (1998).

[16] Franck (1996).

extant branches of international law, including human rights. In other words, there are important forms of Third World resistance that remain beyond the discursive framework of international law. I do not claim that these movements are invariably 'progressive'; indeed, many of these movements do enact forms of cultural politics that are very problematic for the rights of minorities, women, or other groups. Nevertheless, even these movements often emerge as a reaction against the failure of preceding geo-political orders and regimes and, as such, enable a collective questioning of what went wrong. The Iranian revolution is a good example: while it proved to be violent and dictatorial, it has enabled Iranians to attempt to develop culturally legitimate ways of conceiving social and political progress that do not replicate the mistakes of the Shah regime, including a total alienation from Islam and a violent modernization process.

To substantiate this suggestion, a series of conceptual tools from social movement literature are introduced and linked up with international legal debates to show how thinking about international law through social movements is much more rewarding than through states (as realists/positivists do) or individuals (as liberals/naturalists do). The central purpose of the inquiry here is how does one write this resistance into international law? The concept of 'cultural politics' is introduced here and it is suggested that international law must decenter itself from the unitary conception of the political sphere on which it is based, which takes the state or the individual as the principal political actor. Then, I examine four areas in which the praxis of social movements radically challenges human rights, which functions as the sole approved discourse of resistance, as argued in the previous chapter: (a) the constitution of an 'alternative' human-rights discourse from the praxis of social movements that is unrepresentable within the extant human-rights paradigm. The praxis of social movements problematizes the traditional pro-sovereign/anti-sovereign posture of international lawyers by showing how it is possible to realize human rights without relying on the state, and, at the same time, avoid adopting an anti-state posture that is characteristic of the mainstream rights discourse; (b) the redefinition of civil society and democracy: social movements move international law beyond formalist definitions of democracy – such as electoral rights – and negative definitions of civil society as the arena of non-governmental activity, to a richer, positive definition based on a cultural politics of identity, autonomy, and territory. Taking a social movement perspective, I suggest, shows that the notion of civil society is not restricted to NGOs. I also introduce Nancy Fraser's concept of "subaltern counterpublics" to argue for a reinvigoration of the concept of civil society in international law; (c) disrupting the property-rights nexus and asserting local control over property resources: social movements have compelled the articulation of alternative conceptions of property and economic arrangements in several western and non-western countries that starkly reveal the inadequacies of extant conceptions about property and markets, and pose serious challenges to liberal internationalism; (d) social movements contradict one of the central tenets of current liberal orthodoxies, that increasing globalization leads inexorably to a marginalization of the local and towards transnationalism; instead, they show that increasing globalization may very well lead to an increase in the importance of the "local" as the agent of socio-political change in developing countries. This "local" could be local government structures (such as Panchayats in India) or unique forms of government–civil-society combinations that challenge the very definition of the state.[17] Nowhere is this more apparent than in the recent popularity of autonomy, decentralization, and devolution in several developing countries.

The second component of the main argument in this chapter is that while the international legal system continues to be organized on a 'global' basis, it is also increasingly being revealed as inadequate, and is resisted, coopted, and transformed by social movements at the local and – for want of a better term – 'glocal' levels. This has serious implications for the spatial boundaries within which international law is conceptualized, elaborated upon, and argued over. I suggest that international law is incapable, at present, of meeting this challenge.

Social movements and international law: a theoretical introduction and a redefinition of the political

Let me begin by providing a contextual introduction to the theoretical challenges that arise when we adopt a social movement perspective towards international law. The current interest in social movements must be traced to the historical context in which forms of popular mobilizations began to transform the Third World. During the 1950s and 1960s, the principal forms of popular mobilizations in the Third World were organized around the 'nation,' aimed mainly at national liberation from colonial rule, and around "class," aiming at structural transformation

[17] For a great example of this, see Tendler (1997) chapter 6.

of the colonial/comprador economic and social orders within Third World countries. This mass radicalism lay behind the elite Third World radicalism one witnessed at the UN, calling for a NIEO. This was accompanied and followed by large public mobilizations in Western countries such as the civil rights, black nationalist, women's rights, and gay and lesbian rights movements in the US, the green movement in West Germany, and the 1968 student protests in France. However, by the early 1970s, after the engineered 'fall' of Allende in Chile, the splintering of the Third World coalition in the mid-1970s, the containment of nationalist and class movements by the two Super Powers, and the genuine grassroots disillusionment with the violence of the nation-building project in many Third World countries, new forms of popular mobilization began to emerge, based on new forms of domination and exploitation (such as migrant labor, urban squatters, women). These forms of mobilizations were beginning to transform the political, economic, and social landscape of many Third World countries, and, yet, they could not be analyzed within the Marxist paradigm, which had provided the tools for interpreting radical social change in the Third World for several decades. The literature on social movements emerged largely as a response to these new forms of mobilizations, even as it attempted to explain the exhaustion of left ideology. This explains the attempt to distinguish the new forms of popular mobilizations as 'new social movements' (based on identity politics) from presumably 'old' social movements such as national liberation movements or the class-based movements. By the end of the 1990s, identity-based movements themselves had run out of steam and had come under severe questioning from, among others, post-Marxists. This followed the discovery that the 'move to markets' in development policy in the early 1990s conveniently coincided with the move away from class to identity. The whole spectrum of literature that discusses the above political and social developments is what I refer to broadly as social movements literature. This literature is complex, varied, and spread across several disciplines including sociology, comparative politics, anthropology, and critical development studies.

This literature contains a multitude of views about what constitutes a social movement, and what distinguishes a 'new' from an 'old' movement. To take one example, Mario Diani identifies the following general elements in a social movement: (1) it involves networks of informal interactions between a plurality of actors; (2) it is engaged in political or cultural conflicts; (3) it organizes on the basis of shared beliefs and collective identities.[18] This definition raises several important issues. First, there is the issue of what causes one movement to mobilize more successfully than another – that is, what kinds of networks of interaction are necessary for converting popular discontent or sporadic disaffection into a viable movement. A general answer that is provided is that 'social movement organization' or NGOs provide the glue to the coordination of actors with multiple motives to join the movement.[19] This does not mean that NGOs lead social movements[20] or that they themselves constitute social movements.[21] Amnesty International is not a social movement, but may form a part of particular social movements in particular locations, a movement to abolish capital punishment, for example. Second, the plurality of actors in social movements includes organizations, groups of individuals, and individuals, all of whom may have different motivations for joining such social movements. The anti-globalization movement – recently witnessed in Washington, DC – is an example of this plurality: it contains western labor activists worried about loss of jobs but also unions who push for protectionism, environmental activists concerned about the eco-damage of global business practices, but also anarchists who throw bombs at Starbucks, human-rights activists who worry about the unaccountability of corporations and international organizations, but also governments who exploit these fears to promote geopolitical interests, Third World social movements for whom the struggle against globalization is a struggle to live, and a number of other hangers-on who do not have any immediate stake but who just like to be part of the show. Exploring and understanding these different motivations is crucial to a proper appreciation of how international legal norms and processes work in practice. Third, the notion of conflict is understood, as Diani notes, in different ways by different scholars.[22] Some view conflict as primarily an interpersonal and cultural one,[23] while others view it as one directed towards economic and political change.[24] In the context of the Third World, most social movements emerge through a conflict with capitalist development. Barry Adam points out:

[18] Diani (1992). [19] Tarrow (1998) 15.

[20] As Tarrow asserts, a "bimodal relationship between leaders and followers . . . is absent from movements" (Ibid. 15).

[21] Diani (1992) 13–14. See Fisher (1997). [22] Diani (1992) 10. [23] Melucci (1989).

[24] Tarrow theorizes that movements respond to political opportunity and advance their causes through direct confrontation with formal political spheres. See Tarrow (1998) 18. Post-Marxists emphasize how movements emerge through their ongoing struggles with the state and capital. See Adam (1993).

> to ignore the dynamics of capitalist development, the role of the labor markets in reorganizing spatial and familial relations, and the interaction of new and traditional categories of people with dis/employment patterns is to ignore the structural prerequisites which have made the new social movements not only possible, but predictable.[25]

The literature also points out that how a conflict plays out – the strategies used, the means deployed and shunned, and simply what gets counted as 'political' – will depend on each society's own historical methods of protest – what Tarrow calls 'contention by convention'.[26] This calls for a very contextual understanding of resistance, unlike the totalizing category of rights, which presumes that resistance is expressed only in the secular, rational, and bureaucratic arenas of the modern state, especially through the judiciary. Thus, Parisians build barricades[27] and Indians stage *dharnas* and *satyagrahas*. 'Political culture' as a concept is critical for understanding what gets counted as 'political' when conflicts arise in particular societies. Instead, international law (and law in general) reduces complex conflicts in non-western societies to the "rationalist, universalist and individualist" political culture of the west.[28] The final element of Diani's definition is that movements organize on the basis of shared beliefs and collective identities. This raises the issue of how such identities get formed in the first place. Some suggest that a 'consensus mobilization' is an ongoing part of a movement's formation,[29] while others acknowledge that irreconcilable differences lead to a "process of realignment and negotiation between actors."[30] To me, it appears that both these processes occur in many social movements, often simultaneously. As gaps between different actors widen and consensus eludes them, realignment of identities begin to occur. This process is wholly different from the 'right to identity' approach adopted by international law, which looks at identity as merely an individual choice.

Beyond liberalism and Marxism: toward a cultural politics

It then goes without saying that the new forms of mobilization in the Third World could not be analyzed using liberal categories such as rights. First, liberal theory assumed a sharp distinction between public and private, privileging only that which belonged to the public sphere for legal protection. As the feminist slogan 'personal is political' vividly showed, this

[25] Adam (1993) 322. [26] Tarrow (1998) 18. [27] Ibid. 19.
[28] Mouffe (1993) 2. [29] Tarrow (1998) 22–23. [30] Diani (1992) 9.

simply failed to take account of relations of power in the domestic or private arenas. This was based on a sharply delimited arena of the 'political,' which has been shown by feminists, among others, as inadequate. Second, liberal theory assumed all legitimate power to be united in a 'sovereign will' and all political activity to be conducted through institutional arenas such as legislatures and through institutions such as political parties. This was revealed in the experience of Third World mass movements to be disciplinary (as it ruled out other arenas of doing politics) and promoting a corrupt version of etatism. European social theorists, especially Jürgen Habermas, Alain Touraine, Claus Offe, and Alberto Melucci, had criticized this liberal tendency to unify the political space. Habermas in particular, had theorized about new social movements, drawing on the experience of German Green movements, and postulated the idea of the 'public sphere' where, he argued, opinion formation takes place, prior to will formation in the sanctioned political arenas. This 'public sphere' has been a useful tool for conceptualizing social movements. Third, liberal theory assumed the unity of the social actor (as a consumer, producer, citizen, etc.) and created formal arenas where the interests of such social actors would be represented. The praxis of social movements in the Third World shows that the heterogeneity and plurality of the social actor is an essential feature of mass mobilization, which the representational model can not accommodate without doing violence to its heterogeneous character. Fourth, liberal theory assumed a harmonious view towards economic growth, as it assumed that the post War welfare state would shoulder the responsibility of humanizing it. This was based on the understanding that the contradictions created by the institutions of civil society – property, market, the family, and so on – would be 'neutrally' resolved by the state. Instead of achieving this result, the state simply colonized civil society and, indeed, all life spaces. This was particularly true in Latin America and Asia, which followed state-led industrialization as part of an import substitution strategy. Social movements in the Third World have arisen then partly as an attempt to liberate these life spaces from the state, and partly to politicize the very institutions of civil society so that it is no longer dependent upon ever more regulation and control.

How did Marxist theory figure in this? After all, Marxism had provided the theoretical tools for analyzing the social conflicts in the Third World for almost half a decade. The short answer simply is, as I have suggested, social movements in the Third World emerged substantially as a response to the failure of Marxism as a liberatory discourse. This was due to many factors. First, Marxism assumed the identity of social agents (peasant, labor, etc.) through fixed social structures that privileged some categories over others (for example, the proletariat as the vanguard). This meant for example, that a struggle that lacks a 'real' class basis – 'bourgeois feminism' or 'kulak farmers' – could not be comprehended. Due to this, Marxism was fast becoming irrelevant to the most important social struggles in the Third World that were organized around environmental degradation, oppression of women, and dispossession of labor and assets from farmers. Second, Marxism was wedded to an evolutionary view of society and therefore tended to interpret all social struggles in terms of a move from feudalism to capitalism, for example. In addition to being rigid and essentialistic, this historical determinism missed the real nature of many Third World social movements, which combined struggles over material aspects (economic struggle) with struggles over symbolic meanings (cultural struggle). In addition, this evolutionary view bordered on ethnocentrism as it automatically assumed the superiority of specific forms of western modernity over non-western tradition. This was rejected by several social movements in the Third World such as the Zapatistas, who organized around a particularly strong cultural identity. Third, Marxism shared with liberal theory, the understanding of a unified political space and, by consequence, the state as the main agent of social and economic change. Consequently, the purpose of mass mobilization, it was theorized, was the capture of state power. This was reinforced by the etatism of Third World development models in the post World War II period such as import-substitution and export-promotion. Social movements, on the other hand, reject the state as the main agent of socio-political transformation and do not seek state power as an end in itself. Instead, they seek to recover their own political space in which they can set the pace and direction of economic change. Fourth, Marxism began to get out of touch with the new forms of economic arrangements and new forms of struggles that accompanied them, not only in advanced industrial societies, but also in the Third World. These new economies, revealed most clearly by the emergence of foreign direct investment, trade and capital markets, began to show that the sphere of capital accumulation and its processes were wider than those of commodity production and exchange. It was wider in at least two ways: first, capital accumulation was increasingly on a global scale, whereas commodity production had been theorized within the boundaries of the nation state; second, capital accumulation was beginning to include substantial amounts of labor, (domestic labor, informal immigrant labor, in low-wage apparel industries) and wealth (nature itself) that were not included in commodity production and exchange.

In short, there was a global economy in the making. Marxism was simply unable to supply the theoretical tools to comprehend and respond to it. The social movements that emerged in the Third World emerged largely as a response to the new, harsh forms of global economy. Indigenous peoples movements, fishworkers' movements, farmers' movements, and anti-globalization protests are, then, a result of the failure of Marxism as a coherent left doctrine. I'll suggest, following Gail Omvedt,[31] that what is needed is a historical materialism of all groups adversely affected by the new global economy (I do not discuss this more here).

Social movements arise, then, as a challenge to liberalism and Marxism, and, therefore, by extension, to extant theories of international law. These theories extend from the utopian (liberal/western/naturalist) to the apologist (Marxist/Third Worldist/positivist). The utopians imagine a world without sovereignty (but not necessarily without the state) in which the individual is the primary political actor. The apologists on the other hand, take the political community of the nation state as the primary political actor and seek to imagine an international legal order that is at the same time created and constrained by their sovereignty. Social movements reverse both these ways of imagining an international order: they seek to preserve the autonomy implied in the positivist vision, but by abandoning the nation state as the collectivity that would guarantee such autonomy; they also share the naturalists' deep suspicion of the leviathan, but allow a multiplicity of arenas including the community (rather than the individual alone) as political actors. Instead of the unified political space allowed by these extant theories, social movements seek to redefine the very boundaries of what is properly 'political.'

Indeed, all social movements enact a unique form of politics that I would label "cultural politics." By saying this, I do not mean to privilege those movements that are more clearly cultural as 'authentic.' In the past, this resulted in a false dichotomy between 'new' and 'old' social movements: the former based on identity and new forms of politics (such as human rights, gay, environment, etc.) while the latter movements struggled for resources and the need to cope with the contradictions of the capitalist economy (such as urban squatters', peasant, and fishworkers' movements). Rather, for all these movements identities are strongly associated with survival strategies. This gives rise to a much richer, contextual, and relational form of politics. As an important recent collection of essays puts it:

[31] Omvedt (1993) xvi.

> We interpret cultural politics as the process enacted when sets of social actors shaped by, and embodying, different cultural meanings and practices come into conflict with each other... Culture is political because meanings are constitutive of processes that, implicitly or explicitly, seek to redefine social power. That is, when movements deploy alternative conceptions of women, nature, race, economy, democracy, or citizenship that unsettle dominant cultural meanings, they enact a cultural politics.[32]

This definition makes it clear that politics is much more than a set of actions taken in formal political arenas (such as legislatures); rather, it is a decentered phenomenon that encompasses power struggles, which are enacted in the private, social, economic, and cultural arenas in addition to the formal arenas. By challenging and resignifying what counts as political and who gets to define what's political, social movements foster alternative conceptions of the political itself.

To illustrate more clearly what this rich, relational definition of the 'political' means for international law, let me outline its elements:

(a) politics goes beyond what we do in formal arenas, and therefore beyond formal voting rights and representation. However, human-rights law and mainstream political science continue to focus on what happens in the formal institutions to the exclusion of non-institutional mobilizations. For example, a leading democracy theorist states that political institutionalization is "the single most important and urgent factor in the consolidation of democracy."[33] This narrow outlook governs several areas of international law including peacekeeping and peace building, international economic law, good governance, and humanitarian interventions to save "failed states."

(b) Struggles over meanings and values in the domain of culture are also political. The personal is finally political. This reverses a bias against culture that international law has historically exhibited.

(c) Political struggles are relational; they are not individual. This abandons the 'billiard ball' model of politics that has governed liberal rights theory and realist international legal theory. To resignify alternative conceptions of the body or the woman, one needs to look at the way groups and communities mobilize in concrete circumstances.

(d) Conflict is at the heart of politics. This element, which is borrowed from Marxism, reverses the liberal theory's presumption in favor of harmony between social classes (and a resultant covering up of

[32] Alvarez, Dagnino, and Escobar (1998) 7. [33] Diamond and Plattner (1993).

underlying conflicts). These conflicts, which arise at both the material and symbolic levels, are not between nation-states, but between classes. This element lends a much needed left-oriented perspective to counter the pro-cosmopolitan, pro-global, capitalist bias of international law.

(e) By positing a cultural politics, social movements effectively foster alternative modernities. As Fernando Calderón puts it, some movements pose the question of how to be both modern and different:[34] by mobilizing meanings that can not be defined within standard paradigms of western modernity, they challenge international law's authority to pronounce on what is modern and traditional.

(f) Finally, identities do not result merely from individual choice, but from relational activities between a group of people who come together to achieve a common purpose in the form of a movement. In this sense, the 'rights' to identity are inherently relational.[35] This is entirely foreign to both the utopian and apologist approaches to international law.

It may then appear that the praxis of social movements centrally challenges the very foundations of international law, and provides a more realistic and hopeful way of imagining a post-Westphalian order, as Richard Falk has called it. Instead of the universal categories of sovereignty and rights, social movements offer a pluriversal defense of local communities. In doing that, they reveal the limitations of a Kantian liberal world order based primarily on individual autonomy and rights, and a realist world order based primarily on state sovereignty.

Rethinking international human-rights law: social movements as counter-hegemonic strategies

In this section, I argue for an interdisciplinary approach to international human-rights law from the perspective of social movements theory in social anthropology. The discussion is located in the context of the emergence of various types of protest and resistance movements in the Third World during the last two decades or so. Despite the emergence of such movements and a vast body of literature analyzing those movements,

[34] Fernando Calderón, quoted in Alvarez, Dagnino and Escobar (1997) 9.

[35] Recent rights and property scholarship in the US has moved to articulate a social relations approach, as I discuss below. See in particular, the work of Jennifer Nedelsky, Joseph Singer, and Jack Beerman.

international human-rights law has remained virtually isolated from them. Indeed, even the international human-rights and international law scholarship that has attempted to do interdisciplinary work so far, has not focused on social anthropology in general, and social movements research in particular.[36] Given the anti-state rhetoric of much of international human-rights law, and the emphasis placed on the role of NGOs and civil society in human-rights theory and practice, it is rather puzzling why international lawyers and human-rights activists have not taken social movements research seriously. This section will seek some answers to these questions. Much of the extant interdisciplinary work, which emerged as part of an attempt to understand the growing influence of 'global civil society' on international politics, relies on international relations (IR) theory, with its state-centered rhetoric and realist or liberal normative framework.[37] As such, it does not appreciate the fundamental, epistemological challenge that social movements pose to international law. Scholars analyze the emergence of social movements within the liberal paradigm of human rights, rather than seeing the praxis of social movements as a challenge and alternative to the rights discourse. I shall argue that social movements do in fact constitute alternatives to the rights discourse.

I shall begin by rehearsing some themes from the last chapter to provide background. To begin, despite its anti-state rhetoric, the theory and practice of international human rights law is actually built on the doctrine of sovereignty. Indeed, its counter-sovereignty posturing only led it into an empty and contentious cul-de-sac of theoretical impasse and practical limitation, that affirmed the centrality of sovereignty, by denying it. In particular, the critical weaknesses of the received historiography of rights, as I see it, are two: its neglect of internal social resistance as human-rights praxis, due to its exclusive focus on the state, and its uncritical acceptance of the counter-sovereignty liberal rights rhetoric, without examining the socioeconomic and cultural foundations of rights and sovereignty. These weaknesses have greatly reduced the transformatory potential of international human-rights discourse, and instead made it into a handmaiden of particular constellations and exercises of power.

These weaknesses are due to the nature of the rights discourse, the vocabulary of international human-rights praxis, and its relationship to sovereignty and property. As I argued, the mainstream rights discourse

[36] Exceptions are Falk (1987); Hunt (1990); Aziz (1995); Stammers (1999). For partial attempts to engage with social movements, see Otto (1996a); Weston (1992).

[37] Lipshutz (1992); Wapner (1994); Symposium Issue (1994); Spiro (1995).

has had a deeply conservative effect on the transformatory potential of international human rights. This it did in many ways. First, according to Lockian liberal theory, rights were conceived of negatively as individual spheres of autonomy, vis-à-vis the State. This is exactly the way property rights were conceived of under anti-bellum laissez-faire capitalism, and the way sovereignty was understood in post-Westphalian world order. This idea of negative rights is at the core of human rights discourse in the form of civil and political rights. By their nature, these negative rights did not question the structural or sociopolitical root causes of human-rights violations such as patterns of land ownership, militarization, local autonomy, or control over natural resources. Second, the other rights that did call into question the resource-base of human-rights violations, namely, economic, social, and cultural rights, were treated as 'second generation' rights whose implementation depended on a standard of 'progressive realization' and not immediate implementation. Third, the group rights such as self-determination, which had the potential of disrupting the conservative nature of human rights praxis, were tamed by subjecting them to two rules: first, that they would not violate existing territorial integrity of states, and second, they would not include economic self-determination.

This situation underwent a significant change in the 1970s and 1980s. First, development theory moved from trickle-down growth to growth with redistribution and basic needs to participatory human development. During the same time, human-rights discourse moved from an exclusive emphasis on civil and political rights, to a position that all rights are indivisible and interdependent, and then finally to a set of 'third generation' rights such as the right to development. This convergence – from the polarities of economics and politics – brought about a crisis in human-rights theory, even as it opened up exciting new areas for human-rights practice. This crisis resulted from the fact that rights such as right to development, go to the root of the legitimacy of the state and the viability of the doctrine of sovereignty by questioning the developmental basis of the state including the prominent role of the state in the development process. Yet, this crisis appears to have been overcome for the moment.

The primary reason why the new stream of critique has been successfully coopted by human-rights discourse is because of two reasons: first, the new stream did not question the very model of development that the state was pursuing and the dominant role of the state in that process; and second, the new stream was also framed as rights discourse thereby losing much of its transformatory potential, without attempting to rethink the very Lockian terms of that discourse to reflect pluriversal ways of achieving human dignity and freedom. Before such rethinking occurs, articulation of any emancipatory project in the language of rights is limited within its rationalistic and disciplinary terms, which emphasize individual autonomy over relationships and trust. The model of development pursued by the Third World was based on western ideas of rationality and progress which had to be questioned in order to formulate a critical praxis of human rights. Rights discourse, with its historical connection to ideas of property and sovereignty, had to be replaced with other strategies or discourses, in order to get over its conservative influence. All this did not happen.

Viewed against this historiography, social movements offer much that is different and interesting from a human-rights point of view. First, much of the social movements theory and practice is radically skeptical of development in that social movements do not aim to catch-up with the West, but seek to determine what kind of growth is best for them, under what conditions such growth should occur and whether there should be limits to such growth. In this sense, they contradict western ideas of rationality and progress, which are based on the principle of scarcity and the policy of ever-expanding growth. Second, substantial parts of social movements theory and practice is not state-centered. This is not only because many social movements do not aspire for State power, but also because the practice of many social movements transcends the sovereignty–counter-sovereignty dualism that typifies human rights discourse. Third, social movements theory and practice offer an interesting and different way of thinking about how to realize the emancipatory or liberating potential of rights discourse without succumbing to the conservative influences of its property-sovereignty roots. Finally, social movements research is also likely to contribute to international human-rights law in two major areas of critique: in the area of feminist critiques of the public–private distinction, the notion of 'cultural politics' developed above is likely to offer an alternative to the liberal politics of the mainstream human-rights discourse, due to its decentered political sphere and the plurality of social actors. It shows how it may be possible to develop a human rights praxis without falling victim to the public–private distinction. Also, in the area of Third World critiques of cultural relativism, social movement theory and practice are likely to show whether and how it is possible to develop a human-rights praxis without succumbing to the utopian universalism of the mainstream or the crass apologia of the relativists. It does this by showing how debate about identities and values is influenced and affected by debate about strategies and resources. I shall now elaborate on these themes.

It must be noted here that I do not, by any means, either claim that social movements exist as a homogeneous category with a limited and identifiable set of actors, rationale, structures, strategies, and values. On the contrary, they are extremely diverse and dramatically vary from country to country or even from region to region. But I would suggest that it is this plurality and contradiction that make the social movements such an interesting and useful area of study for human rights which has remained a totalizing, universalizing monolithic discourse for too long.

Social movements as critique of development and sovereignty

The following seven main characteristics of social movements may be offered to distinguish them from the shortfalls of the dominant human-rights discourse outlined above. First, social movements offer a fundamental critique of the extant developmental models, with their concomitant postulates of rationality (the place of the expert), progress (the "catching-up syndrome"), and linear meta narrative. A good example of such a movement is the Narmada Bachao Andolan (NBA), in India. But other examples of sociopolitical resistance that has offered a critique of the dominant model of development include the base communities built around liberation theology in Latin America, Islamic revival movements in Sudan or Afghanistan, Gandhist, environmentalist, and cultural revivalist movements in India, as well as the Green movement in West Germany.[38]

These movements appear, on the whole, to reject the rational-technological model that underlies the dominant development discourse. It must be noted here that these movements are significantly different from other Third World movements, say in the 1950s, that pinned their hopes on community development. To these social movements, rejection of the western model involves the rejection of Marxism as well, at least in its theory of linearity, mode of production, and the Stalinist version of the vanguard. Further, these social movements also differ from the old model of community development or pure relativism, in the emphasis they put on the relationship between development and a theory of democracy[39] (I elaborate on this point later). This distinguishes it from the new stream

[38] Banuri (1990). [39] Sheth (1987); Benhabib (1996).

'right to development' discourse in human rights as it problematizes the very notion of development.

Second, several social movements focus their struggles at the material and symbolic levels, thus enacting a 'cultural politics' as outlined above. Examples include the Working Women's Forum (WWF), India's largest poor women's movement, which is the subject of the detailed case study that follows this chapter, the urban squatters movement in Brazil, the PCN (the Process of Black Communities, a movement of Black indigenous people in the Pacific coast of Colombia), and the Zapatistas in Mexico. The struggles of these movements cannot be interpreted solely according to instrumental rights reasoning, or within the Marxist framework as a struggle of classes. Instead, the exercise of rights for the participants of these movements has a dual purpose: it is important on its own terms as it enables them to affirm their dignity as human beings; it also enables them to use the rights discourse to seek the ends of their struggle. The liberal politics of rights discourse has no theoretical basis to accommodate this Fanonian–Nandyian cultural–psychological aspect of social struggles.

Third, significant parts of social movement theory and practice are not state-centered. This derives from several reasons. First, many social movements generally do not aspire for state power as an end in itself.[40] Whether one takes the example of the NBA and Chipko movements in India, CO-MADRES or the Encuentros in Latin America, the Venezuelan ecology movement, or the Zapatistas in Mexico, this seems to be the case. The last one is a particularly good example: a movement of Mexican Indian population organized around cultural identity – ethnicity, language, relationship to nature – that nevertheless did not seek secession from Mexico. It is quite off the mark to analyze such movements within either the inter-state framework of international law (using secession and recognition doctrines) or the liberal framework (using constitutional rights). Indeed this is one of the major characteristics that distinguishes the social movements from their historical counterparts such as labor movements in the nineteenth century or peasant rebellions in the twentieth century, which aimed to take state power ultimately. The state may, of course, play an important role in the formation of those movements (as in the Venezuelan environmental movement), or in strategic or tactical decisions made by those movements. Many social movements also work

[40] There are examples of movements that do aspire for state power, such as the Dalit movement in India, but this does not reflect the more general trend.

with the state in implementing its developmental policies (as C.P. Bhatt did in the Chipko movement, or Arch-Vahini did in the Narmada dam agitation in Gujarat). But, this does not detract from the fact that many social movements do not seek state power since they perceive themselves as 'nonparty political formations' as Rajni Kothari puts it.[41] This does not mean that they repudiate state power and seek to gradually displace it either. The goal is neither the Marxists' withering away of the state or the liberal 'civil society' that displaces the state and the demos as the real arena of public action. Such a non-state-centered form of resistance and protest is quite different from the mainstream human-rights discourse, which is built on the liberal view that all political activity is either pro-sovereign or anti-sovereign. In that sense, the social movements approach helps one to transcend the sovereignty–counter-sovereignty dualism of human-rights discourse described above.

This does not mean that these social movements are nonpolitical, however. In fact, the politics of the social movements seems to be a decentered one in which the slogan 'personal is political' takes on a real meaning. Their political agenda seems to be a democratization of their political institutions, the family, community, the workplace, and the society at large. Many identity-based movements including feminist movements in India and Latin America, or the homosexual movement in Brazil, appear to organize themselves on this understanding of politics. This helps in overcoming the division of political space in liberal political theory between the public and the private that underlies human-rights discourse.

Fourth, several social movements reject violence as a means and several others appear to be ambivalent about it.[42] The Zapatistas in Mexico, the Jharkhand movement in India, and the movement of the rural landless people in Brazil all fall into this category. All of these had the option of exercising violence, but have explicitly spurned it. This sets them apart from Marxist or Maoist theories which explicitly endorsed the smashing of all existing structures. While the use of violence is necessarily a tactical decision, there is considerable evidence of a qualitative difference in the attitude of popular mobilization towards it.

Fifth, the rise of social movements also exhibits a general frustration with liberal democracy and formal institutional politics. This loss of faith is intricately tied to the failure of the Third World state to deliver on the promises of development, but also reflects a more fundamental critique of

[41] Kothari (1993). [42] Falk (1987).

the limitations of these institutions. This sets it apart from the mainstream rights discourse, which is based on a narrow vision of liberal democracy that is realized through the right to vote, stand for election, and so on.[43] As Smitu Kothari (1995, p. 448) puts it

> It is not enough to espouse electoral democracy, and even affirmative policies for economically and socially underprivileged groups, in the absence of a basic restructuring of society toward greater egalitarianism. The challenge is neither distribution nor redistribution, but restructuring such that there is greater equity in the access and control over productive resources. In the absence of this, democracy has little meaning.

Instead, social movements seek to redefine the very definition of democracy, by reconstituting the basis of civil society through counter-hegemonic action. I elaborate on this theme below in the section on civil society.

Sixth, most Third World social movements I have studied are intermeshed in transnational "legal fields"[44] without becoming "international" or even "transnational" in conventional terms. They inhabit and exploit the international when it visits them in the locations, but have no desire to expand it to build cross-border alliances. In this image of international law, a relationship does not become international or transnational only when it crosses a state's boundaries. Rather, relationships are already constituted by and within enclaves of international law which exist within nation states. For example, the PCN in Colombia has structured its mobilization within the terms of the biological diversity debate generated by the ratification of the Convention on Biological Diversity; the WWF in my case study inhabited a sphere of 'international women's rights' within India; the Zapatistas inhabit 'indigenous peoples' rights' within Mexico. None of these movements wish to become transnational as they are locally based movements; but they adopt an eclectic, strategic attitude towards the international when it visits them in their villages, slums, and forests. This image of international law is completely different from the liberal rights image, whose cognitive limits are defined by the boundaries of nation states. As such, civil society becomes 'global' or 'international' only when it has some activity in more than one state. This understanding simply reproduces the spatial ordering of the statist international order and attempts to squeeze all human conduct through it.

[43] Mutua (1996a).

[44] For the use of this term, see Trubek et al. (1994); Bourdieu (1987).

Seventh, social movement theory and practice offer an interesting and new way of thinking about how to redeem the emancipatory promises of the liberal rights discourse without succumbing to its sovereignty–property roots that I discussed above. This would also assist in addressing the charge that human rights are the politics of the elite and not mass politics. From the farmers, dalits, women, environmentalists, and ordinary villagers of India to the peasants in the Andes, what distinguishes social movements from human rights is that *they result from the actual struggles of those peoples, and not from an abstract a priori conception.* Such struggles reflect a convergence between theory and action, that human-rights scholars and activists have longed for but that has been generally unavailable. These struggles show how individuals and communities can achieve their autonomy and self-realization by participating in shaping their own destiny without being constrained by theoretical boundaries. And yet, in order to offer a sufficiently detailed and well-worked out program as an alternative to the liberal rights discourse, social movements need to anchor themselves on a theory of justification that provides normative direction and coherence to activism. Social movements appear to lack such a general theory, though I have discussed some theoretical directions in chapter 1 including the notion of counter-hegemony articulated by Antonio Gramsci.

Viewing social movements as counter-hegemonic discursive practices will enable them to focus on the various hegemonic power formations in political and personal lives. The emphasis, henceforth, would be on the actual terrain that power operates on, rather than some predetermined given one such as the "public" or even the "political." That would enable one to focus on issues of class, gender, sexuality, or the urban–rural divide which have been submerged by the totalizing power of the liberal rights discourse. We could then interrogate the contextuality of the local struggles, and the differences in the experience of local oppressions that are hidden from view.

Navigating the critique: feminism, cultural relativism, and social movements

One of the constructive outcomes of an interdisciplinary marriage between social movements and human rights discourse lies in its potential for avoiding or transcending some of the main critiques against the mainstream human-rights discourse. The main forms of those critiques are as follows. First, feminist scholars have critically engaged the public v. private binary that underlies the framework of the mainstream discourse[45] and criticized its gendered rhetoric, practice, and institutional apparatus.[46] As noted above, social movement politics, with its decentered-ness and the resultant collapse of the public–private distinction, offers a credible alternative to the politics of the rights discourse. Besides, much of the social movement praxis is conscious of the patriarchal foundations of political, economic, social, and personal spheres of lives, and attempt to combat them by its struggle. This explains why a substantial part of social movements theory and practice has been offered by feminist engagements.

Second, Third World leaders, scholars, and activists have leveled charges of neocolonialism and imperialism against human-rights discourse and decried its Western roots[47] and asserted cultural relativism as a defense.[48] In fact, as Makau Wa Mutua has noted,[49] the most fierce debates in human rights are today over culture. Coupled with this is the argument that the Western human-rights model attempts to export a Western liberal–democratic model, as many of the classic political and civil rights such as the right to vote periodically, can only be exercised under such regimes.

Social movement theory and practice offer a powerful counterpoint to this argument. They do so in two ways. First, social movements offer a local and indigenous (and therefore cultural-legitimate) way of questioning the violence of the postcolonial developmental state. These forms of questioning may vary from culture to culture; they may include overt forms of protest as in Brazil or they may include everyday forms of resistance as in Malaysia, as James Scott has pointed out.[50] In other words, social movements indicate an alternative way of resistance and protest that is *not grounded in a western human-rights ideology*. Second, as argued above, social movement praxis also enables the construction of a democratic theory from the actual struggles of the people that helped defeat the monopoly that the liberal-democratic model has on the imagination.

Third, Resource Mobilization theory, when combined with New Social Movement theory, offers an explanation and a justification of various forms of mobilization and protest in Third World countries that depend more on strategies, resources, and alliances. One example would be the NBA allying itself with Environmental Defense Fund and other western

[45] Engle (1993); Romany (1993). [46] Charlesworth, Chiakin, and Wright (1991).
[47] Bell (1996). [48] Ghai (1994). [49] Mutua (1996b).
[50] Scott (1990); Scott and Kerkvliet (1986).

environmental groups to lobby the World Bank and the US Congress. Another would be the Zapatistas allying themselves with various groups outside Mexico, and using the internet, email (and other 'western' technology) to wage their struggle. Such examples show that the cultural relativism argument does not explain the local–global nexus that often enables local resistance movements to flower and succeed. This factor will be discussed more in the section on globalization.

Critique of etatism: distinguishing liberal and social movements approaches

One apparent commonality between social movements' and liberal international legal theoretical literatures would seem to be the critique of etatism and regulation. The latter argue for a reconceptualization of sovereignty in which it is "disaggregated," and the formulation of a legal order in which it becomes the "capacity to participate in an international regulatory process."[51] Social-movement theorists argue that the state itself is a source (not an agent as in Marxist theory) of exploitation and violence towards the subalterns, partly because it is the product of a eurocentric modernity and partly because it is the principal means through which modernization process (democracy and development) is held to occur. As Pramod Parajuli puts it, social movements challenge the " 'philanthropic ogre' of the modern nation-state [and] seek autonomous social governance."[52] This may lead some to argue that liberal internationalism and social movements share much in common. I shall argue against that supposition and suggest that liberal internationalists are not so much against the state, as against sovereignty – especially the autonomy of national units. I shall also suggest that the social movements' critique of the state is entirely different from liberal internationalism's selective counter-sovereignty discourse.

First, the liberal internationalists base their work on a simplistic division of the world between liberal and non-liberal states, thus not only arrogating to themselves the power to determine the categories which divide the globe, but also re-enacting the familiar nineteenth-century colonialist division between civilized and uncivilized states. Thus, Anne-Marie Slaughter argues that her new conception of "disaggregated

[51] Slaughter (1995) 537. I take her scholarship as the paradigm of liberal international legal scholarship.
[52] Parajuli (1990) 175.

sovereignty" applies only between liberal (white? western? capitalistic? developed?) states; as for non-liberal states, "more traditional conceptions" of sovereignty apply in their relations with liberal states.[53] Their sovereignty is "constrained less by individuals and groups in transnational society than by other states or by international institutions."[54] Besides the fact that this attempt violates the basic legal postulate of equality of states, the experience of Third World social movements shows this claim to be empirically untrue: as my discussion of the Polonoroeste and Narmada projects in Part II showed, Third World sovereignty is perhaps even more subject to the constraints created by individuals and groups in 'transnational society' (with all its fuzziness). More importantly, the praxis of many social movements attempts to articulate an embedded, place-based cosmopolitanism that can not be comprehended within the cognitive confines of the liberal–non-liberal distinction.

Second, the liberal internationalists function entirely within a United Statesean world view that makes their theories almost ethnocentric. For instance, this theory takes the presence of certain institutions to be given (such as parliaments, judiciaries, bureaucracies) and argues for a principle of non-interference in their institutional competence, a thinly disguised version of American separation-of-powers doctrine. Social movements do not take any institution to be necessary. Their attitude is often strategic, contingent and opportunistic towards institutions of the state – they constrain or work with whichever institutions happen to show more support for their interests at any given time. Social movements also seek to reconfigure the very meaning of the 'public,' showing no great interest in received institutional designs. By contrast, liberal internationalists take certain institutions of the state as given and fetishize them as emerging transnational actors – a paradox for a purported counter-sovereignty discourse that sees the state as the antithesis of internationalism.

Third, liberal internationalism conceives of each institution of the state as having dual regulatory and representative functions.[55] This (along with its institutional fetishism discussed above) makes it clear that its central target is sovereignty and not the state. In fact, if sovereignty is the capacity to participate in an international regulatory process, logically the state needs strengthening, not weakening, so that it can carry out its regulatory responsibilities under international treaties.[56] By contrast, social movements oppose the increasing bureaucratization of their life-worlds,

[53] Slaughter (1995) 536. [54] Ibid. [55] Ibid. 534.
[56] For such an argument recently, see Fox (1999).

and, consequently, view etatism as a regressive strategy. They emphasize the representative aspect of self-governance over the regulatory one, and staunchly defend their autonomy. Indeed, social movements are so suspicious of bureaucratization that their own internal structures are very often fluid, horizontal and without hierarchical leadership, thus clearly different from NGOs. This quirky combination of a defense of external sovereignty (through autonomy) and an opposition to etatism, is a new Third World approach, which, I have argued, constitutes a departure from and challenge to extant approaches to international law.

What then is a possible theoretical basis for comprehending social movements that oppose etatism while preserving autonomy? Specifically, why do social movements oppose the bureaucratization of their life-worlds as a central aspect of their power struggles? I suggest that while an answer to this question is not yet obvious, an understanding of Foucault's notion of governmentality may provide a clue about their strategy towards power. In his essay, "Governmentality," Foucault defines "governmentalization of the State" as "the ensemble of institutions, procedures, analyses and reflections, the calculations and tactics that allow the exercise of this very specific albeit complex form of power."[57] In this view, power has a bureaucratic form that is not merely confined to a monolithic state. In fact, Foucault argues against a "reductionist vision of the relative importance of the state's role" which may make us imagine the state as a "target needing to be attacked."[58] Reducing the state into a target may be convenient for activists and policy-makers, but it does not correspond to the reality of the exercise of power in modern society which goes beyond state structures. As Foucault argues,

> the state . . . does not have this unity, this individuality, this rigorous functionality, nor, to speak frankly, this importance; maybe, after all, the state is no more than a composite reality and a mythicized abstraction, whose importance is a lot more limited than many of us think.[59]

This understanding of the state is derived from his notion of power which is web-like, encompassing all human relations, rather than confined to structures. If this is true, power is not merely exercised by state structures (in police action, passage of laws, etc.), it is embedded in every form of bureaucratic, routinized relationship. In this way, power is not unidirectional, but pluri-directional. As Colin Gordon puts it, the governmentality perspective gives rise to "a range of distinct modes of pluralization

[57] Foucault (1991) 102. [58] Ibid. 103. [59] Ibid.

of modern government which contribute towards the relativization of the notational boundary line between state and society."[60] Real freedom then, could be achieved by freeing ourselves from the routine bureaucratization of our everyday lives and recovering the life-worlds that have been lost. This unique understanding of power is what makes the social movements adopt a critical attitude towards etatism as an emancipatory strategy. This is fundamentally different from liberal internationalists, who want to emancipate society by expanding the state, in a process of etatization without autonomy.

Social movements and the discourse of civil society: reconfiguring democracy

The discourse of civil society, principally emerging from the democratic transitions of Latin America, Asia, and Eastern Europe in the 1980s and 1990s, would seem to offer a theoretical basis for analyzing social movements as extra-institutional forms of collective action that seek to renew democratic action.[61] The emergence of these "new global communities"[62] is also seen to have the potential to democratize international law, principally through NGOs.[63] However, this "NGOization" of civil society discourse is problematic for several reasons, is too narrow and essentially misses the radical potential of a social-movement perspective to transform international law. One way of reconceptualizing a social-movement-based notion of civil society, is to think of the public spheres inhabited by civil society as "subaltern counterpublics," as Nancy Fraser has suggested.[64]

It must be noted that the concept of democracy has entered international legal discourse.[65] Though none of the human-rights treaties call for any particular political regime in which they may be enjoyed (indeed, until the end of the Cold War it was customary for international lawyers to assert this non-ideological character of human rights), it is asserted by many that human rights promote and are dependent upon western-style liberal democracy.[66] The impact of this new turn on international law may be seen in calls for a "right to democratic governance,"[67]

[60] Gordon, Burchell, and Miller (1991) 36 (italics in the original).

[61] The substantial literature on civil society in the 1990s includes: Cohen and Arato (1992); Hall (1995); Seligman (1992); Keane (1988a); Keane (1988b); Gellner (1994); Rosenberg (1994); Bell (1989); Taylor (1990); Walzer (1991, 1992); Christenson (1997).

[62] Spiro (1995). [63] See, e.g., Charnowitz (1997). [64] Fraser (1994).

[65] Crawford (1994); Franck (1992). [66] Mutua (1996a). [67] Franck (1992).

multilateral and regional programs for democratization through good governance and peace building, and the argument for a pro-democratic intervention. These efforts have been ideologically biased by their formalistic definition of democracy that has tended to emphasize voting rights, and western-style representative institutions – in short the normative and institutional framework for the existence of classic western liberal rights.[68] Thus, democracy promotion efforts have consisted often of strengthening state institutions (parliaments), political parties, and media,[69] to the neglect of what happens in extra-institutional arenas, or even in other institutional arenas such as workplaces. To the extent that there is a focus on those arenas, it is under the rubric of promoting 'civil society,' usually through funding for NGOs. At the doctrinal level, the mainstream focuses on traditional sources of international law such as treaties, custom or general principles, enumerated in article 38(2) of the Statute of the ICJ, all of which look to the practice of states. The liberal mainstream expands on this to focus on various 'soft law' sources such as voluntary codes of conduct adopted by MNCs, inter-agency agreements at sub-state levels, and, to a lesser extent, the impact of NGO networks on the normative structure of international law.[70] While the latter may appear to shift international law's focus on to the extra-institutional arenas that I have drawn attention to, in actuality such a shift is not occurring. As I argue below, focus on NGOs is not the same as a focus on social movements, since NGOs are, by definition, institutional actors who derive their legal identity from the national systems where they are incorporated.

The track record of international relations is somewhat different, where democracy is increasingly seen as critical to the maintenance of the world order through the 'democratic peace' thesis,[71] and solidified through institutional and legal reform, and the constitution of a civil society (national or global). However, its definitions of civil society have tended to confine it to a narrow negativist view of non-governmental arena (consisting of markets and NGOs) excluding certain economic actors (such as trades unions) or non-institutionalized collective action in the form of social movements. Nevertheless, the celebration of civil society as the new harbinger of political and economic reforms in the Third World must be examined closely to see its benefits and pitfalls, and how it may be reconstituted. I suggest that the notion of civil society, as it is presently

[68] Fox and Nolte (1995). [69] Diamond (1995) 15.
[70] For an example of the first two, see Slaughter (1997). An example of the latter is Keck and Sikkink (1998).
[71] Doyle (1983).

constituted, is too narrowly focused on NGOs, and this "NGOization" of civil society severely limits its radical democratic potential.

Let us begin with the notion of civil society as it is used in contemporary legal discourse. Habermas defines it as follows:

> Civil society is composed of those more or less spontaneously emergent associations, organizations and movements that, attuned to how societal problems resonate in the private life spheres, distill and transmit such reactions in amplified form to the public sphere. The core of civil society comprises a network of associations that institutionalizes problem-solving discourses on questions of general interest inside the framework of organized public spheres. These "discursive designs" have an egalitarian, open form of organization that mirrors essential features of the kind of communications around which they crystallize and to which they lend continuity and permanence.[72]

These associations could indeed include social movements and NGOs. But Habermas makes it clear that he has a much narrower concept of civil society in mind: first, he distinguishes his definition from the much older social contract, western definition of civil society best exemplified by Adam Ferguson,[73] Hegel, Marx, and Gramsci that included social labor, commodity exchange, commerce, as well as spontaneous civil associations. The new definition, he asserts, no longer includes the economy but "those nongovernmental and noneconomic connections and voluntary associations that anchor the communication structures of the public sphere in the society component of the life world."[74] Second, he makes it clear that the institutionalization of this civil society is possible only through basic human rights of the western model: indeed, that "a robust civil society can develop only in the context of a liberal political culture... it can blossom only in an already rationalized life world."[75]

The results of this qualified vision of civil society are twofold: it imposes a liberal limit on the nature of public action that is admitted to the privileged arena of civil society, thereby enabling the exclusion of voices that do not qualify as liberal. The result of this may be seen clearly in the liberal attitude towards most social movements, but especially in the Algerian context where a clearly democratic vote for Islamic rule was rejected as illiberal. Second, by institutionalizing civil society through a liberal rights discourse, he compels an "NGOization" of social movements through the

[72] Habermas (1996) 367.
[73] Ferguson (1767) (first English language treatment of the subject).
[74] Habermas (1996) 366–67. [75] Ibid. 368, 371.

acquisition of legal identity. To claim rights, one must first be recognized as an actor in the legal system, and Habermas asks social movements to do just that. This Habermasian vision represents, I claim, the current understanding of civil society in international-law and international-relations scholarship. In this vision, civil society constitutes a small and privileged arena of liberal NGOs.

This understanding completely overlooks the important analytical and conceptual differences between NGOs and social movements, and their political context.[76] Indeed, the experience of social movements shows that the notion of civil society is a much more complex and contested terrain than that which Habermas suggests. First, NGOs may form part of social movements, but they do not themselves constitute movements, as pointed out earlier. Some umbrella-type NGO may be formed to represent a social movement for strategic and operational purposes, but that remains a movement, nevertheless. The NBA is not one NGO, but a coalition of NGOs, activists, intellectuals, and affected people who came together under one roof. Despite the obviousness of this point, confusions between NGOs and social movements continue to persist.[77] Second, civil society is not a homogeneous concept, but a terrain of struggle that is often bedeviled by undemocratic power struggles and exclusionary practices. NGOs are often formed by English-language-speaking, cosmopolitan local activists who know how to relate to western donors (who provide most of the NGO funding) and write fundraising proposals, while social movement activists do not often have this power. Indeed, the relationship between NGOs, local social movements and global development agencies remains problematic and has been criticized.[78] Third, often a social movement perspective is seen as adequate to analyze civil societies within nation-states, but in analyzing 'global' or 'transnational' civil society, the role of NGOs becomes important. This raises problematic issues concerning a western bias in the NGO world, and in the very constitution of 'global' spaces, including in international law. Finally, most NGOs actively seek or are neutral about foreign funding, while many social movements such as NBA actively avoid/oppose it. This must be seen in the context of emerging critiques of NGO–donor relationships, which point out that as NGOs move closer to aid agencies through a reliance on foreign funding, they become more bureaucratic and experience a fall off in flexibility and ability

[76] See Fisher (1997).

[77] See, e.g., Clarke (1998) 36–37 (arguing that NGOs have filled the political vacuum created by the weakness of political parties in India since the mid-1970s).

[78] See essays by Lins Ribeiro and Sonia Alvarez in Alvarez, Dagnino, and Escobar (1998).

to innovate.[79] In India, NGOs which have foreign connections are often regarded as "antinationalist agents of capitalism and western political and cultural values."[80] Almost all major social movements in India including Chipko, NBA, NATSR, and NFF (National Fishworkers Federation) have avoided foreign funding for this reason. As such, confining civil society to NGOs may have the unfortunate effect of narrowing the field to entities that do not command much legitimacy in the Third World.

Instead of this narrow conception of civil society, I propose a broader definition that accommodates social movements, NGOs, and even some economic actors (such as trades unions), and one that allows for contestation. Here I draw upon Nancy Fraser's notion of "subaltern counterpublics" which she defines as "parallel discursive arenas where members of subordinated social groups invent and circulate counter discourses, which in turn permit them to formulate oppositional interpretations of their identities, interests and needs."[81] In this view, there's not one, but several competing plural publics, which are constituted by groups which experience themselves as being excluded from the public sphere and civil society – women, workers, squatters, fisher people, gays, and lesbians.[82] As she correctly argues, these counterpublics have a dual function: on the one hand they function as spaces of withdrawal and regrouping, where identities are affirmed to recover human dignity which has been denied in the overarching public sphere; on the other hand, they also function as spaces in which alternative conceptions of rights, body, and politics are re/formulated with a view to influencing the wider public sphere.[83] This definition, which stresses the need to recognize a plurality of civil societies that may exist in these counterpublics, is much more capable of representing the actually existing practices of social movements.

Liberal rights theory is not capable, as it currently stands, of accommodating the plural bases of actually existing democracy in the Third World, exemplified by social movements. To understand how this democracy works, one must then look beyond elections and NGOs to the actual practices of social movements in the redefined civil societies. This redefinition of the notion of civil society, based on the praxis of social movements, is essential for moving international law beyond formalist and negativist definitions of democracy.

[79] Edwards and Hulme (1997) 278. [80] Fisher (1997) 454. [81] Fraser (1994) 84.

[82] She acknowledges that not all counterpublics are virtuous, but suggests that, nevertheless, their proliferation is a good thing in stratified societies as it means a widening of discursive contestation (ibid).

[83] Ibid. 85.

Property and territory: autonomy without sovereignty?

As noted earlier, social movements' 'turn to culture' in the last two decades has emphasized rights to identity, territory, autonomy, and alternative conceptions of modernity and development. This has brought them into direct conflict with the discourse of private property, which has acquired a principal place in international development policy, and, therefore, in liberal theories of international law for many reasons. Nowhere is this more apparent than in the case of indigenous peoples who have begun asserting their control over local property resources, thus conflicting with the developmental goals of many states, which aim to promote private or state property ownership and exploitation of such resources. But this is even the case in urban areas, which witness struggles by neighborhood communities and movements to reassert their control over local economic development, often by asserting their local sovereignty over their neighborhoods, trumping that of local governments and private developers. This has begun posing serious challenges to extant conceptions of property rights in international development policy, which are based on narrow, individualist, economistic notions of absolute rights to exclude, use, and transfer. Instead, social movements have begun forcing states to recognize alternative conceptions of property that recognize that property is a social and cultural institution based on human relationships. In addition, in asserting their collective rights to territory, many social movements explicitly disavow the language of sovereignty (and therefore of self-determination and secession), and instead seek autonomy. These aspects are of great relevance to international law for historical and contemporary reasons.

Historically, international law has always been at the heart of the discourse about sovereignty and property in the Third World. Beginning with medieval discourse about the rights of infidels (Pope Innocent IV), and extending through sixteenth- and seventeenth-century discourse about the rights of Indians (Vitoria, Las Casas), nineteenth-century discourse about the standard of civilization (Westlake), and twentienth-century discourses about development and democracy, international law has played a central role in denying the rights of Third World peoples to assert their rights over their own territories. When these states did attempt to transform international law by asserting rights to territory – for example through the Permanent Sovereignty over Natural Resources (PSNR) doctrine in the post-independence period to nationalize western investments – western international lawyers usually responded negatively by denying the legal status of these new doctrines. The promotion of absolute property rights in the 1980s and 1990s by western donors and multilaterals must then be seen in this historical context. Here, the promotion of individual property rights is directed at weakening the dominium of Third World sovereignty, or the ability of collectivities to exercise control over individual and corporate ownership of resources. This clash between individual and collective interests in land and other resources is sought to be mediated through the discourse of property rights in international development policy, as though neutral, apolitical choices are possible through that discourse.

This notion of private property rights in international development policy is based on the model of a rational, autonomous, profit-maximizing, efficient individual who works to better herself. According to utilitarian justifications that underlie this image of neoclassical economic theory, the society becomes better off when each betters herself, as the sum of individual good becomes the collective good.

This notion of an autonomous individual is reinforced by the rights language in which property interests are expressed. In this liberal conception, rights function as barriers that protect individuals from intrusions by other individuals, collectivities, or the state. The critical element here is the boundary between autonomous individuals, and the law's function is seen as the protection of these boundaries, and the judiciary's function, that of policing. These liberal rights theories seek to mediate conflict, not nurture self-creation, sustenance, and community building. The individuals protected by them appear disconnected. This excessive individualistic bias of property rights has been criticized quite heavily.[84]

Social movements offer an entirely different understanding of property and rights. This is primarily because of their unique understanding of autonomy, which focuses on relationships rather than separation and boundaries.[85] This conception of autonomy as relationship emphasizes links rather than boundaries. Many of them do seek to assert autonomy over their territories, thus capturing the thrust of more traditional Third World efforts to control territory; but they go beyond that by redefining the very meaning of autonomy as an inclusive phenomenon. The importance of autonomy as a central aspect of property must be pointed out. From the perspective of the developmental state, nothing is more dangerous

[84] For a critique from economic theory and psychology, see Piore (1995).

[85] For a wonderful account of how rights may be conceived as relationships through a reconceptualization of autonomy along the lines suggested here, see Nedelsky (1993).

than individual and community autonomy, as it removes the power of control over resources and property from the hands of the bureaucrats to the local people. As one Indian minister said upon being confronted with a local dam-building effort by farmers in the Krishna River valley using local, small-scale technology: "If peasants build dams, then what will the state have left to do?"[86] Indeed, devolving the power over territory to local communities strikes at the very raison d'être of the developmental state, as development is what the state and experts do *for* the people, not what the people do for themselves. The control over territory is the basis of sovereignty and property, and autonomy eats that control away. This is precisely the kind of property rights of which social movements have compelled recognition.

This approach to the understanding of property rights is hardly new. In fact, there is an emerging tradition of scholarship in US property law, drawing on feminist legal theory, critical race theory, law and society, and critical legal studies, dubbed the "social relations approach," which reconceptualizes property as a social and cultural institution based on relations between individuals and communities regarding control of valued resources.[87] By defining property as a relational concept, these scholars have repudiated the autonomous, selfish and rationalistic individual-based conception of property and rights.[88] This notion of property rights is useful for understanding the praxis of social movements as collective action that enacts a cultural politics.

Some examples of social movements that have actually compelled the recognition of such property rights may be mentioned.[89] In India, the NATSR, a social movement of indigenous peoples, successfully compelled the Parliament to extend the *panchayat raj* amendments (village self-rule) to the tribal areas in 1996 through a constitutional amendment.[90] In the

[86] Omvedt (1993) 242.

[87] The leading exponent of this view is Joseph Singer. See Singer (1997) 20; Singer (1987–88, 2000, 2001). See also Nedelsky (1993).

[88] See Minow (1990).

[89] I focus on the Third World, given the nature of this book. But examples can be found in the West as well. In the US, the most famous example is perhaps the Dudley Street Neighborhood Initiative (DSNI), formed in Roxbury, Massachusetts. Formed during the mid-1980s as a response to neighborhood decay and crime through abandonment of private property by developers, a social movement of inner-city residents organized to obtain the power of eminent domain from the city mayor, in order to take over the abandoned lots and convert them into usable property. This was the first instance when eminent domain was devolved to the neighborhood level due to the pressure generated by a social movement. See Medoff and Sklar (1994).

[90] The Provisions of the Panchayats (Extension to the Scheduled Areas) Act, 1996.

amendment act, the tribal *Gram Sabhas* (village councils) are given the authority to exercise full collective rights over their territory including the right to veto and approve any development project such as mining or logging. This is nothing short of extending autonomy and self-rule to the local level, by decentralizing the power of eminent domain.

In Colombia, the 1991 Constitution granted, among others, the black communities of the Pacific region, collective rights to the lands they have traditionally occupied. This was followed by the 1993 Law of Cultural and Territorial Rights for the Black Communities (Ley 70 of August 1993), which was elaborated through a long negotiated process. This reform was made possible through an intense agitation carried out by a social-movement network called the Process of Black Communities (PCN). As a recent analysis of this social movement puts it, the constitutional reform is "the first important space of black community organizing on the basis of cultural, ethnic, and territorial demands; it entailed the construction of an alternative proposal by the black communities centered on ethnic and cultural rights."[91] The rights asserted by the PCN consisted of the right to be black (identity), the right to space for being (territory), the right to the exercise of being-identity (autonomy), the right to their own development as they see fit, and solidarity with other subaltern struggles.[92] It is, in short, a practical project of territorial defense and alternative modes of development, through an assertion of collective property rights. While the impact of these legislative measures varies in practice (it is also too early to tell in the examples I cited here), they represent significant challenges to the extant ways of thinking about property, autonomy, and sovereignty. As I have suggested in this chapter, the cultural politics of social movements such as PCN pose serious challenges to liberal categories such as rights and property in their received modes, by articulating alternative visions of modernity and development that may be pursued through these categories, and thereby reconceive these very categories themselves.

Social movements, globalization and space: ambivalence and contradictions

In this section, two propositions are advanced that run counter to liberal internationalist orthodoxy that increasing globalization amounts to a realization of the Kantian dream of global cosmopolitanism triumphing over local governance, through the emergence of transnational legal

[91] Grueso, Rosero, and Escobar (1998) 199. [92] Ibid. 202–03.

governance. First, increasing globalization leads in many countries to more, not less emphasis on the role of the local as an agent of socio-cultural and economic transformation. This can be clearly seen in the significant number of countries wherein autonomy arrangements and devolution schemes of various kinds have been enacted, due to pressures generated by local social movements. Second, even as capitalism is increasingly organized on a global basis, resistance to it is also emerging on an extra-territorial basis through social movements.[93] I say extra-territorial because the praxis of the social movements is not often organized at a transnational or global basis, but often combines center and periphery, or just parts of the periphery.[94] In other words, globalization is turning out to be an internally contradictory phenomenon, which produces the conditions for its propagation as well as resistance against itself. This has been described by Richard Falk as "globalization from below," and by Peter Evans as "counter-hegemonic globalization".

Let us begin by noting that two broad contradictory processes are said to be occurring throughout much of the Third World: globalization and localization.[95] Globalization is said to be driven primarily by economic factors such as the emergence of global financial markets, a rapid expansion of the knowledge economy and the construction of a global normative and institutional architecture for trade.[96] The chief characteristics of this process are the weakening of the national sovereignty of states, the increasing porosity of borders in the movement of capital, goods and certain categories of labor, and new international legal norms and institutions that regulate these new developments. Localization is thought to be enabled primarily by a confluence between global development policy emphasis in favor of participation and democracy, vigorous local self-determination movements along ethnic and indigenous lines among others, and an increasing global network of norms and processes that legitimize local governance, peoples' autonomy and individual human rights. Localization is primarily evidenced by an increasing emphasis on new forms of federalism, a turn to devolution and autonomy within

[93] It goes without saying that such resistance is also organized on a local basis. For that argument see Sklair (1998). Indeed, the transnationalization of resistance is derived from and often intended to strengthen existing local resistance. For this argument, see Evans (2000).

[94] Here I follow Hannerz (1991) 116.

[95] See Evans (2000).

[96] There is also a political and cultural dimension to globalization, but I focus here on economic globalization primarily, as, without it, the other two would seem much less threatening. For an important critique of economic globalization, see Rodrik (1997).

nation states, and the emergence of global cities with their own material and symbolic sovereignty.[97]

There is substantial evidence of this trend in India and Latin America. India provides a rich variety of data. On the one hand, India has entered into a number of global economic agreements, including under the WTO and under World Bank's persuasion, relating to intellectual property, trade in services, and other matters that have compelled the passage of a number of special laws and measures. On the other hand, India has also adopted or is on the verge of adopting a number of other laws that are called for under various international treaties relating, for example, to biodiversity or women's rights. While this process is underway, several constitutional, legal, and policy changes have taken place in the area of local governance, substantially expanding the powers available to local communities and authorities. Recent examples include the extension of the *panchayat raj* system to the scheduled tribes' areas in 1996 (described above), the formation of village-level self-governance units in Andhra Pradesh, the devolution of financial autonomy to village and town development committees in Kerela, and the very recent experimentation with local governance in Madhya Pradesh in connection with the Narmada valley displaced communities. In Latin America, the 1991 Colombian constitutional amendment providing for local control over property resources for the black communities on the Pacific coast, decentralized budgeting reforms in Brazil, and the ongoing struggle of the Zapatistas in Mexico underline the same tendency that, as these countries have globalized, there is more and more recognition of the local as an important agent of change. This has not come easily or voluntarily: rather, it has resulted from concrete struggles of social movements. International relations and international law scholarship that celebrates globalization either simply misses the concrete moves towards local governance in the Third World or is profoundly ideological.

At the second level, counter-hegemonic globalization is also made possible due to the very structure of globalization. As Saskia Sassen and others have noted, cheap transportation and communication facilities (including the internet) have enabled cross-border movement of people, ideas, strategies, and initiatives.[98] As Peter Evans has argued, the old aphorism "think globally and act locally" is now being turned around: activists think locally by pursuing local solutions to local problems, but act globally, to generate political momentum to support the local changes.[99]

[97] On the emergence of the global city, see Sassen (1998) chapter 1.
[98] Ibid. section I. [99] Evans (2000) 3.

There are several ambiguities and contradictions associated with this imagery of resistance. Indeed, one of the common aspects of many social movements in the Third World, whether they be in India or Latin America, appears to be the transnational linkages between different actors that sustain the movements, from environmental to feminist, and enable them to pursue their objectives. The local–global nexus that often serves to ensure the success of a social movement, such as the Encuentros in Latin America, is not merely celebrated in social movement theory and practice but it seems to be accepted as a central tenet of what social movements are all about. This fact is often located in the discussion of the phenomenon of globalization, that moment of 'time-space compression' which is touted as the dominant geopolitical event in the post-Cold-War era.[100]

Simultaneously, one sees several converging trends as well. For example, there is the sense of the millennial triumph of the neoliberal free market ideology that denotes the 'end of history.' That ideology also calls for free flow of transnational capital and private property rights, factors that are central to a consideration of practical issues such as fund-flows in the NGO sector from the North to the South. Meanwhile, the debate on development has now moved to embrace the liberal-democratic model and the mainstream rights discourse through the device of 'good governance' which is now acknowledged by multilateral development institutions and bilateral donors as key to development. Also, one witnesses the proliferation of political aid conditionalities imposed by the IMF, EU, or other donors that attempt to replace the hegemony of Cold War rhetoric with that of western-style democracy, with its contingent set of institutions.

What should one, then, make of social movements during this moment? Do they present an opportunity for a creative way to build a local–global nexus that somehow transcends the imperialistic purposes of 'globobabble,' or will they prove to be the Trojan horses that would reinvite the colonizer inside Third World societies? I don't really know. I would only argue that a blind opposition to either approach is likely to be a major folly. On the one hand, the transnationalization of resistance to global capitalism has been made possible through several factors that are internal to globalization itself. Therefore, a wholesale anti-imperialistic dismissal of globalization will completely miss the most important means of resistance to global capitalism. On the other hand, globalization is also not a neutral phenomenon as it functions, but a 'hegemonic' phenomenon[101] that is situated within a matrix of lop-sided relationships between the

[100] Robertson (1992). [101] Evans (2000).

center and the periphery.[102] Therefore, social movements should assess the needs and interest of the actors, the necessity for strategy, and the tactical use of international networks, while critically examining their own relationship with the 'global,' especially with regard to their own autonomy in matters of funding. After all, if the NBA in India had taken any money from foreign sources, it would very likely have immediately lost its legitimacy and 'voice.'

A final note on the role of the state in globalization. Contrary to the manner in which the mainstream globalization discourse views the state, as a fast disappearing relic of the sixteenth century, social movements reveal the complex ways in which the state could actually prove to be an ally and in fact contribute to the building of protest or resistance. The Venezuelan ecology movement, which resulted from state initiatives that began with a law, is a good example of this fact. On the other hand, the state itself may be influenced by the complex ways in which social movements build coalitions and join a common struggle. An example would be the Encuentros where the Latin American states sent their representatives to participate in meetings after witnessing the outpouring of support from civil society. Yet another way in which the state intersects with social movements is in the constant 'drifting' of individuals from government to movements and NGOs and back. Indeed, this drifting occurs even between the 'global' and the 'local': witness Medha Patkar's (the leader of the NBA in India) appointment as one of the commissioners of the World Commission on Dams.

This approach to the role of the state corresponds much more to the reality of resistance to globalization, which is staged in many sites where institutional and non-institutional actors join together in strategic, ad hoc coalitions. These sites can no longer be understood within the category of the 'nation state.' At the same time they are not 'global' sites in most cases, but peripheral or semi-peripheral sites which function adroitly within the political spaces created by globalization. In other words, as globalization has posed a challenge to the spatial ordering of the world by disrupting the centrality of the territorial nation state as the primary actor, resistance to it is also emerging along different spatial orderings which are not necessarily organized on a 'transnational' or 'global' basis. As I suggested earlier, in this new image of international order, there are particular enclaves of the 'international' that exist in different locations. International law simply does not have the theoretical framework or doctrinal tools to make sense of this complex reality.

[102] Hannerz (1991) 107.

Conclusion

This chapter has argued that social movements pose a central challenge to international law in several areas. First, they seek to displace the liberal theory of international politics with a 'cultural politics' that seeks alternative visions of modernity and development by emphasizing rights to identity, territory, and autonomy. Second, they show that the mainstream human-rights discourse is extremely limited which does not have the cognitive ability to 'see' much of the resistance of social movements. Engaging with the theory and practice of social movements is necessary to convert human-rights discourse from its narrow, state-centered, elitist basis to a grassroots-oriented praxis of the subalterns. Third, social movements challenge extant conceptions of private property in international development policy and offer alternative conceptions of property that emphasize autonomy of communities. To that extent, they also challenge the nexus between property and sovereignty in law by showing how to realize autonomy without being imprisoned by the language of sovereignty. Fourth, the emergence of social movements cannot be understood through the category of civil society as it is presently understood in extant scholarship. In particular, I suggested that the "NGOization" of civil society has effectively rendered many social movements invisible, and that the notion of civil society be reconceived, following Nancy Fraser, as subaltern counterpublics to reinvigorate democracy. I also pointed out that the praxis of social movements is entirely different from liberal internationalist claims about global civil society as a counter sovereignty discourse. Finally, it was suggested that social movements contradict the central tenets of the liberal internationalist vision of globalization – that globalization leads to a reduction in the importance of the local. Instead, paradoxically, globalization has led to more, not less, emphasis on the local, but also resistance to globalization manifests itself extra-territorially through globalization itself. This chapter has been in the nature of an exploration which has attempted to make sense of the complex reordering of world politics and international law in the post Cold War and post 9/11 period. This exploration shows that a theory and practice of international law that takes social movements seriously as actors is urgent and essential. The place-based praxis of social movements has emerged as an important site of re/formulation and transformation of the space-based global legal discourse.

9

Markets, gender, and identity: a case study of the Working Women's Forum as a social movement

This case study summarizes the findings of my field research with the Working Women's Forum (WWF), a large women's movement in South India. The research consisted of field visits over several years, extensive interviews during the entire period with the staff, members, and the leaders of the WWF, observatory research in the cooperatives, and research on extensive documentary materials and literature provided by the WWF. I also offer analysis of my findings in addition to locating them in the wider literature on social movements and development. The study concludes by noting the difficulty of placing the WWF within the received categories of international law and municipal law as well as the various ways in which the praxis of the WWF challenges received notions about economic development and human rights.

Description of the structure and activities of the WWF

The WWF was started in 1978 by its current President, Ms. Jaya Arunachalam, and several working women, primarily as a union of women in the informal sector with an initial membership of 800. Since then it has grown into a movement of 591,000 poor women in three southern states of India: Tamil Nadu, Karnataka, and Andhra Pradesh. Its operation reaches over 2,061 villages and 1,651 slums in 4,158 different areas organized into 45,000 groups in 15 branches. As such, it currently appears to be the largest women's movement in India, surpassing the better-known and much-studied Self-Employed Women's Association (SEWA).

From its beginnings as a small union of poor women organized around the issue of credit, the WWF has now expanded to perform multiple roles that combine the activities of a micro-credit/banking agency (making loans), a trade union (organizing for collective bargaining with the government and the private sector for better terms and conditions of employment), a women's NGO (engaging in advocacy on key issues of concern and making representations and media drives), and a socio-political women's movement (waging collective grassroots struggles against oppressive patriarchal structures and other cultural and political obstacles, as well as providing a sense of solidarity to the women). These activities reflect the determination of the WWF that a holistic and integrated approach is necessary in order to secure relief from the multiple and intersecting oppressions that working poor women face in their daily lives: class exploitation, caste hierarchies, male dominance, poor physical health, and a closed world that renders them isolated and vulnerable. As a result, the WWF is structured as follows:

a. **Indian Cooperative Network for Women (ICNW).** Established as a separate legal entity under laws of the federal government, this has the responsibility of providing micro-credit to poor working women. It was initially known as Working Women's Cooperative Society (WWCS), and was registered under the laws of the state of Tamil Nadu. It was registered under federal laws in order to escape the harassment faced by the members from the officials of the state government.
b. **National Union of Working Women (NUWW).** Established as a Trade Union of poor working women in 1982 under the Trade Unions Act, in order to improve their living and working conditions.
c. **WWF as family planning and health care provider.** Under the organizational structure of the WWF, several projects have been conducted to provide healthcare and to promote family planning among poor working women.
d. **WWF as a movement/NGO.** Registered under the Societies Registration Act, the WWF performs the role of an NGO in areas such as advocacy, while mobilizing the large numbers of women on collective political/cultural issues such as caste. Thus the WWF has conducted a large numbers of mass inter-caste marriages, has organized rallies and demonstrations on specific causes, and has actively attempted to influence public opinion on issues of concern, including through the use of media.

The organizational structure of all of the above components merge into 160 staff members and 174 organizers (elected from the members) who are supervised by a Standing Committee of seven members and a President (who is Jaya Arunachalam). According to Ms. Arunachalam and her staff, 95% of the WWF come from the grassroots including middle managers. However, only two out of the seven Standing Committee members appeared to be from the grassroots. In addition, there does not appear to be any mechanism for replacing the President. The staff and the organizers themselves are well-motivated and work for low pay: the staff get between Rs.1,500–Rs.3,500 per month and the organizers get between Rs.300–Rs.500. The organization is reasonably well equipped, with two jeeps at the HQ and one jeep per branch. Administrative and management costs appeared to be well under control, at not more than 30%.

As noted, the initial purpose of WWF was to promote the economic status of very poor working women in the informal sector by organizing them as workers of a distinct sector and by providing them credit. Even though more than 90% of India's women workers belong to the informal sector, the male-dominated mainstream Trade Unions did not show any interest in either the informal sector or women. Besides, the Trade Unions were dominated by leftist ideals of solidarity of the working class, which made any effort to organize working women, as a separate category of workers, suspect in their eyes. But, the women in the informal sector, who worked as hawkers and vendors, providers of urban services, home-based petty manufacturers and petty traders, as well as rural agricultural workers, faced specific barriers and handicaps that arose from their status as women. Such barriers included caste and class-based barriers which restricted their mobility, behavior, and access to resources, and which resulted in keeping these women at the lowest socio-economic level, forcing them to live in marginal/survival conditions. As a result, the WWF initially started with the objective of improving the economic security of the poor women. But as noted above, it soon became clear that the barriers faced by the women were not merely economic, class-based ones, but multi-dimensional in which cultural norms and assumptions, political oppressions, and socially rigid stereotypes contributed to their condition of marginal existence. Therefore, an integrated and holistic approach was devised in which the women struggle against all these forms of oppressions using different tactics, through their multiple subjectivities, to create what Robert Chambers calls "counter-culture."[1] I shall now describe in some detail the workings of the different components of the WWF and offer some preliminary analysis.

ICNW: the transformatory power of economic freedom

In India, women have traditionally found it difficult to function as actors in the marketplace. The structure of the economy favors wholesale markets with established lines of goods and credit, which are usually monopolized

[1] Quoted in UNICEF-Working Women's Forum (1989).

by men. In addition, the women are expected to devote most of their time to domestic responsibilities which puts severe limits on the amount of time they can devote to their businesses. There are also rigid social norms about the type of businesses that women 'typically' do that often constrain the range of choices available to women. As a result, the women engage in petty, seasonal, or low-volume trading which are considered high credit risks. In order to secure even this high risk credit, the women used to rely on money-lenders who charged exorbitant interest rates that drove them deep into debt. Despite the presence of nationalized banks that were mandated to lend to the poor, the women found them in practice to be unresponsive, impersonal, and rude, due to the fact that most of the women were illiterate. The banks were also unwilling to lend to women without having the men sign as co-guarantors. In addition, the banks were also not interested in processing the substantial number of small loans that the poor women requested, due to the large amount of paperwork involved.

As a result, the ICNW provides credit to these women. The key element in the structure is the neighborhood loan group. Anyone wishing to join the WWF must become a member of one of these groups. Each group consists of ten to twenty members, all women from the same neighborhood. A group leader is elected by the group. Once a group is formed, it is registered with the WWF and each member files an application form and pays a low membership fee (Rs.12/year). The members must attend groups meetings consistently, repay loans regularly, and act as mutual guarantors for the loans of all the group members. The loan procedure is as follows: all the group members apply together for loans, after the group leader has assessed the need, capacity, and productivity of each member, and after the members have reviewed each other's ability to earn. The applications are referred by the group leader to the local area organizer of the WWF. The applicants then go to the local WWF office to fill out a simple one-page loan application with the help of the group leader, area organizer, general secretary, and the loan officer. The latter submit the applications to the local bank branches and inform the area organizers. The area organizers take the applicants to the bank on the date of disbursement of loans and help them go through the process of filling out the right forms. The loans are taken at 4% DIR interest rate at a ten-month repayment schedule. The group leader collects and deposits repayments from the members to the banks.

Though the money comes from the banks, the WWF, as the intermediary, ultimately decides who gets a loan and who may default or adjust a repayment schedule. The approach by the WWF varies significantly in this regard from commercial banks. For example, the WWF is flexible about the purposes for which the loans are actually put to use: a majority of poor women divert some part of the loan amount towards consumption needs (food, clothes, as well as cultural necessities such as marriages or festivities). Commercial banks would not allow that. Also, the WWF permits rescheduling of loans for reasons that may be considered unacceptable by banks: fluctuations in the supply of goods due to monsoon floods, marriages, childbirth, medical procedures, accidents and disasters, as well as religious festivals. This has not affected the loan recovery rates: they remain around 95%, much higher than commercial recovery rates. Basically the whole system works on the basis of peer pressure buttressed by a sense of solidarity that results from a sensitized understanding of the real problems of these women.

The issue of credit is usually analyzed only in economic terms. However, for the WWF and the women who are its members, the value of credit transcends economic rationale. For the WWF, the ability to provide credit is the basis of its mobilizing potential, since the main reason women join the WWF is to gain access to credit. For the women members, credit has a significant and sometimes unexpectedly pleasant effect on their social and domestic status, in addition to its undoubted positive impact on the health and economic security of the women. The women and their families eat better, avoid money-lenders, invest in better clothes, medicines, education, jewelry (which is a primary means of savings in India), in addition to improving and diversifying their businesses. The presence of the WWF has eliminated the need for male co-guarantors of loans, liberating the women from dependence on their men. Many WWF members report that as their capacity to bargain increases due to their solidarity, they have gained greater trust, respect, and power inside their families and communities. The symbolic effects of their new roles have, in other words, unintended but welcome social and political consequences. They also have very significant impact at a personal level on the attitudes and personalities of many of these women, due to the sense of power and the feeling of responsibility that the WWF provides them.

NUWW: the supply of ideology

Though the NUWW has specific programs for its members such as pension and insurance schemes, and health and education programs for child labor rehabilitation, the main reason for the NUWW wing of the WWF appears to be to supply left-of-center ideology to the movement. The organization of women in the form of a trade union enables the women to engage in their programs in a class-conscious way. This sets the WWF apart from pure issue-based or identity-based movements. At a first glance, it may seem paradoxical that a micro-credit/lending organization should embrace leftist ideology. But upon a closer look, based on interviews with the women as well as upon observation of their socio-economic status within the overall structure of economic relationships in South India, it becomes obvious that in order to succeed, the other activities of the WWF (credit, socio-political change, cultural struggle, legal advocacy, etc.) need to be formulated in an oppositional mode to the particular type of capitalism that is prevalent in South India. The WWF appears to believe that it is possible to do the above by positioning itself at yet another level of identity: a class-conscious, leftist, trade union. While this organizational identity supplies the WWF with ideology, political orientation, as well as organizational form, it must be emphasized that the WWF does not affiliate itself with any leftist political party or make any moves towards capturing political power from its base as a trade union.

Movement: social and political mobilization, cultural struggle and identity

As a large collectivity of more than 591,000 women, the WWF is India's largest women's movement. The staff and the leadership of the WWF are acutely conscious of the critical role played by identity in its success. The strong pro-women ideology that the WWF has exhibited, has provided a sense of solidarity and self-confidence to the women, in addition to laying the foundation for several pro-women programs that in turn promote mobilization and enable popular struggles. The focus on their identity as women, has enabled the WWF to expand its activities to areas that are culturally and linguistically different. As examples, one may cite the expansion of the WWF into the community of women lace artisans of Narsapur in Andhra Pradesh (a neighboring state), and into the community of non-farming rural women of Bidar district in Karnataka (another neighboring state).

But while identity-based mobilization has proved successful with the WWF, it must be pointed out that the causes for the expansion of the WWF have differed substantially. In the first instance (Dindigul district in Tamil Nadu), WWF activities such as non-farm employment schemes for rural women were started due to the fact that Ms. Jaya Arunachalam's husband's ancestors owned ancestral lands in the same area. In at least three other instances (Adiramapattinam in Tamil Nadu, Narsapur in Andhra Pradesh, and Bidar district in Karnataka), activities for fisher-women, lace artisans and rural agricultural women (respectively), resulted from the interventions of international development agencies (FAO, ILO/Ford Foundation, and UNICEF respectively). Thus the WWF did not spontaneously spread to these areas because it happened to be a 'women's movement,' but rather the spread resulted from a complex configuration of external interventions, internal mobilizations (both of which were based on a perception of the WWF as an identity-based movement), accidental/personal connections, and other such factors. The story of this micro-politics is fascinating in itself and deserves further study.

It may be thought that many of the activities of the WWF involve struggles on the cultural terrain, due to the very fact of attempting to effect far-reaching socio-political changes that seek to alter the power relations between sexes in South Indian society. Despite this, many of the WWF members and staff appear to have a limited focus on cultural issues, understanding them as rather peripheral to their main activities. According to them, their activities focus on culture through education and training (using posters, plays, etc.), because they attempt to sensitize women and men to the negative consequences of oppressive institutions such as caste. This can be contrasted to the culture-neutral way in which they interpret their main focus of activity, viz., the promotion of women's economic freedom, or the cultural-ideological thrust of modern 'development' practice of which the WWF's activities are an integral part in South India.[2]

Thus the WWF exhibits some characteristics of a social movement and appears to lack some others. In its use of identity-based mobilization, in its fluidity and fragmentation of membership, in its complex relationship with the government/state (more follows on this), in the transnational linkages that it has created – as a women's movement, a trade union, as well as an alternative development institution – it is clearly a social movement.

Women's NGO: incorporation, foreign funding, coalition-building

As Eric Hobsbawm once noted, the Achilles' heel of any social movement is its lack of institutionalization. While the fluid and fragmentary nature

[2] There is a voluminous literature on cultural critiques of development ideas and institutions emerging more recently. For prominent examples, see Ferguson (1994); Escobar (1995).

of a movement enables its profusion, the lack of an institutional channel through which the energy of the movement can be guided can result in the dissipation of the direction and pace of the movement. As a result, many scholars have noted the useful roles that NGOs play: they may often initiate or sustain social movements;[3] or they may be the institutional vehicles for protest and collective action.[4] As a result, it is not surprising that the WWF is also registered as an NGO. As noted in the beginning section, the WWF is now registered under a central law in order to escape the harassment that it faced from the Tamil Nadu state officials. This provides an interesting example of the political and institutional space provided by the gaps and ambiguities in the legal system (in this case playing the state government against the central) that can then be exploited by an NGO such as the WWF.

In addition to the institutional identity and the organizational capacity that incorporation provides it, the WWF also benefits from its NGO status in other ways. First, it enables coalition-building with like-minded groups in India and outside, as noted in the previous section. This coalition-building with women's groups and development groups gives the WWF much leverage and standing vis-à-vis the government. In addition, its position as a women's NGO also provides ideological and political space by enabling it to be submerged within the rhetoric of human rights (freedom of association and gender equality). Second, it facilitates fund-raising from donors, by positioning itself as a 'women's NGO' or a 'development NGO.' In the current climate of continuing fascination among the development institutions with the rhetoric of participatory development and grassroots, the NGO identity is strategically helpful to the WWF.[5] Its success in this regard can be noted by a quick look at the number of donors that it has had: examples include (besides the central government and several state governments), SIDBI (Small Industries Development Bank of India), NADB (National Development Bank) and NABARD (National Bank for Agriculture and Rural Development) (domestic institutions), the Dutch government, German assistance, the Ford Foundation, SIDA, ILO, UNICEF, UNFPA (UN Population Fund), and UNDP. It must also be noted here that according to the staff of the WWF, there has been no serious internal debate within the movement about the pros and cons of foreign funding. This can be contrasted, for example, to other Indian

[3] Lehman (1990). [4] Diani (1992).
[5] For an exhaustive survey of the NGO debate, see Fisher (1997).

movements or NGOs which remain very sensitive to the whole issue of foreign funding, with many strongly opposed to bilateral funding.

Methodology of work: grassroots responsibilities

Several common strands can be seen in the methodology of the work of the WWF. Its mobilization is identity based; its initiators belong to the same class background as the target population; the initial approaches are made through an offer of credit for employment; its tactics are locally based and culturally well attuned to the realities of power in the area; its goals are realistic and need based; and, finally, its organizational structure is based on the principle of promoting the leadership from the grassroots. The final aspect of the methodology of its work is very important, as it provides external legitimacy and internal credibility to the WWF. Internal to the WWF, the division of work among the staff reflects the realities of South Indian society in which it must work. The leaders, who are well educated and belong to the upper class and castes, are in charge of public relations including media, relationship with the government and international agencies (as interlocutors), and policy planning. The middle managers, who are literate and belong to the lower middle class (but from various castes), are in charge of implementation of programs and projects, administration, recruitment, and liaison with local officials. The members, most of whom are illiterate and belong the poorest and the most exploited communities and castes, are the beneficiaries – they are the 'working women.' This alliance of women from different strata in society has worked well to its advantage in the case of the WWF.

This methodology makes it very different from just an NGO (choosing either advocacy or service delivery) or a trade union (collective bargaining). Indeed, its methodology, coupled with its hybrid forms of organization, makes it impossible to categorize the WWF as a particular entity.

Relationship with the government and political parties

Despite the appellation 'non-governmental,' NGOs (and movements that consist of NGOs) are often in complex, ambivalent, and dynamic – sometimes cooperative and sometimes contentious – relationship with the government.[6] That is certainly the case with the WWF. Generally

[6] For a discussion, see ibid. 451.

speaking, its development-oriented activities such as credit, health, and population-control programs are often performed in intimate connection with the development objectives and activities of the government, whereas its advocacy efforts as an NGO as well as its mobilization as a movement are often in tension with the government. Whether in organizing a rally against bus-fare hikes or in favor of more government programs for slum-dwellers, the WWF is often pitted against powerful interest-groups within the government that work to frustrate their objectives. However, this tension with the government has remained a constructive one for the WWF in that the oppositional methods used and the objectives pursued by the WWF have been within the accepted parameters of the government. This could be contrasted, for example, to the hostility exhibited by the state towards the activities of a very different movement, the Narmada Bachao Andolan (NBA), which has focused on a radical critique of and opposition to a specific development activity of the state, viz., dam-building.[7] This is not the case with the WWF which is perceived more as a 'soft' NGO/movement by the government which serves as a vehicle for the WWF to promote its own activities.

The only major instance of a real conflict between the WWF and the government appears to have happened with the Tamil Nadu government under Chief Minister Jayalalitha (also a woman). Under that government, WWF members and staff alleged harassment from government officers who were intent on taking over control of all the cooperatives in the state including those of the WWF. Due to that experience, the WWF registered under a central law as the ICNW which enabled it to escape state government control.

To sum up, while the initial activities of the WWF, including its ability to organize freely, could not have started without the public space provided by the Indian legal/political system,[8] the experience with the Tamil Nadu government shows how governments often see NGOs as undermining state hegemony and attempt to bring them under control.[9] Finally it must be noted that the WWF has had a very mixed success in influencing either government policies or legislation in a long-term manner and very little impact on political processes and structures. As noted above, much of the work of the WWF is very much in line with governmental programs and objectives, though in certain instances – such as the protest against bus-fare hikes – the action by the WWF has forced the government to reverse

[7] On the Narmada dam and the struggle over it, see generally Fisher (1995).

[8] A point made by Banuri (1993) 49–67. [9] Fisher (1997) 451.

its decisions. As to its impact on political processes and structures, almost two decades of women's activism by the WWF has not altered the political balance of forces, the political culture, the number of women in politics, and the issues on the public agenda in the state in any significant way. This is readily conceded by the members and staff of the WWF. This fact stands in contrast to the celebratory rhetoric – of civil society, democratization, and alternative political culture – with which NGOs such as the WWF are often greeted. What is closer to truth is that the WWF is a middle-of-the-road social movement that nevertheless has some radical long-term potential for altering power relations in society.

Finally, the WWF is not affiliated to any political party, though the President, Ms. Jaya Arunachalam, is a long-time member of the Congress party, which has provided institutional and political space to the WWF. The interesting aspect of the current position of the WWF towards political parties is that it is going through a self-examination whereby it is considering whether to float a political party at the national level. Its leaders have begun looking at models of progressive parties in other countries – such as the Green Party in Germany.

Challenges posed by WWF to extant paradigms

This study of the WWF has raised a number of questions that go to the heart of several accepted notions in different disciplines and areas. While this study is not the place to examine these challenges in great detail, I mention the following as examples of the kind of challenges that social movements pose, as I have argued in previous chapters.

Challenge to economic growth/development The praxis of the WWF centrally challenges several orthodoxies of economic growth. First, the success of the WWF challenges a dominant view that capital-intensive industrialization is the only model of economic growth. The very poor urban and rural women of the WWF have shown that viable economic activity is possible in the informal sector in a self-sustaining and productive way that meets developmental goals. Second, the WWF's focus on supporting women's existing economic enterprises rather than attempting to train them and create new jobs is contrary to one of the orthodoxies of economic growth which holds that workers in the informal sector need to be moved to the formal sector through job creation (a labor/employment policy) and training. This orthodoxy creates the momentum for a capital-intensive economic-growth model that will declare smaller enterprises (petty trading, hawking) illegal, and replace them with larger more 'viable' units. Third, the praxis of the WWF also shows that its grassroots-oriented and participatory approach works better than top–down, government-led development efforts. Despite the rhetoric of participation, development institutions and governments have yet to relinquish their control over development activities to the grassroots. The WWF's experiment functions, as a result, to challenge this control.

Challenge to human rights Human-rights theory and practice have always had trouble accommodating groups or activities that are not primarily concerned with civil liberties in a traditional western sense. Thus while the initial freedom of association of WWF members as well as their commitment to gender equality will be considered by most human-rights scholars and practitioners to be 'genuine' human rights, most of the activities of the WWF – promotion of economic freedom, trade unionizing, health and family-planning programs, cooperation with the government, or culture-focused activities such as inter-caste marriages – will not be considered so. The mainstream human-rights movement remains trapped in a version of liberalism that makes it impossible for it to come to terms with what the WWF does. Human-rights discourse does not concern itself with economic freedom because its main focus is on civil and political rights (economic rights being 'progressively realizable'); it does not focus on trade unionizing (despite lip-service) because it does not have a class angle to it (and is in fact pro-capitalist, as some have argued); it treats health and family-planning programs as 'merely' development programs (with its liberal assumption of a division between politics and economics); it can not understand how human-rights activities could be conducted in cooperation with the state (due to its anti-state bias); and it has traditionally concerned itself with culture only for the purpose of denying its validity (and proving its own universality in that process). The praxis of the WWF causes intense discomfort to mainstream human-rights thinking. That partly explains why the WWF has almost no links with the 'human rights' groups in India.

Challenge to feminist groups/movements Most western and many Indian women's NGOs have traditionally had a rights focus whereby their main activities have revolved around top–down legislative and policy changes through the state. Those NGOs have also traditionally consisted of elite women from the upper classes/castes, working for the 'upliftment' of the less fortunate lower-class/-caste women. In addition, women's NGOs have also usually taken a hard-line towards cultural issues, treating them, as they often deserved, as obstacles to be overcome by the universal rhetoric of women's rights. At least in all these aspects, the WWF is significantly different. Its members do not have a rights focus and their activities are grassroots oriented and self-initiated. 95% of the members of the WWF come from the poorest and the most exploited castes in the society and they work for their own 'upliftment.' The practice of the WWF is also to work within the cultural norms of the areas where they work in so far as this serves their overall objectives. These differences are perhaps the reason why the WWF is not considered by other groups as a feminist group.

Challenge to international law Recent writings in international relations[10] and international law[11] have highlighted the growing transnational issue networks consisting of local and international NGOs and social movements as proof of an emerging international civil society and instruments of global governance. As I have argued, a central notion behind this imagery of the world order is that sovereignties and states become fragmented and NGOs and movements become part of distinct issue-based global-governance networks that help each other in managing the world. According to this view, NGOs and movements are the vanguard of the new international order. Another central liberal understanding of the new world order hinges on the belief that planetary affiliations (such as gender, environment, or human rights) are challenging local, culture-based, nationalist ones. In addition, even as international law has celebrated the emergence of the transnational issue-networks, it has promoted the legal regime for the universalization of western liberal democracy as well as western-style capitalism. Thus, legal writers claim the emergence of a 'right' to democratic governance[12] (in the western style), and international lawyers busy themselves with the construction of the WTO, perhaps the largest international institutional experiment in the post World War II period, invented solely for the promotion of western-style capitalism.

The praxis of the WWF shows, however, that many of these claims and understandings about the new world order are inaccurate, premature, contradictory, or impossible in practice. While the WWF has certainly built transnational links with women's and development groups, as mentioned earlier, it is far from accurate to say that such links represent the foundations of lasting and structured global networks that can actually accomplish specific tasks. But more importantly, the nature of the activities of the WWF shows that, far from fragmenting sovereignty, it reinforces

[10] See, e.g., Lipschutz (1992); Sikkink (1993).
[11] See, e.g., Slaughter (1997); Charnowitz (1997).
[12] See Franck (1992).

its value and centrality to the lives of the people – especially if one were to understand sovereignty in a Foucaultian sense to mean governance capabilities (and not in the liberal sense of formal superiority in an independent sphere). The claim about planetary affiliations would also seem to be vastly exaggerated with respect to the WWF. Its members find it difficult enough to move their activities to culturally distinct regions in South India where different languages are spoken. It would be far from accurate to say that the WWF members – or its leaders – entertain grand global visions of gender solidarity.

Finally, it must be noted that the actual realization of the economic and political models that are currently promoted by the West is likely to deal a serious blow to the activities of the WWF. The New Economic Policy (NEP) that was inaugurated in the summer of 1991 in India that reflects the Washington consensus of privatization, marketization, liberalization, stabilization, and structural adjustment has had a serious impact on the lives of poor women who are members of the WWF. Examples include the hike in transport costs (for vegetable vendors and petty traders) arising out of a cutback in subsidies; lower access to resources and information by the women due to their loss of employment outside the home and thus being pushed into home-based production; lesser access to nutrition and basic necessities such as food, clothes, shelter, and water due to inflation and privatization; lesser access to higher education due to privatization since parents prefer to send their sons to college rather than their daughters due to the high costs involved; and cutbacks in the budget for non-formal and mass literacy programs. These changes have made it much harder for the WWF to meet its objectives and goals.

Similarly, the promotion of the universal western liberal democratic model – of the American variety – may also have the serious consequence of depoliticizing the issues that have been the staple of the WWF's activities, such as economic freedom; emphasizing the importance of NGOs and foreign funding as a real measure of freedom; replacing the empowerment approach with the anti-discrimination approach for women's rights which is much narrower; and, finally, treating all culture-based economic and political interventions as wrong and replacing them with a purportedly universal (western) model.

The above observations indicate the need for a serious look at the ideological/political orientation of international law. If international law wants to celebrate the grassroots and the emergence of a transnational civil society, it needs a critical self-examination of its own ideological and political assumptions – otherwise, its objectives are in conflict.

Challenge to domestic law The praxis of the WWF has truly exposed the weaknesses of the Indian domestic legal regime in many areas. In banking, the successes of the WWF have been proof of the failure of the assumptions that underlie traditional banking regulations, with their narrow assumptions of creditworthiness, the market activities that banks find profitable, the reasons that banks accept for rescheduling of loans, not to mention their male-centered elitism toward rural and poor women. These assumptions have shown that banks are in need of a serious overhaul to make them more people oriented and efficient. In labor law, again, the successes of the WWF are in fact proof of its own failure as well as the failure of the Indian left in general. It is a well-known critique of the Indian labor law regime that trade unionization has failed in India. To that one might add that it is particularly so in the case of women and those in the informal sector. The WWF has shown the gendered nature of the labor law regime in India that also needs a fundamental reform. From a human-rights/civil-liberties perspective, the experience of the WWF with the Tamil Nadu government has shown the need for a more comprehensive legal protection of freedom of association at the state and central levels, as well as adequate monitoring and enforcement mechanisms. From an urban/city-planning perspective, the record of the WWF proves the dismal record of the state and local governments in South India in providing basic amenities like drinking water, housing, and health facilities. The presence of the WWF has brought better health, hygiene, and employment opportunities to the women in slums, for example. However, this fact is hardly reflected in the local legislation pertaining to cities and towns, both in the allocation of responsibilities (the primary focus being the local governments rather than civil society organizations) as well as in the method of implementation.

Thus, the praxis of the WWF has created a serious crisis in many domestic legal regimes that needs to be addressed quickly and effectively.

Conclusion

This chapter is a preliminary effort at understanding India's largest women's movement, the WWF, in the context of the literature on development, social movements, and law, as well as the momentous economic and political changes that are occurring in India. The research shows that the praxis of the WWF poses serious challenges to accepted notions of economic development, human rights, international law, and domestic law. The research also shows that while the WWF has much radical potential in the long term, it is unrealistic to understand it as anything more than a middle-of-the-road social movement. The case study reveals the way in which identity-based social movements, such as the WWF, have challenged extant legal and economic structures as part of a process of survival in the extreme margins of peripheral societies. I have suggested that these challenges cause intense discomfort to received ideas in law, human rights and economic development even though the WWF's methods, actions, and goals are hardly radical (like those of the NBA, for example). The traditional discourses of liberation – development and human rights – have almost nothing to offer to the women who constitute the membership of the WWF. Instead, these women have articulated their own version of resistance that remains incomprehensible to the established narratives of liberation. I have attempted to recover this alternative narrative of resistance and write it into the very text of law.

PART IV

Epilogue

Mainstream international law, including the 'new international law' – differs from the concerns raised in this book in a number of ways. First, international law has traditionally seen the Third World in geographic, spatial terms, through the category of the state. As such it has tended to see the Third World's interaction with itself through that lens only. As I have suggested, however, patterns of Third World resistance changed significantly over the twentieth century and resistance can no longer be adequately grasped without adopting a social movement perspective to global and local change. Second, at a general level, international law has never been concerned primarily with social movements, save in the context of the self-determination and formation of states. It has treated all other popular protests and movements as 'outside' the state, and, therefore, illegitimate and unruly. This division has been based on a liberal conception of politics, which sharply distinguishes between routine institutional politics and other extra-institutional forms of protest. While there may have been some justification for this attitude before, now this model of politics stands heavily criticized in the social sciences. Due to its liberal conception of politics and its inability or unwillingness to factor in the impact of collective movements and forms-of-identity struggles other than nationalism, international law has remained strangely artificial and narrow. The exploration of a social movement perspective will, it is hoped, correct this institutionalist bias in international law. Third, international law's attitude to development has been fairly benign so far. Both First World and Third World lawyers have treated the modernizing and civilizing imperatives of development as ontologically acceptable. The only disagreement, in the form of the NIEO debates, has been over the pace and the implementation of the promises of development. The examination of the development–social movement dialectic in this book shows that the response to development interventions from the Third World, in the form of social movements, was much less benign. Indeed, I would suggest that a post-developmental approach for international law is essential if it is to remain relevant to the most significant social struggles of our times in the Third World. Fourth, international lawyers have had a particular historical approach to the construction of the main elements of post-War modern international law. That approach has oscillated between a selective and eurocentric humanism – in the form of human rights – and an ahistorical functional pragmatism – in the form of international economic law. According to this approach, international human rights is the product of western humanist reaction to the horrors of the Nazi era, but is intellectually grounded in western political theory of Locke, Kant, and Rousseau. It bears no relationship to the 'old' international law of colonialism, and owes nothing to anti-colonial struggles as intellectual forbears. Instead, I suggested that the discursive field of human rights – its symbols, apparatuses, and doctrines – was significantly shaped during the inter-war transition from colonialism to development, as well as by the apparatuses that were developed to manage anti-colonial resistance movements. Similarly, international economic law is presented as the law of international economic institutions such as GATT/WTO and Bretton Woods, with no connection either to the 'old' colonial international law, or, for that matter, to development. The analysis in this book showed that international institutions including important economic institutions – the Mandate system of the League, UNCTAD, multilateral and bilateral development agencies, the Bretton Woods institutions, and post-Cold-War institutions to promote democracy and peace – grew out of and were primarily shaped by the development encounter and Third World resistance.

From a broader, disciplinary perspective I also engaged in this task with at least two goals in mind: first, I was interested in investigating the contemporary theoretical crises of an international legal order, oscillating perennially between normativity and concreteness,[1] but, more acutely, evidencing a loss of faith in two key emancipatory variables: the nation state, and development. This is nowhere more apparent than among Third World legal scholars. To that extent, this book is a contribution to the re-articulation of a distinctive Third World approach to international law. In this, I was guided by the question: how does one de-elitize international law by writing resistance into it, to make it 'recognize' subaltern voices? Second, I was animated by the implications of the near-disappearance of the Marxist paradigm in international law for creative Third World legal scholarship.[2] This has occurred not merely due to the rather simplistic

[1] Koskenniemi (1989) 2–8. [2] With the exception of Chimni (1993); (1999).

"end of history" argument, but also due to the rise of cultural-identity politics across the world, in the form of what Thomas Franck has called, "post-modern tribalisms."[3] The question then is do these political actors – social movements – provide a way to rethink the relationship between economic, moral, political, and cultural issues in legal and institutional practice as well as formations of identity? I have suggested that they indeed do.

Concretely, two themes explored at length in this book remain invisible to mainstream international law scholarship. First, the main elements of twentieth-century international law – international institutions that represent the pragmatist approach and human-rights law that represents the liberal approach – have been centrally constituted by the evocation of and continuous interaction with the resistance posed by the category 'Third World.' Second, this resistance of the 'Third World' has undergone significant changes over the twentieth century and can no longer be understood without an understanding of social movements. In other words, both the realist statist paradigm and the liberal individualist paradigm are unhelpful in appreciating much of what happens in the Third World.

The liberal individualist paradigm seems on the surface to have the capability to appreciate the changing nature of Third World resistance through, for example, the idea of civil society. But, there are serious limitations to the way the notion of civil society is understood in mainstream literature and this threatens to constitute itself through familiar exclusionary tactics that make much of the praxis of social movements invisible. Indeed, instead of seeing Third World resistance through social movements as a confirmation of liberal internationalism, a closer understanding reveals them to be irruptions of and alternatives to it. This is so because the praxis of social movements offers a fundamental epistemological challenge to the premises of liberal internationalism. Social movements seek to redefine the 'political' in non-institutional, non-party, cultural terms. They seek to redefine the 'economy' in place-based, rather than space-based, terms. And they seek to redefine 'law' in radically pluralistic terms. Liberal internationalism runs contrary to all of these: its notion of politics remains highly institutionalized and monoculturally western; its notion of economy is built on the overpowering of place-based survival strategies by space-based efficiency notions; and its understanding of law is almost ethnocentrically narrow and is built on significant exclusions of categories of marginalized peoples.

[3] Franck (1993).

Looking at international institutions, they have unprecedented authority over different parts of the globe in the current era of cosmopolitanism. From administering Kosovo to taking over East Timor, to restructuring entire governance institutions of Third World countries, the ambit and range of institutions are unparalleled. With that increase in duties, however, come responsibilities, both ethical and legal, not only to listen and respond to the voices of the subalterns, but also to know the limits of cosmopolitanism as a cure-all.[4] The latter is important to bear in mind as it is often thought in international legal circles that a shift in power from the sovereign to international institutions is per se progressive and can only better serve the interests of those who live under the sovereign. This 'move to empire'[5] is perhaps inevitable in a profession which has been built on overcoming the legacies of absolute sovereignty. But to replace absolute sovereigns with absolute supra-sovereigns in the form of institutions is hardly the solution. More importantly, international institutions are not autonomous from the 'local' pressures that generate circumstances for institutional interventions. Rather, they are themselves constituted through a complex and ambivalent relationship with the 'local,' increasingly manifested in the form of social movements in the Third World. This is what I have argued in this book.

Yet this does not lead to the dismissal of international institutions as important actors in international law. On the contrary, by being closely interwoven with 'local' social movements that generate pressures for change, international institutions may yet have the potential to contribute to that change. The World Bank's turn to poverty alleviation and environmental protection, while imperfect and the result of external pressures mounted by social movements, and the assumption of democratic duties by the UN have assisted local social and democratic change by creating and supporting political space for such claims to be made. A number of recent examples suggests this two-way relationship between social movements and international institutions: (a) The World Bank Complaints Panel and the Narmada and Polonoroeste struggles; (b) The World Commission on Dams and countless developmental struggles for survival against the onslaught of development in the Third World; (c) the Ottawa Treaty against Anti-personnel Landmines and the effective advocacy for it by an international social movement of grassroots groups; (d) the anti-nuclear and peace movements and their successful attempt to approach

[4] For an incisive critique of the cosmopolitan sensibility, see Kennedy (1999).

[5] For an important analysis of the relationship between colonialism, empire, and the politics of story-telling about international law's evolution, see Berman (1999).

the International Court of Justice in the Nuclear Weapons advisory opinion case. I do not mean that this two-way process heralds a new era in international relations or is always unambiguously "good." The purpose here is simply to tell a very different and a distinctly non-western story about international law and institutions, and to raise some questions about the politics of story telling in international law, which has excluded the role of social movements so far.

The 'arrival' of social movements in international law does not mean that the state has become an insignificant actor in the Third World. Far from it. The state remains powerful and an important site of ideological and political contestations in most Third World countries. However, it is undeniable that the nature of Third World resistance has undergone a radical transformation due to the emergence of local social movements as independent actors. The response by international institutions to this resistance has reflected the importance of this change, by engaging the multiple sites where the 'Third World' is located for these institutions.

Several implications follow from this book for the history, theory, and method of international law. They cannot possibly be explored at length here but let me note the following by way of exploration. The history of international law has been written so far from the perspective of states, stressing the role played by institutions and leading western scholars and leaders, and guided by a concern for the interests of the global cosmopolitan class. This means, for example, that the resistance to colonialism is analyzed (when and if at all) as a macro-level diplomatic process at the state level. I have sought to ask whose history is it? Instead of this approach, one could imagine building a 'history from below' that studies the everyday life of international interventions, including the resistance to such ideas by ordinary people. This means not simply that the practice of historiography must become more inclusionary; it also means that the very focus of historiography must change from the macro to the micro, from the episodic to the mundane.

This 'history from below' may also lead to a 'theory from below.' Instead of constructing the structure of international law from ideas and intellectual strategies alone, one could imagine a history from below leading to a theory of peoples, cultures, and power. This theory would need to transcend the limitations of realist statism and liberal individualism, and build on the radical cultural politics of social movements to enable alternative visions of governance that do not privilege particular social actors. This is necessary to transform international law from an international law of domination to one of resistance in the aid of marginalized communities and peoples. This project is in defense of an international law from below.

Clearly a new form of politics, a new form of organization of power, and new methods of expressing resistance are emerging from the grassroots and are only likely to intensify in the present millennium, as Seattle and Washington showed recently. It is important for the discipline of international law to rethink its categories and learn how to take the 'local' more seriously in its problematic and contested relationship with the Third World.

LIST OF REFERENCES

"Aaland Island Question Report" (1920) *Official Journal of the League of Nations*, Special Supp. No.3, October (1920)

Abu-Odeh, Lama (1992) "Post-Colonial Feminism and the Veil: Considering the Differences," *New England Law Review* 26, 1527

Ackerman, Bruce, and David Golove (1995) "Is NAFTA Constitutional?" *Harvard Law Review* 108, 799

Adam, Barry (1993) "Post-Marxism and the New Social Movements," *Canadian Review of Sociology and Anthropology* 30 (3), 317

Alexandrowicz, C. H. (1967) *An Introduction to the History of the Law of Nations in the East Indies* (Oxford: Clarendon Press)

Alford, William (2000) "Exporting 'the pursuit of happiness,' " *Harvard Law Review* 113, 1677

Allot, Philip (1990) *Eunomia: New Order for a New World* (New York: Oxford University Press)

(1995) "The International Court and Voice of Justice," in Vaughan Lowe and Malgosia Fitzmaurice (eds.), *Fifty Years of the International Court of Justice: Essays in Honor of Sir Robert Jennings* (Cambridge: Cambridge University Press)

Alston, Philip (1988) "Making Space for New Human Rights: the Case of the Right to Development," *Harvard Human Rights Year Book* 1

(1992) *The United Nations and Human Rights: a Critical Appraisal* (Oxford: Clarendon Press; New York: Oxford University Press)

(ed.) (1996) *Human Rights Law* (New York, New York University Press)

Alston, Phillip and James Crawford (eds.) (2000) *The Future of UN Human Rights Treaty Monitoring* (Cambridge: Cambridge University Press)

Alvares, Claude and Ramesh Billorey (1988) *Damming the Narmada* (Penang, Malaysia: Third World Network, APPEN)

Alvarez, Alejandro (1929) "The New International Law," *Transactions of the Grotius Society*, April 16, 35

Alvarez, Jose (2000) "Multilateralism and its Discontents," *European Journal of International Law* 2, 393

Alvarez, Sonia E. (1998) "Latin American Feminisms 'Go Global': Trends of the 1990s and Challenges for the New Millennium," in Sonia E. Alvarez,

Evelina Dagnino, and Arturo Escobar (eds.) *Cultures of Politics/Politics of Cultures: Re-Visioning Latin American Social Movements* (Boulder, Colo.: Westview Press)

Alvarez, Sonia E., Evelina Dagnino, and Arturo Escobar (eds.) (1998) *Cultures of Politics/Politics of Cultures: Re-Visioning Latin American Social Movements* (Boulder, Colo.: Westview Press)

American Society of International Law (1975) Panel on "The Charter of Economic Rights and Duties of States," *American Society of International Law Proceedings*, 225

Amin, Samir (1976) *Unequal Development: an Essay on the Social Formations of Peripheral Capitalism* (New York: Monthly Review Press)

(1990) *Delinking: Towards a Polycentric World* (London: Zed Books)

Anand, R. P. (1980) "Development and Environment: the Case of the Developing Countries," *Indian Journal of International Law* 24, 1

(1987) *International Law and the Developing Countries: Confrontation or Cooperation?* (Dodrecht, Boston: Kluwer Academic Publishers)

Andrews, David, Anthony R. Boote, Syed S. Rizavi, and Sukhwinder Singh (2000) *Debt Relief for Low-Income Countries: the Enhanced HIPC Initiative* (Series: International Monetary Fund Pamphlet Series No. 51)

Anghie, Antony (1995) "Creating the Nation State: Colonialism and the Making of International Law" (unpublished SJD Dissertation, Harvard Law School)

(1996) "Francisco de Vitoria and the Colonial Origins of International Law," *Social and Legal Studies* 5, 321

(1999) "Finding the Peripheries: Sovereignty and Colonialism in Nineteenth Century International Law," *Harvard International Law Journal* 40, 1

An-Na'im, Abdullahi Ahmed (1990) "Human Rights in the Muslim World: Socio-Political Conditions and Scriptural Imperatives," *Harvard Human Rights Journal* 3, 13

(ed.) (1992) *Human Rights in Cross-Cultural Perspectives. A Quest for Consensus* (Philadelphia: University of Pennsylvania Press)

Appadorai, A. (1955) *The Bandung Conference* (New Delhi: Indian Council of World Affairs)

Apter, David (1997) "Political Violence in Analytical Perspective," in David Apter (ed.), *The Legitimation of Violence* (New York: New York University Press)

Arendt, Hannah (1970) *On Violence* (New York: Harcourt Brace Jovanovich)

Arndt, Heinz Wolfgang (1983) "The Trickle-down Myth" (1983) *Economic Development and Cultural Change* 32 (1), 1

(1989) *Economic Development: the History of an Idea* (Chicago: University of Chicago Press)

Asad, Talal (1997) "On Torture, or Cruel, Inhuman and Degrading Treatment," in Richard A. Wilson (ed.), *Human Rights, Culture and Context: Anthropological Perspectives* (London; Chicago: Pluto Press)

Ashley, Richard (1980) *The Political Economy of War and Peace: the Sino–Soviet–American Triangle and the Modern Security Problematique* (London: F. Pinter; New York: Nichols Pub. Co.)

Aufderheide, Pat, and Bruce Rich (1985) "Debacle in the Amazon," *Defenders, U.S.*, March–April

Aziz, Nikhil (1995) "The Human Rights Debate in an Era of Globalization: Hegemony of Dis-course," *Bulletin of Concerned Asian Scholars* 27, 9

Banuri, Tariq (1990) "Development and the Politics of Knowledge: a Critical Interpretation of the Social Role of Modernization Theories in the Development of the Third World," in Frédérique A. Marglin and Stephen Marglin (eds.), *Dominating Knowledge: Development, Culture, and Resistance* (Oxford: Clarendon Press; New York: Oxford University Press)

(1993) "The Landscape of Diplomatic Conflicts," in Wolfgang Sachs (ed.), *Global Ecology: a New Arena of Political Conflict* (Atlantic Highlands, N.J.: Zed Books)

Baran, Paul (1957) *The Political Economy of Growth* (New York: Monthly Review Press)

Barlow, Maude and Tony Clark (1998) *MAI: the Multilateral Agreement on Investment and the Threat to American Freedom* (New York: Stoddart; General Distribution Services)

Barnett, Robert (1993) "Exchange Rate Arrangements in the International Monetary Fund: the Fund as Lawgiver, Adviser, Enforcer," *Temple International and Comparative Law Journal* 7 (1), 77

Barro, Robert (1994) "Democracy: a Recipe for Growth?" *Wall Street Journal*, December 1

Bary, W. Theodore de (1998) *Asian Values and Human Rights: a Confucian Communitarian Perspective* (Cambridge, Mass.: Harvard University Press)

Basu, Amrita (ed.) (1995) *The Challenge of Local Feminisms: Women's Movements in Global Perspective* (Boulder, Colo.: Westview Press)

Batsell, Walter Russell (1925) "The United States and the System of Mandates," *International Conciliation* (Carnegie Endowment for International Peace) 213 (October)

Bauer, Joanne, and Daniel Bell (eds.) (1999) *The East Asian Challenge for Human Rights* (New York: Cambridge University Press)

Bauer, Peter Tamas (1976) *Dissent on Development* (Cambridge, Mass.: Harvard University Press)

Bauer, Peter, and B. S. Yamey (1977) "Against the new economic order," *Commentary* 25 (April)

Baviskar, Amita (1995) *In the Belly of the River: Tribal Conflicts over Development in the Narmada Valley* (Delhi; New York; Oxford University Press)

Baxi, Upendra (1972) "Some Remarks on Eurocentrism and the Law of Nations," in R. P. Anand (ed.), *Asian States and the Development of Universal International Law* (Delhi: Vikas Publications)

(1988) "Taking Suffering Seriously," in *Law and Poverty: Critical Essays* (Bombay: N. M. Tripathi)

(1991) "From Human Rights to the Right to be Human: Some Heresies," in Smitu Kothari and Harsh Sethi (eds.), *Rethinking Human Rights: Challenges for Theory and Action* (Delhi: Lokayan)

(1998) "Voices of Suffering and the Future of Human Rights," *Transnational Law and Contemporary Problems* 8 (Fall), 125

Bedjaoui, Mohammed (1979) *Towards a New International Economic Order* (New York: Holmes and Meier)

Beiner, Ronald (ed.) (1995) *Theorizing Citizenship* (Albany, N.Y.: State University of New York Press)

Bell, Daniel (1989) " 'American Exceptionalism' Revisited: the Role of Civil Society," *Public Interest* 38

(1996) "The East Asian Challenge to Human Rights: Reflections on an East-West Dialogue," *Human Rights Quarterly* 18, 641

Belleau, Marie-Claire (1990) "Les Juristes inquiets: Critical Currents of Legal Thought in France at the End of the Nineteenth Century" (unpublished SJD dissertation, Harvard Law School)

Benhabib, Seyla (1996) *Democracy and Difference: Contesting the Boundaries of the Political* (Princeton, N.J.: Princeton University Press)

Bentwich, Norman (1930) *The Mandates System* (London: Longmans, Green and Co.)

Bergsten, C. Fred (1976) "Interdependence and the Reform of International Institutions," *International Organizations* 30 (Spring), 362

Bergsten, C. Fred, George Berthoin, and Kinhide Mushakoji (1976) *The Reform of International Institutions: a Report of the Trilateral Task Force on International Institutions to the Trilateral Commission* (New York, N.Y.: The Commission)

Berman, Nathaniel (1988) "Sovereignty in Abeyance: Self-Determination and International Law," *Wisconsin International Law Journal* 7, 51

(1992) "Modernism, Nationalism, and the Rhetoric of Reconstruction," *Yale Journal of Law and the Humanities* 4, 351

(1993) " 'But the Alternative is Despair': Nationalism and the Modernist Renewal of International Law," *Harvard Law Review* 106, 1792

(1999) "In the Wake of Empire," *American University International Law Review* 14, 1515

(2000) "The Nationality Decrees Case, or, of Intimacy and Consent," *Leiden Journal of International Law* 13, 265

Bermann, George (1994) "Taking Subsidiarity Seriously: Federalism in the European Community and the United States," *Columbia Law Review* 94, 331

Bhagwati, Jagdish (ed.) (1977) *The New International Economic Order: the North–South Debate* (Cambridge, Mass.: MIT Press)

Bourdieu, Pierre (1977) *Outline of a Theory of Practice* (Cambridge, New York: Cambridge University Press)

(1987) "The Force of Law: toward a Sociology of the Juridical Field," *Hastings Law Journal* 38 (July), 805

Boutros-Ghali, Boutros (1993) "Human Rights: the Common Language of Humanity," in UN World Conference on Human Rights, The Vienna Declaration and Programme of Action

Bowles, Samuel, and Herbert Gintis (1986) *Democracy and Capitalism: Property, Community, and the Contradictions of Modern Social Thought* (New York: Basic Books)

Bradlow, Daniel D. (1993) "International Organizations and Private Complaints: the Case of the World Bank Inspection Panel," *Virginia Journal of International Law* 34, 553

(1996) "The World Bank, the International Monetary Fund and Human Rights," *Transnational Law and Contemporary Problems* 6, 47

Bradlow, Daniel D., and Sabine Schlemmer-Schulte (1994) "The World Bank's New Inspection Panel: a Constructive Step in the Transformation of the International Legal Order," *Heidelberg Journal of International Law* 2, 392

Bright, Charles, and Susan Harding (eds.) (1984) *Statemaking and Social Movements: Essays in History and Theory* (Ann Arbor, MI: University of Michigan Press)

Broad, Robin (1988) *Unequal Alliance: the World Bank, the International Monetary Fund and the Philippines* (Berkeley, Calif.: University of California Press)

Brunelli, Gilio (1986) "Warfare in Polonoroeste," *Cultural Survival Quarterly* 10, 37

Bull, Hedley (1984) "The Revolt Against the West," in Hedley Bull and Adam Watson (eds.), *The Expansion of International Society* (New York: Oxford University Press)

Bull, Hedley, and Adam Watson (1984) *The Expansion of International Society* (New York: Oxford University Press)

Burbach, Roger (1997) *Globalization and its Discontents: the Rise of Postmodern Socialisms* (London and Chicago: Pluto Press)

Cabral, Amilcar (1970) "National Liberation and Culture" (Eduardo Mondlane Memorial Lecture, Syracuse University, February 20)

Calderón, Fernando, Alejandro Piscitelli, and José Luis Reyna (1992) "Social Movements: Actors, Theories, Expectations," in Arturo Escobar and Sonia E. Alvarez (eds.) *The Making of Social Movements in Latin America* (Boulder, Colo.: Westview Press)

Carothers, Thomas (1999) *Aiding Democracy Abroad: the Learning Curve* (Washington, D.C.: Carnegie Endowment for International Peace)

Carter, Barry, and Philip Trimble (1995) *International Law* (2nd edition) (Boston, Mass.: Little, Brown)

Carty, Anthony (1986) *The Decay of International Law? a Reappraisal of the Limits of Legal Imagination in International Affairs* (Manchester: Manchester University Press)

Cass, Deborah Z. (1992) "The Word that saves Maastricht? The Principle of Subsidiarity and the Division of Powers within the European Community," *Common Market Law Review* 29, 1107

Cassese, Antonio (1995) *Self-Determination of Peoples: a Legal Reappraisal* (Cambridge: Cambridge University Press)

Caufield, Catherine (1996) *Masters of Illusion: the World Bank and the Poverty of Nations* (New York: Henry Holt)

Chace, James (1984) *Endless War: How We Got Involved in Central America and What Can Be Done* (New York: Vintage Books)

Chacko, C. J. (1958) "India's Contribution to the Field of International Law Concepts," *Recueil des Cours* 93, 117

Charlesworth, Hilary (1992) "The Public–Private Distinction and the Right to Development in International Law," *Australian Yearbook of International Law* 12, 190

Charlesworth, Hilary, Christine Chinkin, and Shelley Wright (1991) "Feminist Approaches to International Law," *American Journal of International Law* 85, 613

Charnowitz, Steve (1997) "Two Centuries of Participation: NGOs and International Governance," *Michigan Journal of International Law* 18, 183

Chatterjee, Partha (1993) *The Nation and its Fragments* (Princeton, N.J.: Princeton University Press)

Chayes, Abram, and Antonia Handler Chayes (1995) *The New Sovereignty: Compliance with International Regulatory Agreements* (Cambridge, Mass.: Harvard University Press)

Cherokee Nation v. The State of Georgia, 30 U.S. 1; 8 L. Ed. 25

Chimni, B. S. (1993) *International Law and World Order: a Critique of Contemporary Approaches* (New Delhi: Sage Publications)

(1999) "Marxism and International Law: a Contemporary Analysis," *Economic and Political Weekly* February 6

Chowdhuri, R. N. (1955) *International Mandates and Trusteeship Systems: A Comparative Study* (The Hague: Martinus Nijhoff)

Christenson, Gordon (1997) "World Civil Society and the International Rule of Law" (1997) 19 *Human Rights Quarterly* 724

Clarke, Gerard (1998) "Non-Governmental Organizations (NGOs) and Politics in the Developing World," *Political Studies* 46, 36

Claude, Inis, Jr. (1971) *Swords into Plowshares; the Problems and Progress of International Organization* (New York: Random House)

Cohen, Jean, and Andrew Arato (1992) *Civil Society and Political Theory* (Cambridge, Mass.: MIT Press)

Conrad, Lorry (1989) "The Legal Nature and Social Effects of International Monetary Fund Stand-by Arrangements," *Wisconsin International Law Journal* 7(2) (Spring), 407

Corbett, Percy (1924) "What is the League of Nations?" *British Yearbook of International Law*, 119–48

Cornia, Giovanni A., Richard Jolly, and Frances Stewart (eds.) (1987) *Adjustment with a Human Face* (Oxford: Clarendon Press)

Cover, Robert M. (1983) "Forward: Nomos and Narrative," *Harvard Law Review* 97, 4

Cranston, Maurice (1973) *What are Human Rights?* (New York: Taplinger Pub. Co.)

Crawford, James (1979) *The Creation of States in International Law* (Oxford: Clarendon Press)

(1994) Democracy in International Law: Inaugural Lecture Delivered March 5, 1993 (Cambridge: Cambridge University Press).

Crenshaw, Kimberle (1988) "Race, Reform, and Retrenchment: Transformation and Legitimation in Antidiscrimination Law," *Harvard Law Review* 101, 1331

Dahl, Robert (1956) *A Preface to Democratic Theory* (Chicago, Ill.: University of Chicago Press)

Dahrendorff, Ralf (1999) "The Third Way and Liberty," *Foreign Affairs* (September/October)

Dam, Kenneth (1982) *Rules of the Game: Reform and Evolution in the International Monetary System* (Chicago, Ill.: University of Chicago Press)

Davies, Michael C. (ed.) (1995) *Human Rights and Chinese Values: Legal, Philosophical, and Political Perspectives* (Hong Kong and New York: Oxford University Press)

Dell, Sidney (1983) "Stabilization: the Political Economy of Overkill," in John Williamson (ed.) *IMF Conditionality* (Cambridge and Washington, D.C.: Institute for International Economics)

(1985) "The Origins of UNCTAD," in M. Zammit Cutajar (ed.) *UNCTAD and the North-South Dialogue: the First Twenty Years: Essays in Memory of W. R. Malinowski* (Oxford: Pergamon Press)

Diamond, Larry (1995) *Promoting Democracy in the 1990s: Actors and Instruments, Issues and Imperatives: a Report to the Carnegie Commission on Preventing Deadly Conflict* (Washington, D.C.: The Commission)

Diamond, Larry, and Marc F. Plattner (eds.) (1993) *Capitalism, Socialism and Democracy Revisited* (Baltimore, Md.; The Johns Hopkins University Press)

Diani, Mario (1992) "The concept of Social Movement," *The Sociological Review* 40, 1

Donnelly, Jack (1988) "Human Rights at the United Nations, 1955–1985: the Question of Bias," *International Studies Quarterly* 32, 275

(1989) *Universal Human Rights in Theory and Practice* (Ithaca, N.Y.: Cornell University Press)

Dore, Issaak (1985) *The International Mandate System and Namibia* (Boulder, Colo.: Westview Press)

Doyle, Michael (1983) "Kant, Liberal Legacies, and Foreign Affairs, Part I" *Philosophy and Public Affairs* 12 (Summer), 3 and "Part II" *Philosophy and Public Affairs* 12 (Autumn), 4

Doyle, Michael W., Ian Johnstone, and Robert C. Orr (eds.) (1997) *Keeping the Peace: Multidimensional UN Operations in Cambodia and El Salvador* (New York: Cambridge University Press)

Drago, Luis (1907) "State Loans in the Relation to International Policy," *American Journal of International Law* 1, 692

Dreze, Jean, and Amartya Sen (1989) *Hunger and Public Action* (Oxford: Clarendon Press)

Dubash, Navroz, Mairi Dupar, Smitu Kothari, and Tundu Lissu (2001) *A Watershed in Global Governance? An Independent Assessment of the World Commission on Dams* (Washington, D.C.: World Resources Institute)

Dupuy, R. (ed.) (1980) *The Right to Development at the International Level* (Alphen aan den Rijn: Sijthoff and Noordhoff)

Dutkiewicz, P., and R. Shenton (1986) " 'Etatization' and the Logic of Diminished Reproduction," *Review of African Political Economy* 37, 108

Dworkin, Ronald (1978) *Taking Rights Seriously* (Cambridge, Mass.: Harvard University Press)

Eckholm, Eric (1984) "World Bank urged to halt aid to Brazil for Amazon development," *New York Times*, October 17

Eder, Klaus (1993) *The New Politics of Class: Social Movements and Cultural Dynamics in Advanced Society* (London and Newbury Park, Calif.: Sage Publications)

Edwards, Michael, and David Hulme (1997) *NGOs, States and Donors: Too Close for Comfort?* (New York: St. Martin's Press)

Eisenhower, Dwight (1965) *Waging Peace, 1956–1961: the White House Years* (Garden City, N.Y.: Doubleday)

Eisenhower, Milton S. (1963) *The Wine is Bitter: the United States and Latin America* (Garden City, N.Y.: Doubleday)

Engle, Karen (1992a) "International Human Rights and Feminism: when Discourses Meet," *Michigan Journal of International Law* 13, 517

(1992b) "Female Subjects of Public International Law: Human Rights and the Exotic Other Female," *New England Law Review* 26, 1509

(1993) "After the Collapse of the Public/Private distinction: Strategizing Women's Rights," in Dorinda Dallmeyer (ed.), *Reconstructing Reality: Women and International Law* (Washington, D.C.: American Society of International Law)

(2001) "From Skepticism to Embrace: Human Rights and the American Anthropological Association from 1947–1999," *Human Rights Quarterly* 23, 3

Enke, Stephen (1963) *Economics for Development* (Englewood Cliffs, N.J.: Prentice-Hall)

Epp, Charles (1998) *The Rights Revolution: Lawyers, Activists and Supreme Courts in Comparative Perspective* (Chicago, Ill.: University of Chicago Press)

Escobar, Arturo (1992) "Planning," in Wolfgang Sachs (ed.), *Development Dictionary: A Guide to Knowledge as Power* (London: Zed Books)

(1995) *Encountering Development: the Making and Unmaking of the Third World* (Princeton, N.J.: Princeton University Press)

Escobar, Arturo, and Sonia E. Alvarez (eds.) (1992) *The Making of Social Movements in Latin America* (Boulder, Colo.: Westview Press)

Esteva, Gustavo (1987) "Regenerating Peoples' Space," *Alternatives* 12, 125

(1992) "Development," in Wolfgang Sachs (ed.), *Development Dictionary: a Guide to Knowledge as Power* (London: Zed Books)

Esteva, Gustavo, and Madhu Suri Prakash (1998) *Grassroots Postmodernism: Remaking the Soil of Cultures* (London: Zed Books)

Evans, Peter (2000) "Fighting Marginalization with Transnational Networks: Counter-hegemonic Globalization," *Contemporary Sociology* 29, 1: 230–41

Evans-Pritchard, E. E. (1965) *Theories of Primitive Religion* (Oxford: Clarendon Press)

Falk, Richard (1981) *Human Rights and State Sovereignty* (New York: Holmes and Meier)

(1983) *The End of World Order* (New York: Holmes and Meier)

(1987) "The Global Promise of Social Movements: Explorations at the Edge of Time," *Alternatives* 12, 173

(1998) *Law in an Emerging Global Village: a Post-Westphalian Perspective* (New York: Transnational Publishers Inc.)

(2000) *Human Rights Horizons: the Pursuit of Justice in a Globalizing World* (New York: Routledge)

Fanon, Frantz (1963) *The Wretched of the Earth* (New York: Grove Press)

Ferguson, Adam (1767/1995) *An Essay on the History of Civil Society*, ed. Fania Oz-Salzberger (Cambridge: Cambridge University Press)

Ferguson, James (1990) *The Anti-Politics Machine: "Development," Depoliticization and Bureaucratic Power in Lesotho* (Cambridge and New York: Cambridge University Press)

Finger, Seymour M. (1976) "United States Policy toward International Institutions," *International Organizations* 30 (Spring), 347

Fisher, William F. (1997) "Doing Good? The politics and antipolitics of NGO Practices," *Annual Review of Anthropology* 26, 451

Fisher, William F. (ed.) (1995) *Toward Sustainable Development? Struggling Over India's Narmada River* (Armonk, N.Y.: M. E. Sharpe)

Forsythe, David (1977) *Humanitarian Politics: the International Committee of the Red Cross* (Baltimore, Md.: Johns Hopkins University Press)

(1980) *Humanizing American Foreign Policy: Non-profit Lobbying and Human Rights* (New Haven, Conn.: Yale University Press)

Foucault, Michel (1973) *The Birth of the Clinic: an Archaeology of Medical Perception* (New York: Pantheon Books)

(1972) *The Archeology of Knowledge* (New York: Pantheon Books)

(1979) *Discipline and Punish* (New York: Vintage Books)

(1980) *Power/Knowledge: Selected Interviews and Other Writings, 1972–1977* (New York: Pantheon Books)

(1991) "Governmentality," in Graham Burchell, Colin Gordon, and Peter Miller (eds.), *The Foucault Effect: Studies in Governmentality: with Two Lectures by and an Interview with Michel Foucault* (Chicago, Ill.: University of Chicago Press)

Fox, Gregory (1999) "Strengthening the State," *Indian Journal of Global Legal Studies* 7, 35

Fox, Gregory, and Georg Nolte (1995) "Intolerant Democracies," *Harvard International Law Journal* 36 (Winter), 1

Fox Piven, Frances, and Richard Cloward (1977) *Poor People's Movements: Why They Succeed, How They Fail* (New York: Pantheon Books)

Franck, Thomas M. (1986) "Lessons of the Failure of the NIEO," *International Law and Development* (Proceedings of the Canadian Council on International Law), 82

(1988) "Legitimacy in the International System," *American Journal of International Law* 82, 705

(1990) *The Power of Legitimacy amongst Nations* (New York: Oxford University Press)

(1992) "The Emerging Right to Democratic Governance," *American Journal of International Law* 86, 46

(1993) "Postmodern Tribalism and the Right to Secession," in Catherine Brölmann, R. Lefeber, and Mzeick (eds.), *Peoples and Minorities in International Law* (New York: Kluwer Academic Publishers).

(1995) *Fairness in International Law and Institutions* (Oxford: Clarendon Press)

(1996) "Clan and Super Clan: Loyalty, Identity and Community in Law and Practice," *American Journal of International Law* 90 (July), 359

Frank, André Gunter (1973) "The Development of Underdevelopment," in Charles Wilbur (ed.), *The Political Economy of Development and Underdevelopment* (New York: Random House)

(1967) *Capitalism and Underdevelopment in Latin America: Historical Studies of Chile and Brazil* (New York: Monthly Review Press)

Fraser, Nancy (1994) "Rethinking the Public Sphere: a Contribution to the Critique of Actually Existing Democracy," in Henry Giroux and Peter McLaren (eds.), *Between Borders: Pedagogy and the Politics of Cultural Studies* (New York and London: Routledge)

Friedman, Wolfgang (1964) *Changing Structure of International Law* (New York: Columbia University Press)

Fukuyama, Francis (1992) *The End of History and the Last Man* (New York: Free Press)

(2000) "Social Capital and Civil Society," IMF Working Paper (Washington, D.C.: International Monetary Fund, April)

Furedi, Frank (1994) *Colonial Wars and the Politics of Third World Nationalism* (London and New York: I. B. Tauris)

Furnivall, J. S. (1956) *Colonial Policy and Practice: a Comparative Study of Burma and Netherlands India* (New York: New York University Press)

Galtung, J. (1980) "The Basic Needs Approach," in Katrin Lederer in cooperation with Johan Galtung and David Antal (eds.), *Human Needs: a Contribution to the Current Debate* (Cambridge, Mass.: Oelgeschlager, Gunn and Hain)

Gandhi, Mohandas K. (1997) *Hind Swaraj and Other Writings*, ed., Anthony Parel (Cambridge: Cambridge University Press)

Garcia, Maria Pilar (1992) "The Venezuelan Ecology Movement: Symbolic Effectiveness, Social Practices and Political Strategies," in Arturo Escobar and Sonia Alvarez (eds.), *The Making of Social Movements in Latin America* (Boulder, Colo.: Westview Press)

Gathii, James Thuo (1998) "Review Essay: Eurocentricity and International Law," *European Journal of International Law* 9, 184

(1999a) "Empowering the Weak, Protecting the Powerful: a Critique of Good Governance Proposals" (unpublished SJD Thesis, Harvard Law School)

(1999b) "Good Governance as a Counter Insurgency Agenda to Oppositional and Transformative Social Projects in International Law," *Buffalo Human Rights Law Review* 5, 107

Gellner, Ernest (1994) *Conditions of Liberty: Civil Society and its Rivals* (New York: Allen Lane/Penguin Press)

Gendzier, Irene (1985) *Managing Political Change: Social Scientists and the Third World* (Boulder, Colo.: Westview Press)

Gerster, Richard (1982) "The International Monetary Fund and Basic Needs Conditionality," *Journal of World Trade Law* 16, 497

Ghai, Yash (1994) "Human Rights and Governance: the Asia Debate," *Australian Yearbook of International Law* 15, 1

(1999) "Rights, Social Justice and Globalization in East Asia," in Joanne Bauer and Daniel Bell (eds.), *The East Asian Challenge for Human Rights* (New York: Cambridge University Press) 252

Ghils, Paul (1992) "International Civil Society: International Non-Governmental Organizations in the International System," *International Social Science Journal* 44, 417

Gold, Joseph (1971) " 'To Contribute Thereby to . . . Development . . .' Aspects of the Relations of the International Monetary Fund with its Developing Members," *Columbia Journal of Transnational Law* 10, 267

(1979) *Conditionality*, Pamphlet No. 31 (Washington, D.C.: International Monetary Fund)

Gong, Gerrit (1984) *The Standard of "Civilization" in International Society* (Oxford: Clarendon Press)

Goodin, Robert (1979) "The Development–Rights Tradeoff: Some Unwarranted Assumptions," *Universal Human Rights* 1, 33

Gordenker, L. (1972) "The Secretary General," in James Barros (ed.), *The United Nations: Past, Present, and Future* (New York: Free Press)

Gordon, Colin, Graham Burchell, and Peter Miller (eds.) (1991) *The Foucault Effect: Studies in Governmentality: with Two Lectures by and an Interview with Michel Foucault* (Chicago, Ill.: University of Chicago Press)

Gordon, Robert (1984) "Critical Legal Histories," *Stanford Law Review* 36, 57

Gordon, Ruth (1997) "Saving Failed States: Sometimes a Neocolonialist Notion," *American University Journal of International Law and Policy* 12, 903

Gramsci, Antonio (1971) *Selections from the Prison Notebooks of Antonio Gramsci*, eds. and trans. Quintin Hoare and Geoffrey Nowell Smith (New York: International Publishers)

Greenberg, David (1980) "Law and Development in the Light of Dependency Theory," *Research in Law and Sociology* 3, 129, 152

Grueso, Libia, Carlos Rosero, and Arturo Escobar (1998) "The Process of Black Community Organizing in the Southern Pacific Coast Region of Colombia," in Sonia E. Alvarez, Evelina Dagnino, and Arturo Escobar (eds.), *Cultures of Politics/Politics of Cultures: Re-Visioning Latin American Social Movements* (Boulder, Colo.: Westview Press)

Guha, Ramachandra (1989) *The Unquiet Woods: Ecological Change and Peasant Resistance in the Himalayas* (Berkeley, Calif.: University of California Press)

Guha, Ranajit (1988) "On Some Aspects of the Historiography of Colonial India," in Ranajit Guha and Gayatri C. Spivak (eds.), *Selected Subaltern Studies* (New York: Oxford University Press)

Guha, Ranajit and Gayatri Chakravorti Spivak (eds.) (1988) *Selected Subaltern Studies* (New York: Oxford University Press)

Guha-Roy, S. N. (1961) "Is the Law of Responsibility of States for Injuries to Aliens a Part of Universal International Law?," *American Journal of International Law* 55, 863

Guitián, Manuel (1981) *Fund Conditionality: Evolution of Principles and Practices*, Pamphlet No. 38 (Washington, D.C.: International Monetary Fund)

(1992) *The Unique Nature of the Responsibilities of the International Monetary Fund*, Pamphlet No. 46 (Washington, D.C.: International Monetary Fund)

Haas, Ernst (1964) *Beyond the Nation State: Functionalism and International Organization* (Stanford, Calif.: Stanford University Press)

(1953) "The Attempt to Terminate Colonialism: Acceptance of the UN Trusteeship System," *International Organizations* (February)

Habermas, Jurgen (1971) *Legitimation Crisis*, trans., Thomas McCarthy (Boston, Mass.: Beacon Press, 1975)

(1981) "New Social Movements," *Telos* 49, 33

(1996) *Between Facts and Norms: Contributions to a Discourse Theory of Law and Democracy*, trans., William Rehg (Cambridge, Mass.: MIT Press)

Haggard, Stephen (1997) "Democratic Institutions, Economic Policy and Development," in Christopher Clague, *Institutions and Economic Development: Growth and Governance in Less Developed and Post-Socialist Countries* (Baltimore, Md.: Johns Hopkins University Press)

Hall, H. Duncan (1948) *Mandates, Dependencies and Trusteeship* (Washington D.C.: Carnegie Endowment for International Peace)

Hall, John (ed.) (1995) *Civil Society: Theory, History and Comparison* (Cambridge: Polity Press)

Halley, Janey (1998) "Gay Rights and Identity Imitation: Issues in the Ethics of Representation," in David Kairys (ed.), *The Politics of Law* (3rd edition) (New York: Pantheon Books)

Handler, Joel (1978) *Social Movements and the Legal System: a Theory of Law Reform and Social Change* (New York: Academic Press)

Handler, Joel, and Yeheskel Hasenfeld (1997) *We the Poor People: Work, Poverty, and Welfare* (New Haven, Conn.: Yale University Press)

Hannerz, Ulf (1991) "Scenarios for Peripheral Cultures," in Anthony D. King (ed.), *Culture, Globalization and the World-system: Contemporary Conditions for the Representation of Identity* (Binghamton, N.Y.: Dept. of Art and Art History, State University of New York at Binghamton)

Helman, Gerald, and Steven Ratner (1992) "Saving Failed States," *Foreign Policy* 89, 3

Henkin, Louis (1979) *How Nations Behave: Law and Foreign Policy* (New York: Columbia University Press, 2nd edition)

(1990) *The Age of Rights* (New York: Columbia University Press)

(1997) "Conceptualizing Violence: Present and Future Development in International Law," *Albany Law Review* 60, 571

Hershey, Amos (1907) "The Calvo and Drago Doctrines," *American Journal of International Law* 1 (January–April), 26

Hewlett, S. A. (1979) "Human Rights and Economic Realities: Tradeoffs in Historical Perspective," *Political Science Quarterly* 94, 463

Higgins, Rosalyn (1969–81) *United Nations Peacekeeping* (4 vols.) (Oxford: Oxford University Press)

(1994) *Problems and Process: International Law and How We Use It* (Oxford: Clarendon Press)

Hildyard, Nicholas (1997) *The World Bank and the State: a Recipe for Change?* (London: Bretton Woods Project)

Hirschman, Albert O. (1970) *Exit, Voice and Loyalty: Responses to Decline in Firms, Organizations and States* (Cambridge, Mass.: Harvard University Press)

(1977) *The Passions and the Interests: Political Arguments for Capitalism before its Triumph* (Princeton, N.J.: Princeton University Press)

(1981) "The Rise and Fall of Development Economics," in *Essays in Trespassing: Economics to Politics and Beyond* (Cambridge: Cambridge University Press)

Hobsbawm, E. J. (1959) *Primitive Rebels, Studies in Archaic Forms of Social Movement in the Nineteenth and Twentieth Centuries* (New York: W. W. Norton)

Hochschild, Adam (1998) *King Leopold's Ghosts: a Story of Greed, Terror, and Heroism in Colonial Africa* (Boston, Mass.: Houghton Mifflin)

Hooke, A. W. (1982) *The International Monetary Fund: its Evolution, Organization and Activities*, Pamphlet No. 37 (Washington, D.C.: International Monetary Fund)

Hopkins, Raul, Andrew Powell, Amlan Roy, and Christopher L. Gilbert (1997) "The World Bank and Conditionality," *Journal of International Development* 9, 507

Horn, Norbert (1982) "Normative Problems of a New International Economic Order," *Journal of World Trade Law* 16, 338

Horowitz, Morton (1992) *The Transformation of American Law, 1870–1960* (Cambridge, Mass.: Harvard University Press, 1977)

Hossain, Kamal, and Subrata Roy Chowdhury (eds.) (1984) *Permanent Sovereignty Over Natural Resources in International Law: Principle and Practice* (New York: St. Martin's Press)

Howard, Rhoda (1995) *Human Rights and the Search for Community* (Boulder, Colo.: Westview Press)

Hsiung, J. C. (1986) *Human Rights in East Asia: a Cultural Perspective* (New York: Paragon House Publishers)

Hunt, Alan (1990) "Rights and Social Movements: Counter-hegemonic Strategies," *Journal of Law and Society* 17 (3), 309–28

Huntington, Samuel (1991) *The Third Wave: Democratization in the Late Twentieth Century* (Norman, Okla.: University of Oklahoma Press)

Huntington, Samuel, and Joan Nelson (1976) *No Easy Choice: Political Participation in Developing Countries* (Cambridge, Mass.: Harvard University Press)

International Commission on Intervention and State Sovereignty (2001) Report titled "Responsibility to Protect," International Development Research Center, Canada, December

International Covenant on Civil and Political Rights, New York, December 16, 1966, in force March 23, 1976, 999 UNTS 71

International Monetary Fund (1945) Articles of Agreement for the International Monetary Fund, December 28, 1945, *UNTS* 2, 39, 40

(1946) Decision of the Executive Board, No. 71–72, compiled in *Selected Decisions and Selected Documents of the International Monetary Fund* (Washington, D.C.: International Monetary Fund, May 31)

(1997a) *1997 Annual Report* (Washington, D.C.: International Monetary Fund)
(1997b) *Guidelines to Staff* (Washington, D.C.: International Monetary Fund August)
(1997c) *Good Governance: The International Monetary Fund's Role* (Washington, D.C.: International Monetary Fund)
(1999a) "Communiqué of the Interim Committee of the Board of Governors of the International Monetary Fund, September 26, 1999" Available at www.imf.org
(1999b) "Debt Initiative for the Heavily Indebted Poor Countries (HIPCs)", September 5, 1999. Available at http://www.imf.org/external/np/hipc/hipc.htm#hipc1
International Status of South West Africa Case, ICJ Reports (1950)
Isham, Jonathan, David Kaufmann, and Lant Pritchett (1997) "Civil Liberties, Democracy and the Performance of Government Projects" *World Bank Economic Review* 11 (May), 219
Israel, Fred L. (ed.) (1967) *Major Peace Treaties of Modern History 1648–1967* (Philadelphia, Pa.: Chelsea House)
Jackson, John H. (1997) "The Great 1994 Sovereignty Debate: United States Acceptance and Implementation of the Uruguay Round Results," *Columbia Journal of Transnational Law* 36, 157
Jackson, John H., William J. Davey, and Alan O. Sykes, Jr. (1995) *Legal Problems of International Economic Relations: Cases, Materials and Texts on the National and International Regulation of Transnational Economic Relations* (3rd edition) (St. Paul, Minn.: West Pub. Co.)
Jacobson, Harold Karan (1962) "The UN and Colonialism," *International Organization* (Winter), 37–56
James, Harold (1998) "From Grandmotherliness to Governance: the Evolution of IMF Conditionality," *Finance and Development* 35 (December)
Jeldres, Julio (1993) "The UN and the Cambodian Transition," *Journal of Democracy* 4 (October), 104
Jenks, Wilfred (1958) *The Common Law of Mankind* (New York: Praeger)
Jessup, Philip C. (1948) *A Modern Law of Nations: an Introduction* (New York: Macmillan)
(1956) *Transnational Law*. Storrs Lectures on Jurisprudence (New Haven, Conn.: Yale University Press)
Jhabvala, Farroukh (1987) "On Human Rights and the Socio-Economic Context," in Frederick E. Snyder and Surakiart Sathirathai (eds.), *Third World Attitudes Toward International Law* (Dordrecht: Martinus Nijhoff)
Jones, Creech, J. A. (ed.) (1959) "The Colonial Issues in World Politics," in *New Fabian Colonial Essays* (London: Hogarth Press)
Kahin, George (1956) *The Asian-African Conference, Bandung, Indonesia* (Ithaca, N.Y.: Cornell University Press)

Kapur, Devesh, John Lewis, and Richard Webb (eds.) (1997) *The World Bank: its First Half Century* (vol. 1) (Washington, D.C.: Brookings Institution)

Kausikan, Bilahari (1993) "Asia's Different Standard," *Foreign Policy* 92, 24

Keane, John (1988a) *Democracy and Civil Society: on the Predicaments of European Socialism, the Prospects for Democracy, and the Problem of Controlling Social and Political Power* (London and New York: Verso)

Keane, John (ed.) (1988b) *Civil Society and the State: New European Perspectives* (London and New York: Verso)

Keck, Margaret, and Kathryn Sikkink (1998) *Activists beyond Borders: Advocacy Networks in International Politics* (Ithaca, N.Y.: Cornell University Press)

Kennedy, David (1980) "Theses about International Law Discourse," *German Yearbook of International Law* 23, 353

(1987) "The Move to Institutions," *Cordozo Law Review* 8, 841

(1993) "Autumn Weekends: an Essay on Law and Everyday Life," in Austin Sarat and Thomas Kearns (eds.), *Law and Everyday Life* (Ann Arbor, Mich.: University of Michigan Press)

(1994) "The International Style in Postwar Law and Policy," *Utah Law Review* 1, 7

(1995) "A New World Order: Yesterday, Today and Tomorrow," *Transnational Law and Contemporary Problems* 4, 330

(1996) "International Law in the Nineteenth Century: History of an Illusion," *Nordic Journal of International Law* 65, 385

(1999) "Background Noise? The Politics Beneath Global Governance," *Harvard International Review* 21, 56

(2000) "When Renewal Repeats: Thinking against the Box," *New York University Journal of International Law and Politics* 32 (Winter), 335

Keynes, J. M. (1920) *The Economic Consequences of the Peace* (London: Macmillan)

Khan, L. Ali (1996) *The Extinction of Nation-States: a World without Borders* (The Hague: Kluwer Law International)

Killick, Tony (1984) *The IMF and Stabilization: Developing Country Experiences* (New York: St. Martin's Press)

Kingsbury, Benedict (1998) "Sovereignty and Inequality," *European Journal of International Law* 9, 599

Kirgis, Frederic L., Jr. (1993) *International Organizations in their Legal Setting* (2nd edition) (St. Paul, Minn.: West Pub. Co.)

Koh, Harold H. (1997) "Why do Nations Obey International Law?" *Yale Law Journal* 106, 2599

Korten, David (1995) *When Corporations Rule the World* (Bloomfield, Conn.: Kumarian Press; San Francisco, Calif.: Berrett-Koehler Publishers)

Koskenniemi, Martti (1989) *From Apology to Utopia: the Structure of International Legal Argument* (Helsinki: Lakimiesliiton Kustannus)

(1990a) "The Pull of the Mainstream," *Michigan Law Review* 88, 1946

(1990b) "The Politics of International Law," *European Journal of International Law* 1, 4

(1999) "International Law and Imperialism," the Josephine Onoh Memorial Lecture, the University of Hull Law School, February, 16

Kothari, Rajni (1987) *Human Rights – A Movement in Search of a Theory*, 5 Lokayan Bulletin 17 Reprinted in Philip Alston (ed.) *Human Rights Law* (New York: New York University Press, 1996)

(1989) *State against Democracy: in Search of Humane Governance* (New York: New Horizons Press)

(1993) "*Masses, Classes and the State*," in Poona Wignaraja (ed.), *New Social Movements in the South: Empowering the People* (London and Atlantic Highlands, N.J.: Zed Books; New Delhi: Sage)

Kothari, Smitu (1995) "Damming the Narmada and the Politics of Development," in William Fisher (ed.), *Toward Sustainable Development? Struggling over India's Narmada River* (Armonk, NY: M. E. Sharpe)

(1996) "Social Movements, Ecology and Democracy," in Fen O. Hampson and Judith Reppy (eds.), *Earthly Goods: Environmental Change and Social Justice* (Ithaca, N.Y.: Cornell University Press)

Kothari, Smitu and Harsh Sethi (eds.) (1991) *Rethinking Human Rights: Challenges for Theory and Action* (Delhi: Lokayan, 1991)

Krantz, Frederic (ed.) (1985) *History from Below: Studies in Popular Protest and Popular Ideology in Honour of George Rudé* (Oxford: Blackwell)

Kunz, J. (1955) "Pluralism of Legal and Value Systems and International Law," *American Journal of International Law*, 370

(1957) "The Changing Law of Nations," *American Journal of International Law*, 77

Laclau, Ernesto, and Chantal Mouffe (1985) *Hegemony and Socialist Strategy: towards a Radical Democratic Politics*, trans., Winston Moore and Paul Cammack (London and New York: Verso)

Landell-Mills, Joslin (1988) "IMF, Helping the Poor: the International Monetary Fund's New Facilities for Structural Adjustment," International Monetary Fund, Washington, D.C.)

Lauterpacht, Hersch (1950) *International Law and Human Rights* (Hamden, Conn.: Archon Books)

Legal Consequences for States of the Continued Presence of South Africa in Namibia (South West Africa) not with standing Security Council Resolution 276, ICJ Reports (1970)

Lehman, David (1990) *Democracy and Development in Latin America: Economics, Politics and Religion in the PostWar Period* (Cambridge: Polity)

Lewis, Arthur (1955) *The Theory of Economic Growth* (Homewood, Ill.: T. D. Irwin)

Lillich, Richard and Hurst Hannum (1995) *International Human Rights: Problems of Law, Policy and Practice* (3rd edition) (Boston: Little Brown)

Lindley, Mark Frank (1926) *The Acquisition and Government of Backward Territory in International Law; Being a Treatise on the Law and Practice Relating to Colonial Expansion* (London and New York: Longmans, Green)

Linkenbach, Antje (1994) "Ecological Movements and the Critique of Development: Agents and Interpreters," *Thesis Eleven* 39, 63–85

Lipschutz, Ronnie D. (1992) "Reconstructing World Politics: the Emergence of Global Civil Society," *Millennium: Journal of International Studies* 21, 389

Logan, Rayford W. (1945) *The Senate and the Versailles Mandate System* (Westport, Conn.: Greenwood Press)

Lord Cromer, E. B. (1913) "The Government of Subject Races," in *Political and Literary Essays, 1908–1913* (London: Macmillan and Co.)

Lugard, Sir Frederic (1922) *Dual Mandate in British Tropical Africa* (Edinburgh and London: Blackwood)

Lummis, Douglas (1992) "Equality," in Wolfgang Sachs (ed.), *Development Dictionary: a Guide to Knowledge as Power* (London: Zed Books)

Lutzenberger, José (1985) "The World Bank's Polonoroeste Project – a Social and Environmental Catastrophe," *The Ecologist* 15, 69

MacIntyre, Alasdair (1981) *After Virtue: a Study in Moral Theory* (London: Duckworth)

MacKinnon, Catherine (1993) "On Torture: a Feminist Perspective on Human Rights," in Kathleen Mahoney and P. Mahoney (eds.), *Human Rights in the Twenty-first Century: a Global Challenge* (Dodrecht and Boston, Mass.: Kluwer Academic Publishers)

Mamdani, Mahmood (1996) *Citizen and Subject: contemporary Africa and the Legacy of Late Colonialism* (Princeton, N.J.: Princeton University Press)

Mamdani, Mahmood, Thandika Mkandawire, and E. Wamba-dia Wamba (1993) "Social Movements and Democracy in Africa," in Poona Wignaraja (ed.), *New Social Movements in the South* (London and Atlantic Highlands, N.J.: Zed Books; New Delhi: Sage)

Mander, Jerry, and Edward Goldsmith (eds.) (1996) *The Case against the Global Economy and for a Turn toward the Local* (San Francisco, Calif.: Sierra Club Books)

Margalith, Aaron M. (1930) *The International Mandates* (Baltimore, Md.: Johns Hopkins University Press; London: H. Milford, Oxford University Press)

Marks, Stephen (1981) "Emerging Human Rights: a New Generation for the 1980s?" *Rutgers Law Review* 33, 435

Marx, Karl (1959) "The British Rule in India," in Lewis Feuer (ed.), *Marx and Engels: Basic Writings on Politics and Philosophy* (New York: Anchor Books, Doubleday and Co. Inc.) 474

(1978) "On the Jewish Question," in Robert C. Tucker (ed.), *The Marx-Engels Reader* (2nd edition) (New York: Norton)

Mavrommatis Palestine Concessions Case, PCIJ Series A, No.2

Maybury-Lewis, David (1981) *In the Path of Polonoroeste: Endangered Peoples of Western Brazil* (Cambridge, Mass.: Cultural Survival)

Mayer, Ann Elizabeth (1994) "Universal versus Islamic Human Rights: a Clash of Cultures or a Clash with a Construct?" *Michigan Journal of International Law* 15, 327

Mazrui, Ali (1990) *Cultural Forces in World Politics* (London: J. Currey; Nairobi, Kenya: Heinemann; Portsmouth, N.H.: Heinemann)

(1994) "The Message of Rwanda: Recolonize Africa?" *New Perspectives Quarterly* (Fall)

McCormick, Neil (1993) "Beyond the Sovereign State" (1993) *Modern Law Review* 56, 1

McDougal, Myres S., and Harold D. Lasswell (1959) "The Identification and Appraisal of Diverse Systems of Public Order," *American Journal of International Law* 53, 1

McNamara, Robert (1981) "Speech to the United Nations Conference on the Human Environment," in Robert S. McNamara (ed.), *The McNamara Years at the World Bank* (Baltimore, Md.: Johns Hopkins University Press)

Meadows, Donella, and Dennis Meadows (1972) *The Limits to Growth; a Report for the Club of Rome's Project on the Predicament of Mankind* (New York: Universe Books)

Medoff, Peter, and Holly Sklar (1994) *Streets of Hope: the Fall and Rise of an Urban Neighborhood* (Boston, Mass.: South End Press)

Melucci, Alberto (1989) *Nomads of the Present: Social Movements and Individual Needs in Contemporary Society* (London: Radius)

Mertus, Julie (1999) "From Legal Transplants to Transformative Justice: Human Rights and the Promise of Transnational Civil Society," *American University International Law Review* 14, 1335

Mickelson, Karin (1998) "Rhetoric and Rage: Third World Voices in International Legal Discourse," *Wisconsin International Law Journal* 16, 353

Military and Paramilitary Activities in and against Nicaragua (Nicaragua v. U.S.), Merits, ICJ Reports (1986)

Mill, James (1820) *The History of British India* (London: Printed for Baldwin, Cradock and Joy)

Minow, Martha (1990) *Making all the Difference: Inclusion, Exclusion and American Law* (Ithaca, N.Y.: Cornell University Press)

Mitrany, David (1933) *The Progress of International Government* (New Haven, Conn.: Yale University Press)

(1946) *A Working Peace System: an Argument for the Functional Development of International Organization*, 4th edn. (London: National Peace Council)

Morgenthau, Hans (1940) "Positivism, Functionalism and International Law," *American Journal of International Law* 34, 260

Morse, Bradford, and Thomas R. Berger (1992) *Sardar Sarovar: Report of the Independent Review* (Washington, D.C.: World Bank)

Morsink, Johannes (1999) *The Universal Declaration of Human Rights: Origins, Drafting, and Intent* (Philadelphia, Penn.: University of Pennsylvania Press)

Mortimer, Robert (1984) *The Third World Coalition in International Politics* (New York: Praeger)

Mouffe, Chantal (1993) *The Return of the Political* (London and New York: Verso)

Muchlinski, Peter (1987) "Basic Needs Theory and Development Law," in Francis Snyder and Peter Slinn (eds.), *International Law of Development* (Abingdon, Oxon: Professional Books)

Muldoon, James (1979) *Popes, Lawyers and Infidels: the Church and the Non-Christian World, 1250–1550* (Philadelphia, Penn.: University of Pennsylvania Press)

Muntarbhorn, Vitit (1999) "National Human Rights Action Plans in the Asia-Pacific Region: Identifying Commonalities as Guidelines for the World?" (Paper submitted at the Workshop on the Development of National Plans of Action for the Promotion and Protection of Human Rights in the Asia-Pacific Region, Bangkok, Thailand, July 5–7)

Murphy, Craig, and Enrico Augelli (1993) "International Institutions, Decolonization and Development," *International Political Science Review* 14 (1), 71

Mutua, Makau wa (1995a) "The Banjul Charter and the African Cultural Fingerprint: an Evaluation of the Language of Duties," *Virginia Journal of International Law* 35, 339

(1995b) "Why Redraw the Map of Africa: a Moral and Legal Inquiry," *Michigan Journal of International Law* 16, 1113

(1996a) "The Ideology of Human Rights," *Virginia Journal of International Law* 36, 589

(1996b) "The Politics of Human Rights: Beyond the Abolitionist Paradigm in Africa," *Michigan Journal of International Law* 17, 591

Myrdal, Gunnar (1957) *Economic Theory and Underdeveloped Regions* (London: G. Duckworth)

(1968) *Asian Drama: an Inquiry into the Wealth of Nations* (New York: Pantheon Books)

(1970) *The Challenge of World Poverty; a World Anti-Poverty Program in Outline*, Christian A. Herter lecture series (New York: Pantheon Books)

Nandy, Ashis (1983) *The Intimate Enemy: the Loss and Recovery of Self Under Colonialism* (Delhi and New York: Oxford University Press)

(1987) "Reconstructing Childhood," in *Traditions, Tyranny, and Utopias: Essays in the Politics of Awareness* (Delhi and New York: Oxford University Press)

(1992) "State," in Wolfgang Sachs (ed.), *Development Dictionary: a Guide to Knowledge as Power* (London: Zed Books)

Narmada Bachao Andolan v. Union of India, Supreme Court (Judgment dated October 18, 2000)

Nedelsky, Jennifer (1993) "Reconceiving rights as Relationship," *Review of Constitutional Studies* 1, 1

Nelson, Paul J. (1995) *The World Bank and Non-Governmental Organizations: the Limits of Apolitical Development* (New York: St. Martin's Press)

North, Douglas (1990) *Institutions, Institutional Change and Economic Performance* (Cambridge: Cambridge University Press)

Nowak, Manfred (1993) *UN Covenant on Civil and Political Rights: CCPR Commentary* (Strasbourg Va., Arlington, Va.: N. P. Engel)

O'Brien, Robert, Anne Marie Goetz, Jan Aart Scholte and Marc Williams (2000) *Contesting Global Governance: Multilateral Economic Institutions and Global Social Movements* (Cambridge: Cambridge University Press)

Oberschall, Anthony (1993) *Social Movements: Ideologies, Interests, and Identities* (Englewood Cliffs., N.J.: Prentice-Hall)

OECD (1995) *Participatory Development and Good Governance*

Offe, Claus (1984) *Contradictions of the Welfare State* (London: Hutchinson)

(1985) "New Social Movements: Challenging the Boundaries of Institutional Politics," *Social Research* 52

Oloka-Onyango, Joseph (1999) "Globalization and Human Rights" (draft dated 1999, on file)

Omvedt, Gail (1993) *Reinventing Revolution: New Social Movements and the Socialist Tradition in India* (Armonk, NY: M. E. Sharpe)

Oppenheim, Lassa (1960) *International Law: a Treatise* (ed.) H. Lauterpacht (8th edition) (London: Longmans)

Ostrom, Elinor (1997) "Investing in Capital, Institutions and Incentives," in Christopher Clague (ed.), *Institutions and Economic Development: Growth and Governance in Less Developed and Post-Socialist Countries* (Baltimore, Md.: Johns Hopkins University Press)

Otto, Diane (1996a) "Nongovernmental Organizations in the United Nations System: the Emerging Role of International Civil Society," *Human Rights Quarterly* 18, 107

(1996b) "Subalternity and International Law: the Problems of Global Community and the Incommensurability of Difference," *Social and Legal Studies* 5, 337

(1997a) "Rethinking Universals: Opening Transformative Possibilities in International Human Rights Law," *Australian Yearbook of International Law* 18, 1

(1997b) "Rethinking the 'Universality' of Human Rights Law," *Columbia Human Rights Law Review* 29, 1

Panchayats (Extension to the Scheduled Areas) Act (1996), Act No. 40, entered into force December 24, 1996, available at http://ncscst.nic.in/panchayats.htm

Panikkar, Raimundo (1982) "Is the Notion of Human Rights a Western Concept?" *Diogenes* 120, 75–102

Paolini, Albert (1999) *Navigating Modernity* (Boulder, Colo.: L. Rienner Publishers)

Parajuli, Pramod (1990) "Power and Knowledge in Development Discourse: New Social Movements and the State in India," *International Social Science Journal* 43, 173

Pastor, Manuel, Jr. (1987) "The Effects of IMF Programs in the Third World: Debate and Evidence from Latin America," *World Development* 15, 249

Patel, Anil (1995) "What do the Narmada Valley Tribals Want?" in William F. Fisher (ed.), *Toward Sustainable Development? Struggling Over India's Narmada River* (Armonk, N.Y.: M. E. Sharpe)

Paul, C. N. (1989) "International Development Agencies, Human Rights and Humane Development Projects," *Alternatives* 14, 90

Payer, Cheryl (1974) *The Debt Trap: The IMF and the Third World* (New York: Monthly Review Press)

(1982) *The World Bank: a Critical Analysis* (New York: Monthly Review Press)

Peerenboom, R. P. (1993) "What's Wrong with Chinese Rights? Toward a Theory of Rights with Chinese Characteristics," *Harvard Human Rights Journal* 6, 29

Picciotto, Robert (1997) "Putting Institutional Economics to Work: from Participation to Governance," in Christopher Clague (ed.), *Institutions and Economic Development: Growth and Governance in Less Developed and Post-Socialist Countries* (Baltimore, Md.: Johns Hopkins University Press

Pierson, Christopher (1992) "Democracy, Markets and Capital: Are there Necessary Economic Limits to Democracy?" *Political Studies*, XL, Special Issue

Piore, Michael (1995) *Beyond Individualism* (Cambridge, Mass.: Harvard University Press)

Polak, Jacques (1991) "The Changing Nature of IMF Conditionality," International Finance Section, Dept. of Economics, Princeton University

Polanyi, Karl (1944) *The Great Transformation* (New York: Rinehart and Co. Inc.)

Porras, Ileana (1994) "The Rio Declaration: a New Basis for International Cooperation," in Philippe Sands (ed.), *Greening International Law* (New York: New Press)

Pritchett, Lant, and Daniel Kaufmann (1998) "Civil Liberties, Democracy and the Performance of Government Projects," *Finance and Development* 26 (March)

Procacci, Giovanna (1991) "Social Economy and the Government of Poverty," in Colin Gordon, Graham Burchell and Peter Miller (eds.), *The Foucault Effect: Studies in Governmentality: with Two Lectures by and an Interview with Michel Foucault* (Chicago, Ill.: University of Chicago Press)

Proudhon, Pierre-Joseph (1876) *What is Property? An Inquiry into the Principle of Right and of Government* (Princeton, Mass.: B. R. Tucker)

Pufendorf, Samuel Frieherr von (1703) *De jure naturae et gentium* (Of the Law of Nature and Nations) (London: Printed by L. Lichfield)

Putnam, Robert (1993) *Making Democracy Work: Civic Traditions in Modern Italy* (Princeton, N.J.: Princeton University Press)

Quashigah, Kofi, and Obiora Chenedu Okafar (eds.) (1999) *Legitimate Governance in Africa: International and Domestic Legal Perspectives* (The Hague: Kluwer Law International)

Quaye, Christopher (1991) *Liberation Struggles in International Law* (Philadelphia, Penn.: Temple University Press)

Rahnema, Majid (1991) "Global Poverty: a Pauperizing Myth," *Interculture* 24, 4

(1992) "Poverty," in Wolfgang Sachs (ed.), *Development Dictionary: a Guide to Knowledge as Power* (London: Zed Books)

Rahnema, Majid with Victoria Bawtree (eds.) (1997) *The Post-Development Reader* (London: Zed Books)

Rajagopal, Balakrishnan (1991) "A Quantitative Analysis of the Roll-Call Data at the UN Commission on Human Rights, 1947–1991," American University, Washington College of Law paper, Fall

(1992) "The Case for the Independent Statehood of Somaliland," *American University Journal of International Law* 8 (Fall), 653

(1993) "Crossing the Rubicon: Synthesizing the Soft International Law of IMF and Human Rights," *Boston University International Law Journal* 11, 81

(1998) "Review Essay: the Allure of Normativity," *Harvard Human Rights Journal* 11, 363

(1998–99) "Locating the Third World in Cultural Geography," *Third World Legal Studies*, 1

(1999a) "International Law and the Development Encounter: Violence and Resistance from the Margins," *American Society of International Law 93rd Proceedings*, 16

(1999b) "Taking Seattle Resistance Seriously," Opinion, *The Hindu* (December 11)

(2000a) "From Resistance to Renewal: the Third World, Social Movements and the Expansion of International Institutions," *Harvard International Law Journal* 41 (2), 529 (Symposium Issue on International Law and the Developing World: a Millenial Analysis, Spring)

(2000b) "The Supreme Court and Human Rights," Opinion, *The Hindu* (December 6)

Rappard, William E. (1946) "Human Rights in Mandated Territories," *The Annals of the American Academy of Political and Social Science* 243, 118

Ratner, Steven (1993) "The Cambodian Settlement Agreements," *American Journal of International Law* 87, 1

Rawls, John (1999) *The Law of Peoples* (Cambridge, Mass.: Harvard University Press)

Renteln, Alison Dundes (1990) *International Human Rights; Universalism versus Relativism* (Newbury Park: Sage Publications)

Republic of Indonesia, Ministry of Foreign Affairs (1956) *Asia-Africa Speaks from Bandung*

Ribeiro, Gustavo Lins (1998) "Cybercultural Politics: Political Activism at a Distance in a Transnational World," in Sonia E. Alvarez, Evelina Dagnino, and Arturo Escobar (eds.), *Cultures of Politics/Politics of Cultures: Re-Visioning Latin American Social Movements* (Boulder, Colo.: Westview Press)

Rich, Bruce (1994) *Mortgaging the Earth: the World Bank, Environmental Impoverishment, and the Crisis of Development* (Boston, Mass.: Beacon Press, 1994)

Rich, B., T. Stoel, and B. Brambe (1985) "The Polonoroeste Project," *The Ecologist* 15, 78

Rich, Roland (1983) "The Right to Development as an Emerging Right," *Virginia Journal of International Law* 23, 320

Risse, Thomas, Stephen Ropp, and Kathryn Sikkink (eds.) (1999) *The Power of Human Rights: International Norms and Domestic Change* (Cambridge: Cambridge University Press)

Ritsher, Walter Holmes (1934) *Criteria of Capacity for Independence* (Jerusalem: Syrian Orphanage Press)

Robertson, Roland (1992) *Globalization: Social Theory and Global Culture* (London: Sage)

Rodrik, Dani (1997) *Has Globalization Gone too Far?* (Washington, D.C.: Institute of International Economics)

(1998) "Democracies Pay Higher Wages" (NBER Working Paper No. 6364)

Röling, Bernard Victor Aloysius (1960) *International Law in an Expanded World* (Amsterdam: Djambatan)

Romany, Celina (1993) "Women as Aliens: a Feminist Critique of the Public–Private Distinction in International Human Rights Law," *Harvard Human Rights Journal* 6, 87

Romulo, Carlos (1956) *The Meaning of Bandung* (Chapel Hill, N.C.: University of North Carolina Press)

Rosenberg, Gerald (1991) *The Hollow Hope: Can Courts Bring about Social Change?* (Chicago, Ill.: University of Chicago Press)

Rosenberg, Justine (1994) *The Empire of Civil Society: a Critique of the Realist Theory of International Relations* (London and New York: Verso)

Rothstein, Robert (1979) *Global Bargaining: UNCTAD and the Quest for a New International Economic Order* (Princeton, N.J.: Princeton University Press)

Roy, Arundhati (1999) "The Greater Common Good," *Frontline* 16 (May 22–June 4), 11

Rozental, Andres (1976) "The Charter of Economic Rights and Duties of States and the New International Economic Order," *Virginia Journal of International Law* 16, 309

Sachs, Wolfgang (1990) "The Archaeology of the Development Idea," *Interculture* 23, 1

(1992b) "Environment," in Wolfgang Sachs (ed.) *Development Dictionary: a Guide to Knowledge as Power* (London: Zed Books)

Sachs, Wolfgang (ed.) (1992a) *Development Dictionary: a Guide to Knowledge as Power* (London: Zed Books)

Sahlins, Marshall (1972) *Stone Age Economics* (Chicago, Ill.: Aldine-Atherton)

Said, Edward (1978) *Orientalism* (New York: Vintage Books)

(1993) *Culture and Imperialism* (New York: Knopf)

Santos, Boaventura de Sousa (1995) *Toward a New Common Sense: Law, Science and Politics in the Paradigmatic Transition* (New York: Routledge)

(1997) "Toward a Multicultural Conception of Human Rights," *Zeitschrift Fuer Rechtssociologie* 18, 1

Sarat, Austin, and Thomas Kearns (1995) *Identities, Politics, and Rights* (Ann Arbor, Mich.: University of Michigan Press)

Sartre, Jean Paul (1963) Preface to *The Wretched of the Earth*, Frantz Fanon (New York: Grove Press)

Sassen, Saskia (1998) *Globalization and its Discontents: Essays on the new Mobility of People and Money* (New York: New Press)

Sathirathai, Surakiart, and Frederick E. Snyder (eds.) (1987) *Third World Attitudes Toward International Law* (Dordrecht: Martinus Nijhoff)

Sauvant, Karl (1981) *Changing Priorities on the International Agenda: the New International Economic Order* (Oxford and New York: Pergamon Press)

Schachter, Oscar (1976) "The Evolving International Law of Development," *Columbia Journal of Transnational Law* 15, 1

(1983) "Human Dignity as a Normative Concept," *American Journal of International Law* 77 (October), 848

(1991) *International Law in Theory and Practice* (Dordrecht: Nijhoff)

(1997) "The Decline of the Nation-State and its Implications for International Law," *Columbia Journal of Transnational Law* 36, 7

Schermers, Henry G. (1980) *International Institutional Law* (Leiden: Sijthoff)

Schild, Veronica (1998) "New Subjects of Rights? Women's Movements and the Construction of Citizenship in the 'New Democracies,'" in Sonia Alvarez, Evelina Dagnino, and Arturo Escobar (eds.), *Cultures of Politics/Politics of Cultures: Re-Visioning Latin American Social Movements* (Boulder, Colo.: Westview Press)

Schreuer, Christoph (1993) "The Waning of the Sovereign State: towards a New Paradigm for International Law," *European Journal of International Law* 4, 447

Schumacher, E. F. (1973) *Small is Beautiful: Economics as if People Mattered* (New York: Harper and Row)

Schumpeter, Joseph (1942) *Capitalism, Socialism and Democracy* (New York and London: Harper and Brothers)

Scott, James (1985) *Weapons of the Weak: Everyday Forms of Peasant Resistance* (New Haven: Yale University Press)

(1990) *Domination and the Arts of Resistance: Hidden Transcripts* (New Haven: Yale University Press)

(1998) *Seeing like a State: how Certain Schemes to Improve the Human Condition Have Failed* (New Haven Conn.: Yale University Press)

Scott, James, and Benedict Tria Kerkvliet (eds.) (1986) *Everyday Forms of Peasant Resistance in South-East Asia* (London and Totowa, N.J.: Frank Cass)

Seligman, Adam (1992) *The Idea of Civil Society* (New York: Free Press; Toronto: Maxwell Macmillan Canada; New York: Maxwell Macmillan International)

Sen, Amartya (1983) "Development: Which Way Now?" *Economic Journal* (December)

(1997) "Human Rights and Asian values," *The New Republic*, July 14 and 21

(1999a) *Development as Freedom* (New York: Knopf)

(1999b) "Human Rights and Economic Achievements," in Joanne Bauer and Daniel Bell (eds.), *The East Asian Challenge for Human Rights* (New York: Cambridge University Press)

Sen, Amartya, and James D. Wolfensohn (1999) "Let's Respect Both Sides of the Development Coin," *International Herald Tribune* (May 5), 3

Sethi, Harsh (1993) "Survival and Democracy: Ecological Struggles in India," in Ponna, Wignaraja (ed.), *New Social Movements in the South: Empowering the People* (London and Atlantic Highlands, N.J.: Zed Books; New Delhi: Sage)

Shalakany, Amr (2000) "The Analytics of the 'Social' in Private Law Theory: a Comparative Study," (unpublished SJD Dissertation, Harvard Law School)

Shaw, Martin (1992) "Global Society and Global Responsibility: the Theoretical, Historical, and Political Limits of 'International Society' " *Millenium: Journal of International Studies* 21, 421

Sheth, D. L. (1987) "Alternative Development as Political Practice," *Alternatives* 12, 155

Sheth, D. L., and Ashis Nandy (eds.) (1996) *The Multiverse of Democracy: Essays in Honour of Ranji Kothari* (New Delhi and Thousand Oaks, Calif.: Sage)

Shihata, Ibrahim F. I. (2000) *The World Bank Inspection Panel: in Practice* (Oxford and New York: Oxford University Press)

(1995) "The World Bank and the Environment: Legal Instruments for Achieving Environmental Objectives," in *The World Bank in a Changing World* (Dodrecht and Boston, Mass.: Kluwer Academic Publishers)

Shivji, Issa (1989) *The Concept of Human Rights in Africa* (London: Codesria Book Series)

(1995) "Constructing A New Rights Regime: Promises, Problems And Prospects" 8 *Social and Legal Studies* 253 (June)

Shue, Henry (1996) *Basic Rights: Subsistence, Affluence, and U.S. Foreign Policy* (2nd edition) (Princeton, N.J.: Princeton University Press)

Sibley, David (1995) *Geographies of Exclusion: Society and Difference in the West* (London and New York: Routledge)

Sikkink, Kathryn (1993) "Human Rights, Principled Issue-Networks and Sovereignty in Latin America," *International Organizations* 47 (3) (Summer), 411

Simma, Bruno, and Philip Alston (1992) "The Sources of Human Rights Law: Custom, Jus Cogens and General Principles," *Australian Yearbook of International Law* 12, 82

Simon, William H. (1984) "Visions of Practice in Legal Thought," *Stanford Law Review* 36, 469

Singer, Joseph (1987–88) "The reliance interest in property," *Stanford Law Review* 40, 577

(1997) *Property Law: Rules, Policies and Practices* (2nd edition) (New York, N.Y.: Aspen Law and Business) 20

(2000) *Entitlement: the Paradoxes of Property* (New Haven: Yale University Press)

(2001) *The Edges of the Field: Lessons on the Obligations of Ownership* (Boston, Mass.: Beacon Press)

Singh, Someshwar (2000) "UN Human Rights Commissioner Responds to the WTO" (Third World Network: Available at http://www.twnside.org.sg/title/responds.htm, Aug 29, 2000)

Sklair, Leslie (1998) "Social movements and global capitalism," in Frederic Jameson and Masao Miyoshi (eds.), *The Cultures of Globalization* (Durham, N.C.: Duke University Press)

Slater, David (ed.) (1985) *New Social Movements and the State in Latin America* (Amsterdam: CEDLA; Cinnaminson, N.J.)

Slaughter Burley, Anne-Marie (1993) "International Law and International Relations Theory: a Dual Agenda," *American Journal of International Law* 87, 205

Slaughter, Anne-Marie (1995) "International Law in a World of Liberal States," *European Journal of International Law* 6, 503, 537

(1997) "The Real New World Order," *Foreign Affairs* 183 (September/October)

Smith, Jackie, Charles Chatfield, and Ron Pagnucco (eds.) (1997) *Transnational Social Movements and Global Politics: Solidarity beyond the State* (Syracuse, N.Y.: Syracuse University Press)

Sohn, Louis (1973) "The Stockholm Declaration on the Human Environment," *Harvard International Law Journal* 14, 423

(1982) "The New International Law: Protection of the Rights of Individuals rather than States," *American University Law Review* 32 (Fall), 1

Special Issue on Dams on the River Narmada (1991) *Lokayan Bulletin* 9, 3/4

Spiro, Peter J. (1995) "New Global Communities: Nongovernmental Organizations in International Decision-Making Institutions," *Washington Quarterly* 18, 45

Spivak, Gayatri C. (1988) "Can the Subaltern Speak?" in Cary Nelson and Lawrence Grossberg (eds.), *Marxism and the Interpretation of Culture* (Houndmills, Baringstoke, Hampshire: Macmillan Education)

Stammers, Neil (1999) "Social Movements and the Social Construction of Human Rights," *Human Rights Quarterly* 21, 980

Steiner, Henry (1991) *Diverse Partners: Nongovernmental Organizations in the Human Rights Movement: the Report of a Retreat of Human Rights Activists* (Cambridge, Mass.: Harvard Law School Human Rights Program; [Toronto], Ont., Canada: Human Rights Internet)

Steiner, Henry, and Philip Alston (1996) *International Human Rights in Context: Law, Politics, and Morals* (1st edition) (Oxford and New York: Oxford University Press)

Stiglitz, Joseph (1999) "Participation and Development: Perspectives from the Comprehensive Development Paradigm," Remarks at the *International Conference on Democracy, Market Economy and Development* February 27, Seoul, Korea, 3 (available on-line at http://www.worldbank.org/html/extdr/extme/js-022799/index.htm)

Streeten, Paul (1981) *Development Perspectives* (New York: St. Martin's Press)

Symposium Issue (1993) "Conference on Changing Notions of Sovereignty and the Role of Private Actors in International Law," *American University Journal of International Law and Policy* 9, 1

Symposium Issue (1994) "Social Movements and World Politics," *Millenium* (Special Issue, Winter)

Symposium Issue (1996) "The Decline of the Nation-State and its Effects on Constitutional and International Economic Law," *Cordozo Law Review* 18, 903

Symposium Issue (2001) "Reactions of the Report of the World Commission on Dams," *American University International Law Review* 16

Sunstein, Cass (1997) "Introduction: Questioning Constitutional Justice. The Legitimacy of Constitutional Courts: Notes on Theory and Practice," *East European Constitutional Review* 6 (Winter), 61

Tarrow, Sidney G. (1994) *Power in Movement: Social Movements, Collective Action and Politics* (Cambridge and New York: Cambridge University Press)

(1998) *Power in Movement: Social Movements and Contentious Politics* (Cambridge and New York: Cambridge University Press)

Taylor, Charles (1990) "Modes of civil society," *Public Culture* 3, 95

Temperley, Harold William Vazeille (ed.) (1969) *A History of the Peace Conference of Paris* (London and New York: Oxford University Press)

Tendler, Judith (1997) *Good Government in the Tropics* (Baltimore, Md.: Johns Hopkins University Press)

Teson, Fernando (1985) "International Human Rights and Cultural Relativism," *Virginia Journal of International Law* 25, 869

(1993) "Feminism and International Law: a Reply," *Virginia Journal of International Law* 33, 647

(1997) *Humanitarian Intervention: an Inquiry into Law and Morality* (New York: Transnational Publishers)

Third World Network (1997) *The Multilateral Agreement on Investment (MAI): Policy Implications for Developing Countries*, April (Available at http://www.twnside.org.sg/)

Tilly, Charles (ed.) (1975) *The Formation of National States in Western Europe* (Princeton, N.J.: Princeton University Press)

Touraine, Alain (1988) *Return of the Actor: Social Theory in Postindustrial Society* trans. Myrna Godzich (Minneapolis, Minn.: University of Minnesota Press)

Trubek, David (1973) "What is an Omelet? What is an Egg? Some thoughts on Economic Development and Human Rights in Latin America," *American Society of International Law Proceedings* 67 (5) (November), 198

Trubek, David, R. Bucharan, Y. Dezalay, and J. Davis (1994) "Studies of the Internationalization of Legal Fields and the Creation of Transnational Arenas," *Case Western Reserve Law Review* 44, 407

Tyrer v. United Kingdom, E.C.H.R., Series A, No.26 (1978)

Udall, Lori (1995) "The International Narmada Campaign: a Case Study of Sustained Advocacy," in William F. Fisher (ed.), *Toward Sustainable Development? Struggling Over India's Narmada River* (Armonk, N.Y.: M. E. Sharpe)

Unger, Roberto Mangabeira (1975) *Knowledge and Politics* (New York: Free Press)

(1996) *What should legal analysis become?* (London, New York: Verso)

Vagts, Detlev F. (1997) "International Agreements, the Senate and the Constitution," *Columbia Journal of Transnational Law* 36, 143

Vries, M. G. de (1986) *The IMF in a Changing World – 1945–1985* (Washington, D.C.: International Monetary Fund)

Wade, Robert. (1996) "Japan, the World Bank and the Art of Paradigm Maintenance: the East Asian Miracle in Political Perspective," *New Left Review* 217 May–June

(1997) "Greening the Bank: the Struggle over the Environment, 1970–1995," in Devesh Kapur, John Lewis, and Richard Webb (eds.), *The World Bank: its First Half Century* (vol. 1) (Washington, D.C.: Brookings Institution)

Walker, R. B. J. (1990) "The Concept of Culture in the Theory of International Relations," in Jongsuk Chay (ed.), *Culture and International Relations* (New York: Praeger)

(1993) *Inside/Outside: International Relations as Political Theory* (Cambridge and New York: Cambridge University Press)

Walzer, Michael (1991) "A Better Vision: the Idea of Civil Society," *Dissent* 38, 293

(1992) "The Civil Society Argument," in Chantal Mouffe (ed.) *Dimensions of Radical Democracy: Pluralism, Citizenship, Community* (London and New York: Verso)

Wapner, Peter J. (1994) "Environmental Activism and Global Civil Society," *Dissent* 41, 389

Ward, Barbara (1962) *The Rich Nations and the Poor Nations* (New York: Norton)

Weber, Max (1958) *The Protestant Ethic and the Spirit of Capitalism*, trans., Talcott Parsons (New York: Scribner)

Weeramantry, Christopher (1992) *Nauru: Environmental Damage under International Trusteeship* (Melbourne: Oxford University Press)

Weintraub, Sidney (1976) "What do we Want from the United Nations?" *International Organization* 30 (Autumn), 687

Weiss, Thomas George, and Leon Gordenker (eds.) (1996) *NGOs, the United Nations, and Global Governance* (Boulder, Colo.: Lynne Rienner)

Welch, Claude (1995) *Protecting Human Rights in Africa: Roles and Strategies of Nongovernmental Organizations* (Philadelphia, Penn.: University of Pennsylvania Press)

Weston, Burns (1992) "Human Rights," in Richard Claude and Burns Weston (eds.), *Human Rights in the World Community: Issues and Action* (Philadelphia, Penn.: University of Pennsylvania Press)

White, Freda (1926) *Mandates* (London: J. Cape)

White, Lucie (1993) "On the Guarding of Borders," *Harvard Civil Rights-Civil Liberties Law Review* 33, 183

(1997) "Democracy, in Development Practice: Essays on a Fugitive Theme," *University of Tennessee Law Review* 64, 1073

Wignaraja, Poona (ed.) (1993) *New Social Movements in the South: Empowering the People* (London and Atlantic Highlands, N.J.: Zed Books; New Delhi: Sage)

Williams, Gavin (1981) "The World Bank and the Peasant Problem," in Judith Heyer (eds.), *Rural Development in Tropical Africa* (New York: St. Martin's Press)

Williams, Patricia (1991) *The Alchemy of Race and Rights* (Cambridge, Mass.: Harvard University Press)

Williams, Robert A. (1990) *The American Indian in Western Legal Thought: the Discourses of Conquest* (New York: Oxford University Press)

Williamson, John (ed.) (1983) *IMF Conditionality* (Washington, D.C.: Institute for International Economics)

Wilson, Richard (ed.) (1997) *Human Rights, Culture and Context: Anthropological Perspectives* (London and Sterling, Va.: Pluto Press)

Wolfensohn, James D. (1998) Remarks at the joint World Bank/UNESCO Conference on Culture and Sustainable Development: Investing in the Promise of Societies (Washington, D.C., September 28)

(1999) "A Proposal for a Comprehensive Development Framework" (a discussion draft, January 21, available on-line at www.worldbank.org)

Wood, Angela (1999) *Perestroika of Aid? New Perspectives on Conditionality* (London: Bretton Woods Project)

World Commission on Dams (2000) *Dams and Development: a New Framework for Decision-Making* (London: Earthscan)

World Commission on Environment and Development (1987) *Our Common Future* (Oxford and New York: Oxford University Press)

Wright, Quincy (1930) *Mandates under the League of Nations* (Chicago, Ill.: University of Chicago Press)

Wright, Richard (1956) *The Color Curtain: a report on the Bandung Conference* (Cleveland, Oh.: World Pub. Co.)

Zakaria, Fareed (1994) "Culture is Destiny: a Conversation with Lee Kwan Yew" (1994) *Foreign Affairs* 73 (March/April), 113

UN Documents

United Nations (1960) UNGA Res. 1514

United Nations (1962) "Declaration on Permanent Sovereignty over Natural Resources," UNGA Res., 1803 GAOR, 17th Sess. Supp. No. 17, UN Doc. A/52 97

United Nations (1964) UNGA Res. 1975 (XIX), December

United Nations (1970) ESC Res. 1503, 48 UNESCOR, Supp. (No 1A), UN Doc. E/4832/Add. 1

United Nations (1971) "Report of the 1969 Meeting of Experts on Social Policy and Planning," *International Social Development Review, 3*

United Nations (1972) UNGA Res. 2849, UNGAOR, 26th Sess. Supp. No. 29, UN Doc. A/2849

United Nations (1974a) "Charter of Economic Rights and Duties of States," UNGA Res. 3281, 29 GAOR, Supp. 30, UN Doc. A/9030

United Nations (1974b) "Declaration on the establishment of a New International Economic Order), UNGA Res. 3201, Sixth Spec. Sess. GAOR, Suppl. 1, UN Doc. A/559

United Nations (1974c) "Program of Action of the Establishment of a New International Economic Order," UNGA Res. A/3202 (S-VI)

United Nations (1977) UNGA Res. 32/130, December 16

United Nations (1979) Report of the Secretary General on the Right to Development, E/CN.4/1334.

United Nations (1985) The History of UNCTAD, 1964–1984

United Nations (1986) "The NIEO and the promotion of human rights," Study by Ferrero, Special Rapporteur of the Sub-Commission on the Prevention of Discrimination and Protection of Minorities (1986)

United Nations (1990a) "Question of the Realization of the Right to Development," Report prepared by the Secretary-General E/CN.4/1990/9/Review1 (1990)

United Nations (1990b) *The Blue Helmets: a Review of United Nations Peacekeeping* (2nd edn.) (New York: United Nations, Dept. of Public Information)

United Nations (1992) *Rio Declaration on Environment and Development*, UN Doc. A/Conf.151/5/Review1, 1992 (New York: United Nations Dept. of Public Information)

United Nations (1993) Report of the Secretary-General on the Work of the Organization, A/48/1, September 10

United Nations (1995a) *Agenda for peace* (2nd edn.)

United Nations (1995b) "Support by the United Nations System of the Efforts of Governments to Promote and Consolidate New or Restored Democracies," Report of the Secretary-General, A/50/332, August 7

United Nations (1996) Agenda for Democratization

United Nations (1997a) Agenda for Development

United Nations (1997b) "Question of Human Rights and States of Emergency," Tenth annual report and list of states which, since January 1, 1985, have proclaimed, extended or terminated a state of emergency (presented by Mr. Leandro Despouy, Special Rapporteur appointed pursuant to Economic and Social Council resolution 1985/37, E/CN.4/Sub.2/1997/19, June 23)

United Nations (1998a) Subcommission on prevention of discrimination and Protection of Minorities (E.CN.4/SUB.2/RES/1998/12) 20 August

United Nations (1998b) "Situation of human rights in Cambodia," Report of the Special Representative of the Secretary-General for Human Rights in Cambodia, E/CN.4/1998/65.

United Nations (1999) "Slavery: UN leader wants apology to Africa" (*UN Wire*, UN Foundation, September 16)

United Nations (2000) "Globalization and its impact on the full enjoyment of human rights," Report submitted by J. Oloka-Onyango and Deepika Udagama, in accordance with Sub-Commission resolution 1999/8, E/CN.4/Sub.2/2000/13

United Nations (2001a) Durban Declaration and Programme of Action, World Conference against Racism, Racial Discrimination, Xenophobia and Related Intolerance, September

United Nations (2001b) "Globalization and its impact on the full enjoyment of human rights," Preliminary report submitted by J. Oloka-Onyango and Deepika Udagama, in accordance with Sub-Commission resolution 1999/8, and Commission on Human Rights Decision 2000/102, E/CN.4/Sub.2/2001/10 (July 2)

United Nations Development Program (1997a) "Governance for Sustainable Human Development"

United Nations Development Program (1997) "Reconceptualizing governance"

United Nations Development Program (1998a) "Integrating human rights with sustainable human development"

United Nations Development Program (1999) "Globalization with a Human Face" (Human Development Report)

United Nations Development Program (2000) "Human Rights and Human Development" (Human Development Report)

UNICEF-Working Women's Forum (1989) *Decade of the Forum* (UNICEF-WWF Publication)

USAID (2000) "USAID FY 2000 Accountability Report B-1, Part B: Financial Statements and Notes" (2000) (Available at http://www.usaid.gov/pubs/account/fy_2000/2000_accountability_report_part_b.pdf

World Bank (1992) "Operational Directive 4.15: Poverty Reduction" (1992), compiled in *The World Bank Operational Manual* 2 (December 1992)

World Bank (1993) *The East Asian Miracle*

World Bank (1994) *Governance: The World Bank's Experience*

World Bank (1998) *Human Rights and Development: The Role of the World Bank*

INDEX